DATE			
AUG 9 '82			

Colour, Class
and the
Victorians

Colour, Class and the Victorians

English attitudes to the Negro
in the mid-nineteenth century

Douglas A. Lorimer

Leicester University Press
Holmes & Meier Publishers, Inc.
1978

First published in 1978 by Leicester University Press

Designed by Douglas Martin
Set in Intertype Baskerville
Printed in Great Britain by
Western Printing Services Ltd, Bristol
Bound by Redwood Burn Ltd, London and Esher

British Library Cataloguing in Publication Data
Lorimer, Douglas A
Colour, class and the Victorians.
1. Blacks – Great Britain – History
2. Attitude (Psychology) 3. Great Britain –
Race relations
I. Title
301.45'19'6 DA125.N4
ISBN 0-7185-1161-1

First published in the United States of America by
Holmes & Meier Publishers, Inc.
30 Irving Place, New York, N.Y. 10003

Library of Congress Cataloging in Publication Data
Lorimer, Douglas A
Colour, class and the Victorians.
Bibliography: p.
Includes index.
1. England – Race relations. 2. Blacks – England –
Public opinion. 3. Public opinion – England.
4. Social classes – England. I. Title.
FA125.N4L67 1978 301.15'43'30145196 78-6396
ISBN 0-8419-0392-1

For my parents

CONTENTS

Acknowledgments

During the course of my research and writing, I have accumulated a great debt to a great many persons and institutions. Without the financial assistance of H. R. Macmillan, the University of British Columbia, the Canada Council, and Wilfrid Laurier University, it would have been impossible for me to undertake let alone complete this study. My research efforts also depended upon the expert guidance and co-operation of many archivists and librarians including the staffs of the Institute of Historical Research, the British Library, and the Public Record Office. I am equally thankful to the following societies and institutions and their librarians for their help and for their permission to cite from their archives: the Anti-Slavery Society whose papers are housed in Rhodes House Library, Oxford; the Church Missionary Society; the Imperial College of Science and Technology for use of the Huxley Papers; the Royal Anthropological Institute of Great Britain and Ireland for permission to quote from the records of the Ethnological and Anthropological Societies of London; University College, London, for the Bright Letters, and the Brougham and Beesly Papers; and Dr Williams's Library for use of the Estlin Papers. I am also grateful to Wilfrid Laurier University Press for permission to republish part of an earlier essay which is now included within chapter 4.

I also owe a great deal to the members of the history department of the University of British Columbia who guided, cajoled, and prodded me through my undergraduate and graduate studies. In particular I would like to thank Dr Robert Kubicek, Dr John Norris, and especially Dr James Winter, my thesis supervisor, for their patience, criticism, and advice. Professors Michael Banton of Bristol, John Flint of Dalhousie, and Murray Young of New Brunswick, were kind enough to give detailed comments on the original manuscript which have greatly helped in the task of revision. I owe a special thanks to Dr Michael Biddiss whose expert advice and precise criticism have given me a wider perspective. I would also like to thank Peter Boulton and his staff at Leicester for their assistance in preparing the manuscript for publication. Although they may not be aware of it, my colleagues, Dick Fuke and Jim Harkins, by their patient listening and informed remarks have helped me to clarify and modify my ideas. For the onerous task of typing the various versions of the manuscript I am indebted to a whole team of secretaries at Wilfrid Laurier led by Jean Gourlay and Marg Meston of the history department. Finally I owe a special thanks to Joyce who in her dual capacity as spouse and fellow historian is always my most perceptive and encouraging critic. In spite of all the help I have received errors undoubtedly remain. For these I am solely responsible.

Douglas A. Lorimer
Waterloo, Ontario
January 1978

1

Introduction

The subjects of this study are white not black. Victorian attitudes to race were as much a product of developments in the white world of England as a result of the multi-coloured world of the Empire.

The Victorians debated the 'Negro Question' at considerable length and with much passion, because they saw it as a test case of racial theories and ideas. As a result of the anti-slavery movement, nineteenth-century Englishmen had a well-defined stereotype of blacks and at least a tradition of concern and interest in their welfare. From the contrast of black and white, the Victorians also assumed that Africans and their New World descendants were at the opposite ends of the racial spectrum from the pale-skinned natives of the British Isles. In 1880, Professor W. H. Flower, a prominent anthropologist, noted that 'the African negro has, on account of his structure being better known than that of any other of the lower races, always been taken as the antithesis of the white man of Europe, and in numerous treatises on the subject the differences between them have often either been exaggerated or softened down, according to the bias of the writer'.[1] The Victorians looked upon the Negro as the photographic negative of the Anglo-Saxon, and they seemed to get a clearer perception of their own supposed racial uniqueness from the inverted image of the black man. Because it told them so much about themselves, they engaged in an intense debate on the Negro Question, and consequently a study of this issue can reveal much about Victorian racial attitudes in general.

Nineteenth-century English spokesmen incorporated all black men into the single category of the 'Negro'. They made no precise distinction between differing populations in Africa, or between Africans and Afro-Americans. At least until 1870, the mid-Victorians took a greater interest in slavery and race relations in the New World than in African affairs, and therefore their stereotyped conceptions relied less upon the association of Africans with savagery than upon the identification of blacks with slavery and plantation labour. During the 1850s and 1860s, a reaction set in against the sentimental caricature of the abolitionists, and a more derogatory stereotype of the Negro became more prevalent. This change occurred before the exploits of explorers and the search for colonies revived interest in the African continent. In 1866, for example, the *Daily Telegraph* commented that while the heroics of English explorers merited the highest praise, the continent of Africa was a 'bore', for 'No one can be really much interested in a black wilderness, inhabited by foul, fetid, fetish-worshipping, loathsome, and lustful barbarians', To the *Daily Telegraph*, this unrelenting monotony of savagery and filth – dotted, by the way, with 'sixpennyworth of rum and water' and 'Obeah-men' returned to Africa from the Caribbean – meant that 'the African . . . has rendered even heroism uninteresting, and the Nile prosaic'.[2] Familiar with descriptions of 'Quashee' in the West Indies, the mid-Victorians thought explorers in Africa had little to tell them about the Negro. In its attempt to explain the growth of racialism in the mid-nineteenth century, this study will show a similar inclination to give greater weight to New World experience than to the renewed interest in Africa.

This interest in the American Negro was largely a result of the evangelical and humanitarian attack on slavery in the early nineteenth century. The success of the anti-slavery movement further strengthened its appeal, until spokesmen belonging to all political persuasions looked back upon it as one of the brightest chapters in recent English history. The movement had acted as an influential pressure group upon parliamentary opinion in the 1830s, but by the late 1840s it had lost much of its effectiveness. Nonetheless, the protective role adopted toward the Negro continued to be a respected, and for a great many people, an important part of their moral and civilizing mission in the world.

By the 1850s and 1860s, a new and aggressively racist movement, in the guise of the young science of anthropology, challenged the tradition of protective benevolence towards the black man. The old and, as many thought, dead question of the nature and status of the Negro was revived, and applied to the new issues of the mid-century. The continued economic decline of the West Indies apparently proved the incapacity of blacks for freedom and added to the growing disdain for the sentimental abolitionists. At the same time, the slave crisis in America and racial conflicts in the West Indies focussed English attentions upon the Negro. The American Civil War created deep and revealing divisions in opinion through all levels of English society, and put in question the sincerity of English denunciations of slavery. From 1865 to 1868, the controversy over Governor Eyre and the Jamaica Insurrection split the Victorian intelligentsia, and raised in dramatic form the question of the due and proper limits of authority, at a time when the ruling classes in Britain were themselves considering the extension of the franchise to the lower orders. The 1850s and 1860s saw the birth of scientific racism and a change in English racial attitudes from the humanitarian response of the early nineteenth century to the racialism of the imperialist era at the close of the Victorian age.[3]

It is commonly assumed that this growth of racialism was a product of the pressing needs of imperial rule.[4] In order to justify British control over various indigenous peoples, the Victorians, so it is argued, developed the ideology of the civilizing mission and the white man's burden which at one blow sanctified British imperialism and reduced the indigenous populations to perpetual subservience. This interpretation raises certain difficulties. It relies upon the assumption that the English were sufficiently aware of the needs of Empire to respond in an appropriate manner. During the 1850s and 1860s, the colonies of white settlement seemed destined for self-government, and India and tropical crown colonies seemed a necessary but onerous burden assumed out of economic interest, and carrying with them the moral duty of civilizing alien races in British ways. The desire to expand imperial conquests and responsibilities and the attempt to achieve a greater unity in the Empire did not occur at this time, but toward the end of the century.[5] During the mid-Victorian period, when a more strident racialism began to develop, the Empire simply did not have sufficient hold over the attentions of the English public to produce in them a new and pervasive racist ideology.

This misconception arises in part from the nature of the historical evidence. Colonial and overseas adventurers duly recorded their observations in memoirs, narratives, periodical articles, and press reports, and thereby communicated their responses to English readers, secure and comfortable in the familiar armchair of club or parlour. From these published sources, it would appear that more insular Englishmen absorbed the racial attitudes of their countrymen overseas, but did little to reshape those impressions to fit their own preconceptions and outlook.[6] By looking at the racial attitudes of Englishmen securely at home and untouched by personal experience of the Empire, this study hopes to show that domestic as well as imperial influences shaped Victorian racial attitudes.

In the mid-nineteenth century, a new vigorous racist ideology challenged the humanitarian traditions of the anti-slavery movement, and preached a new doctrine of racial supremacy. Growing out of the armchair investigations of the new science of anthropology, and reinforced by the romantic speculations of historians seeking in folk myths the elusive qualities of the national character, this new ideology of racism, which declared that moral and intellectual as well as physical traits were biologically determined, confused cultural and physical characteristics, and gave 'race' an all-inclusive meaning so that it became, in the minds of its exponents, the most significant determinant of man's past, present and future.

The intellectual history of scientific racism is fairly well known, and like the needs of imperial rule, it is commonly thought to have had a significant impact upon Victorian racial attitudes. The difficult task for the historian is to find out how the erudite works of a few anthropologists and historians came to influence a wider public. For this reason, an attempt will be made to get beyond the description of ideas and opinions about race, in order to assess attitudes and the interrelationship between opinions, emotional responses, and the resultant behaviour stemming from these thoughts and feelings.[7] From this perspective, both the influence of scientific racism and the underlying assumptions of its proponents can be examined. It is hoped that this assessment will lead to a more precise measure of the place of racist thought and imperial experience in the formation of Victorian racial attitudes.

Victorian writers on the racial question treated races as biologically defined groups, and confused the relationship between physical traits and cultural or learned behaviour. From today's perspective, 'race' has greater significance as a sociological rather than as a biological phenomenon, and consequently a 'race', according to Pierre L. van den Berghe, is best described as 'a group that is *socially* defined but on the basis of *physical* criteria'.[8] From this definition it follows that a racial group needs readily-perceived physical distinctions in order to be identifiable, but that the significant attributes assigned to that group stem not from its appearance but from its social environment and status. Many Victorian commentators claimed to be able to distinguish not only highly visible features such as skin colour, but also supposed differences in head shape and size, and to be able to infer from these traits intellectual and psychological characteristics. Therefore, they were quite certain they could perceive the unique features of Anglo-Saxons, Celts, especially the Irish, Jews, and various European nationalities, as well as distinguish between 'white' and 'coloured' races. When referring to the 'Negro', therefore, we have in mind Victorian conceptions of Africans and their New World descendants, and not some scientifically defined entity. In these Victorian perceptions, the significant attributes of the Negro were not physical, but rather the social and cultural traits derived from the association of blacks with the status of American slaves, West Indian plantation labourers, and African 'savages'.

Victorian commentators on race, whether scientists, travellers, missionaries, philanthropists, or politicians, came largely from the respectable ranks of English society, and their perceptions of race were influenced by the assumptions and values of their predominantly middle-class background.[9] In an age when Disraeli could speak of two nations and mean a people of one nationality but divided by political power, wealth, social position, and levels of civilization, the question of authority and the place of the civilizing mission applied not only to the rule of white British over subject coloured peoples, but also to the government of the wealthy over the poor in Britain itself. The nineteenth-century discussion of the racial question rested upon values and assumptions moulded by this hierarchical, class-conscious, social order. The question, 'does a black man equal a white man?' had little meaning in an age when few thought all white men deserved equality.

In the mid-nineteenth century, few commentators espoused egalitarian principles, but they still believed that the individual through industry, self-help, and education could improve his social standing. They asserted that these avenues for self-improvement were open to all individuals, blacks as well as whites, but the belief in self-advancement applied less readily to groups than to individuals. When considering the 'Negro race', commentators lost sight of individual diversity and simply assumed all blacks were inferior to all whites. Their assumptions about the characteristics of the Negro race made them less willing to recognize the abilities of individual blacks, and some suggested that even 'a self-improved Negro' could not rise to the elevated status of a gentleman. An increasing number of spokesmen in the mid-nineteenth century asserted that gentlemen by definition were white, and that a black or brown skin, irrespective of an individual's wealth, learning or manner, marked that individual as a member of the inferior orders. The transition in racial attitudes from an earlier ethnocentric response to a more openly racist one occurred when a white skin became an essential mark of a gentleman. This change occurred not so much in response to the needs of

Empire, as out of new attitudes toward social status emerging within English society.

Although Victorian observers readily assigned racial characteristics to various ethnic groups, they tended to adopt, at least until the 1860s, an ethnocentric rather than a racist stance. The term 'racist' is best limited to those societies which see themselves superior by reason of their biological inheritance, whereas the more common ethnocentric assumption of cultural superiority still admits the possibility of the outsider conforming to the supposedly superior norm.[10] In the first half of the nineteenth century, English spokesmen compared alien cultures to their own, and judged foreigners to be inferior if they failed to match British standards. Rarely finding strangers who passed this test, missionary activists and abolitionists attempted to convert these foreigners to a British, and therefore a civilized, way of life. After the mid-century, and especially from the 1860s onwards, English spokesmen adopted a more stridently racist stance, as they placed foreigners into racial categories, and judged them inferior by reason of their inherited characteristics. Conversely, it was assumed that the English were members of the Anglo-Saxon race, and were superior due to their innate physical, intellectual and emotional make-up. In this new racialist vision, the ethnocentric hope of civilizing the world in conformity to British standards seemed to be the naive fantasy of an aged, sentimental, and now senile generation.

The Victorians freely expressed their dislike and suspicion of foreigners. Catholics and Jews were an alien element in Anglo-Saxon, Protestant Britain. In the insular world of the nineteenth century, 'Niggers began at Calais', and if Englishmen were forced to choose, they claimed to prefer fairer northern Europeans to southern ones, and these lighter-skinned Mediterranean peoples to the 'lesser breeds without the law'. 'Nigger', which usually referred to someone of African ancestry, was applied with increasing frequency in the mid-nineteenth century to anyone with a complexion darker than an Anglo-Saxon shade of whiteness.[11] Charles Lamb, in his *Essays of Elia*, first published in 1820, remarked that he only imperfectly sympathized with blacks:

In the Negro countenance you will often meet with strong traits
of benignity. I have felt yearnings of tenderness towards some of
these faces – rather masks – that have looked out kindly upon one
in casual encounters in the streets and highways. I love what
Fuller beautifully calls – these 'images of God in ebony'. I should
not like to associate with them – to share my meals and my
good-nights with them – because they are black.[12]

In the same essay, Lamb observed that he was 'a bundle of prejudices', and that he felt both attracted and repelled by Scotsmen, Jews, and Quakers, as well as blacks.

The widespread dislike of strangers, and contempt for dark-complexioned persons in particular, derived more from xenophobia and ethnocentrism than from prejudice. In the definition of Michael Banton, prejudice is 'an emotional and rigidly hostile disposition towards members of a given group', and is thus a product of the psychological needs of the prejudiced individual.[13] It cannot of itself explain discriminatory behaviour. An individual may practice racial discrimination not from prejudice, but from conformity to social conventions.[14] With these considerations in mind, Banton draws a distinction between prejudice and antipathy, 'A predisposition unfavourable to a particular group resulting from ignorance, conflict of interests or some other objective cause'.[15] In the historical development of racial attitudes, prejudice may explain the behaviour of specific individuals; xenophobia, ethnocentrism, or antipathy produced from some objective cause more correctly describe the more flexible and broadly-based attitudes of larger social and cultural groupings.[16]

In the nineteenth century, the black intruder into the Englishman's world faced no traditional or institutional bars against his presence, and yet as the century advanced Negro residents and visitors faced increasing hostility and more frequent discrimination. This transition from the xenophobia of the earliest contacts from the sixteenth to the eighteenth centuries, to an increased antipathy in the late nineteenth century, was not simply a result of the growth in the number of prejudiced individuals, but a consequence of a change in accepted social conventions about conduct toward blacks.

Nineteenth-century publications recorded opinions about Negroes, but rarely indicated the emotional responses or behaviour of Victorians toward Africans and Afro-Americans. Remote from the inter-racial contacts of the Empire, and rarely meeting blacks in Britain, the Victorians perceived the physical characteristics of the Negro largely through the verbal descriptions of lecturers and writers. Many of these spokesmen had travelled or resided in Africa or the multi-racial societies of the New World, and their recorded opinions are not a reliable guide to the attitudes of Englishmen in general. In order to assess these attitudes, recorded opinions about the Negro must be weighed against Victorian behaviour toward blacks.

Opinions in themselves are dangerous and difficult to handle.

They are often less important for the ideas they convey than for the purpose they serve. For example, the Rev. John Cunningham, in a sermon in Exeter Hall in 1848, identified Africans with the curse of Ham not to prove that blacks should be slaves, but to prove the prophetic power of the Scriptures. Here, Cunningham used slavery to vindicate the Bible, not Holy Writ to justify slavery.[17] Inconsistencies in opinion also make generalizations suspect. Among Members of Parliament in the 1860s, John Arthur Roebuck expressed the most thorough social Darwinian view of racial conflict. In New Zealand, he declared, 'the Englishman would destroy the Maori, and the sooner the Maori was destroyed the better'.[18] Yet in 1863, Roebuck took up the case of A. Fitzjames, a black Trinidadian lawyer educated at Middle Temple. The Governor of Sierra Leone had dismissed Fitzjames from his post of Acting Chief Justice, and Roebuck called for an inquiry into the incident.[19] Opinions, and the attitudes they express, can only be understood when placed in their context of time and place. In 1861, Palmerston, who had spent a lifetime directing British policy against the slave trade, and who was then treading a delicate path between North and South in the American Civil War, read Livingstone's description of Victoria Falls, and wrote to Lord John Russell, his Foreign Secretary: 'What a Triumph for the Nigger over the Yankee to have a waterfall so much finer than Niagara'.[20] Palmerston had little use for democratic Americans, and spent a great deal of time poring over reports on the slave trade, but it would be dangerous to infer that he preferred 'Niggers' to 'Yankees'.

Opinions, then, were often inconsistent, and more frequently the inflated expressions of national pride. In order to reduce the problem of inferring attitudes from opinion, this study, where possible, uses manuscript rather than published sources. This use of manuscript materials provides at least a partial solution to the problem of interpreting attitudes from publications self-consciously composed for a select readership, and certainly unpublished sources have helped put opinions about the Negro in a more appropriate perspective. In their correspondence, Englishmen rarely expressed the violent racist invective included in some nineteenth-century newspapers. It would appear from this contrast that the press, indulging in sensationalism to arouse readers' interest, gives an exaggerated, distorted view of racial attitudes.

Manuscript sources also have their limitations. Abolitionists rarely discuss slavery or the Negro in their letters, for their correspondents tend to be people of a similar persuasion and therefore they share common, though invariably unstated, assumptions. Manuscript materials have been helpful in adding to and confirming the published accounts of black residents and visitors in Britain, in revealing the abolitionists' struggle against the decline of their reputation and support, in assessing the attitudes of established scientists toward the exponents of scientific racism, and in gaining an impression of the attitudes of politicians and other observers during the discussion of the Negro in the American Civil War and the Jamaica Insurrection.

Published sources in themselves are of interest of course, because they recorded impressions and influenced opinion. I have attempted to survey a fairly wide range of anti-slavery, missionary, and scientific periodicals, as well as daily and weekly newspapers, and the more learned reviews. In this survey, I have also tried to weigh religious and political affiliation, circulation and social background of readership in the assessment of opinion and in the placing of that opinion within the context of Victorian England. I have relied upon secondary materials for an understanding of social and intellectual developments within English society, and where possible, I have used nineteenth-century sources to substantiate these generalizations.

By necessity a study of this kind relies upon a great variety of sources, and since these materials cannot be handled by a quantitative method, they provide only an 'impressionistic' glance at nineteenth-century attitudes. Social scientists, fully aware of this limitation upon the historical approach to the subject, have called for further studies in the history of race relations.[21] This historical study, it is hoped, will at least challenge some common misconceptions about Victorian racial attitudes.

In order to assess the forces behind the nineteenth-century change from ethnocentrism to racialism, and in order to limit the difficulties of inferring attitudes from opinions, it is necessary to gain some impression of the feelings and behaviour of Englishmen upon meeting blacks. Chapters 2 and 3 will look at the experience of Negroes in Britain, their observations about the Victorians, and the comments of Englishmen about these black residents and visitors. Once this assessment of Victorian behaviour is established, a more accurate appraisal of opinion is possible. Chapter 4 will look at the stereotype of the Negro given circulation by philanthropic and popular sources of opinion, and will assess the role of a new, more derogatory caricature upon racial attitudes.

In spite of efforts to get at popular views of the Negro, the bulk of source material remains the reports of an articulate minority from the respectable ranks of society. The social background of this group shaped their perception of racial distinctions and race relations. The inter-relationship between social attitudes and the perception of racial characteristics will be examined in Chapter 5, and the forces of change within English society and their influence upon the decline of humanitarian interest in the Negro will be studied in Chapter 6. Changes within the domestic social environment also had an influence upon scientific ideas about race. Chapter 7 will study the growth of scientific racism, and assess the influence of the scientists' social background upon their assumptions about racial differences. From the perspective of the social climate of the 1860s, a clearer idea can also be gained of the reception of scientific racism by educated mid-Victorians.

The scientific discussion of race involved a select minority of mid-nineteenth-century Englishmen. The issue of race seemed remote from the immediate concerns of the larger public, and therefore the racial question more frequently intruded upon their consciousness when events abroad proved sensational enough to command attention. The most extensive discussion of the Negro took place in the political forum, and thus political controversies gave the clearest display of differences in Victorian opinions about the black man. From an examination of English reactions to the Negro in the American Civil War, in Chapter 8, and the Governor Eyre Controversy, 1865–8, in Chapter 9, something can be learned of the differences in opinion in the society at large. This study also provides a gauge of the influence of domestic political and social values upon opinions about blacks, and gives some indication of the forces working to change racial attitudes.

From this study, then, it is hoped that something can be learned about the forces within English society which lay behind the growth of a more strident racialism during the 1850s and 1860s. The first task is to gain a measure of Victorian behaviour by looking at the experience of blacks in Britain.

2

Racial Discrimination in England: the Black Experience, 1600–1900

For the mid-Victorians, the 'Negro Question' was a contentious, yet irrepressible issue. Negrophobe warred against Negrophile, and in this acrimonious atmosphere the combatants made exaggerated claim for and against Africans and their New World descendants. The warring factions left little indication of how closely their stated opinions coincided with their true feelings, or of how much their ideas influenced their behaviour. Fortunately, various blacks who visited or resided in the United Kingdom have left a record of their observations and experiences. Through these black observers of the English and from the comments of Englishmen about them, some empirical assessment can be made of the degree of racial discrimination in the United Kingdom and of the development of English racial attitudes from the eighteenth to the late nineteenth centuries.

From the first trading contacts with Africa in the mid-sixteenth century, Englishmen expressed ethnocentrically-based dislike of the African's physical appearance. This aversion also assumed the character of moral judgment, for English observers associated Africans with heathenism and natural bestiality. As the slave trade from West Africa and the institution of slavery in the New World became established, increasing references appeared to the older Judaic and medieval Christian association between the Negro and the curse of Ham.[1]

Some scholars have argued that these early expressions of xenophobia demonstrate that racism antedates the establishment of black slavery in the New World. Others have gone a step further and have drawn a link between efforts to expel alien blackamores from

Elizabethan England in 1596 and 1601, and the restrictive Common-
wealth Immigration Acts of the 1960s, and have concluded that
English racism has demonstrated a remarkable continuity over the
past 400 years.[2] This record of prejudice and discrimination would
seem to suggest that English racism was relatively unaffected by the
transformation from a preindustrial to an industrial social order
from the seventeenth to the nineteenth centuries. The continuity
of this discrimination would also seem to bring into question the
claim of some sociologists that the character of race relations is
determined by social structure, and reaffirm the contrary claim that
cultural attributes, for example H. Hoetink's somatic norm image,
a group's perception of its own physical type, have a greater role in
determining the character of race relations.[3]

Racism gains this appearance of a remarkably continuous historical record from the application of present-day standards of racial
justice to past ages quite different in their social structure and mores.
Evidence for racism rests upon a demonstration that individuals or
ethnic groups received unequal treatment on the basis of their
physical appearance. Historically, unequal treatment has been not
the exception but the rule in both racially mixed and racially
homogeneous communities. Therefore it is not difficult to prove the
existence of discrimination, but it is more difficult to demonstrate
that race alone was the basis of this unequal treatment. For example,
what would constitute racially tolerant as distinct from discriminatory behaviour in eighteenth-century England? The numerous ranks
and orders of this society do not fit the conventional scheme of three
distinct classes, but rather are better described as a vertical status
hierarchy. In this kind of society individuals felt less of an identification with their social peers than an acute awareness of their place
between those immediately above and below them on the social
ladder. Discrimination in this social hierarchy operated for or
against individuals in accordance with their social rank, and more
particularly, on the basis of their individual connections of patronage
and dependency. For the white or black servant the keys to social
security or advancement were not skin colour, but the status and
favour of one's master and patron. Ideas of liberty for all individuals
as distinct from property-owners gained ground in the course of the
century, and as this principle matured, slavery itself came under
attack. On the other hand, notions of social equality, which underlie
the present-day moral outrage against racism, were morally out-
rageous to the dominant and most articulate groups in eighteenth-
century England, and were espoused only by a few enlightened

radicals. Even among artisans and the labouring poor hierarchical distinctions operated, and a stronger sense of egalitarianism as well as cooperation only emerged during the traumatic social transformation effected by the industrial revolution.[4] Given the differences in social structure and the consequent differences in conceptions of individual liberty and social equality, there is a danger that discriminatory acts in the eighteenth century may be mistakenly interpreted as similar to more recent forms of racism in urban-industrial societies with a liberal democratic ethos.

To prove that racism against blacks existed in eighteenth-century England, one would need to establish first that Englishmen thought that the distinct physical traits of Africans indicated that blacks were significantly different from whites in their mental and psychological makeup. Second, one would require evidence that blacks were treated as a group, and treated in a different fashion from whites. The existence of a racial stereotype of the 'Negro' in eighteenth-century England, and the fact that the status of slave was attached uniquely to blacks, suggest the existence of racism. On the other hand, a closer examination of the situation of blacks reveals that the white host community did not treat them as a uniform group, and that the experience of individual blacks was often comparable to that of individual whites.

Racism in the form of a loose collection of ideas aiming to show that blacks were distinct from and inferior to whites did emerge in the latter half of the eighteenth century. But these ideas were largely a reaction against the more prevalent ethnocentrism of the age which assumed human nature to be both uniform and universal, and which ascribed both cultural and physical variations from the European norm to the effect of differing environments. The prevailing literary stereotype of the Negro no longer conveyed the xenophobia of the earlier sixteenth-century accounts of West Africa, for during the seventeenth century English observers had revised some of their earlier erroneous and adverse impressions. By the eighteenth century, this revision had gone to the opposite extreme and Africans were included in the literary and philosophic cult of the noble savage, a more positive but no less ethnocentric stereotype.[5]

In origin and in its fullest development, this literary convention applied to the American Indian, but from the appearance of Mrs Behn's *Oroonoko* in 1688 to the full flowering of the abolitionist movement in the late eighteenth century, many writers, including Blake, Burns, Coleridge, Cowper, Southey, and Wordsworth, as well as many lesser-known poets, depicted Africans as noble savages.[6]

Oroonoko's nobility derived more from his likeness to European standards than from his African traits:

His Face was not that of brown, rusty Black which most of that Nation are, but a perfect Ebony, or polish'd Jett. His Eyes were the most awful that cou'd be seen, and very piercing; the White of 'em being like Snow, as were his Teeth. His Nose was rising and *Roman*, instead of African and flat. His Mouth, the finest shap'd that could be seen; far from those great turn'd Lips, which are so natural to the rest of Negroes.[7]

English writers depicted the Negro hero, suitably Europeanized in physical appearance, as uncorrupted man, enjoying his natural freedoms and rights in his African home.

In their campaign against the slave trade and slavery, philanthropists made use of the noble savage convention. But by the 1820s and 1830s, the African was to English eyes less a noble savage than a child of nature, or a natural Christian who by his inherited temperament practised the virtues of humility, patient suffering, and brotherly love.[8] In reaction to this rising attack on slavery and energetic defence of the Negro, the defenders of slavery made the first attempts to provide a systematic, rationalized proof of black inferiority.[9]

The most effective polemicist for the West India interest and the most outspokenly racist defender of slavery was Edward Long. His writings on the history and life of Caribbean slave societies appeared in the 1770s, and conveyed a stereotype of the Negro as a slothful, unreliable worker made industrious by slavery. He added to this conventional picture of the slave a vision of Africa as 'that parent of everything that is monstrous in nature', and of blacks as 'libidinous and shameless as monkies or baboons'.[10] From his observations in Jamaica, Long claimed that Africans constituted a separate species having a closer kinship to the apes than did Europeans. His prejudiced outbursts were a product of his West Indian experience and personal sexual anxieties and represented one extreme of racial opinion in eighteenth-century England.

It is difficult, perhaps impossible, to assess to what extent Englishmen with no personal experience of slavery in the West Indies shared Long's point of view. At the very time that Long's views reached the reading public, the humanitarian attack on slavery began to take shape, and a far more extensively circulated defence of blacks as men rather than as slaves began to win a sympathetic response from a wide range of English opinion. By the last quarter of the eighteenth century, English opinion about the nature and proper status of

Africans was divided, and thus no simple generalized description can encompass the variety of racial attitudes prevalent at that time. In spite of the initial xenophobic response of travellers to tropical Africa, English attitudes toward blacks from the sixteenth to the end of the eighteenth century did not display a rigid continuity. Racial attitudes changed not simply as a result of experience in Africa, or even of New World slavery, but also as a consequence of the changing outlook of Englishmen at home.[11]

Until the beginning of the nineteenth century, there were more Africans in Europe than Europeans in Africa. The first blacks arrived in England at least as early as the sixteenth century, and after 1660 the number of these dark strangers rose rapidly, as wealthy planters returned from the prosperous sugar colonies with the visible signs of their riches and power, their black slaves.[12] Contemporary observers conjectured that there were as many as 30,000 black slaves in England in the mid-eighteenth century, but scholars have generally accepted Lord Mansfield's more conservative estimate of 14–15,000 at the time of the Somerset case in 1772. The majority of these were probably concentrated in London, and in relation to the population of the city at that time, even 14,000 blacks constituted a sizeable and easily recognized minority group.[13] West Indian planters retiring to the home country and anxious to retain their accustomed domestics imported most of these black servants into England. The planter aristocracy believed that the Negro's 'natural disposition' made him more obedient and trust-worthy than his obstreperous English counterpart. In spite of this confidence in the abilities and temperament of their black servants, masters frequently complained of drunkenness, lechery, and dis-loyalty of this class of domestics. These complaints were in no way unique, for they were part of the perennial problem of the servant, and applied equally to black and white. In fact, in many cases, the Negro servant's black skin was a positive advantage; it made him of special value to his owner.

Black slaves in England derived a special status from their striking appearance and exotic association as representative natural or uncorrupted men. Invariably named Pompey, the black page, dressed in the colourful silks and turban of the East, became the pampered favourite in many an aristocratic household. The Sackvilles first hired a Negro page in the early seventeenth century, and retained at least one of these black servants until the late eighteenth century. By that time, such Negro domestics had become so common that the family obtained a more original Chinese servant.[14]

Pampered as household pets, many of these black servants fared reasonably well under the attentions of their aristocratic mistresses. Almost all received some education, and a few gained extensive training in the arts of gracious living.[15] Under the patronage of the Duchess of Queensbury, Soubise, a slave boy brought to England from St Kitts, became a noted equestrian, and gained an entrance into the most fashionable circles of London society. The gossips chatted disapprovingly of the Duchess' favouritism toward a Negro, but Soubise only alienated his patroness when he denied his slave origin and claimed instead descent from the African aristocracy. Soubise then became a riding and fencing master at Eton, and there he found his aristocratic pupils preferred him to their white instructors.[16] Ignatius Sancho, another liberated slave nurtured under the care of an aristocratic family, also mixed freely in fashionable and literary circles. Although he had many English friends and was fully anglicized in his tastes and habits, Sancho remained concerned about the suffering of his coloured brethren. In his extensive correspondence with his literary friends, who included Sterne, Sancho encouraged them to take up the cause of the oppressed Negro. In a letter to another black, Sancho counselled:

Look around upon the miserable fate of almost all of our unfortunate colour – superadded to ignorance – see slavery, and the contempt of those very wretches who roll in affluence from our labours. Super-added to this woeful catalogue – hear the heart-racking abuse of the foolish vulgar. – You, S——e, tread as cautiously as the strictest rectitude can guide ye – yet you must suffer from this – but armed with truth – honesty – and conscious integrity – you will be sure of the plaudit and countenance of the good.[17]

Even Sancho's favoured social position did not exempt him from insults against his race. Nonetheless, the racial prejudice encountered by Sancho and other blacks taken under the care of aristocratic patrons bore little relation to the racism of the contemporaneous slave societies of the New World, or of the more recent pattern of racism in urban industrial settings. In eighteenth-century England, encounters with racial bigotry were occasional, and were the product of the prejudiced outbursts of individuals, rather than a consequence of institutionalized discrimination.[18]

Attitudes toward inter-racial sexual relations often provide an indication of the intensity of racism. In eighteenth-century England, some writers, most notably Edward Long, expressed shock at the willingness of English women to cohabit with black males, and

warned of the shame and degradation consequent from miscegenation.[19] These expressions of prejudiced opinion may exaggerate the
extent of inter-racial marriages, but if in fact mixed unions were
fairly frequent the significance of these diatribes against miscegenation needs to be reassessed. The opinions of Edward Long and his
friends may be less typical, and the very existence of mixed marriages
may indicate a larger measure of toleration.

In 1731, the *Gentleman's Magazine* reported the marriage of
Robert Widah, a black, said to be a great officer belonging to the
Prince of Pawpaw in Africa, to Mrs Johnson, an English woman.
Members of both races served as attendants in the wedding party.[20]
Only a few blacks in eighteenth-century England were of such note
as to have their wedding announced in the *Gentleman's Magazine*,
or to have their life and letters published. The vast majority left
little trace of their individual lives and experiences, and remain as
anonymous as their fellow English domestics and labourers. From
the scraps of evidence that do exist, it would appear that black
domestics mixed freely with their English colleagues. As the majority
of these black slave-servants were men, they found their wives and
consorts among English women, and apart from the criticism of such
unions by defenders of slavery, these racially mixed couples faced
some but not widespread opposition from their masters and fellow
domestics.[21] In the mid-eighteenth century, a strict bar existed not
against the marriage of blacks and whites, but against the mis-
cegenous unions of Irish Catholics and English Protestants.[22] Among
the poor of London a fair measure of racial toleration seems to have
existed. The London mob, whose habitual xenophobia was summed
up in the chant, 'No Popes, no Jews, no Wooden Shoes', befriended
black fugitives, and frequently harboured runaway slaves from their
pursuers.[23] A significant proportion of black casual labourers and
indigents married English women. In 1787, philanthropists and
government officials, planning both to establish a colony in West
Africa and to expel black indigents from London, sponsored the first
expedition to Sierra Leone. Of the 459 persons who sailed for the
new colony, 112 were white. Most of these whites were women
married to blacks, and not as once claimed prostitutes compelled to
join the settlement. Of the 61 families identified in a study of the
colonists by Mary Beth Norton, 44 were interracial.[24]

The autobiography of James Albert Ukawsaw Gronniosaw, an
African, who ultimately settled in England after an adventurous
life as a prince in his homeland, as a slave in Barbados and New
York, and as a sailor in the Royal Navy, provides a more detailed

glimpse of life among the labouring poor. In England, Gronniosaw had a constant struggle to find regular employment, and experienced times of severe poverty. On these occasions he depended upon the charity of Quaker philanthropists. He married an English widow, a weaver, in spite of the objections of his friends who thought his bride too poor for him. Although the ex-slave faced many hardships in England, he reported no incidents of racial discrimination. The struggle of the African prince, his English wife and their growing family to find work and to survive periods of severe hunger and poverty was the common predicament of the labouring poor.[25]

The hardships endured by a minority of blacks in eighteenth-century England were unique in one way. They alone were slaves. This slave status provides the clearest indication that some degree of institutionalized racism existed in eighteenth-century England. Even the claim that Lord Mansfield's decision in the Somerset case of 1772 abolished slavery in England is founded upon an historical mis-conception. Mansfield merely declared that a servant could not be forced to leave the country against his will. Slavery was abolished outright in Scotland in 1788, but according to English law, slaves brought to England from the colonies enjoyed freedom only so long as they stayed within the country. If an immigrant black servant voluntarily returned to the slave colonies, he could be legally resold as a slave until slavery itself was abolished in 1833.[26] As a conse-quence of these legal niceties, as well as the difficulties of enforcing them, the practice of keeping and selling slaves in England continued after 1772, and philanthropists continued to rescue and protect fugitive slaves into the early years of the nineteenth century.[27]

The reluctance of the courts to come out directly against slavery may have been due in part to a racial antipathy towards blacks, but the extreme conservatism of the law when tampering with property rights was also in evidence. Certainly Lord Mansfield's caution in dealing with the legal status of slavery in England stemmed from his concern about the rights of property owners.[28] The very uncertainty of the law about slavery in England was a consequence of the fact that the legal status of slave was an import from the slave colonies, and this legal ambiguity in itself reflects the relative weakness of institutionalized racism in England when compared to contempora-neous multiracial societies in the New World. Furthermore, this reluctance of the law to tamper with property rights, and the assumption behind this hesitancy that blacks could be treated as chattels and not as human beings, sparked off a campaign to have the law specifically prohibit the slave trade and slavery. In the early

1780s, reaction to the notorious case of the slave ship *Zong*, when the ship's master cast 132 slaves overboard in order to collect the insurance, led philanthropists to mount an organized campaign to demand that Parliament outlaw the slave trade.[29] Some degree of institutionalized racism clearly existed in eighteenth-century England, but by the end of the century the moral and legal sanctions for slavery were on the defensive against the combined forces of a rising humanitarian crusade, and a weakening political support for this form of racial exploitation.[30]

The standard of living of blacks in England did not alter greatly as a consequence either of the changes in the law or of the growth of humanitarian opposition to slavery. With the marked decline in the importation of slaves after the Somerset case, black domestics still found a demand for their services, and with changes in the law, many left the service of their old masters and found work as wage-earners. A considerable influx of black immigrants also occurred at this time, as a consequence of the American War of Independence. These new arrivals came as loyalists, demobilized soldiers, or in the largest numbers as disbanded sailors. Finding themselves unemployed and unwanted in London, these destitute newcomers formed the 'blackbirds' of St Giles who appealed to Granville Sharp and other philanthropists for aid. The authorities and the hard-pressed philanthropists attempted to rid London of this group of alien paupers by organizing the emigration scheme to Sierra Leone. Although in 1786 over 300 of the black poor were loaded into ships and sent to found the colony, this class of indigent continued in London, and as late as 1816 the authorities were still concerned about their presence in the metropolis.[31]

In response to the problems of securing a livelihood and of protecting themselves against re-enslavement, as well as out of a common identity shaped by their African heritage and slave past, blacks in eighteenth-century London formed their own community. They closely watched the court cases involving slavery, and gave James Somerset personal and moral support by attending the prolonged hearings which decided his fate.[32] Black leaders also kept a watchful eye over philanthropic and government plans to ship indigent blacks to Sierra Leone. Two prominent black spokesmen, Ottobah Cugoano, and Gustavus Vasa, the commissary for the expedition until his criticism of the management of the scheme led to his dismissal, advised fellow blacks against joining the venture.[33] In consideration of the limited options open to blacks in the late eighteenth century, the British Isles offered a safer domicile than either West Africa or the Americas, where a more certain threat of enslavement and a more virulent racism awaited any black migrant. Out of this relative freedom from slavery and racism in England, there developed an exaggerated belief, widely held by fugitive slaves in the nineteenth century, that Britain was a haven free from racial prejudice and discrimination.

In England itself, the increase in the number of blacks and the problem of black indigents led critics of these immigrants to become more vocal. At the beginning of the nineteenth century, William Cobbett inveighed against the number of 'debased Foreigners' in England, 'distinguishing particularly, *Jews, Negroes,* and *Mulattoes.*' Cobbett raised the loudest complaint not against the black poor, but against the elevation of some wealthier blacks into polite society: 'many, too many, of the rich, in the wildness, in the insolent caprice of their luxury, chose to regard them, as beings not only equal, but somewhat superior, to even the middling classes of the people'.[34] He observed that the admission of blacks into the army 'necessarily degrades the profession of the soldier', and that a 'shocking' number of English women were prepared to accept not only black lovers, but much worse, black husbands: 'Amongst white women, this disregard of decency, this defiance of the dictates of nature, this foul, this beastly propensity is, I say it with sorrow and shame, *peculiar to the English.*'[35]

Cobbett's prejudiced remarks were the exception, not the rule. Hester Piozzi, 1741–1821, a friend of Dr Johnson's and a devotee of literary affairs, thought the intermixture of the races in English society was 'preparing us for the moment when we shall be made one fold under one Shepherd.'

Well! I am really haunted by *black shadows.* Men of colour in the rank of gentlemen; a black lady, cover'd in finery, in the Pit at the Opera, and the tawny children playing in the Squares. . .afford ample proof of Hannah More and Mr Wilberforce's success towards breaking down the *wall of separation.*[36]

In the new edition of her novel, *Belinda,* Maria Edgeworth, acting upon the advice of her father, deleted the marriage of Juba, a black servant, with Lucy, a white servant girl:

many people have been scandalised at the idea of a black man marrying a white woman; my father says that gentlemen have horrors upon this subject, and would draw conclusions very unfavourable to a female writer who appeared to recommend such unions; as I do not understand the subject, I trust to this better judgment.[37]

Mr Edgeworth's sensitivity to colour differences and to public reaction revealed more about his own feelings and his West Indian experience than about the prevalent attitude of the time. His daughter's innocence on the subject represented a more typical response. The English reaction to colour differences at the end of the eighteenth century varied widely. No definite pattern of behaviour was established, and even those who exploited blacks overseas did not necessarily practice discrimination in England. When visiting Liverpool in 1811, Paul Cuffee, a black American sea captain and trader, found that even slave traders did not show disrespect for a black man of some standing.[38]

In eighteenth-century England, racially prejudiced individuals undoubtedly existed, but on the whole, no clear pattern of institutionalized or socially sanctioned discrimination was in evidence.[39] After 1790, occasional outbursts of anti-Negro feeling increased, but these scattered incidents hardly constituted a significant change in attitudes. The level of racial antipathy probably followed the general trend of increased social antagonism. The rising campaign against the slave trade provoked a counter-offensive against the Negro, and at the same time reaction against the Revolution in France and radical activists at home led to a heightened awareness of the divisions within English society. The Haiti Rebellion of 1791 crystallized both these reactions. The successful slave insurrection left the West Indian plantocracy quaking, and the tremors were also felt by their friends among the privileged circles in England.

In the late eighteenth and early nineteenth centuries, a change took place not so much in English behaviour as in the social status of blacks in England. At this time social relationships within the whole of the society were being transformed by industrialization. The paternal ethos of the traditional enlarged household gave way to the less secure and more individualistic world of the self-made entrepreneur and the wage-labourer. The paternal protection and close-knit circle of the aristocratic or wealthy household ceased to provide black residents with avenues for assimilation and advance. With the advent of an industrial society, blacks in England found themselves more isolated as individuals, seeking a living in the more anonymous and less hospitable environs of the growing cities. One consequence of this change was that there was less contact between blacks and wealthy, literate Englishmen. As a result, English commentators made fewer observations about black residents and visitors.

At the same time, the anti-slavery movement placed the Negro more prominently before the public. As a slave in the Americas, the black man became the symbolic victim of the most sinful and tyrannical of social systems. In English minds, slavery was identified with sin, and with an outmoded, almost feudal, paternalism, which crushed the individual's sovereignty over his own life and actions. In the new age of *laissez-faire*, individual liberty and self-advancement, Englishmen saw the Negro's oppression in slavery as the symbol of all the forces which thwarted individual liberty in their own society. This change in social structure and values left blacks in Britain more isolated, but at the same time the rise of the anti-slavery and missionary movements in the evangelical revival created a new consciousness of the black man's suffering in slavery.

Determined to disprove claims of black inferiority, and intent upon spreading Christianity and commerce to Africa, philanthropists brought African children to England for their education. As European trade with Africa increased, African merchants also saw the economic advantages of learning the language, customs, and business methods of the white trader, and, therefore, sent their sons and daughters to England to learn European methods. In 1788, a report on African students in Liverpool stated there were 50–70 of these students in the city, and a similar number were in Bristol and London.[40] At the end of the eighteenth century, these Africans encountered occasional incidents of racial intolerance. Prince John Frederick Naimbana, son of the king of Koya Temne, in England to receive an education under the care of Henry Thornton and the Sierra Leone Company, publicly rebuked a critic of the African race:

> If a man should sell me and my family for slaves, he would do
> injury to as many as he might kill or sell; but if any one takes
> away the character of black people, that man injures black people
> all over the world; and, when he has once taken away their
> Character, there is nothing which he may not do to people ever
> after.[41]

Naimbana's rejoinder hit at the core of racism, and, though the African prince had to counter the racial prejudice of individuals, neither he nor other black students had to face widespread discrimination, and on the whole these black visitors were favourably received.[42]

In 1798, Zachary Macaulay brought back 30–40 African children from Sierra Leone to be educated in Clapham. Although Cobbett poured his abuse upon this scheme of 'negro-pampering', Macaulay found his neighbours in Clapham took great interest in his students.[43] American and West Indian blacks also came to Britain for their education. James McCune Smith, excluded from higher education in the United States, attended Glasgow University where he gained his B.A. in 1835, his M.A. in 1836, and M.D. in 1837.[44] Some West Indian children of mixed ancestry had English fathers who sent them to live and be educated with their English relatives. The number of these students and their admittance into even the most prestigious educational and professional institutions demonstrated that at least on an official or public level no colour bar existed.[45] Privately, however, many Englishmen undoubtedly felt a xenophobic aversion to these dark-complexioned strangers, and some simply assumed themselves superior to the black and brown races of man.

In the 1830s, when the abolitionist movement was at its height, philanthropists, although preoccupied with the question of slavery, were also aware of the problems of racial prejudice and discrimination. A religious tract of 1830 instructed English children in the 'correct' behaviour toward their black 'brothers and sisters'. The tract, entitled 'The Negro Boy', described the reactions of two English children upon meeting a black boy in the street, and then assessed how some black pupils and their English classmates got on together at school. The pamphlet assumed that the initial natural reaction towards blacks would be hostile, and that this hostility could only be overcome by education and understanding. As a lesson in Christian charity and race relations, the tract provides little indication about the attitudes of English children to their black classmates, but it does say a great deal about the xenophobic assumptions and feelings of its adult author.[46]

Not even the most ardent abolitionists were free from these feelings of aversion. Thomas Clarkson recalled that 'When Christophe's wife and daughters, all accomplished women, were brought or introduced by him to Wilberforce, and others in High Life, there was a *sort of shrink* at admitting them into Society.'[47] After Henri Christophe's overthrow and suicide in Haiti, his widow and two daughters spent three years, 1821–4, in exile in England. For several months the exiles stayed with the Clarksons, whose hospitality contrasted favourably with the reception given by other members of the Clapham Sect. Wilberforce wrote to Mrs Clarkson: 'I hope you will not suffer any motives of feeling or delicacy ... to obstruct your rendering our Haytian friends the solid service they would doubtless receive from your accompanying them.' Wilberforce unfortunately had 'no time to spare', and his wife had 'not at present spirits to undertake an office which would require a considerable share of them.'[48] Although Zachary Macaulay's daughters 'remembered Madame Christophe as a handsome woman with remarkably dignified and quiet manners', Macaulay felt the need to reassure his wife: 'you need be under no apprehensions respecting Madame Christophe. She is not likely to come near us. But if she had, you might have rested perfectly at ease on the score of morals. I have no doubt whatever that the young women are perfectly modest and virtuous.'[49] Thomas Clarkson also had some reservations about the Christophe's black maid, for he doubted 'whether my servants would harmonize with a person of this description.'[50] In spite of the priggish fears of the Clapham Sect, which were as much a product of their concern for social propriety as a matter of xenophobia or prejudice, the Christophes enjoyed a pleasant and friendly stay in England.

Apparently the English kept their antipathies to themselves, for blacks entered even the most respectable social circles with no discernible objection to their presence. Mrs Wilkins, a former resident of Trinidad and a convert to the anti-slavery cause, recalled her reaction when first meeting a black gentleman in English society:

It was the first time in my life that I had seen a person of colour enter a room on equal terms with myself; and my surprise and discomfort were by no means diminished when the daughter of our hostess introduced him to me as a partner for the next quadrille. If the footman had presented himself for that purpose I could not have been more startled, and had I met this gentleman at Court it could not have saved him from the feeling of aversion and contempt with which I instinctively regarded him.[51]

Mrs Wilkins put her reaction down to her upbringing in a slave society, but some of the English people in the same room probably felt equally ill at ease. Their discomfort was not simply a result of their reaction to racial differences, for, as Mrs Wilkins observed, association with the lower classes on such intimate terms produced a similar reaction.

English commentators frequently saw similarities between race and class differences. Writing in 1823, Hannah Kilham, who among other philanthropic works produced a scheme to train African school-mistresses in England, found it necessary to challenge assumptions about the Negro's inferiority. In order to reassure her readers about the capacity of African children, she clearly distinguished between Negroes in England and those in their native land:

In England, people see only a few of those who have been slaves, or mostly beggars, and too often judge from such specimens of Africans in general . . . could the incredulous as to African capacity have seen . . . the bright, intelligent countenances of

many of the children . . . they would certainly doubt no longer as
to the capability of instruction among the Africans. But what
judgement would even be formed of the English nation were only
the most unfavourable specimens presented to view?[52]
Comparing her African experiences with her work among the poor
of St Giles, Hannah Kilham commented: 'The lowest ranks of
society would be, in some respects, more difficult subjects for instruction than many are in those called heathen lands, and they
would want the same care even from the beginning in the attempt
to civilize and Christianize them'.[53] In Hannah Kilham's view, the
task of 'elevating' or 'civilizing' the lower orders was much the same
whether they were black or white. Her readers may not have shared
her vision of the civilizing mission. The comparison between uncivilized Africans and the brutish lower orders of England may have
only confirmed her readers in their feelings of superiority over all
black men and over the vast majority of Englishmen. In fact, the
similarity between racial attitudes and domestic social attitudes
makes it very difficult to discern how far discriminatory acts were
the product of racial or social antipathies. The hierarchy of social
grades within English society provided a ready foundation on which
to build a hierarchy of races, but in the first half of the nineteenth
century assumptions of racial superiority apparently did not lead to
discrimination. The watchful abolitionists reported few incidents
of intolerant behaviour, and even these acts were only recorded to
prove that racial discrimination was unfounded and unjust.[54]

Some abolitionists identified blacks with inferior status, and
therefore refused to accept ex-slaves on an equal footing with
themselves. When painting 'The Anti-Slavery Convention', in 1840,
Benjamin Haydon devised a test of abolitionist attitudes. As each
noted philanthropist sat to be sketched for the painting, Haydon
asked him where Henry Beckford, an ex-slave from Jamaica, should
be placed in the picture. First the painter tested John Scoble and
John Tredgold, Secretaries of the British and Foreign Anti-Slavery
Society. Both men objected to the Negro occupying a prominent
place on the same level as the leading abolitionists.[55] But when
Haydon tested William Garrison and his leading British supporter,
George Thompson, the painter found they made no objection. For
Haydon, 'that was not enough. A Man who wishes to place the
Negro on a level must no longer regard him as *having been* a Slave!
and not feel annoyed at sitting by his side.'[56] The abolitionists'
concern for the slave did not necessarily lead to an acceptance of the
free Negro as a brother and equal. With limited experience of

meeting blacks, some British abolitionists undoubtedly felt a xenophobic aversion to their dark-skinned friends. A few regarded a
black skin and slave origins as a sign of inferiority, but rarely did they
openly display these feelings through hostile or insulting behaviour.

A condescending paternalism rather than xenophobia or racial
prejudice characterized the abolitionists' attitudes to black acquaintances. Zilpha Elaw, an American Negro evangelist who toured
England from 1840 to 1846, reported of her meeting with the Board
of the British and Foreign Anti-Slavery Society:

> It was really an august assembly; their dignity appeared so
> redundant, that they scarcely knew what to do with it all. Had I
> attended there on a matter of life and death, I think I could
> scarcely have been more closely interrogated or more rigidly
> examined; from the reception I met with, my impression was,
> that they imagined I wanted some pecuniary or other help from
> them; for they treated me as the proud do the needy.[57]

Other than this interview, the evangelist had little to do with the
anti-slavery movement. In her mission to the English, she toured
most extensively in the North and North-East, and preached most
frequently at Nonconformist and especially Primitive Methodist
chapels. Although the police broke up one of her street meetings,
she experienced little opposition, and expressed her gratitude to her
many English friends for their hospitality. As an evangelist, she
encountered more opposition to her sex than to her race. Some
clergy and laity barred her from their worship, because they thought
a woman should not preach the Gospel. In her travels, Zilpha Elaw
experienced no other form of opposition, and mentioned no instance
of racial discrimination.

The patronizing tone displayed by the members of the Broad
Street Committee was not a result of any exceptionally low opinion
or strong aversion they had toward blacks. The evangelist's dark
complexion was not the sole determinant of the philanthropists'
behaviour. Her sex and social position, as well as her race, influenced
the attitude they adopted toward her. First, as a woman preacher,
she not only contravened accepted notions of the woman's place, but
also broke established religious conventions. Quite apart from
tolerating women preachers, the abolitionists did not allow women,
or rather ladies, on to the floor of anti-slavery meetings. The fair sex
was only permitted to watch meetings from the gallery. Further,
Zilpha Elaw, as a woman with limited means and of some but not
much learning, was the obvious social inferior of the distinguished
Board of the Anti-Slavery Society. Her activities in Primitive

Methodist chapels served to emphasize the social distance between herself and the Quaker bankers and solid Church of England men among the abolitionist leaders. The inequalities within English society fostered assumptions of superiority, and encouraged a condescending outlook among the respectable classes. These attitudes influenced the Victorian gentleman's reaction to blacks, and provided a foundation upon which assumptions of racial superiority could build.

The nature of the Victorians' contact with blacks in England encouraged this tendency to identify a dark complexion with inferior status. Other than a few exceptional visitors from Africa, the West Indies, and the United States, the blacks whom the Victorians most frequently encountered were clearly members of the lowest segment of English society.

Probably the largest group of permanent black residents in nineteenth-century England were the descendents of the slaves of the eighteenth century. As there was no large exodus of this group, they presumably remained and intermarried with the indigenous population. The various censuses of the nineteenth century did not record the race of either aliens or British-born residents.[58] In the absence of quantitative data, conclusions about the numbers and experience of blacks must be drawn from a few scattered references, and unfortunately even in this material little mention is made of the descendants of the black slaves.

The most distinguished descendant of these eighteenth-century servants was Thomas Birch Freeman, a Methodist missionary to West Africa. Freeman's life shows how racial attitudes changed during the course of the nineteenth century. His father, known simply as Tom and described as a full Negro, worked as a gardener on a country estate near Winchester, and his mother was an English servant in the same household. The younger Freeman became a convert to Methodism, and trained as a missionary. Before setting off to Africa in 1837, he married an English woman, Elizabeth Boot, of Ipswich. Freeman's severest encounter with racial discrimination came late in his life. In the 1880s, a group of young missionaries confident in their newly-formed conviction of white superiority ousted Freeman from his position of respect and authority.[59] Among black Englishmen of the nineteenth century, Freeman was the exception, for only his distinguished work as a missionary brought his background to light. The remainder of the descendants of the eighteenth-century slaves worked as servants and labourers, and left little trace of their individual histories.

Occasionally, black servants did come before the public eye, or were mentioned in the press. Andrew Bogle, who served Sir Edward Doughty for 40 years, was twice called upon to give evidence in the case of the Tichborne claimant, one of the most famous and lengthy of Victorian trials.[60] Bogle was among the last of a fast-disappearing class in English society, for by the 1870s black servants were far less prominent and far fewer in number than they had been earlier in the century. In 1875, a writer in *All the Year Round* observed that 'The negro footman is now rarely seen; and it indeed would appear that there has been a considerable departure of the "black man" from among us'; and yet the same writer looked back to his youth and remarked that 'Some of us must surely possess youthful reminiscences of these Caesars and Pompeys of the past.'[61] Linda Brent, a black American who served as a nurse in England for ten months, reported that 'During all that time, I never saw the slightest symptom of prejudice against color.'[62] Changes in fashion meant that black servants no longer received the special attention paid to them in the eighteenth century, but apparently they encountered no exceptional hardships because of their distinctive colour.

Black sailors, a more transient and impoverished racial minority in Victorian England, experienced much harsher conditions. Sailors from the West Indies, the United States, and Africa served in the East Indian and Atlantic trades and made frequent calls at British ports, at times staying for several months before gaining another voyage. Blacks also served in the Royal Navy and the army, and in fact both services actively recruited, not to say compelled, liberated slaves in West Africa to sign on for lengthy terms of service.[63] In 1804, Cobbett complained of black soldiers stationed in England, but neither West Indian or West African regiments served there later in the century. The African Institution, in 1816, applied for some provision to be made for black sailors in Greenwich and Portsmouth made destitute after being disbanded from the Royal Navy.[64] Black sailors continued to serve in the navy and in the merchant marine throughout the century, and were a common sight in the streets of English ports.

In fact, black sailors were so well known in these ports that when wanting to employ men of African origin, Englishmen first looked for them in the dockyards. Hannah Kilham, in her researches into African linguistics, readily found two African sailors to help her with the transcription of African languages into writing. Similarly, a large number of the 158 blacks recruited for the Niger Expedition in 1841 were found in English ports. When the British and Foreign

Anti-Slavery Society sought employment for David Holmes, a destitute American slave in London, they turned first to the docks. Both Holmes and his friend, Dan, found employment as sailors.[65]

From a number of cases of black British sailors imprisoned in the Southern United States, further information can be gleaned about the social background of this transient population. Of the 40 cases the Foreign Office investigated between 1823 and 1851, four sailors gave British ports as their home addresses. Henry Steward gave his birthplace as Liverpool, and Daniel Fraser, born in the West Indies, but resident in Scotland from the age of four, was fluent in Gaelic.[66] John Brown, a fugitive slave who fled to England, claimed that a black British sailor enslaved on a Georgia plantation had inspired him with his vision of British liberty and freedom from colour prejudice. This sailor, John Glasgow, claimed he was a resident of Lancashire, and was married to an English woman whom he had left behind on a small farm. In another case investigated by the Foreign Office in 1851, the British Government paid $500 to buy William Houston's freedom. Houston had been jailed by the Southern authorities and then sold into slavery. He was born in Gibraltar, and as a boy had moved to Liverpool with his mother, a woman of African descent, and his two brothers and three sisters. His mother ran a lodging house for sailors in Liverpool, and his two brothers were tailors in London. The Rev. Jeremiah Asher, a black Baptist preacher from Philadelphia who toured England to raise funds for his church, recounted the experience of two other Liverpudlians, a black American sailor and his English wife. She moved from Liverpool to Philadelphia to be with her husband only to find that no one would associate with a white woman married to a black man. Faced with this hostility, the couple moved back to Liverpool.[67]

Although most of the black British seamen who entered American ports served on traders to the West Indies, a considerable number either registered British ports as their permanent residence, or served on vessels which traded to Britain. In the year 1852, 63 black British sailors had been imprisoned in the Southern States, and from 1857 to 1859, 158 black sailors called in at Charleston. In the anti-conscription riots in New York in 1863, 63 British Negroes gained protection on board the French flagship in the harbour. By 1859 the imprisonment of black sailors by the Southern authorities had created so great a problem that the Board of Trade issued a warning to masters in every port in the United Kingdom advising them of the difficulties posed by these discriminatory laws. The steps taken by the government to advise ship masters acknowledged the sign-

ificance of the black seafaring population in Britain.[68] The English
population in the seaports apparently sympathized with the black
sailors. In 1857, Negro crew members fought with their white officers
on an American vessel anchored in the Mersey. The blacks thought
the ship was bound for Antigua, when in fact it was headed for
Mobile, Alabama. At the magistrate's hearing, the court room
spectators were openly sympathetic to the black sailors, and the
local press also took the side of the crew against their white officers.[69]

In their living conditions and treatment in Britain, these blacks
apparently fared no worse than foreign European sailors, and
probably as well as English seamen. The seafaring population in the
nineteenth century had a hard existence at best, and a level of
subsistence may be reached where distinctions in standards of life
become rather pointless. Certainly West Indian sailors who were
familiar with the language and customs of the English did not
experience the difficulties encountered by Arab and East Indian
sailors. One estimate in 1878 put the number of coloured sailors
engaged in long voyages in the British Merchant Service at 20,000,
of whom 5,000 were Lascars working for the Peninsular & Orient
Company. The Lascar seamen, separated by language and religion
as well as by race, experienced the worst conditions of isolation and
neglect of any alien community in Victorian England. Left stranded
in London over the winter before they could get a ship back to India,
isolated by their ignorance of English, and enjoined by their religion
to associate only with the faithful, many ended up in the Coldbath
Fields House of Correction convicted of vagrancy, and some were
found dead in the streets of the metropolis, killed by disease,
starvation, and exposure.[70] The experience of black sailors offers no
parallel.

Victorian commentators on race by and large agreed that the
mysterious dusky Indian deserved a place far higher in the hierarchy
of racial types than did the black savage Negro. In the realities of
race relations in the cosmopolitan ports, these intellectual generalizations had little relevance. Neither racial classification nor skin
colour was the most significant determinant of the degree of hardship and alienation suffered by foreign and coloured sailors. In
fact, the Asian seamen's association with the Victorian underworld
in the brothels, gambling rooms, and opium dens of Shadwell gave
other groups of coloured seamen an unwarranted notoriety.[71] To
members of the respectable classes, anyone with a dark skin was
classed as a 'black'. His origin might be African, Arab, East Indian,
Chinese, or Polynesian, or a mixture of any one of these with

European ancestry. Ironically, the association in the minds of respectable Victorians between coloured sailors in general and the most
notorious elements of English society added to the growing conviction that the black and brown races were inferior to civilized whites.[72]

In this most cosmopolitan and egalitarian segment of London
society, the various races intermingled freely. A member of the
London City Mission reported that:

> It would surprise many people to see how extensively these dark
> classes are tincturing the colour of the rising race of children in
> the lowest haunts of this locality: and many of the young fallen
> females have a visible infusion of Asiatic and African blood in
> their veins. They form a peculiar class, but mingle freely with the
> others. It is an instance of depraved taste, that many of our fallen
> ones prefer devoting themselves entirely to the dark race of men,
> and some who are to them [sic] have infants by them.[73]

Henry Mayhew took pains to emphasize that the haunts of sailors
were not the worst London had to offer. He found the theatres and
music halls which sailors frequented in the East End much superior
to the decrepit hang-outs of thieves and prostitutes in Soho. In one
of these dance halls of the East End, which Mayhew considered far
above the standard of the lowest dives, he found 'a sprinkling of
coloured men and a few thorough negroes scattered about here and
there.' In his researches, Mayhew also found some mulatto women
who as prostitute-thieves lived by 'plundering coloured sailors of
their money and clothes.'[74] At least until the late nineteenth century,
the various races among the cosmopolitan world of the London
poor mixed with the English population with much the same freedom
as they had done in the eighteenth century.

As well as finding blacks in the haunts of sailors, on London streets
Mayhew encountered black crossing-sweepers, dark-skinned sellers
of religious tracts, and supplicating ex-slaves. Earlier in the century,
when the anti-slavery campaign was at its peak, these black mendi-
cants were so successful in gaining alms that some English beggars
blackened themselves to enhance their appeal. By the time of
Mayhew's survey in the early 1850s, these English imposters of the
Negro had changed their garb for that of the black minstrel. Mayhew
estimated that 50 buskers circulated through London streets with
black faces and curly hair, and of these only one was a genuine
Negro.[75] Mayhew had a good opinion of black servants and
labourers:

> There are but few negro beggars to be seen now. It is only
> common fairness to say that negroes seldom, if ever, shirk work.

Their only trouble is to obtain it. Those who have seen the many negroes employed in Liverpool, will know that they are hard-working, patient, and too often underpaid. A negro will sweep a crossing, run errands, black boots, clean knives and forks, or dig, for a crust and a few pence. The few imposters among them are to be found among those who go about giving lectures on the horrors of slavery, and singing variations on the 'escapes' in that famous book 'Uncle Tom's Cabin'. Negro servants are seldom read of in police reports, and are generally found to give satisfaction to their employers. In the east end of London negro beggars are to be met with, but they are seldom beggars by profession. Whenever they are out of work they have no scruples, but go into the streets, take off their hats, and beg directly.[76]

Mayhew's observations about black casual labourers correspond to the experience of a number of escaped slaves who came to England from the United States in search of freedom from the Fugitive Slave Law, racial discrimination, and economic hardship. Some of these managed to secure a living, but, being subject to the economic uncertainties which plagued the lives of casual labourers and tradesmen, some fell on hard times and appealed to the British and Foreign Anti-Slavery Society for aid. In the Report of the Ladies' Society to Aid Fugitives from Slavery for 1854, the cases of eight destitute Negroes in England were described. Six of these fugitives had found employment in a variety of jobs, including work as a waiter, an apprentice bonnet-blocker, a rope-maker, a carpenter, and a ship's cook, before ill-health or unemployment forced them to appeal to the abolitionists for help.[77] It would therefore appear that when work was available, employers were willing to hire blacks. Other fugitives shared a life of appalling destitution along with the most impoverished elements of the English population. Dinah, a fugitive American slave, still suffering from injuries inflicted upon her in slavery, could only labour irregularly at needlework, and was looked after by a poor English woman who also gained a living by sewing.[78] In the early 1860s, the number of these fugitives in England increased sharply as a consequence of the American Civil War. In order to find employment for these destitute blacks, and to advance a philanthropic cause, the African Aid Society and the Aborigines Protection Society proposed that these indigents be given their passage to Liberia where their labour and skills were needed.[79]

Mayhew interviewed a number of black beggars he encountered in the streets of London. One of these street characters was a crippled crossing-sweeper from Jamaica who had served for nine years in the navy and merchant marine. After an injury at sea, which necessitated the amputation of both legs, he settled in London, and worked, when able, as a crossing-sweeper. At other times, he begged. He and his wife, an English coloured woman from Leeds, disliked their living quarters and their Irish neighbours: 'If you don't go out and drink and carouse with them, they don't like it; they make use of bad language – they chaff me about my misfortune – they call me "Cripple"; some says "Uncle Tom" and says "Nigger"; but I never takes no notice of 'em at all.'[80] Another black beggar interviewed by Mayhew complained of problems in securing employment and lodgings, and also about the prejudice of his fellow workers. He was a freedman from New York who came to England with his brother after hearing that the English treated 'niggers as good as whites'. He first found work with a travelling circus, but soon left when ill-treated. He then became dependent upon casual labour as a porter, and when unemployed he begged. He remarked that some lodging houses refused to keep black boarders, and on occasion his fellow workers made jokes about his colour, or called him 'nigger'. Racial discrimination may have added to this man's hardships, but his experiences were not necessarily typical. His brother managed to find a good position as a servant, and lived in relative prosperity.[81] The individual black living among the cosmopolitan poor of London or the seaports found his troubles aggravated by discrimination in housing and employment, but his sufferings were not solely caused by racial intolerance. His poverty placed him in the ranks of the residuum where almost a third of the English population shared similar hardships.

In spite of incidents of discrimination, the black poor did not suffer from universal or even widespread objections to their colour, and, as isolated individuals rather than as an identifiable group, blacks mixed reasonably freely with the commonality of Englishmen. Outbursts of anti-Negro feeling only occurred after the First World War, when an increase in the number of African and West Indian sailors in London, Liverpool, Manchester and particularly Cardiff, together with a shortage of jobs in the merchant service led to violence. During the nineteenth century, blacks in England never constituted a threat to any interest or group, nor did they present a convenient scapegoat for the failures and frustrations of society. Irish Catholics, and later in the century Jewish immigrants, were more readily at hand for that purpose. Even in the anti-alien agitation of the late nineteenth century, anti-immigrant campaigners, apart from a few anti-semitic extremists, deliberately avoided blatant appeals to race prejudice.[82] To the black poor and Negro sailors, the barriers of language, culture, and social class proved greater obstacles to economic security and social acceptance than did distinctions of colour.

For the great majority of blacks in nineteenth-century England, changes in English ideas about race had only a marginal influence upon their lives. The most decisive change in black status had come with the Industrial Revolution, and the separation of individual blacks from the patronage and influence of the wealthy. For some the abolitionists continued to provide a protective charity, as the philanthropists kept a watchful eye on the growth of racial discrimination and provided some assistance for blacks in need. After 1870 these philanthropic agencies were less actively interested in the plight of the black poor, or in the question of racial discrimination. The black poor were thus left more to their own devices, but because they were isolated as individuals and represented no threat to any group interest they faced no greater racial hostility. The relationship between individual blacks and respectable Victorians continued to be governed less by a consciousness of racial differences between black and white than by the reality of social disparities between rich and poor.

3

Black Gentlemen
and the
Mid-Victorians

For respectable Victorians, racial distinctions only became an important determinant of attitudes when individual blacks could claim to be educated, polished gentlemen, and therefore could not be treated as representatives of the lower orders. A group of articulate, refined, and gentlemanly blacks visited England during the nineteenth century, and faced Victorian gentlemen as equals. During the mid-century these visitors were hospitably received, but as the century advanced English gentlemen adopted a more arrogant attitude, and for specifically racial reasons rejected the claims of these blacks for equal status. It was not so much the black poor, but rather these black gentlemen who more directly encountered the growth of racial antipathy in the second half of the nineteenth century, and it is from their experience that something can be learned of the nature of Victorian racialism and its development.

Up to the mid-century, Englishmen reacted to black strangers with a certain uneasiness and apprehension. Their suspicions were heightened by lingering questions about the Negro's nature and status, but rarely did these fears express themselves in discriminatory or hostile behaviour. Blacks found acceptance in the best social circles, and with the climax of the anti-slavery movement in the 1830s, philanthropists made greater efforts to prove that racial discrimination was unjustified. English behaviour upon meeting blacks was not simply determined by an adverse reaction to their dark skins and other distinctive physical traits. Social standing as much as racial differences determined the attitude adopted toward individual blacks.

From the 1840s to the end of the American Civil War, the presence of ex-slaves and Negro abolitionists as speakers or as platform guests played an important part in British anti-slavery agitation. In making preparations for the Anti-Slavery Convention of 1853, Wilson Armistead, the president of the Leeds Anti-Slavery Society and publicist on the Negro and slavery, hoped that 'a very general invitation will be given to Black and coloured people, those of talent and enterprise, whose presence (a good sprinkling of them) would add much to the interest, and consequent effect of the occasion'.[1] In the 'Exeter Halls' not only of the metropolis, but of Manchester, Liverpool, Glasgow, Dublin, and most other large centres of population, Frederick Douglass, William Wells Brown, Josiah Henson, Samuel R. Ward, William and Ellen Craft, Sarah Remond, and other prominent black Americans put the case of their enslaved brethren, and through their eloquence moved their spell-bound audiences from pathos and tears, to righteous indignation and tumultuous cheering. Not only before the massed hundreds and thousands of these gatherings, but also in the village halls and chapels, they advocated their cause before a remarkably extensive area of the country. During his five years in Britain, William Wells Brown travelled over 25,000 miles and gave over 1,000 lectures to benevolent societies, religious organizations, literary groups, and mechanics' institutes.[2] Frequently equipped with a panorama illustrating the conditions of slave life, highlighted by examples of tortures, and supplied with a stack of the narratives of their escapes, these ex-slaves were effective agents for their cause, provided a popular entertainment, and gained a comfortable income for themselves. The lectures became so popular that dark-skinned men posing as ex-slaves began touring the country. In 1853, the *Anti-Slavery Reporter* and the *Anti-Slavery Advocate* warned against three such imposters who took money on false pretences, ruined the reputation of deserving blacks, and reduced the income of acknowledged anti-slavery charities.[3]

These itinerant lecturers financed themselves by fees from their lectures, and by sales of their narratives. Some of these narratives had a remarkable sale in Great Britain, and attested both to the prominence of the authors and to the widespread sympathy with the anti-slavery cause. Frederick Douglass's narrative went through five British editions in 1846–7, selling over 13,000 copies, and by 1850 30,000 copies had been bought in Britain and America. Charles Gilpin, the English publisher of William Wells Brown's narrative, sold 12,000 copies of the work in 1850.[4] Frequently these biographies or autobiographies included a final chapter describing the fugitives' travels in

Britain. These black tourists invariably contrasted their freedom from insult in monarchical Britain with their experience of discrimination in democratic America. Undoubtedly the violent racism of nineteenth-century America, in both North and South, led these black visitors to interpret the absence of institutionalized discrimination in Britain as a lack of racial antipathy among the British. Providing they had the funds to afford it, they had access to all public amenities and, in the private sphere, they found the most eminent classes in English society welcomed them and displayed no sign of aversion to their presence. The narrators were acutely aware of their readership in both Britain and America, and they may have exaggerated their favourable reception for effect. The contrast between the two countries complimented their British friends, and denounced the prejudice of their fellow Americans. On the other hand, these narrators reported so few incidents of racial discrimination, and so overwhelmingly agreed on their freedom from prejudice while in Britain, that one must give some credence to their observations. The character of the ex-slaves leads one to accept the veracity of their reporting. As men and women who had escaped from slavery, they were in no sense cowardly about opposing a new injustice. Their British friends, as good Evangelicals and Nonconformists, enjoyed an outspoken attack on an acknowledged evil, and did not avoid opportunities for a little self-incrimination and purgation of guilt over the sins of their fellow countrymen. The contrasting picture of prejudiced America and tolerant Britain encouraged British abolitionists to become watchdogs over any evidence of discrimination and to denounce it as un-British as well as unjust. The visiting anti-slavery lecturers were therefore relatively free to denounce discrimination when they encountered it. They had few occasions to do so, for they found the mid-Victorians surprisingly tolerant.[5]

For some American blacks, England became a refuge from racial persecution. William Allen, a teacher from New York, was forced to flee from America when he married Mary King, one of his white students. The Allens arrived in England in 1853, and stayed for the remainder of their lives. Allen, with the help of his English friends, operated a day school for local youngsters in north London, the Caledonian Training School in Islington, and remained an active spokesman against slavery and a defender of the Negro race.[6] After the passing of the Fugitive Slave Law in 1850, William and Ellen Craft, along with other fugitive slaves, fled to England to avoid recapture. Through the hospitality of Joseph Estlin, a physician and Garrisonian abolitionist from Bristol, and the friendship of Lady

Byron and Harriet Martineau, the Crafts gained an education and introduction into English society. At the British Association in 1863, and much to the delight of that learned gathering, William Craft challenged the analogy between the Negro and the ape put forward by James Hunt, an outspoken racist, and president of the Anthropological Society of London. The Crafts remained in England until after the end of the American Civil War, but eventually returned to their native Georgia.[7] Through their residence in England, the Allens and the Crafts demonstrated their faith in mid-Victorian racial tolerance. Many more black writers and lecturers expressed the same conviction through their narratives.

The fugitive slaves most frequently reported incidents of discrimination on board the transatlantic liners which carried them to and from Europe. Influential abolitionists had to overcome the objections of the shipping agent to the Crafts' colour before the two ex-slaves could gain a passage. William Wells Brown similarly experienced discrimination on board ship, and the Rev. Samuel Ringgold Ward, confined to his stateroom in case he upset the other passengers, received a daily visit from Thackeray, a sympathetic fellow traveller. In London, Ward's residence at a hotel caused six Americans to leave.[8] The *Anti-Slavery Advocate*, outraged at the spread of 'American' race feeling in England, reported another incident where a Manchester hotel had asked a black West Indian to have his meals separately so as not to offend a guest from the Southern States. The black visitor simply went to another hotel. The *Advocate* claimed this incident was the first discriminatory act of its kind to be reported in England.[9]

English commentators and the American fugitives identified any instances of racial discrimination with the influence of American tourists. In 1845 the Cunard line, fearing the reaction of their American passengers, refusing to acknowledge Frederick Douglass's first-class ticket, and forced him to travel steerage. Before his return to the States in 1847, Douglass found Cunard's Liverpool agent again refused to give him first-class accommodation. Douglass wrote to *The Times*, and with his abolitionist friends created sufficient public outcry to gain a public apology from Samuel Cunard himself. Even *The Times*, an organ not altogether friendly to the Negro, objected to a British company 'trucking to an unworthy prejudice of our transatlantic neighbours', and declared that Cunard's bad faith toward Douglass was 'as dishonourable, as the prejudice against him is ignorant and contemptible.'[10] Douglass thought that any instances of racial intolerance he encountered abroad came from

American tourists, and he considered the Cunard incident an exception to the enthusiastic and friendly welcome he received everywhere he travelled in Britain.

On several occasions, Douglass repeated the observation that during his long stay in England he met no antagonism on account of his race. He recalled that experience as:

> having enjoyed nearly two years of equal social privileges in
> England, after dining with gentlemen of great literary, social,
> political, and religious eminence – never, during the whole time
> having met with a single word, look, or gesture, which gave me
> the slightest reason to think my colour was an offence to
> anybody.[11]

Douglass did not receive this favourable treatment simply because of his good manners and his eloquence. He did not avoid contentious issues or heated controversy. In Scotland, he led the attack on the Free Church's acceptance of money from slaveholding congregations in the Southern States. He similarly attacked the Evangelical Alliance. At a Temperance Convention held in Covent Garden, he assailed the racial prejudices of the American Temperance Movement. Yet in spite of his outspoken challenges, no one replied with a denunciation of Douglass's race or colour, and in fact many of those who met the distinguished fugitive were greatly impressed by him.[12]

Another fugitive slave, William Wells Brown, who lived in England from 1849 until 1854, also described the British as tolerant hosts. In 1850, when he attended the Paris Peace Conference organized by pacifist groups, Brown noted only his fellow Americans made objections to his presence. French and English delegates treated him favourably, and he was introduced to Victor Hugo and Richard Cobden. Having travelled extensively in the United Kingdom lecturing on slavery and teetotalism, Brown claimed that 'the prejudice which I have experienced on all and every occasion in the United States ... vanished as soon as I set foot on the soil of Britain.'[13] He contrasted his experience with the treatment he received as soon as he returned to Philadelphia:

> I had partaken of the hospitality of noblemen in England, had sat
> at the table of the French Minister of Foreign Affairs; I had
> looked from the strangers' gallery upon the great legislators of
> England, as they sat in the House of Commons; I had stood in the
> House of Lords when Her Britannic Majesty prorogued her
> Parliament; I had eaten at the same table with Sir Edward
> Bulwer Lytton, Charles Dickens, Eliza Cook, Alfred Tennyson,
> and the son-in-law of Sir Walter Scott; the omnibusses of Paris,

Edinburgh, Glasgow, and Liverpool, had stopped to take me up; ... but what mattered that? My face was not white, my hair was not straight; and, therefore I must be excluded from a seat in a third-rate American omnibus.[14]

Brown had established his literary connections through his honorary membership in the Whittington Club. He prided himself on being able to mingle freely with all levels of English society, and he claimed to have met radical politicians as well as the nobility, and to have lectured to working-class audiences on slavery and temperance. Brown especially noted the number of blacks in the streets of Britain who could walk freely without fear of insult. At the Great Exhibition of 1851, he remarked on the number of Asians and Africans in the crowds, and took special delight in the way American visitors were upset by his having an English woman accompanying him. The only reference to any peculiar reaction to his appearance was certain curiosity at his colour. In Dublin, waiting with crowds to see the Queen, Brown noted: 'My own colour differing from those about me, I attracted not a little attention from many; and often, ... would find myself eyed by all round.'[15] Other than these inquisitive stares, Brown met with no sign of racial animosity.

Other black Americans also reported favourably on English conduct towards them, but the few who made critical comments about their hosts' reactions provide a more informative insight into the nature of mid-Victorian racial attitudes.[16] The Rev. Samuel Ringgold Ward, who came to Britain in 1853 as the agent of the Anti-Slavery Society of Canada, uncovered some signs of antipathy, but observed that the British seemed to react more sharply to class than to racial differences. Since he had experienced discrimination in the free Northern States and in Canada, he denied that slavery caused prejudice. He claimed that the source of American antagonism toward blacks was the lower-class origin of the early settlers, and observed that 'the same class will abuse a Negro in England or Ireland now.' He found that immigrant 'Englishmen, Irishmen, and Scotchmen, generally become the bitterest of Negro-haters, within fifteen days of their naturalization', but that, on the other hand, 'the middling and better classes of all Europe treat a black gentleman as a gentleman'[17]: 'the British gentleman is a gentleman everywhere, and under all circumstances.... Among gentlemen, the black takes just the place for which he is qualified, as if his colour were similar to that of other gentlemen.'[18] Ward's North American experience and his Nonconformist conscience influenced his observations. He contrasted the cleanliness and sobriety of the Welsh with the degradation and drunkenness of the Catholic Irish poor, and favourably compared the kirk-attending Scottish workers' knowledge of slavery with the ignorance of their non-churchgoing English brethren. He remarked on the squalor of London, Glasgow, and Dublin, and wished that *The Times* and other sources of anti-Negro opinion would plead for blacks the extenuating circumstances of poverty, ignorance, drink, and neglect which apologists applied to the British poor. He objected to the usual accusation that Negroes were debased by nature. In Ward's opinion, the black community in the United States would gain respect only when they had the wealth to command it.[19]

British abolitionists did not escape Ward's criticism. He complimented Lord Elgin for his philanthropy, because he 'is not one of those who claim any special favours for the coloured man, or who expect any special worship *from* him. This is about the sum of some people's philanthropy touching the Negro.'[20] Ward contrasted the sincere abolitionist with the sentimentalist. These shallow friends of the Negro, Ward claimed, soon became pro-slavery men when they went to America. On the whole, Ward complimented the English on their hospitality and their ability to make a guest feel at ease: 'In this country it is difficult to understand how little difference is made in the treatment of black men, in respect to their position. Englishmen do not expect servants to ride in first-class carriages; but a person of wealth or position, of whatever colour, has, in this respect, just what he pays for.'[21] Through his social connections and ability as a distinguished anti-slavery lecturer, Ward had both the position to command respect, and the money to pay his way. Consequently, he found the English friendly, tolerant hosts.

After two decades of these tours by black abolitionists, the British and Foreign Anti-Slavery Society, in 1864, began to have doubts about the value of Samuel Ward and other black lecturers:

Now we believe far more harm than good is done to the anti-slavery cause by these itinerant lecturers, many of whom are either rank imposters, or men who, having originally a legitimate claim to sympathy, have been spoilt by over-patronage, have lingered in the country till the interest in them has exhausted itself, and then being without resources, have fallen back on their 'wits', and made the best they could of them.[22]

The *Anti-Slavery Reporter* advised British friends of the slave to exercise discretion in their charity to Negroes, but made a distinction between the Rev. Howard Mitchell, Howard Day, S. R. Ward, and Reuben Nixon, all ex-slaves or lecturers who had lost favour or had been found to be frauds, and 'the Sella Martins, the Professor Allens, the William Crafts, the Highland Garnetts, and others, whose probity had withstood the severe test of success after undergoing the trials incidental to praiseworthy, though, for a time unsuccessful self-help.'[23] To the Quaker bankers of the Board of the British and Foreign Anti-Slavery Society a black anti-slavery lecturer dependent on his fees and on charity had not attained the elevated status of independent means and respectability. In the same way, the Board had reservations about George Thompson, an English fee-earning lecturer on free trade and anti-slavery, a radical Member of Parliament from 1849 to 1854, and something of a professional demagogue. Only financial independence could secure genuine respect, and few, if any, black abolitionists could claim sufficient wealth to free themselves from the taint of having an economic interest in anti-slavery agitation.

In spite of the British abolitionists' reservations about the financial dependents of black spokesmen, Ward and his fellow lecturers mingled freely with a broad segment of English society. From the homes of the nobility to working men's institutes, in churches, and chapels, they not only received the hospitality of their abolitionist friends but were welcomed into the charmed circle of politics, literary societies, and learned associations. Their black complexions did not bar them from polite society, nor did their favourable reception mean Englishmen lacked colour consciousness. At times the ex-slaves were treated as objects of pity or curiosity, and often their race and slave origin gained them special treatment, but not all blacks, and not even all Negro abolitionists, shared equally in the special favours of their hosts. The most eminent of these visitors, for example, Frederick Douglass and William Wells Brown, gained a more ready admittance into good society than many lesser-known fugitives. A black skin and a slave birth could not open the door to polite society. By their experience in American anti-slavery circles, or by education in England, these distinguished abolitionists had gained the friends, the influence, and the training in the social graces to make them acceptable guests in these distinguished circles. Their success lay in their ability to conform to conventions of correct behaviour. In manner, in speech, in dress, in their own confidence and social ease, and even in their mental outlook, they were eminently qualified, and therefore acceptable in the best circles of Victorian society. When William Wells Brown came to define what he meant by equality, he ended up stressing individual effort and enterprise in much the way that Lord Palmerston had in his often quoted Don Pacifico speech. For Brown, for Palmerston, and for most respectable Victorians the key was not equality but liberty. According to Brown, 'every man must make equality for himself. No society, no government, can make equality for him. I do not expect the slave of the South to jump into equality; all I claim for him is that he may be allowed to jump into liberty, and let him make equality for himself.'[24] When the mid-Victorians considered the questions of race and equality they usually tried to create a hierarchical classification of racial types with the Anglo-Saxon clearly at the top and the Negro somewhere near the bottom. This racial theorizing did not have much bearing upon mid-Victorian behaviour. The experience of eminent black abolitionists shows that the mid-Victorians did not treat all blacks alike. A fortunate few received the respect commanded by their abilities and their social accomplishments. In the mid-nineteenth century it was still bad manners to object to the colour of a black gentleman.

The experience of fugitive slaves who came to England without the education and preparation in North American abolitionist circles, without experience in the arts of gracious living, and without the necessary introductions to influential Englishmen, contrasted sharply with that of their more favoured brethren. Black lecturers on the evils of slavery did not leave a favourable impression with all members of the English public.

In 1852, the editor of the *Wolverhampton Herald* wrote a number of abusive articles on the lectures of Henry Box Brown, a fugitive slave who had earned his name by his escape to freedom in a box. Brown sued the editor of the newspaper and was awarded £100 damages. Brown founded his claim upon the expectation that he would earn £50–£70 per week from his lectures, but after the libellous review in the Wolverhampton paper his audience declined considerably. The newspaper had described Brown as a 'bejewelled "darkie" ', whose 'gross and palpable exaggeration' of the condition of slavery could only 'generate disgust at the foppery, conceit, vanity, and egotistical stupidity of the Box Brown school.' In a second article, headed 'Nigger Panorama', the *Herald* had included a long passage purporting to be an excerpt from Brown's lecture in an authentic Southern Negro drawl. 'The celebrated Brown', supposedly, 'played, with ludicrous and semi-baboonish agility, his nocturnal antics to the delight and merriment of the Juvenile ragamuffins', but in court, *The Times* reported that Brown, although wearing some jewellery, was quiet in manner and correctly spoken. A schoolmaster who had attended Brown's performance testified that the ex-slave had spoken quite correctly. In its defence, the *Herald* claimed to be protecting the public against 'such exaggerated, preposterous, and, to a certain extent, indecent exhibitions.' Brown's panorama had shown the whipping of both men and women slaves, and the burning of one slave alive.[25] Although Brown gained reparation in this case, neither black speakers nor their subject were free from ridicule and abuse. In some instances, blacks faced outright discrimination.

In 1850, John Brown, who had escaped from slavery into Canada, sailed to England in search of British freedom and justice. Upon arrival in Liverpool, he travelled to Cornwall to meet some miners with whom he had worked in Michigan. He spent two months near Redruth lecturing on slavery, and then passed on to Bristol where he worked for four weeks as a carpenter. Not satisfied with his progress, he ventured north to Heywood, Lancashire, and found employment with a builder. He soon lost his job there, for 'I found there is prejudice against colour in England, in some classes, as well as more generally in America.'[26] Brown's account of this incident implied that he found his fellow workmen rather than his employer antagonistic to his colour. Brown turned his attentions to the more profitable business of lecturing on slavery. Before working men's institutes and chapel meetings, he advocated the defeat of the slave power in America through the development of free-grown cotton in India, Australia, the West Indies, and Africa. From his earnings as a lecturer, and from the sale of his narrative, he hoped to pay his passage to West Africa and put his plan into effect.[27] Brown, dissatisfied with his progress in English society, and hindered in his advance by some racial hostility, turned his hopes to Africa.

Although some distinguished black abolitionists gained an entrance to privileged social circles, a professional lecturer or a carpenter could hardly hope to aim so high. Henry Box Brown and John Brown did not have the advantages of their distinguished countrymen. Without an established reputation and without the experience or the influential acquaintances in respectable social circles, itinerant black lecturers, such as the two Browns, were left to fend for themselves. In contrast, the more eminent black abolitionists gained British friends and associates of quality and influence, and thus their 'equality' or social status was assured.

In some instances, English abolitionists clearly treated the fugitive slave as an inferior. In 1861 extradition proceedings against John Anderson, a fugitive slave in Canada, greatly excited the British public. Anderson was accused of murdering his master in Missouri while making good his escape from slavery. After a series of urgent questions in Parliament, a confused jurisdictional dispute between English and Canadian courts, and action by the Imperial Government to prevent Anderson's release to the American authorities, the extradition appeal was lost, and Anderson retained his freedom.[28] Some British abolitionists suggested that Anderson should be brought to England to help arouse support for the North in the American Civil War. The British and Foreign Anti-Slavery Society advised against any such move, for they feared the fugitive would become 'a charge upon public or private benevolence', and thought that Anderson's benefactors would 'obtain help for him by converting him into an object of morbid curiosity, while the damage done to the anti-slavery cause by such exhibitions may be extreme.'[29] In spite of these warnings, Harper Twelvetrees and a committee of English abolitionists brought the now famous fugitive to England.

Unfortunately, Anderson proved to be a poorly educated, perhaps illiterate, mason and plasterer with no experience of public speaking, let alone of addressing the vast audiences of Exeter Hall. At the meeting held in this huge auditorium, speakers in welcoming Anderson pointed to his condition as proof that slaveholders neglected the education and welfare of their slaves. The Anderson Committee soon found that the London environment 'hindered' their charge's progress, and therefore they hustled him off to the village of Corby in Northamptonshire. Here, Anderson received some elementary education in reading, writing, arithmetic, and Scripture, and his benefactors noted that 'his temperament had become subdued'. The Committee gained some land in Liberia and proposed that Anderson should make a fresh start in Africa as a landed proprietor. He only reluctantly agreed to the plan. On 22 December 1862, at a Farewell Soirée for the ex-slave's benefit, speakers admonished the fugitive to value his schooling, and to appreciate how his benefactors had elevated him to the dignity of a landholder. Anderson and his fellow Liberians, the philanthropic spokesmen claimed, had a duty to demonstrate 'to the world that the negro race could govern themselves as well as the white race.'

This laid a deep responsibility upon John Anderson and his future fellow citizens, – that in this first attempt at self-government they should conclusively refute the assertion of the slave-owners.
... upon his behaviour in his newly-adopted country would depend, in some degree, the future destiny of the entire negro race; and ... the committee ... would find their reward in his being a sober, prosperous, and respectable citizen.'[30]

The patronizing attitude of Anderson's benefactors hardly evinced an egalitarian spirit, but race alone did not influence their behaviour. Similar sermons of industry, thrift, sobriety, and self-help were handed out to their own white countrymen. Anderson's patrons claimed to judge equality not by the skin colour, but by the evidence of sober, upright, and respectable living. On these criteria, few abolitionists would have accepted Anderson as their equal. They claimed that race did not bar a man from equal status, but demanded that the individual Negro prove his equality by his refined and civilized deportment, and then they would offer him the respect that was his due. In contrast, the racists flatly denied that anyone with a black skin could reach that elevated standard of refinement and civilization. In practice, these doctrinaire claims of racial equality or inferiority shrank in importance. A semi-literate, unskilled, and unsophisticated fugitive slave received the condescending paternalism of his benefactors, whereas a black abolitionist of ability, distinction, and experience, received the consideration and respect which the mid-Victorians thought appropriate to his social station. When a black visitor entered mid-nineteenth century England, his social position, not his colour, determined the quality of his reception.

Between 1840 and 1870 Africans of distinction received as favourable a reception in England as that enjoyed by eminent black Americans. In 1858, the *Aborigines' Friend and Colonial Intelligencer* suggested that there were a sufficient number of African merchants and students in London to form an association similar to the one in existence for American citizens in the metropolis. Four years later the Anti-Slavery Society made plans for a banquet to honour President Benson and ex-President Rogers of Liberia. Lord Brougham was asked to preside and distinguished Africans and men of African descent were to attend.[31]

The presence of these Africans in London was a result of trade between England and West Africa, and of the policy of missionaries, philanthropists, and colonial officials who sought to educate Africans in business and the professions.[32] At this same time within England education, especially in the professions, was becoming increasingly important for the acquisition of gentlemanly status. The education of Africans at the most prestigious institutions of higher learning and professional training necessitated the acceptance of black students into the ranks of respectable, and even gentle, society.[33] William Wells Brown was surprised at the number of black students he met on the streets of British university centres, and at the friendliness of white students towards them. 'In an hour's walk through the Strand, Regent, or Piccadilly Streets in London', he observed, 'one may meet half a dozen coloured young men, who are inmates of various colleges in the metropolis.'[34] When visiting the Infirmary in Edinburgh, Brown

> Was pleased to see among the two or three hundred students three coloured young men, seated upon the same benches with those of a fairer complexion, and yet there appeared no feeling on part of the whites towards their coloured associates, except that of companionship and respect. . . . . I had scarcely left the lecture room of the Institute and reached the street, when I met a large number of students on their way to the college, and here again were seen young coloured men arm in arm with whites.[35]

The number of these students in British institutions of higher learning was partly a result of the ambitious schemes of philanthropists and colonial officials for the promotion of Africans into positions of respect and authority.

After the disastrous Niger Expedition of 1841 Britons interested in the annihilation of the slave trade and in the promotion of legitimate commerce in West Africa were convinced that, for the time being, it was useless for Europeans to fight against the all-conquering tropical diseases. Under the leadership of Henry Venn of the Church Missionary Society, these philanthropists adopted the new tactic of promoting the education of more Africans in England who would then return to their homeland and carry out the work of producing a Christian civilized community.[36] In their programme of education, the philanthropists went beyond sentimental sermonizing on the lowly savage and the poor slave, and evinced their belief in the Negro's ability to fulfil positions of leadership and responsibility. In the 1850s Africans trained in business, the professions, and administration, and backed by philanthropists and goverment officials in London, were promoted into responsible, prestigious positions. Europeans in the colonies made little objection to these appointments. Africans rose to the rank of Lieutenant Governor, and plans were made for African control of the commercial, administrative, and religious life of British areas of influence in West Africa.[37]

In an age when higher education was strictly reserved for the privileged few, proposals for the education of blacks at universities and professional schools had particular relevance to the mid-Victorians' ideas about the social significance of racial differences. The Rev. J. Hampden Gurney, speaking in 1853 to a meeting of abolitionists, proposed the creation of an institution of higher learning

for black West Indians. He thought that 'one of the most important steps toward elevating the coloured race would be to give
them a higher kind of education, so that they might fit themselves,
from their social position and natural gifts, to rise in the scale of
society and show that they were in no ways inferior to whites.'[38]
Gurney held up the examples of the Church Missionary Society
College in Sierra Leone and Codrington College in Barbados, and
recommended the establishment of a college in Bermuda to provide
grammar school and university education for black students of the
United States and the West Indies. In seconding the motion, Mr
Justice T. C. Haliburton, the author of *Sam Slick*, suggested that
such an institution was too good for blacks.

> It was a good idea to have a college for blacks, because they could
> not be educated with whites. He thought, however, that the name
> of a college was too fine. Why not call it an academy? A college
> pre-supposed the admission of gentlemen: but he did not imagine
> any one would say of any black, that he could possibly be a
> gentleman, however well educated, for he sprang from a race
> degraded by their caste as well as by colour. He thought, too, that
> by such high-sounding names they were stirring up the conceit of
> the coloured people, who would soon be aspiring to the hands of
> the daughters of the whites, and seeking to place themselves
> entirely on a level with them, which could not be tolerated.[39]

Much to the delight of the assembled abolitionists, the Rev. Samuel
Ward, as the visible proof of black gentility, attacked Haliburton's
slander on his race, and forced the speaker to retire from the
meeting.[40] The issue at stake was that of the Negro's proper place
in the natural and the social order. On this occasion, the defenders
of the Negro and the supporters of higher education for black
gentlemen won the battle; by the end of the century, Haliburton
and other like-minded men had won the war.

In line with this policy of training a black élite, one scheme sought
to establish on the West coast of Africa a merchant fleet manned
entirely by Africans. When making this proposal in 1849, Sir George
Stephen, a supporter of humanitarian enterprises, and brother of
James Stephen, the permanent under-secretary of the Colonial
Office, hoped to put legitimate commerce firmly in African hands
and thereby end the slave trade. He reassured his readers that there
was nothing odd in Africans commanding vessels or taking other
positions of gentlemanly responsibility:

> liberal education has made large progress in the black and
> coloured population since the abolition of slavery, many of the

Creoles received their education in the European and especially
Scotch universities. We are so little accustomed to meet men of
colour moving in the circle which, somewhat absurdly,
appropriates to itself the title of 'good society', that the idea of a
Negro of refined taste and cultivated mind is with difficulty
received. . . ; yet men whom business or colonial connection has
brought into familiar intercourse with the black and coloured
races, know well that the educated among them are not inferior
to whites in any of those qualities which acquire esteem for the
gentleman or confidence for the merchant.[41]

From 1863 to 1865 Commander A. P. Eardley Wilmot of the West
Coast Africa Station tutored four African youths in the arts of
navigation, and reported that they completed their training in a
'highly satisfactory' manner.[42] Somerset, the First Lord of the
Admiralty, doubted the value of these schemes to train Africans for
the command of vessels. In reply to Lord John Russell, he observed:

I have received your note including Captn E. Wilmot's letter
which recommends that we should have vessels on the coast of
Africa officered as well as manned by natives. I cannot agree with
him. I believe the respect inspired by the sight of a British vessel
of war would be much diminished if we adopted such a system.
The natives are not to be trusted when a conflict occurs and, as I
am informed whenever there is a probability of any fighting it is
necessary to have a large proportion of Europeans.[43]

Somerset felt Africans could not be trusted with the responsibilities
of leadership which the Victorians reserved for gentlemen. In the
1860s philanthropists still actively promoted African education, but
an increasing number of Englishmen began to agree with Somerset
that even educated blacks could not be wholly trusted.

By their unrealistic expectation of complete success, promoters of
these schemes for black advancement were partly responsible for the
declining reputation of the Negro. The plans and activities of Henry
Venn and his colleagues in missionary and anti-slavery societies
expressed confidence in the abilities of blacks. These proposals
equally demonstrated the confident assumptions of their middle-class
outlook. In effect, their schemes aimed at recreating an English
society of black men in Africa or the West Indies through developing
a middle-class élite to act as a reforming influence upon the whole
society. Just as middle-class mid-Victorians confidently viewed
themselves as leaders of civilization and progress through industrial
technology and moral righteousness, so they hoped that a black
middle class would do the same for Africa and the Caribbean. These

promoters of Negro education measured the success of their efforts by the degree to which English ways were successfully imitated. The controversies over emancipation and decline in the West Indies, the state of Sierra Leone, and the value of missionary work, concentrated upon the Negro's nature and abilities rather than upon the social and economic conditions of these diverse areas. The British rarely found that their schemes for black advancement fulfilled their exaggerated expectations and, rather than question their own vision, they revived the question of the Negro's racial inheritance and often found it wanting.[44]

At the same time, the standards of respectable mid-Victorians were changing. Those Englishmen interested in black improvement had demanded success in life and respectability in conduct from white and black alike. During the 1860s and after they added to this demand for respectability and success, the new and more rarified quality of gentility. By its very nature this quest for gentility proved more restrictive, for only a few could gain entrance into this élite rank of leadership and authority. Overseas, black communities had failed to conform even to respectable standards. How then could a few educated blacks, belonging to a primitive race and tainted with servile status, hope to command the respect of gentlemen? With the change in mid-Victorian attitudes, the colour of a man's skin rather than his social accomplishments began to weigh heavier in the English assessment of individual blacks. The Victorians never seriously questioned the Negro's capacity for physical labour. His supposed inferiority only applied to those positions filled by the upper and middle classes, or what Haliburton had styled the places of gentlemen. This change in attitude rested upon an extension of social attitudes already present in Victorian society to include racial differences. Once the assumption was made that blacks could only perform labouring tasks and never approach gentlemanly status, respectable Victorians simply applied to all men with black skins the same judgments, manner, and bearing that they adopted toward their social inferiors within English society. When this association between African descent and lowly social status became more firmly fixed, and was added to the latent suspicions and aversions produced by xenophobia and ethnocentrism, racial attitudes became more rigid and emotive in character, and a new inflexibility and contempt characterized English attitudes to the Negro.

The career of Samuel Ajayi Crowther, whose consecration as Bishop of the Niger in 1864 was the high point in the policy of promoting Africans into positions of leadership, was indicative of this transition in English racial attitudes in the last half of the nineteenth century. When about 15 years old Samuel Crowther, born in Yoruba, was taken on board a Portuguese slaver which was intercepted by the Royal Navy. The slave boy was liberated in Sierra Leone, and in 1826 sent to England and put in care of the Rev. E. Bickersteth, the secretary of the Church Missionary Society. During this time, Crowther attended the parochial school in Islington. Upon his return to Africa, he continued his education in Sierra Leone and began his career as a missionary. In 1841 he served with the Niger expedition as missionary, explorer and translator, and with the Rev. J. Schoen published journals of the expedition. He then returned to London to complete his training at the Church Missionary College, and in 1843 was ordained and returned to Africa. Crowther next returned to England in 1851. Henry Venn urgently recalled him to put pressure on the Government to act against the threatened Dahomean invasion of Abeokuta. Crowther visited Lord Palmerston, at that time Foreign Secretary, and Sir Francis Baring, the first Lord of the Admiralty. He also had a lengthy interview with Prince Albert and the Queen, and lectured students at Cambridge. Venn credited Crowther with having prompted the government to intervene with a naval blockade to protect Abeokuta.[45] After further work as a missionary, explorer, and author in West Africa, Crowther once again returned to England in 1864. On this occasion, he received an honorary Doctor of Divinity degree from Oxford for his translations of the Scriptures into African languages, and with full pomp and ceremony in Canterbury Cathedral the Archbishop of Canterbury consecrated him Bishop of the Niger. On his next visit to Britain in 1870, Bishop Crowther ordained his youngest son, Dandeson, as an Anglican priest. In fact, all six of the bishop's children, three sons and three daughters, received their education in England.[46] Through the 1870s and 1880s, Bishop Crowther made a number of visits to Britain and apparently continued to have a hospitable reception.

In Africa, Bishop Crowther faced opposition from white missionaries. They resisted his appointment and then refused to recognize his authority. With a mixture of personal jealousy and racial arrogance, they argued that no African would respect white missionaries whose leader was a black bishop. The white missionaries viewed their authority as inextricably tied to their status as Europeans. Nonetheless, once Crowther had established himself, even the Rev. Henry Townsend, the bishop's most ardent opponent, acknowledged and respected the African's position.

Crowther's severest trial with European racism came at the end of his career. In 1890, as an active octogenarian who had devoted his life to the church, he faced a new younger breed of white missionary. Inspired by a more rigid evangelical paternalism, and by new anthropological notions of the master race and the childlike attributes of the Negro, these young enthusiasts challenged the positions of the native pastors and circumvented the bishop's authority. Unable to bear their arrogant interference, the aged bishop reluctantly resigned his post.[47] Crowther's lengthy experience depicted the general trend in racial attitudes from the middle to the end of the nineteenth century. The opposition he encountered in the 1850s and 1860s came from Europeans active in Africa. In England, the Church Missionary Society under the direction of Henry Venn supported Crowther against the Europeans' assertions. Apart from Venn, Church Missionary Society officials were not too enthusiastic about having a black bishop, but they were won over to the idea by the consideration that few whites seemed able to endure the tropical climate. In 1892 the CMS executives could not agree to entrust the bishopric to any of the experienced African pastors. As a result, they appointed a more 'reliable' white bishop in Crowther's place.[48] The experience of other Africans in England followed the same pattern. Toward the middle of the century, they reported an hospitable reception. As the century advanced, they increasingly encountered racial insults and intolerance.

This change in attitude was not sudden or even clearly defined. From the late 1860s through to the 1890s, some blacks reported that they were still treated with tolerance; others that they faced insults and discrimination. In 1868, Dr James Africanus Horton – born in Sierra Leone of Ibo parents, educated at King's College, London, and the University of Edinburgh, and an army staff surgeon – described racial antipathy as a peculiarly American rather than English prejudice.

In no part of the Coast is the class distinction of colour so trampled underfoot as at this place [Accra]. Many of the natives are properly educated, and would countenance no tampering with their privileges as 'man and brother'. Some attempts were recently made to originate that Americanized party feeling which existed on other parts of the Coast; but the originators were scouted and almost 'cut' by every one.[49]

For the remainder of his life Horton increasingly faced this 'Americanized' antipathy as Englishmen grew more contemptuous of educated black gentlemen.

Black American visitors continued to report that the English were free of racial prejudice. The Jubilee Singers from Fisk University toured Britain in 1874, 1876, and 1884 in order to raise funds for their university through concerts of Negro Spirituals. They encountered racial discrimination only on board the Cunard liner, and claimed that during their travels in England they met with no racial prejudice. The Singers gained widespread popularity and raised £10,000 during their first visit. At the Duke and Duchess of Argyll's they entertained the Queen, and sang at an official reception given by the Gladstones. They also breakfasted with the Gladstones, and on this occasion mixed freely with church dignitaries, politicians, and members of the nobility.[50] William and Ellen Craft also remained confident in English racial tolerance. They sent their son to England for his education, and advised him

to remain a short time longer in the Old Country, that, is to say, if he could procure employment, it being so very much easier for a man of colour to succeed in the race of life particularly if he had in any way much to do with politics, the Southerons [sic] being still very much envenomed towards men of that class.[51]

Amanda Smith, a black American evangelist who toured England in 1878, also thought the English were remarkably free of racial prejudice. She observed that she could not avoid the curious stares of people, and that 'They were very respectful; they did not laugh, or make remarks...; but they seemed to look as though they pitied me.' At revival meetings, she noted, 'no one acted as though I was a black woman.' Upon being taken ill, and anxious that she should not be a burden to anyone, the evangelist observed, 'I never saw better principled servants in my life than in England. I suppose there is not a lady in England who would think of consulting her servants as to whether she should entertain a coloured person in her home.'[52] In contrast to white Americans, the English may still have appeared tolerant, but they were less free of racial antipathy than they had been earlier in the century.

In 1869 William Allen reported that rival schoolmasters used the colour question to persuade his landlord to sell the building which housed the black teacher's school in Islington.[53] Frederick Douglass compared his earilerrips to Europe with his last visit of 1887. He observed that although most Englishmen and Frenchmen remained 'sound in their convictions and feelings concerning the coloured race', America prejudices had begun to creep in with the black minstrels 'who disfigure and distort the features of the Negro and burlesque his language and manners in a way to make him appear to thousands more akin to apes than to men.'[54] Africans visiting England also noted this change in attitude.

In the 1870s African visitors contrasted the attitude of Victorians at home favourably to that of Englishmen in Africa. Joseph Renner Maxwell – an African graduate of Merton College, Oxford, who matriculated in 1876, received his B.A. in 1879, and was a student at Lincoln's Inn – described his experience in England as 'one of the bright spots of my life.'

> In England amongst the educated classes, even where prejudiced, the Negro is subject to no treatment that is likely to attack him on his most sensitive side. A resident for more than three years at one of the best colleges in Oxford, I was not once subjected to the slightest ridicule or insult, on account of my colour or race, from any one of my numerous fellow students.[55]

Maxwell, who described himself as a 'pure Negro', contrasted this experience with the arrogance and prejudice of the English on the west coast of Africa. His remedy for the problem of racial intolerance was for Africans to marry European women and thereby to reduce racial differences. In part, his thesis rested upon the favourable treatment he received in England. One of the strongest arguments he advanced was the lack of prejudice among 'many, respectable white girls in Europe who will marry black men whom they know to be educated, refined and gentlemanly.'[56] Maxwell's confidence in English racial tolerance received a severe setback in the 1880s. In spite of his gentlemanly education at Oxford, Maxwell found that a Colonial Office ordinance had reduced him to the status of 'native', and thus discriminated against him in the government service.[57]

Edward Blyden, an early writer on African nationalism and negritude, similarly contrasted the tolerant attitude of the English at home with the arrogance of their colonial compatriots. Blyden was born in the West Indies, and became a prominent educator in West Africa. He prided himself on his knowledge of the classics and corresponded with Gladstone on this subject. He contributed to *Fraser's Magazine*, was an honorary member of the Athenaeum, and served as Liberian representative at the Court of St James. Thus Blyden had mixed in some of the most elevated branches of London society. In a letter to the British and Foreign Anti-Slavery Society in 1878, Blyden commented on the contrasting attitudes of Englishmen at home to those in the colonies:

> The observant traveller from the humblest tribe or nation who comes to this country and mingles with the more intelligent and educated classes is struck with the kindness, generosity and liberal

treatment which is everywhere experienced, and the good-will manifested towards the country and people he represents; and contrasting this state of things with the conduct and bearing towards native races of those who represent England, abroad, he comes to the conclusion that either the feeling at home was not deep based on principle or that those who have gone 'across the sea' have changed not only the 'colum' but the 'animum'.[58]

The racial antipathy of the late nineteenth century may have first developed overseas, but increasingly incidents of racial intolerance were reported in England. African students noticed that Englishmen adopted a condescending tone towards them. The Rev. George Mather Nicol, the first Sierra Leonean graduate of Cambridge in 1879, complained of the 'patronizing sneers' of English clergymen when they inquired after the affairs of Sierra Leone.[59] Qualified West Indians complained not only of discrimination in colonial appointments but also of the failure of British philanthropists to take up the fight against racial intolerance. James H. Minns, a black barrister from Nassau who had been educated in England, complained to the British and Foreign Anti-Slavery Society in 1879,

the more intelligent persons of colour who have been put to great expense to obtain a good education in the Mother Country or otherwise, find it in this place difficult to find work suitable to their ability, and the few who succeed in obtaining a Government office, are so narrowly watched, and so easily dismissed for trifles – whilst more favored color are permitted to escape with a reprimand for repeated acts of misconduct.[60]

In the same letter Minns observed that, although the two previous Governors, Watkins and Hennessey, had been impartial in government appointments, the present one, Governor Robinson, 'would do nothing to serve a person of color.' Another West Indian barrister, D. G. Garraway, wrote to the British and Foreign Anti-Slavery Society in 1882, and complained of discrimination in Grenada, of the refusal of West Indian bankers with headquarters in London to hire qualified black employees, and of the reluctance of the Anti-Slavery Society itself to take up the problems of racial prejudice and discrimination.

I am strongly of the opinion that you are mistaken in thinking that your Society would 'lose influence in going out of the Anti-Slavery department.' If you identified yourself more closely with the interests of the coloured people in the West Indies I feel sure that you would in a short time observe that the benefits to be derived would be mutual. It would appear to me however that whilst the majority of Englishmen loudly denounce the slavery of the 'blacks' they cannot help showing their prejudice against 'colour'.[61]

In the mid-century the Anti-Slavery Society had taken a determined stand against any sign of racial discrimination. By 1882, the Society's resolve had deteriorated into apathy. L. A. Chamerovzow, Secretary of the British and Foreign Anti-Slavery Society, wrote to Lord Brougham in 1860: 'The prejudice against colour I have always regarded as the legacy Slavery has bequeathed to Freedom. . . . I am quite of your view that we ought to endeavour to prevent the contamination from affecting our own people here in England.'[62] The two abolitionists thought that their countrymen lacked colour prejudice, and they resolved not to let it develop. Their good intentions did not bear much fruit, for as the century advanced, Englishmen showed less concern for the evils of discrimination, and in their conduct towards blacks in England they were more openly contemptuous.

The experiences of Daniel Hugh Taylor, a Sierra Leonean who practised medicine in England for some years, and Samuel Coleridge-Taylor, his English son and a noted musician and composer, demonstrated the transition in racial feeling toward the close of the century. In the late 1860s Daniel Taylor left the Grammar School in Freetown, and came to England to continue his education at Taunton College in Somerset. After completing his schooling he attended University College, London. By the age of 22 he had qualified as a member of the Royal College of Surgeons and as a licentiate of the Royal College of Physicians. During his student days, Taylor met and courted an English girl, Alice Hare, who served as a lady's companion to a family he often visited. Since the young doctor had little money, the couple married secretly and moved in with a working-class family in Red Lion Square, Holborn. Samuel Coleridge-Taylor was born there on 15 August 1875. Daniel Taylor worked as an assistant to a doctor in Croydon, and proved to be very popular with his English patients. After his superior had moved, Taylor ran the medical practice on his own, but he found the number of his patients declined, as they ceased to have confidence in the black doctor without his white supervisor. As a result, Taylor returned to Africa.[63] During Taylor's residence in England, the degree of racial intolerance had grown considerably. In the last years of the nineteenth century, his son faced even greater antipathy.

Samuel Coleridge-Taylor's experience of racial antagonism in England had a great influence upon his life and work. His distinctive colour and appearance, as well as his celebrity later in life, made him an object of inquisitive stares. Although he never went to Africa, he was proud of his ethnic origin, and as a result devoted much of his work to the study of African, West Indian, and Afro-American folk music. Coleridge-Taylor defended the Negro race against the claims of white superiority and the doctrines of scientific racism. His wife Jessie, an Englishwoman, recalled the difficulties they experienced over the objections of her family to their marriage, and mentioned that they used to receive frequent insults in the streets. Coleridge-Taylor, a quiet man by nature, expressed his annoyance at boys who shouted out 'blackie' after him. On one occasion, when he went to Hastings for a day, he noticed that everyone was exceptionally kind. Upon learning that 'Uncle Tom's Cabin' was playing in town, he 'got out by the next train.'[64] Coleridge-Taylor and his wife encountered these incidents of intolerance during the last decade of the nineteenth and the first decade of the twentieth centuries.

During this same period A. B. C. Merriman Labor, a West African who lectured throughout Africa on his experiences in Britain, was the object of insults and abuse in the streets of London. Although he admitted that some Englishmen still showed goodwill towards blacks, and that some but not all landladies objected to black lodgers, he encountered many forms of insult and discrimination while in London. The worse culprits for spreading anti-Negro feeling, in his view, were those newspaper editors who gave superficial and sensational coverage to African affairs and who raised spurious questions about racial inferiority and the mixing of English women with African students. Merriman Labor also reported that the worst areas of racial antipathy were the lower-class suburbs where a Negro inevitably faced the abusive catcalls of boys and factory girls. At Queen Victoria's Jubilee, he reported, boys threw stones and rotten eggs at visiting black troops.[65] The hostile and abusive London of Merriman Labor and Coleridge-Taylor bore little resemblance to the friendly and hospitable metropolis which had welcomed Frederick Douglass and William Wells Brown in the mid-century.

Back in the 1850s and 1860s, black observers reported that by and large Englishmen did not think colour alone was indicative of character or status. Like their eighteenth-century forefathers, the mid-Victorians accepted an individual black according to his ability to conform to English social conventions. A dark complexion did not inevitably signify lowly social status. The blacks lowest in the social scale, the sailors and poor of London and the ports, experienced the worst conditions of unemployment and overcrowding. Being the most vulnerable, they also suffered most severely from occasional incidents of prejudice and discrimination. Similarly, black preachers and lecturers least versed in the ways of refined society, and lacking both the social attainments and personal connections to secure them respect, found themselves subjected to the arrogance and smug superiority of their supposed friends and benefactors. The fortunate few, the African students and more eminent black abolitionists, gained an entrance into polite society, because they had the social qualifications and acquaintances to make them respectable. In spite of theories claiming the Negro was inferior, the variable conduct of the English at this time showed that these racist speculations had not sufficient support to influence patterns of behaviour. In the absence of any consensus over the significance of racial differences, mid-Victorians simply treated each individual black according to their evaluation of his social standing.

It was this very process of social evaluation which led to the growth in racialism in the second half of the nineteenth century. Mid-Victorians of gentle status admitted a select few blacks of exceptional ability and distinction into the ranks of gentlemen. By the 1860s, an increasing number of Englishmen were growing sceptical about whether even these exceptional individuals should be so favourably treated. Once the idea of a 'black gentleman' became a contradiction in terms, the way to racialism was open. This change in attitude was not a sudden one, but rather a gradual development which ultimately reached the state of the more rigidly hostile attitudes of the late century. Nor did this change involve any new departure in the accepted pattern of social values and judgments. The conventional norms about the correct bearing toward one's social inferiors, whether black or white, were extended to include all blacks regardless of an individual's character and background. A white skin became one essential mark of a gentleman, and blacks of all ranks and degrees were firmly placed in the lowest orders of nature and society.

4

Mid-Victorian Philanthropy
and the Popular Stereotype
of the Negro

Having witnessed Victorian behaviour towards blacks, it may be safe to enter the volatile world of opinion, but one does so with a sense of foreboding. To keep mid-Victorian racial attitudes in perspective, opinions must be constantly weighed against behaviour. English commentators found the Negro Question an irresistible invitation to poetic licence, and as a consequence their opinions give a distorted view of English racial attitudes. The most dedicated, prolific, and culpable of all nineteenth-century opinion-makers on this subject were the philanthropists. A missionary spokesman, caught up in the excitement of his Biblical exegesis, declared:

This man was an Ethiopian, a native of that country which we are accustomed to regard as the very type of alienation from, and antagonism to, the true God and the covenant nation. Lying at a distance remote from the favoured shrine of the Divine presence, peopled by a race on whom rested for long ages a partriarchical curse, how had the tidings of truth reached this land of darkness?[1]

Concerned Victorians set themselves the task of removing Africans and their New World descendants from the patriarchical curse of slavery, and of spreading the light of Anglo-Saxon, Protestant Christianity into the African world of darkness. To achieve these ends, enthusiasts for the anti-slavery cause and missionary enterprise needed to gain the interest and support of the public. The philanthropists attempted to gain this backing through presenting an appealing picture of the oppressed Negro pleading for sympathy and protection. Their appeal quickened English sympathies, but at the cost of intensifying the race consciousness of the Victorians.

The stereotyped images conveyed by anti-slavery activists and missionary promotors were only partly responsible for this paradoxical result. By the middle decades of the nineteenth century, the philanthropists also had to contend with the new force of an expanding popular secular culture. The professional promoters of new cheap sensational fiction and theatrical entertainments took over the philanthropic image of the Negro, and free from moral restraint or didactic purpose, transformed the stereotype of the black man into the more crassly racist figure of the comic minstrel.

The popular Victorian stereotype of the Negro originated with the anti-slavery and missionary movements which grew out of the religious revival of the late eighteenth century. The new enthusiasm which entered religious life directed the attentions of Englishmen to the moral and spiritual condition of the heathen both at home and abroad.[2] One of the most vociferous and certainly one of the most successful branches of this philanthropic endeavour was the anti-slavery movement. Evangelicals and humanitarians looked first to the trans-Atlantic slave trade, and then to the institution of slavery itself. In order to win sympathy for the slave, and to persuade Parliament of the virtue of their cause, the abolitionists employed an unprecedented campaign of propaganda. In the process, the philanthropists further encouraged Englishmen to identify Africans and their New World descendants with the condition of slavery. From countless letter-heads, posters, hand-bills, pamphlets, ornaments, dishes, and trinkets, the Negro appeared in the figure of the chained, kneeling slave, pleading 'Am I not a man and brother?'

In the minds of Englishmen, this association of blacks with slavery continued long after abolition had occurred in British colonial possessions. In the 1850s, 20 years after emancipation, many Englishmen continued to pride themselves upon the justice and beneficence of their action, and continued to concern themselves with the welfare of blacks, both slave and free. Through missionary and anti-slavery organizations, philanthropists attempted to stimulate this interest and sympathy into action, and thus to advance the cause of the abolition of slavery and the conversion of the heathen.

By the 1850s, the focus of anti-slavery attentions was upon America, while missionary endeavour was expanding from the West Indies, and West and South Africa, into the central and eastern regions of that continent. This geographical division of interests did not lead the mid-Victorians to make any precise distinction between their concern for the African heathen and their sympathy for the American slave. The mid-Victorians had not forgotten that the slaves and freedmen of the New World were captives from their

African homeland. Englishmen referred to black Americans as Africans, much in the way that white Americans were termed Europeans.[3]

Both the missionary and anti-slavery movements shared a common interest in the slave trade and slavery. To missionaries in West Africa, and in the 1850s and 1860s in East and Central Africa, the slave trade and slavery were the most powerful enemies of legitimate commerce, civilization, and Christianity.[4] Similarly, abolitionists were concerned with the spiritual as well as the physical condition of the slave. For the more evangelically inclined, the religious implications of slavery often assumed a greater significance than the physical hardships which the slaves endured.[5] One of the prominent themes of abolitionist literature was the lack of any provision for baptism, religious instruction, Bible reading, church membership, or marital vows among the slave population. Furthermore, the anti-slavery movement itself appealed to a religious motivation. For the committed abolitionist, slavery was not simply a cruel and unjust social system, but a sinful institution whose eradication was a Christian duty.[6] David Brion Davis has argued that the abolitionist movement originated in new conception of sin which impelled men to demand the immediate and total end of slavery, an institution which in this new vision contravened the law of God.[7]

No clear distinction existed, then, between the humanitarian interest in the slave and the evangelical concern for the heathen. Still less can one separate the participants in the work of anti-slavery from those involved in missionary labour. With the characteristic enthusiasm with which the philanthropically inclined joined various associations, abolitionists supported missions and missionary supporters sympathized with anti-slavery. Leading abolitionists participated in missionary work in Africa, and annually at their May Meetings missionary societies passed resolutions against slavery and encouraged their members to give moral support to the anti-slavery cause.[8]

The 1850s and 1860s mark the high point of British interest in American slavery. At the same time, the mid-Victorians showed less interest in Africa. Philip Curtin suggests that, during the nineteenth century, 1865 marks the low point of British interest in West Africa.[9] This paramount interest in America is not altogether surprising, but it did mean that a confused association of blacks with both Africa and New World slavery persisted at least until 1870. Through Lancashire's dependence upon American cotton, Britain had close economic ties with the slave system of the Southern States. The flow of immigrants to America meant that many English families had

direct connections with the American people. The frequent correspondence and exchange of visits between English and American
religious and philanthropic leaders, and by anti-slavery activists in
particular, further strengthened these trans-Atlantic ties. The mid-
Victorians also took a special interest in American politics. For the
politically aware, the huge democratic republic was a great political
experiment, which won the admiration of only a few English politicians and the disapproval of many more. As the crisis over slavery
rose to a climax in the 1850s, English interest in the other side of
the Atlantic grew in intensity.[10] This interest meant that even in the
mid-century Englishmen still thought of the Negro as the plantation
slave labourer. In a leader considering Livingstone's travels in
Central Africa, *The Times* claimed that 'the one great service the
world demands from the negro race is the production of cotton'.
But, at the same time, the leader writer doubted if this 'duty' could
be fulfilled independent of slavery, and predicted that the only
result of cotton cultivation in Africa would be 'a change in the
venue of slavery from the Southern States of the American Union
to the vast territory of Africa'.[11] Even *The Times*, the organ of
knowledgeable and supposedly informed opinion, simply assumed
that blacks, cotton, and slavery belonged, like birds of a feather, in
the same flock.

The identification of Africans with slave labour was partly the
consequence of the historical experience of the slave trade and New
World slavery, but also a product of the agitation and propaganda
of anti-slavery and missionary groups. The effectiveness of the philanthropists' appeal depended upon their means of propaganda as
well as its content. To assess the influence of the philanthropists upon
mid-Victorian racial attitudes, it is therefore wise to consider their
medium, before looking at their message.

The anti-slavery organizations relied upon speeches more than
publications to arouse popular support. By 1860 the *Anti-Slavery
Reporter*, the journal of the British and Foreign Anti-Slavery Society
and the leading British abolitionist periodical, was issued monthly
in 700 copies of which only 80 were sold by subscription;[12] the
remainder were given away. In 1858, a correspondent to the *Anti-
Slavery Advocate*, a Garrisonian periodical, claimed that he and his
friends threw both the *Advocate* and the *Reporter* in the waste-
basket, for the material was dull, and the contributions were wasted
on paid officials.[13] With limited circulations and a highly specialized
content, these anti-slavery periodicals interested only the committed
reader. But the periodicals did give anti-slavery information a wider

circulation. In the custom of many Victorian journals, the anti-slavery periodicals included extracts from other, and especially American, abolitionist sources. These periodicals thereby became compendia of anti-slavery information both for the ardent abolitionist and for the interested newspaper editors who in turn extracted items to include in their papers. Along with titillating reports of crime or the latest Papist perversity, newspapers, particularly Nonconformist ones, frequently included short descriptions of slave beatings or heroic slave escapes drawn from anti-slavery journals.[14] The anti-slavery periodicals therefore had an indirect rather than direct influence upon public opinion. They acted as sources of abolitionist news and information which was then conveyed to a wider audience through the speeches of anti-slavery lecturers, or through the occasional reporting of newspaper editors.

Much of abolitionist propaganda aimed not at influencing public opinion at large, but at gaining the ear of politicians or officials who were in a position to shape government policy. Acting as a political pressure group, the anti-slavery societies supplemented their regularly published journals with the occasional issue of pamphlets. These they directed to subjects which were already before the public, or were under parliamentary consideration. At critical moments of the anti-slavery campaign, for example during the American Civil War, the abolitionists aimed their pamphlets at a wider audience, and published them in numerous large editions.[15]

Anti-slavery made a wider appeal through the speeches of prominent abolitionists. Some of these speakers had a considerable reputation for spirited oratory. George Thompson, for example, won a certain notoriety for his demagoguery in both Britain and America.[16] Abolitionist lecturers, some of them fugitive slaves, followed the extensive network of anti-slavery organizations to give speeches in the large centres and in the halls and chapels of country towns and villages. In spite of their acknowledged oratorical gifts, the abolitionists found it difficult to convey the realities of slavery and slave life by the simple means of verbal description. They therefore illustrated their lectures, when possible, by panorama projections depicting the conditions of slavery. Lecturers also exhibited chains and whips to dramatize the more sensational aspects of slavery. In fact the abolitionists showed an astute readiness to exploit the latest techniques capable of influencing opinion. In 1862, the British and Foreign Anti-Slavery Society advertised:

a *fac-simile* photographic likeness of a Louisiana slave's back;
taken five or six months after a terrible scourging, and exhibiting

from the shoulder to the waist great welts and furrows raised or gouged by the lash running crosswise and lengthwise, the victim himself presenting a noble countenance and fine physique.[17]

The *Anti-Slavery Reporter* urged readers to purchase the picture, and to send it to supporters of the Southern Confederacy to convince them of the sinfulness of slavery. This willingness to experiment with new, and especially visual, means to convey their message spoke well for the abolitionists' ingenuity. These innovations were also a result of the difficulties the abolitionists faced in maintaining anti-slavery interest up to the fever pitch of the 1830s and 1840s.

The peripatetic anti-slavery lectures endlessly repeated the same facts, arguments, and examples, with emphasis on the more startling incidents of slave punishment, or the more sentimentally appealing stories of encroachments upon family life. Throughout their discussions of slavery, the philanthropists concentrated upon the nature of the institution itself, rather than upon the racial characteristics of the slave. Intent upon denying the racial inferiority of blacks, the author of *Uncle Tom's Cabin Almanack* had no doubt that a family of Negro slaves would fit readily into a mid-Victorian middle-class household.

Admit a negro family into your home; treat them in a Christian spirit, let them eat your bread and drink of your cup, you can no longer doubt of their essential equality with yourself. That intelligence which the members of the family display in conversation; that deep and lively affection of the husband toward the wife, and of the mother toward her children; that calm and earnest spirit with which the parents join in your domestic devotions, . . . leave on your mind a feeling of wonder that any . . . should have questioned their alliance with the great human family.[18]

And what the the fate of these black men made after the image of the mid-Victorians? In the impassioned oratory of George Thompson, slavery was an institution in which:

millions are kept in the condition of beasts – their humanity ignored – the rights of reason and conscience taken away – the family state annihilated – the marriage right nullified – the parental authority destroyed – female chastity left to the mercy of ruffianly violence – and every man, woman and child among them a piece of merchandise – a nonentity in the State – a dumb cipher in the court of justice – an animated hoeing machine in the field – a kennelled hound at home – a leper in the house of

prayer – an outcast in the graveyard of the white-man – to-day a
slave – a slave forever.[19]

In Thompson's oratory and in the speeches of other abolitionists,
the Negro, depicted verbally rather than visually, appeared as the
black, suffering, and respectable Victorian victim of the most
abominable institution on God's earth.

In their attempts to gain support for the conversion of Africans
and emancipated slaves of the West Indies, missionary groups
suffered difficulties similar to those experienced by anti-slavery
societies. As a consequence, their propaganda also encouraged a
more stereotyped conception of the Negro. Missionary societies relied
upon their journals and periodicals to inform the public of the needs
and achievements of the mission field.[20] These periodicals had much
larger circulation than the anti-slavery journals, for they had a ready
market within the organization of their respective denominations. In
spite of this circulation, missionaries, never content with the support
they received, complained that the magazines failed to attract
readers. In 1860 the Rev. Thomas Smith, a missionary of the Free
Church of Scotland, observed that religious periodicals were of such
a poor quality that they went unread.[21] In order to gain a larger
readership, the Rev. T. B. Whiting advised that:

> Missionary periodicals should be circulated in book-clubs, and in
> every possible way. They should be written in a thoroughly
> interesting and clear manner, and contain not merely dissertations,
> but histories, memoirs, and facts. Letters from the mission-field
> should contain incidents and descriptions. We cannot, of course,
> expect that incidents of an interesting character will always be at
> hand; but our dear brethren will, I trust, pardon my mentioning
> the matter.[22]

Whiting also appealed for stimulating facts and incidents to be
recounted at missionary meetings. This need to interest and amuse
as well as inform their supporters carried with it the danger that
reports might give distorted descriptions of foreign peoples and
places, and thereby increase the cultural and racial arrogance of
their readership.[23]

The tendency to simplify and exaggerate racial characteristics
appeared most clearly in children's missionary literature. Sunday
School children read juvenile versions of missionary journals, and
in their formative years gained ideas and attitudes which helped to
form the more rigid racial attitudes of the later century. In the
1860s writers simplified reports and stories in juvenile missionary
magazines to make them more comprehensible, but editors had not

developed more sophisticated ways to interest and impress their young readers.[24] Along with simplified stereotypes of various ethnic groups, the magazines included heavy-handed attempts to preach the virtues of piety and self-help. As often as not, editors described a young African or Indian convert as a model Christian, and encouraged English children to follow the shining example of the black or brown child in the distant mission field. These magazines were sparsely illustrated by line drawings of a poor quality. Clothing style rather than racial characteristics tended to distinguish ethnic groups, for a line drawing in grey shading provided little indication of skin colour. In contrast to these mid-century productions, the editions of juvenile missionary magazines at the beginning of the twentieth century reveal a far more strident attitude towards race, and a much more sophisticated approach to children. In 1906 a Church Missionary Society publication thus instructed Sunday School teachers:

> Contrast the darkness of Africa with the light of civilization in England. Shew how applicable the title 'The Dark Continent' is to Africa, as inhabited by the Negro race, as the 'Great Unknown Land', and as the Country that, more than any other, has been given over to the 'Works of Darkness'. [25]

By that time, stories were illustrated with larger and more accurate drawings, maps, and photographs. In 'A Missionary Alphabet for Children', a large map of Africa coloured black with tiny white stars contrasted the darkness and sinfulness of the people with the small inroads of the missions.[26] In comparison with these efforts of the beginning of the twentieth century, the mid-Victorian issues appear mild in their appeal to race consciousness and simple in their approach to children.

Adult versions of missionary magazines of the mid-Victorian period employed those same racial stereotypes, and conveyed the same ill-defined ideas about racial groups. In 1851 William Fox, a Methodist missionary, gave a typical description of the degraded and unregenerate state of Africa.

> The gospel is 'the power of God'. It cannot alter the colour of the Negro's skin; but it can change the blackest heart of Ham's descendants, and make it 'white as snow'. There is no shade of guilt too dark, no accumulation of crime too great, and no enormity of transgression, that it cannot remove. None of the sons and daughters of fallen Adam on that sin-stricken, smitten, and afflicted continent, are too far from heaven, or too near perdition, for the gospel to reach and relieve.[27]

The association of Africans with blackness and nakedness, especially in contrast to the fully-clothed Victorians, strengthened the impression that Negroes represented unregenerate mankind, sinful and unwashed. Fox had no doubt that the gospel would win Africans from sin and wash them 'white as snow'. His vision of this redemption, in fact his very language, was as closely tied to ethnocentric assumptions and associations as was his denunciation of black depravity. In spite of their low assessment of Africa and Africans, missionary spokesmen confidently predicted that black men would one day follow the virtuous path of white Anglo-Saxon Protestantism. As proof of this prophecy, missionary literature cited the saintly lives of black converts.[28] In their sermons and journals, spokesmen for missions claimed that the Negro race exemplified a 'natural' Christian character. In a sermon on behalf of the Ladies' Negro Education Society, Alexander Crummell, a black American educated at Oxford and professor of theology at Monrovia, described the 'natural' religious character of Negroes.

> The Negro race manifest this peculiar trait of character: it is a race, I think I may say, remarkably docile, affectionate, easily attached, and when attached, ardently devoted: a race with the strongest religious feelings, sentiments, and emotions: ... These elements of character – these qualities and dispositions shew that God has kindly bestowed a nature upon this race, which is a gracious preparation for the entrance of His Gospel: a nature which, seems, the highest *natural* type of Christian requirement.[29]

Both in their denunciation of Africa's sins, and in their hopes for Africa's salvation, the evangelicals demonstrated an equally ethnocentric response, and encouraged an abstract and contradictory stereotype of the black man.

This contradictory image of the Negro as degenerate savage and natural Christian was a result of the mental and emotional makeup of the evangelicals, rather than a product of the realities of the mission field in Africa or the West Indies. Among both Established Churchmen and Nonconformists, the missionary movement found its most ardent supporters among evangelical Christians. To these committed believers, charity was a call to alleviate the spiritual suffering of man through conquering the power of sin. Being either ignorant or wilfully neglectful of the message of the New Testament, the heathen were in the natural – and therefore sinful and depraved – state of man after expulsion from Eden and fall from grace. Living in peril of eternal damnation, the fallen were in desperate need of salvation. For the missionary supporter the heathen, of whatever race, represented this pathetic figure of sinful fallen man crying for conversion. In 1860, at a conference on missions, the Rev. T. B. Whiting of the Church Missionary Society observed:

We must exalt the missionary spirit to its proper position, on an equality with other Christian duties; as, for instance, with prayer. Active hatred of the reign of sin is part of holiness. Self-denying effort to win sinners from sin and eternal death, is an important element of charity. It is not something which we may or may not do, but which we must do. It is a means of grace to ourselves, and essential to the fullness of spiritual life.[30]

The evangelical conception of sin made the support of missions both a Christian duty and a means to salvation; but, at the same time, enthusiasm for the missionary cause relied upon a vision of the potential convert as the epitome of corrupt, unregenerate man.

The evangelicals' involvement in missionary work, and their approach to the conversion of black sinners, provided a re-enactment of their own spiritual progression from sin through conversion to salvation. Even in the appeal for missionary support, evangelicals saw a danger that sympathy for suffering might supplant righteous indignation. In the *Wesleyan-Methodist Magazine* for 1858, J.B. of Upper Holloway warned that in missionary meetings the pagan often seemed to be 'an object of pity rather than of blame', and asked: 'When viewing man as a sufferer, have we sometimes half forgotten that he is a sinner?'[31] The denunciation of sinners, whether black or white, acted as a purgative by which the saved rid themselves of guilt for past sins or present transgressions. Evangelical racial attitudes, as seen through missionary periodicals, appear to follow the pattern of prejudiced opinion. In this special case, what the social psychologists call 'the mechanics of projection' appear to be at work. In an effort to overcome oppressive feelings of guilt the individual may project his own failings onto another individual or group, and through denouncing those persons relieve himself of his own sense of failing or inadequacy.[32] The evangelical's need for a visible sign of salvation through the experience of conversion, coupled with an abiding puritan conscience, built up a store of feelings of guilt or inadequacy which potentially could find release through a projection of these failings upon others. The evangelical found a release for his own sense of guilt through the denunciation of the sins of others, and similarly found proof of his own worthiness for salvation through arduous and persistent efforts to save the downfallen. The two contrasting and contradictory stereotypes of the black heathen and the Negro convert correspond to the emotional needs of the evangelical, and to the vision of a black and white world divided between the damned and the saved.

Before all evangelicals are condemned as racially prejudiced, certain qualifications should be borne in mind. It is difficult to say how far the evangelicals' attitudes toward Africans or black West Indians were specifically racial in content. Was the emphasis on the darkness of sin and the blackness of Africans any more than an uncritical and unrestrained use of poetic licence by enthusiastic preachers and missionary propagandists? Certainly the evangelicals did not think sin belonged peculiarly to black men. Stories from Africa or the West Indies were sandwiched between similar accounts from India, China, Australasia, or North America. In each case the spiritual and moral, and usually vicious, condition of the particular ethnic group would be described. But for the reader of these diverse reports the particular racial category probably assumed less importance than the broader question of the duty of the white, civilized, Christian Englishman to those in prospect of eternal damnation. In discussing their work, missionaries did not distinguish between racial groups. They compared experiences in India with those in Africa, or difficulties in New Zealand with those in Ireland, and in each area they found similar problems and challenges.[33] At the same time, missionary societies maintained a clear distinction between the white missionary and his flock.

> The European missionary is the founder, instructor and advisor of native Churches; and, except in their mere infancy, ought not to be their pastor. The higher Christian civilization from which he has come; his position as a messenger of foreign Churches, as a man of superior social rank, and as one of a dominant race, render him unfit to be their pastor; while they fall in with his influence as adviser and friend.[34]

In order to justify the formation of independent, self-reliant native churches, mission administrators, in this case, employed the apparently contradictory argument of the racial superiority of the white missionary. But even here, in distinguishing the missionary from his flock, assertions of a racist nature were inextricably entangled with assumptions about the cultural and social superiority of the English missionary.

For the mid-Victorians, the missionary enterprise was not simply a question of spreading the gospel to the so-called 'coloured' races. Exeter Hall rang with calls for the conversion of Roman Catholics and Jews. Home missions to the unredeemed, infidel poor in England were no less important than foreign missions, and thrived upon a similar vision of the degraded, unregenerate state of the lower orders. The Victorians frequently made direct comparisons between the savagery of 'Darkest Africa' and the condition of the poor in their own cities. In an article in the *Wesleyan-Methodist Magazine* of March 1869, one writer claimed that the growth of poverty in large towns was a 'gigantic evil' which 'threatens the civilization to which it is a reproach, is a standing danger to the middle and upper classes, and tends to the deterioration of the race.'[35] Missionaries were certainly as scathing about evils at home as they were about those abroad. In an article of 12 December 1859 the *Record*, an organ of the Evangelical Party within the Established Church, described the sexual licence prevalent in rural areas.

> The immorality which prevails among the agricultural labourers can scarcely be exaggerated. A chaste marriage in many parts is the exception. Decency is almost unknown and the laws of modesty are violated with reckless effrontery. To lift the veil and divulge the practices which are regarded by parents with a lenient and forgiving eye is plainly impossible. We could not give currency to the prurient jokes and ribald conversation which disgrace so many of our country villages, and afford the tempter such facilities in prosecuting his diabolical mission.[36]

This description of sexual excess and depravity might be drawn from a missionary report of a West African settlement, or of a rural community in Jamaica. It was in fact a description of a supposedly typical English village. For the evangelicals, neither black skins nor naked bodies conveyed a more shocking picture of unrepressed sexuality, and therefore depravity, than one they might find within an English setting. In the minds of the evangelicals sin may have been coloured black, but sinners did not belong to any one racial group, or come from a particular region. Nor did the evangelicals so limit their denunciations of man's wickedness.

The picture of the black man conveyed by missionary periodicals reflected the attitudes and interests of their readership, the missionary journals interested and influenced those persons, largely of the middle class, who were already involved in the religious life of their own church or chapel.[37] Within their own society, concerned members of this social group accepted the existence of a social hierarchy which obliged them to work for the conversion of the unregenerate and infidel poor. Missionary periodicals attempted to enlarge their readers' sphere of concern by depicting the crying need of the Negro for salvation. For missionary and anti-slavery supporters, who never ventured from the British Isles into the field of endeavour, this call for action rested upon an appeal to attitudes and values fostered by their own social environment. The philanthropists' propaganda, then, extended these domestic social attitudes to the racial and cultural differences found abroad.[38]

Philanthropic pleading on behalf of blacks created a simplified and exaggerated stereotype of the Negro, which thrived on an awareness of cultural and social, as well as racial, distinctions. The amalgam of forces which created the Negro stereotype cannot of itself account for the hardening of racial attitudes during the 1850s and 1860s. The evangelicals had preached their sermons well before the mid-century, yet a change in racial attitudes occurred only at this later time. Evangelical puritanism no doubt encouraged ethnocentricism, but why did the dual vision of the Negro, and especially the stereotype of the unregenerate savage, influence opinion differently in the 1860s? As will be shown, mid-Victorian racial attitudes underwent change at a time of religious revival. New energies went into the Sabbatarian campaign, purity movements for the reformation of manners and literature, teetotalism, and anti-Catholicism, all of which reflected the reinvigorated puritanism of the age. Stricter demands for conformity to conventional standards of morality and religious observance made men less willing to accept the credentials of black converts, and less hopeful of the moral regeneration of mankind. The active agency of change was not colonial experience, so much as changing attitudes moulded within the metropolitan religious and social climate.

The publications of anti-slavery and missionary societies provide some indication of philanthropic attitudes to race, but the purpose of those books, pamphlets, and magazines was to arouse the sympathy and support of the public at large for the African sinner and suffering slave. The assessment of the influence of these publications upon the popular imagination is an extremely difficult task, but it is probably fair to say that new and more popular forms of literature and entertainment, rather than the middle-class orientated speeches and writings of abolitionist and missionary activists, conveyed the philanthropic images of the Negro to a wider audience.[39]

Until the middle decades of the nineteenth century, literature of all kinds remained costly, and much of it served a didactic purpose. One readily available form of popular literature was the widely distributed tracts and pamphlets of middle-class philanthropic agencies who aimed to teach the lower orders the lessons of moral improvement and self-help. Originating in an alien social environment and often preaching a hostile doctrine, this literature had a limited influence upon working-class readers. With the easing of the social and political strife of the 1840s, the rise of a better standard of living among the literate population, and reduction in the costs of paper and printing, new forms of popular literature and amusement emerged. A new cheap fiction, originating in the 1830s and becoming more formalized by the mid-century, appealed to a widespread readership, and aimed not to teach but to entertain.[40] By the 1850s and 1860s a secular juvenile literature also appeared. Early numbers of boys' adventure magazines included stories from slave life in the American South and the Caribbean, as well as the customary tales of African safaris and cowboy-and-Indian thrillers. These magazines did not receive popular acclaim until the mid-1860s and 1870s, and therefore, although they preached the virtues of empire along with an exaggerated racial conceit, they tended to reinforce rather than initiate the growth of racial arrogance.[41] During these same middle decades of the nineteenth century, the Victorian stage and music hall also began to enjoy greater commercial success by appealing to a wider audience.[42] As a consequence of these developments, philanthropic propaganda now faced powerful rivals in the effort to gain popular attention. During the 1850s and 1860s, these new sources of opinion thrived on anti-slavery appeals and catered to contemporary interest in America. They thereby conveyed with new force American images of the Negro, and ultimately changed the philanthropic stereotype from an object of pity to a figure of fun.

The most remarkable transition from the earlier didactic literature of the philanthropists to the new popular fiction was Harriet Beecher Stowe's *Uncle Tom's Cabin*. Within a year or so of its publication in 1852, the novel had sold over 1½ million copies of numerous editions in the United Kingdom and the Empire. Thus it far surpassed the sale of any other nineteenth-century publication. *Uncle Tom's Cabin* joined the Bible and Bunyan's *Pilgrim's Progress* among the books most commonly owned by prosperous labourers' families, and became the most widely-read moral tract and text-book on nineteenth-century race relations.[43]

Harriet Beecher Stowe's visit to the United Kingdom in 1853 excited even greater enthusiasm for *Uncle Tom's Cabin* and its now famous author. Mrs Stowe received a tumultuous welcome, and recorded that people of all levels of society had read *Uncle Tom's Cabin*, had admired it, and felt sympathy with the slave. To her surprise, she found herself welcomed into the most privileged ranks of English society.[44] On the evening of 8 May 1853, a group of prominent aristocratic ladies gathered with their husbands to give

Mrs Stowe 'An affectionate and Christian address of many thousands of women of England to their sisters, the women of the United States'. This Stafford House Address, handsomely bound in 26 weighty volumes, included some 576,000 supporting signatures. This petition, first proposed by Queen Victoria, and organized by the duchesses of Sutherland and Argyll, declared British womanhood's abhorrence of slavery, and urged American women to work for the abolition of their peculiar institution.[45] The Address was a testimony to the extraordinary popularity of *Uncle Tom's Cabin*, and to its success in reviving flagging interest in anti-slavery.

Many aspects of the Negro stereotype in *Uncle Tom's Cabin* reinforced attributes which missionary and anti-slavery literature had stressed in their appeals for support. Just as little Eva became the epitome of childhood innocence and piety, and Simon Legree joined the ranks of famous nineteenth-century villains, so Uncle Tom and Topsy became the embodiment of 'Negro' character. In an unfavourable review, the *Morning Chronicle* thought that Uncle Tom was a 'perfect monster of morality', because he sought suffering in order to respond to evil with good.[46] Mrs Stowe and the religious press soon came to the defence of Uncle Tom, and argued that such Christian virtue was quite possible in a black slave. In 1853 Harriet Beecher Stowe published *The Key to Uncle Tom's Cabin*, a compendium of first-hand reports and newspaper accounts verifying the accuracy of persons, places, and events in the novel. She defended her portrayal of Uncle Tom by appealing to the notion that the Negro's nature made him naturally sensible to Christianity. 'The negro race is confessedly more simple, docile, childlike, and affectionate, than other races; and hence the divine graces of love and faith, when inbreathed by the Holy Spirit find in their natural temperament a more congenial atmosphere'.[47] Within the novel itself, the author developed this theme through the affectionate relationship between Uncle Tom and the saintly little Eva. The *Christian Observer*, the *Eclectic Review*, and the *Nonconformist* supported Mrs Stowe's contention, and refuted critics who claimed the characters and religious impulse in the novel were overdrawn.[48]

Uncle Tom's religiosity won the favour of the religious press. The comic figure of Topsy, on the other hand, was still more generally popular. In the many adaptations for the stage, which remained popular until the end of the century, Topsy featured as a favourite and prominent character. In missionary magazines, West Indian Sunday School girls appeared as identical little Topsies, and in

Punch Disraeli appeared as a 'Political Topsy'.[49] The *Noncon-formist* thought that the antics of Topsy and the novel's other comic black characters were 'scenes of negro humour that will send our wits diffing in a new vein, and drive the exhibitions of Nigger Melodists to despair.'[50] For the cultivated reviewers in the *West-minster Review* and the *Morning Chronicle*, these comic appeals were the source of the novel's popularity. They agreed that such vulgar humour would appeal only to the populace, and would have no influence upon the independent educated mind.[51] But for many readers of the novel the impish humour of Topsy joined the religio-sity of Uncle Tom as peculiar Negro characteristics.

Many readers and reviewers looked for racial traits in the novel's black characters. A writer in the *English Review* remarked: 'how constantly we are reminded both of the good and evil traits in the *Irish* character by the language and deportment of these sable gentlemen and ladies'.[52] The *Weekly Dispatch* suggested that the novel conveyed 'the meek, gentle, and impressionable traits of Negro nature', and also showed moments of 'their grotesque humour'.[53] On the other hand, the *Eclectic Review* complimented Mrs Stowe for her realism in portraying good and bad Negro characters. In the opinion of this reviewer, the author's realism nearly went too far, for her descriptions of Sambo and Quimbo, Simon Legree's black slave-drivers, were 'almost enough to make us loathe their race'.[54]

Other reviewers were more critical. The *Morning Post* thought the book exaggerated the suffering of the slaves.[55] Charles Dickens suggested Mrs Stowe had weakened her case by 'making out the African race to be a great race'.[56] In a more extended criticism, the *Morning Chronicle* thought the black characters lacked reality, for they remained the tired familiar stereotypes. Nonetheless, this review complimented Mrs Stowe for providing the best version of authentic Negro dialect.[57] This was an important consideration, for at that time novels were read aloud. *Uncle Tom's Cabin* therefore provided an opportunity for English readers to try an imitation of the speech and mannerisms of a black slave. For this reason the *Christian Observer* advised that the novel showed a lack of refinement and womanly delicacy, and doubted if it could be read in the family circle with women present. The reviewer thought Mrs Stowe's disagreeable dialogues were justified only by the attempt to capture a realistic picture of Southern life.[58] In their response to the novel's black characters, English readers, partly affected by Mrs Stowe's descriptions and by their own acceptance of stereotyped notions about Negroes, looked at Uncle Tom and Topsy and the other slaves in the novel less as individuals than as typical examples of a distinct racial group. Along with Charles Kingsley, they welcomed the way in which Mrs Stowe 'had dived down into the depths of the negro heart, and brought out his common humanity without losing hold for a moment of his race peculiarities.'[59]

In enhancing the awareness of racial differences, Harriet Beecher Stowe threatened the very empathy she hoped to build between her white readers and the novel's black heroes. Some writers noted a subtle racial hierarchy working within the novel.[60] Those slaves with the greatest degree of white ancestry – for example, George Harris, a slave artisan and successful fugitive – appeared to be the most intelligent. In contrast, those of blackest hue, Sambo and Quimbo, were the most vicious and degraded. In *The Key* Harriet Beecher Stowe gave some credence to this view. To support the veracity of George Harris's character, she noted: 'It must be remembered that the half-breeds often inherit, to a great degree, the traits of their white ancestors'.[61] In a similar fashion, some abolitionist literature appealed to race consciousness by attempting to arouse a more intense concern for the evils of slavery through portrayals of 'white' slaves.[62] If a light-skinned person with only a trace of African ancestry could be sold into slavery, was not there a danger that even an Englishman, or worse still, an English woman, might fall victim to the slavers' avarice and lust? The anti-slavers attempted to make Englishmen see and feel that the suffering of slaves endangered the moral, and indeed the physical, well-being of whites as well as blacks. Harriet Beecher Stowe's *Uncle Tom's Cabin* conveyed, in a more popular form and with new vividness, the life and character of Negro slaves in the United States, and thereby aroused English sympathies for their plight. At the same time she heightened the Victorians' awareness of the differences between themselves and the novel's black characters. These differences were attributed to the influence both of slavery and of race.

The extraordinary enthusiasm for Uncle Tom could not be satisfied by simple reading of the novel. Publishers, shopkeepers, and enterprising manufacturers soon set out to capitalize on this 'Uncle-Tom-mania'. Uncle Tom Almanacks and Songbooks appeared with fulsome illustrations of famous passages in the novel. Wallpaper depicting Uncle Tom and Topsy in characteristic poses, or Eliza and Harry's famous escape, began to cover nursery walls. Uncle Tom mementos and ornaments cluttered curio shops, and Topsy dolls won the tender care and affection of little English Evas. This craze for the novel and its black characters made its greatest impact upon the stage. As early as September 1852, a dozen adaptations of the novel were presented to the Lord Chamberlain for approval. During the Christmas season of 1852, four different Uncle Tom pantomines appeared in London. Uncle Tom plays had equal success in the provinces, and encouraged the production of new dramas with black characters in a slave setting. The popularity of these stage presentations of *Uncle Tom's Cabin* gave new life to one particularly popular and longlasting form of impersonation of blacks, the minstrel show.[63]

Negro minstrels, white entertainers expert in the art of the burnt cork, had a long-standing success in the second half of the nineteenth century. Although in origin they appealed to anti-slavery sentiment and popularized philanthropic pleading after the fashion of *Uncle Tom's Cabin*, they eventually did much to change popular notion about the black man. Black and white minstrels first appeared on the English stage in 1836.[64] Thomas D. Rice came to England from the U.S.A. and impersonated 'Jim Crow', the supposedly typical American Negro. In the 1840s and 1850s various American troupes toured England, until by the late 1850s and early 1860s a craze for the minstrels had taken hold. By this time more than 15 permanent minstrel companies had been founded, and had become firmly established as part of the English theatrical scene. St James Hall, Piccadilly, first presented a minstrel show in 1859, and in 1865 the Moore and Burgess Minstrels opened a continuous run of 39 years until the theatre was torn down in 1904. In the provinces other troupes had similarly lengthy runs before large and enthusiastic audiences. In 1879, on a special Christmas tour, Hague's Minstrels performed at the huge Bringley Hall, Birmingham. Each day brought two performances, and the total attendance was 19,000. Even Queen Victoria shared her subjects' fondness for minstrel entertainments, for in 1868, the Wilson and Montague Minstrels played a command performance at Balmoral.[65]

Like 'Uncle-Tom-mania', the minstrel shows provided a popular extension of philanthropic views of the Negro. At least until the 1870s, minstrels thrived upon an appeal to the anti-slavery sentiments of their audiences, as well as to the appreciation of their particular brand of music and comedy. The Ethiopian Serenaders, who toured England from America in 1846, specialized in sentimental songs, and made 'Lucy Neal', a slave's lament, one of the favourite tunes of the day. Aaron Banks, a black American comedian who played in English minstrel companies for 20 years after the end of the American Civil War, was a favourite for his rendition of 'Emancipation Day'.[66]

In an even more elevated, pious, and sentimental tone, the Jubilee Singers toured England in 1874, 1876, and 1884 to raise funds for the newly founded Fisk University, an institution of higher education for black students in the United States. They made their largest impact at the revival meetings of Moody and Sankey, two of the nineteenth century's more renowned evangelists. The singers introduced English audiences to Negro Spirituals, and soon these songs appeared in hymnals and songbooks, and became a regular and popular part of chapel music.[67] Whether one judges from the erudite criticisms of W. A. Barratt in the *Musical Times* or from the enthusiastic singing of Karl Marx's children, 'Negro Music', in the form of spirituals or minstrel melodies, had arrived to thrill and amuse old and young, rich and poor alike.[68]

Beyond the music halls and West End theatres, the minstrels introduced their songs to seaside resorts, provincial towns, racehorse tracks, agricultural fairs, and city streets. Henry Mayhew in his studies of the London poor estimated that there were some 250 street ballad singers in the city, and some 50 Ethiopian serenaders.[69] Even amongst those most doubtful of the morality of theatre-going, the minstrel shows, at least those of the more respectable variety, generally enjoyed a reputation for providing entertainment in good taste. Even so *Leisure Hour*, a popular magazine published by the Religious Tract Society, accompanied its favourable account of the minstrels with this warning: 'In low, London neighbourhoods, we have heard songs of rather a broad and coarse kind, and we can only hope that these were not "regular" nigger melodists, but low imitators trading on their popularity.'[70] The minstrels appealed to a wide variety of theatre-goers. They not only provided lively music and droll comedy but also gave, at least early on, what the mid-Victorians considered to be a realistic portrayal of Negro life and character in the United States.

During the late 1850s and 1860s when the minstrel shows were firmly establishing themselves in the British theatre troupes were small, and they presented their songs, dances, speech, and characterization as accurate depictions of the American Negro. In his introduction to an edition of minstrel songs and routines George Moore, an American entertainer who headed one of the leading minstrel troupes playing in London, claimed that he only attempted to give a realistic portrayal of blacks in America. All Negroes, he explained, had peculiar names, were insanely jealous of one another, were highly superstitious, and were fond of music, dancing, gambling and fancy dress.[71] In an article on 'Negro Minstrelsy' in *Chambers's Encyclopaedia* for 1864, the contributor defined minstrel music as 'a species of singing which originated among the negro slaves of the United States, and is now popular at public entertainments'.[72] In 1866 Charles Dilke, who sympathized with the cause of the freed slaves, reported from America:

> I found down in 'Ole Virginnay' that the Nigger traditions of England – derived from Christy's Minstrels are O.K. – for the said Niggers do say 'Yal had', do dance Kentucky 'breakdowns', do wear scarlet waistcoats and do . . . all grin from ear to ear on every possible occasion, what else are you to expect from men whom it was forbidden (till very lately) under terrible penalties to teach even reading.[73]

For the mid-Victorians the Negro remained an exotic and novel being, and they were prepared to accept even the exaggerated and farcical antics of the black minstrels as authentic. In 1866 Samuel Hague, an English entertainer and promoter, attempted to cash in on sympathy for the recently emancipated slaves and the popularity of the minstrel shows. He brought 26 ex-slaves from Georgia to Liverpool and staged a 'genuine Negro' entertainment. Hague's audiences did not take to his attempt at realism, and soon the promoter had the ex-slaves like the white entertainers in the company put on the burnt cork. English audiences were thereby satisfied that they had seen the genuine article, the real black minstrel.[74]

In the interests of entertainment, the minstrel shows soon advanced beyond any pretence at realism. Programmes included Irish ballads, Tyrolean polkas, burlesques of Italian opera, and even black-faced Cossacks who performed a 'boot dance'.[75] Haverly's Mastadon Minstrels at Drury Lane had a company of over 60 minstrel entertainers. The *Saturday Review* in 1884 described these mammoth productions as 'decadent' in comparison with the originals, which were drawn from the imitation of plantation life and aimed 'to reproduce dramatically the mingled simplicity and cunning of the negro.'[76] English audiences may have accepted the minstrel shows as realistic portrayals of Negro character and plantation life, but they went to the performances to be entertained, not to be informed.

The exaggerated character and appearance of the minstrels undoubtedly added to the enjoyment of the music and comedy. Unfortunately, published editions of minstrel songs and routines simply followed the American originals, and there is no way of knowing how English entertainers exploited the racial characterstics of the minstrel figure to add to the humour or to elaborate on contemporary allusions which played an important part in these programmes.[77] The large and inexpensive editions of minstrel songs and routines of the late nineteenth century reflect both the popularity of the minstrel form and the enthusiasm of countless amateur groups who danced and sang before innumerable village fêtes and chapel anniversaries. In 1867, for example, the *Illustrated London News* reported that a group of bank clerks from the City blackened their faces and provided a minstrel show for the entertainment and elevation of the inmates of the Bethnal Green Workhouse.[78]

Both in the professional theatre and on the amateur stage the minstrels conveyed a comic derogatory stereotype of blacks. On his last visit to England in 1887 Frederick Douglass blamed the minstrel shows for the increased racial intolerance that he encountered.[79] Major A. B. Ellis, writing his *History of the First West India Regiment* in 1885, similarly observed that few took the achievements of black soldiers seriously, for most Englishmen formed their ideas about blacks from the popular stage representations:

> The popular idea in Great Britain of the negro is that he is a
> person who commonly wears a dilapidated tall hat, cotton
> garments of brilliant hue, carries a banjo or concertina, and
> indulges in extraordinary cachinnations at the slightest pretext;
> but this is as far from the truth as the creature of the imagination
> in the opposite extreme, evoked by the vivid fancy of Mrs. Beecher
> Stowe.[80]

Popular enthusiasm for the minstrel caricature rather than imperial experience also lay behind the insults which blacks such as Merriman Labor and Coleridge-Taylor sometimes received in the streets of London in the late-Victorian and Edwardian periods.[81]

Certainly late-Victorian illustrations and advertisements made use of the minstrel stereotype and demonstrated a crasser attitude toward blacks. Toy manufacturers advertised mechanical 'Juba' dancers, named after a popular black entertainer, and models of 'mulatto' dolls dressed in the colourful striped costume of the minstrels. Advertisements for black lead pictured a bright-eyed, striding Negro with 'No Dust!' stamped across his chest. A famous before-and-after advertisement, showed how Pears' soap could wash a pickaninny white. Even the black savage who peeked from behind the lime juice cordial sign had more of an impish Topsy-like expression than a frightening cannibalistic countenance.[82] Like the minstrel shows, the advertisements aimed to win friends through humour, but the amusement depended upon a smug insensitivity and racial conceit.

In spite of this derision towards the stereotyped Negro, the minstrel relied as much upon the sympathy as upon the contempt of his audience. George Rehin has suggested that the minstrel form is less important for its specific racial characteristics than for its embodiment of the tradition of the fool or clown in the popular theatre.[83] One of the features of minstrel comedy was the imitation of the mannerisms of the wealthy and the well-connected. The humour came partly from the absurdity of the lowly black taking on the airs and graces of the refined, but also from a sense of identity with the minstrel who made fun of the pretentious. The minstrel presented the black man in a humorous, entertaining, popular, and visual form, and therefore was more effective than the printed word in creating a racial stereotype. But this form of entertainment did not necessarily preach racialism. At most the minstrel caricature, like the suffering slave or unredeemed savage of the philanthropists, encouraged an ambivalent attitude. The minstrel figure was, at once, an object of fun and ridicule as well as a caricature with whom the audience shared a certain identity in the humour, satire, and pathos of song and story.

Whenever the Victorians considered the position of blacks, they could conjure up an image of a patient, suffering slave, a comic minstrel, or a cruel, lustful savage to fit the particular situation. The abolitionists, the missionary promoters, and the professional entertainers gave this composite stereotype a wider circulation so that these rigid, uniform characterizations could be applied to a whole race by more people with greater frequency. These images were only partly a product of race relations in the Empire. Certainly, Exeter Hall and the music hall stage perpetuated an image of the Negro derived from the experiences of New World slavery rather than from the 'new imperialism' of Africa. At times this domestic image was even exported to the Empire. Off the coast of Zanzibar in 1889, a ship's company daubed on burnt cork to entertain passengers bored by the glories of the Empire around them.[84] Imperial experience was certainly important in shaping Victorian attitudes to race, but it is misleading to concentrate on the literature of Empire to the neglect of the domestic social context and popular culture.

The growth in the mid-century of a more crassly racist stereotype of the Negro occurred while English commentators were becoming more assertive about Anglo-Saxon racial superiority. This growth of a more stereotyped vision and the rise of racialism were concurrent, but they did not stand in the relation of cause and effect. The philanthropic and minstrel caricature of blacks reinforced rather than caused this growth of English racial conceit. Just as the stereotype of the Negro can be traced to domestic influences, so this growth in racism can best be explained by the social changes and stresses within the familiar environs of English society.

5

Mid-Victorian Attitudes
to Race and
Class Differences

The population of mid-nineteenth-century England may have been ethnically homogeneous, but to contemporaries the visible differences between classes seemed more striking than their racial similarities. Consequently the mid-Victorians, looking outward through ethnocentric spectacles, often perceived race relations abroad in the light of class relations at home. Blacks became identified with labouring tasks and the lower social orders, and in the process respectable people extended conventional attitudes toward their social inferiors in England to all Negroes. This identification of blacks with inferior status was, in a large part, a result of the historical experience of slavery. Philanthropic and popular stereotypes encouraged this association between blacks and inferior status by giving Negroes a uniform if contradictory set of attributes. Here attitudes to race rested upon assumptions about differences of class; ethnic stereotypes served to reinforce that association.

The mid-Victorians' perception of racial differences as a form of class distinction can be seen clearly in their assessment of slavery. Their response to *Uncle Tom's Cabin* provides a good example of this mode of reasoning. Amidst the tremendous enthusiasm and interest which greeted the novel, English journalists and critics made frequent comparisons between race relations in the slave South and class relations within mid-Victorian England. Harriet Beecher Stowe also used this comparison. In *Uncle Tom's Cabin* Augustine St Clare, a slave-owner of aristocratic but humane sentiments, claimed that the condition of his slaves was no worse than that of the factory operatives in England:

Look at the high and the low, all the world over, and it is the same

story; the lower classes used up, body, soul, and spirit, for the good of the upper. It is so in England; it is so everywhere; and yet all Christendom stands aghast, with virtuous indignation, because we do the thing in a little different shape from what they do it.[1]
This argument was familiar to English readers. From the earliest stages of the anti-slavery agitation, in the late eighteenth century, these comparisons had served as a common defence of slavery, and as a frequent criticism of the abolitionists, who, supposedly, shed bitter tears over the distant slave while neglecting suffering on their doorstep. In the 1830s, for example, Richard Oastler, who served his political apprenticeship in Wilberforce's anti-slavery campaign, made extensive use of this comparison between English labour and slavery to expose the callous attitude of the mill-owners towards their own factory operatives.[2] English reviewers did not take kindly to Mrs Stowe's use of this same comparison. Lord Carlisle, her friend and patron, gave the American writer a gentle reprimand for her analogy between England and the slave South.[3] The comparison detracted from some English readers' enjoyment of the novel, for it meant they could not so readily say that slavery and its evils were uniquely a product of American character and society. Nassau Senior noted how the book, and attacks on slavery in general, appealed to an Englishman's pride in his moral superiority and satisfied a desire 'to gratify anger, revenge, and rapacity, with good conscience.'[4] In spite of these reservations, the English press showed a readiness to explore the similarities between American slavery and English capitalism, and in 1853 the visit of Harriet Beecher Stowe to the United Kingdom provoked an extended discussion of this controversial subject.[5]
American women did not appreciate anti-slavery admonitions from their English sisters. President Tyler's wife and a New York newspaper quickly replied to the Stafford House Address by suggesting that British ladies should put their own house in order before they told their American sisters what to do. The condition of English workers, the American replies suggested, was far worse than that of American slaves.[6] Using the same arguments, English critics also derided the Stafford House Address. In a letter to *The Times*, an irate reader claimed that Mrs Stowe had worn a dress made by the sweated labour of the oppressed needlewomen of London. The famous American author thus demonstrated, he thought, the insensitivity of abolitionists to suffering in England.[7] The radical press also harangued the abolitionists and their aristocratic friends. In the view of these journalists, expressions of sympathy for the American

slave were hypocritical as long as the rich in England neglected the suffering of their own poor.

The comparison of English conditions with the slave life proved useful to the defenders of slavery and to radical critics of the middle-class abolitionists. In an effort to take advantage of the extraordinary popularity of Mrs Stowe's classic, a number of novels appeared with setting and characters similar to *Uncle Tom's Cabin*, but in defence of slavery. These books argued that the black slave was much better off in the South than the free labourer in the Northern States or in England.[8] The radical English press took up this theme not to justify American slavery, but to denounce the 'wage slavery of free labour' in England.

The most extensive and hostile criticism of abolitionist sentiment and the Stafford House Address came from *Reynolds's Newspaper*, a radical weekly with a large circulation. In an article of 10 April 1853 showing how manufacturers exploited loopholes in the Ten Hour Act, the newspaper claimed:

> The truth is that the workers in factories are as much slaves to the money-power as the negroes in the United States are to the lash and the law: and yet there is an abundance of sympathy expended upon the latter, while little enough is bestowed from the same quarter upon the former. When we contemplate the horrors of our factory system, we experience the deepest disgust for the conduct of the Duchess of SUTHERLAND and the rose-water clique at Stafford House, in sending their maudlin sympathies travelling so many miles across the Atlantic, while they exhibit not the slightest evidence of compassion for the slaves whom the money-power rules with a rod of iron in their own native land.[9]

The article claimed that the slavemaster's ownership of his slaves made him more concerned for the welfare of his human chattels than the mill-owner for the condition of his workers. In a leader entitled 'Black Slavery Abroad and White Slavery at Home', George M. Reynolds saw close parallels between English life and the harshest features of American slavery. Within English society the editor pointed to the suffering of factory operatives, needlewomen, and governesses, to the whipping of soldiers and sailors, to the separation of husband and wife in the workhouses, and to the need for the landlord's consent before agricultural labourers could marry. The article extended the comparison: 'in this country the wives and daughters of the poorer orders are considered to be 'fair game' for the shoals of aristocratic rakes and profligates who, living in idleness, having nothing else to do than pursue their vicious pleasures.'[10]

Reynolds' reached the conclusion that 'if the chattel-slaves of the United States were emancipated to-morrow, it would be only to change their condition to that of wage-slaves.'[11] The newspaper in no way defended American slavery, wishing only to expose the hypocrisy of British abolitionists.[12]

Other radical journals followed a similar line of argument. The *Northern Ensign* published a series of articles satirizing Mrs Stowe's *Sunny Memories of Foreign Lands*. The paper used Mrs Stowe's visit to Scotland, and her friendship with the Duchess of Sutherland, to show the difference between the famous novelist's concern for American slaves and her apparent indifference to the misery caused by the Highland evictions off the Sutherland Estates.[13] The *Leader* also denounced the abolitionists' hypocrisy, claiming their stump-oratory satisfied a shallow philanthropic conscience. Anti-slavery harangues did nothing for the slave, and strengthened the slave-owners' resistance to change. Even cotton manufacturers, in the *Leader*'s view, found anti-slavery sentiment compatible with their business interests.[14] In a tone slightly more moderate than *Reynolds'*, the *Star of Freedom*, a lingering Chartist newspaper, argued:

> The slavery of labour in the aggregate, to capital, is almost as prolific of human misery as the bondage of the negro in the slave-states of America. The money despotism of England is as unscrupulous, as inexorably selfish, and as utterly heedless of the death and desolation it creates, as the bloodhounds who subjugate and murder blacks.[15]

The *Star of Freedom* distinguished between English oppression as the indirect consequence of the economic system and American oppression as the direct result of personal rule by master over slave. The abolitionists and their radical critics were in agreement about the evils of slavery. They differed in their assessment of the inequities within English society.

In reply the abolitionists, and the press sympathetic to their cause, justified anti-slavery philanthropy and denied that another form of slavery existed in England. Their efforts to end American slavery, the abolitionists argued, did not detract from charitable activity in England. The *Anti-Slavery Reporter* claimed 'that the philanthropists who take the deepest interest in the cause of the enslaved African race, are amongst the most active and enterprising promoters of the measures which have been adopted to ameliorate the conditions of the humble classes.'[16] Although *Reynolds's Newspaper* thought Lord Shaftesbury a 'branded political traitor and pseudo-philanthropist', the *Christian Times*, in a view more typical of respectable opinion, suggested that the very name of this noble humanitarian, and his association with the Stafford House Address, vindicated British abolitionists from the charge of neglecting charity at home.[17]

Having defended themselves against the charge of hypocrisy, the abolitionists turned to consider the comparison between the Negro slave and the English working man. *Reynolds'* and other radical organs had stressed the similarities between England and the slave South; the abolitionists emphasized differences. Nassau Senior claimed that these were greater between English gentlemen and Southern slave-owners than between black slaves and English labourers. In a review of Harriet Beecher Stowe's *Dred*, Senior observed that slavery had a corrupting and degrading influence upon the masters as well as the slaves. Unlike young English gentlemen, the youthful slave-owner 'receives none of the wholesome discipline of the public school, or the corrective association of a university.'[18] The reviewer of *Uncle Tom's Cabin* in the *Englishman's Magazine* rejected the comparison of English society and the American South altogether. He observed that Anglo-Saxons were the 'hereditary aristocrats of humanity', and felt the oppression of servitude ten times worse than blacks. If, as Mrs Stowe claimed, the American slave lived in conditions comparable to those of the worker in England, the richest and freest of nations, then surely slavery itself was defensible. The reviewer concluded by advising Mrs Stowe to avoid such erroneous and socialistic comparisons.[19] An article in the *British Mothers' Magazine*, a journal published under the sanction of the London Central Maternal Association, put the case against the similarities between black slaves and English workers more crudely. The author denied the similarity between Negro slaves and English paupers: although both were in a degraded state, the slave's condition was an enforced one, whereas the condition of the English poor was 'to a large extent their own fault.'[20] The poor in England benefited from much 'indiscriminate charity', and would remain in a lowly state 'as long as they remain slaves to their appetites and propensities.'[21] The writer suggested that readers should visit working-class women and elevate them morally and spiritually by teaching them the wisdom of thrift, health, cleanliness, temperance, and industry. Once English women had elevated their own working class, they would be in a better position to give some sympathy and advice to American women in their struggle against slavery.[22] Charitable consideration of the status of black slaves and of the English workers did not always decide in favour of the virtues of free white labourers.

Abolitionists refused to recognize that differences of race or skin colour were significant. The essential distinctions were those of social position, education, and character. In a novel, *Uncle Tom in England: or Proof that Black's White*, published to prove that life in England was not comparable to that in the slave South, the author concluded in accordance with sound abolitionist principles:

there is no natural disqualification of the black population, which should deprive them of the right to enjoy equal political and social privileges with ourselves; or, in the words of Uncle Tom, . . . 'as far as our coloured brethren have had the advantages of education and civilization, they have been as peaceful, as orderly, as devout, at those of a fairer skin.'[23]

Proof of black capacity rested with the Negro's acceptance of the white man's ways. The abolitionists thought slavery was fit for no man, whether black or white, and therefore they sought to define what distinguished it from freedom. The *Anti-Slavery Reporter*, and other sympathetic journals, pointed out that the free English labourer had a right to the earnings from his labour. The slave worked only for the enrichment of his master. Any Englishman had freedom of movement; the slave remained tied to his owner's estate. If in England a man suffered unjustly at the hand of another, he had the full protection of the law; the slave had no judicial recourse against the violence of his master.[24]

Abolitionists did admit that suffering and injustice existed in England, but they suggested that the hardship experienced by the poor was in no way comparable to the oppression endured by the slave. According to the *Anti-Slavery Reporter*:

The social evils of slavery exist [in England], not like slavery, as the necessary consequences of laws enacted to render them permanent, but from an unhappy absence of legislation, in some instances, and in others, as the natural result of a variety of circumstances which it is out of the immediate power of legislation to control. Labour is and must be subject for its remuneration to the general rule of supply and demand. Where it is in abundance it will be cheap; where it is scarce, it will be in request and dear. The unfortunate needlewomen and other classes of females, who have been selected as offering pertinent comparisons are, however, not to be placed for one moment in the same category as the slave. The former it is true may work for a low wage, under the hard compulsion of necessity; but what they earn, though it be a trifling is their own; they would get more, if their labour were worth it.[25]

The iron law of supply and demand determined the philanthropists' assessment of the value of labour, and limited their response to the social and economic position of the working class. Their attitude to slavery and race suffered from a similar limitation. For the abolitionists, slavery was a peculiarly sinful and oppressive system, because it was supported by law. The anti-slavers stressed opposition on principle to this hated institution above charity for fugitives or sympathy for the slaves' physical suffering.[26] In a fervent plea against slavery, George Thompson argued that slavery as an institution was a greater evil than suffering or cruelty:

> Labour is not slavery, for freemen labour. Suffering is not slavery
> for freemen suffer. A master may be unjust and extortionate; a
> poor-law guardian may be callous-hearted, and a relieving officer
> may have no bowels of compassion; but the selfishness of
> employers, and the existence of unpitied misery, do not prove the
> existence of a legalized and established system, by which millions
> are kept in the conditions of beasts.[27]

The abolitionists and their friends were at least consistent. For them, the Negro remained preeminently the slave, and therefore attracted sympathy not simply because the slave endured cruelty and hardship, which they admitted existed in England, but because legally-sanctioned slavery denied the black man his individuality and his liberty. This denial struck close at the most cherished values of the middle class, especially Nonconformist groups, who responded to the anti-slavery cause.

Such enthusiasts recognized that this preoccupation with human rights, and not simply with the oppressed Negro, involved an examination of fundamental political and social beliefs. Maria Chapman, an American supporter of Garrison, writing to an English friend in 1859, welcomed the manner in which 'the Leeds Meeting, ... forgetting "fleecy locks and black complexions", demands the *rights of Man*.'[28] Not all those who were concerned for the plight of the Negro were as ardent in their demands as Mrs Chapman. The *Anti-Slavery Reporter* criticized the *African Times* for failing to stand up for the rights of black West Indians. It accused this journal of the African-Aid Society, an agency of the Evangelical Alliance, of confusing English political preoccupations with West Indian realities. According to the *Reporter*, the *African Times* projected its fears of the English lower orders onto the emancipated slaves. The *Reporter* observed:

> no one, to our knowledge has ever demanded that the West-India
> population shall enjoy privileges not accorded to the masses in

England; nor do we see that the possession of nobility of character and of talent by individuals in this country, therefore incapacitated the masses from rightly using the privileges they actually enjoy, or from aspiring after rights they have not yet acquired.[29]

The *Anti-Slavery Reporter*, in contrast to the *African Times*, looked forward to the day when blacks in the West Indies would have the political influence commensurate with their numbers. With one eye on developments abroad, and the other on the advance of parliamentary reform at home, the *Anti-Slavery Reporter* hoped that, following the general election of 1865, 'the next session will not pass without gains, not only to the cause of negro freedom, but to liberty and human rights in general.'[30] Abolitionists and activists for women's rights similarly saw their movements were interconnected.[31] It was this acknowledged interrelationship between pressing moral and political issues and the questions of race and slavery which made the mid-Victorians take an interest in the welfare of the black man which was out of all proportion to their individual involvement in the affairs of the West Indies, Africa, or America.

Chattel slavery denied a man the free use of his own labour, and through the control exercised by the owner it also denied the slave his freedom of will. In effect, another man owned the slave's soul as well as his body.[32] Chattel slavery was therefore the antithesis of the values which mid-Victorians, especially those of middle-class Nonconformist background, held dearest. They believed that the individual had not only the duty but also the inalienable freedom and capacity to determine his own fate, to improve his social position through his own industry and application, and to secure for himself and his family a prosperous and comfortable livelihood. Through the anti-slavery movement mid-Victorians hoped to secure for the slave the individual's inalienable freedom to search for success and salvation. Through the Aborigines Protection Society, philanthropists attempted to secure these rights for the indigenous populations in the colonies.[33] From their belief in the freedom and responsibilities of the individual, these philanthropists opposed the view that a person's birth determined his station in life. They therefore rejected the claim that the individual's ethnic origin determined his place in society, and they attempted to recreate the legal and social prerequisites for social mobility and improvement through self-help, industry, and education. The opposition to slavery and to colonial discrimination became a defence of the status and capabilities of the African and other ethnic groups. The philanthropists in effect attempted to recreate the social and moral environment of mid-

Victorian England in the colonial or foreign setting. Their endeavours were thus closely tied to ethnocentric assessment of African,
West Indian and American societies.[34]

The abolitionists' critique of slavery suffered from the limitations
of this vision. Since slavery was an evil established and supported
by law, its abolition must be an act of law. Apart from proposals for
education and religious instruction, they had little idea of the social
reformation needed to alter the slave's economic and social position.
The emancipated slave would be freed from the legal restraints of
slavery, but would still face the economic and social restrictions
which applied to the English labourer. At best, the freedom conferred by the legal abolition of slavery would enable a fortunate few
to take advantage of limited opportunities for self-help and education. The abolitionists did not foresee that the great majority of
freedmen would continue as they had done in slavery, cultivating
sugar and cotton.

While intent upon pointing out the differences between English
life and conditions of slavery, commentators did accept that in
certain instances the sufferings of slaves and of free labourers might
be equally intense. Throughout these discussions, attention focussed
upon the institution of slavery and the nature of wage-labour. The
question of race seemed momentarily forgotten. Readers sought in
Uncle Tom's Cabin the 'peculiarities' of the African race, and at the
same time found no difficulty in accepting the comparison between
black slaves and white factory operatives. Mid-Victorians accepted
the stereotyped conception of the Negro popularized by the philanthropists, yet they neither rejected the black man's humanity, nor
thought that blacks should be treated differently from white
labourers.

In the mid-nineteenth century Englishmen, at least those from
the respectable and educated social strata, viewed the hierarchy of
class within their own society as part of the natural order, and their
views of race were consistent with this perspective. This readiness to
perceive racial divisions as similar to class distinctions encouraged
the identification of all black men with the uniform attributes and
servile status of labour, and made no allowance for individual
exceptions, such as an eminent black abolitionist or African university student, who did not fit the stereotype. This equation between
race and class was not simply a product of the debate sparked by
Harriet Beecher Stowe's comparison between the slave South and
industrial England. It was a result of the everyday personal experience of middle-class Victorians.

In 1864 the *Saturday Review* made an extended comparison of English society and the Southern Confederacy which suggested that the pervasive and rigid distinctions of class in England had many similarities to racial distinctions in the United States. It observed that the poor of London and agricultural workers in the country were so separated from the rich that they formed a distinct caste.

The Bethnal Green poor, as compared with the comfortable inhabitants of western London, are a caste apart, a race of whom we know nothing, whose lives are of quite different complexion from ours, persons with whom we have no point of contact. And although there is not quite the same separation of classes or castes in the country, yet the great mass of the agricultural poor are divided from the educated and comfortable, from squires, and parsons, and tradespeople, by a barrier which custom has forged through long centuries, and which only very exceptional circumstances ever beat down, and then only for an instant. The slaves are separated from the whites by more glaring and [ineffaceable] marks of distinction; but still distinctions and separations, like those of English classes which always endure, which last from the cradle to the grave, which prevent anything like association or companionship, produce a general effect on the life of the extreme poor, and subject them to isolation, which offer a very fair parallel to the separation of the slave from the whites.[35]

The author observed that within England the wealthy were fortunate in being protected from having too much contact with the poor. It was a good thing that agricultural labourers did not ride in railway compartments, for an English gentleman finding himself in a railway carriage with five such labourers 'would find it hard to stand the smell, however benevolent and pious he might be.' With some evident relief, the writer observed that the poor did not come to church in their 'thronging numbers', for in the presence of the lower orders the rich could not bear the services which 'would reek with a stifling vapour.' The charitable concern of the rich man in England for the state of the poor was comparable with the paternalism of the slave-owner. But, above all, the writer was certain that the humble must know their place.

The English poor man or child is expected always to remember the condition in which God has placed him, exactly as the negro is expected to remember the skin which God has given him. The relation in both instances is that of perpetual superior to perpetual inferior, of chief to dependant, and no amount of kindness or goodness is suffered to alter this relation.[36]

Politically, in the opinion of this commentator, the English had wisely ordered affairs so that the lowly, the ignorant, and the foolish were ruled by the educated and the civilized. He predicted that the working man would receive the vote only 'when an unknown and inconceivable millennium dawns, and he is a well-educated, independent, thriving, moderately-worked, sweet-smelling creature.' The *Saturday Review* was not an organ of extreme opinion, but a respected journal attracting well-educated middle- to upper-class readers of both liberal and conservative sympathies.[37] Among this group, more people were leaving behind the abolitionist rhetoric of their fathers and coming to adopt an attitude towards both class and race much like the writer in the *Saturday Review*.

In their comments upon *Uncle Tom's Cabin*, and upon the similarities between the American South and England, journalists most frequently compared the black slave to the factory operative. The picture of the industrial worker conjured up images of the hot, noisy, confining cotton mill with its rigid discipline and monotonous clock-watched work, and of the equally congested bleak environs of the industrial city with its teeming slums and stinking pollution. To Americans as well as Englishmen, the urban industrial poor was the most familiar example of an oppressed class in English society, and the comparison, not necessarily the most appropriate one, was chosen because it had the greatest emotional impact.[38] The willingness to see the division between respectable society and the urban poor as a kind of racial separation reflected both the contrast of living standards and values, and the lack of direct contact between the middle and working classes.[39] More accurate English comparisons to the slave would have been the agricultural labourer and the domestic servant. The slave, especially as depicted in abolitionist propaganda, worked in the cotton field or in his master's house. The farm labourer and household servant formed a better basis for comparison because their working environments were more similar and because their personal relations with their employers corresponded more closely to those between slave and master. Of course few mid-Victorian commentators on slavery were prepared to think of their personal dependants as slaves, but nonetheless the daily experience of dealing with subordinates in rural villages or suburban households strengthened the assumption that social inequalities were part of the natural order. Together the familiar contact with servants and dependants plus the general awareness of broad class divisions led respectable mid-Victorians to see similarities between race and class relations.

Even within mid-Victorian industrial Britain, agricultural labourers remained the largest single group of workers. Their oppressive living and working conditions in many respects resembled those of American slaves and West Indian plantation hands.[40] In a letter to the *Patriot*, W. Ferguson found it ironical that farm-workers should feel pity for the American slaves, when they themselves suffered similar conditions of poverty, poor housing, restrictions on movement, and deference to their landlord's will.[41] In *Alton Locke*, Charles Kingsley has a farm labourer protest that 'the farmers make slaves on us. I can't hear no difference between a Christian and a nigger, except they flogs the niggers and starves the Christians; and I don't know which I'd choose.'[42] From his visit to a Southern plantation Anthony Trollope concluded that 'any comparison between the material comfort of a Kentucky slave and an English ditcher and delver would be preposterous' – because the slave was so much better off.[43] Richard Cobden, writing to John Bright at the end of 1863, quite prophetically calculated that blacks in the United States stood 20 years ahead of English agricultural workers in the acquisition of political privileges.[44] In an article of 4 December 1869, the *Spectator* similarly observed that 'the negro in the Southern States seems to us in a fair way to make himself a satisfactory place in the world long before our West-Country labourer.'[45] In his weekly column for the *Empire*, a newspaper edited by George Thompson, 'Saxon' compared the Michaelmas hiring fair in country towns to a slave market. He described how agricultural labourers paraded themselves before employers who bargained for their services:

down to this very day, down to the middle of the nineteenth
century, – with all our preachers, all our civilization, all our
schools, and all our Christianity, – the low, vile, and slavish
practice of men and women exposing themselves for money is
perpetuated in our country towns, as one of our venerable and
established institutions. And so much has the thing become natural
to the agricultural districts, that very great numbers of respectable
agriculturalists do not understand that a public market for human
stock is degrading to an enlightened country.[46]

In the cultivation of habits of deference on the part of labourers, and of unquestioned authority on the part of landowners, 'Saxon' saw that rural conditions of labour and employment created a social climate which in many ways resembled the social environment of a multi-racial slave society.[47]

For most readers of missionary and anti-slavery journals, and most audiences at mission sermons and abolitionist lectures, the realities of rural England remained far removed from their comfortable urban and increasingly suburban lives. They were more familiar with the delicate and at times difficult task of managing their household servants. The relationship between the middle-class mid-Victorian family and their domestic servants also bore some resemblance to the relationship between the races in the Southern States or in the West Indies. Certainly within their descriptions of slave life, abolitionists paid little attention to the field-labourer and, like Mrs Stowe in *Uncle Tom's Cabin*, they fixed their gaze upon the relationship between the master and his household slaves. Here was an area familiar to mid-Victorians, at least those of respectable standing, and of interest to middle-class women in particular. In mid-Victorian England domestic servants – the country's second largest occupational group, expanding with the middle-class demand for its services – served as essential aids in the management and comfort of any respectable household. From their position of intimate connection with their betters, they had a pervasive influence upon nineteenth-century social attitudes.[48]

Many features of master–slave relations in the 'Big House' of the plantation resembled master–servant relations in the larger, wealthier households of the mid-Victorians.[49] English liveried servants, known by the names given by their employers rather than their own names, demonstrated the deference and loyalty expected of servile dependents. Employers even assessed servants by their physical characteristics. Male servants, especially coachmen, were valued according to their stature and the shapeliness of their calves.[50] In both societies servants worked seven days a week with limited time off, and daily from early morning to last thing at night. They were at the constant call of their masters, and had less privacy and leisure than their peers in other occupations. During the course of the nineteenth century, corporal punishment of servants in England and in the Southern States declined, but effective discipline could be maintained by the threat of dismissal without references, and in the American South by demotion to field work or sale.[51] British abolitionists could not comprehend how slaveholders could call themselves Christians, and yet within English churches servants sat segregated from their employers.[52] Even some of the grosser evils abolitionists saw within the slave–master relationship were potential dangers within the Victorian household. Within the confines of respectability, abolitionist literature suggested that owners sexually exploited their slave women. In the respectable Victorian household, the master–servant relationship could also encourage a familiarity which passed the bounds of conventional morality. Writers on household management tread delicately round this subject offering dire warnings and sage advice to blushing young maidservants on the dangers of their profession. Mrs Bakewell in her *Friendly Hints to Female Servants* warned that excessive vanity or social ambition would surely lead the servant-girl into the arms of some ruthless seducer with whom she could have no hope of marriage. Undue familiarity on the part of the young maid might innocently tempt young men in the family into the ways of sin. Mrs Bakewell advised servants to know and to keep their place, and to show proper deference and respect to their employers. Mid-Victorian householders did not require the visible distinctions of race to assign a marked place to their servants, nor did they need servants with black skins to ensure that domestics stayed in that assigned place.[53]

On occasion, mid-Victorian writers on the servant question referred to domestics not as a distinct class but as a separate race.[54] In a popular book of advice on how to lead the life of a gentleman, a topic of great and increased importance to the aspiring middle class of the 1860s, J. H. Friswell suggested that men do not want equality but desire to excel and rise above others. He attempted to disprove the doctrine of equality by pointing to the calamity which befell the democratic American Republic in its recent Civil War, and by claiming that all evidence showed a striking inequality between blacks and whites.[55] From these examples, he concluded that humanity could be divided into those born to serve and those born to master. Each had responsibilities toward the other. Servants felt their lot was hard, but it was no more difficult than the onerous duties of the master. Nonetheless, Friswell advised against too arrogant a bearing toward servants, and suggested they were more loyal and co-operative when treated as humble friends rather than as a 'totally distinct creation'.[56] Although Friswell warned against a disdain toward servants which approached racial conceit, the *Saturday Review* in an article of 1860 actually referred to 'the race of domestics'. The author complained that education and popular literature had an unsettling effect on servants' minds, but despaired of any improvement because the children of the destitute were so lowly that they could not even be trained in domestic skills.[57] When commentators examined master–servant relations in the colonies where the two classes were different races, they freely made comparisons with English households. The *Church Missionary and Juvenile Instructor* told its young readers how an English child living in the West Indies had converted her black nurse to Christianity. The magazine then advised its young readers that 'there are many around them in this Christian land in a still more awful state.' The journal inquired: 'are there none who have white nurses who don't "know any thing at all that is good?" '. Its readers were counselled to lead their wayward English nurses into the path of righteousness.[58] Nurses, whether black or white, belonged to a class beneath their charges, and children did not require the visible distinctions of race to be aware of these differences.

During the nineteenth century domestic service, compared to other occupations, declined in status and remuneration. As a consequence, recruitment of servants depended upon the influx of country girls and other semi-skilled persons who could not secure more rewarding and independent employment. At the same time, sterner standards of respectable propriety required a greater reserve in dealing with servants. Consequently a greater social distance between master and servant developed and householders came to view their domestics as ignorant, unruly, feeble-minded children requiring stern discipline. Some masters and mistresses even began to nickname their servants 'slaveys'.[59]

Of course, in the mid-nineteenth century, there was nothing new about domestic servants or agricultural labourers. But for both groups, and particularly the latter, a new relationship with their employers had undermined much of the older paternalistic tradition. The agricultural revolution of the eighteenth and early nineteenth centuries had witnessed a decline in the status of agricultural labourers as 'servants', and as they became dependent upon wage-labour their relationship to their masters became more like the class relationship of urban industrial workers to their employers.[60] Domestic servants always remained in a more dependent, and to some degree a more protected, position. But even here new standards of middle-class propriety plus the problem of recruiting suitable help meant that the older paternalistic ethos of the country house made an uneasy transfer to the tighter-budgeted suburban household, and a more rigid social barrier seemed to separate the middle class family from below the stairs. The day-to-day encounter with these social distinctions, including the frequent brush with the urban poor who seemed to be part of an alien culture, and the familiar dealings with household servants, had an important influence upon the respectable mid-Victorians' perception of race relations abroad.

While this acute awareness of class distinctions underlay mid-Victorian racial attitudes, a more strident racism only materialized when a clear identification occurred between race and class. Until the mid-century at least, respectable Englishmen observed social distinctions between one black and another, and were prepared to accept the credentials of a black gentleman provided he conformed to acknowledged standards of deportment and conduct. An educated West African writing to the *African Times* in 1865 observed: 'The European being a man of education and good breeding felt quite as much at ease in the society of the educated black man as in that of his brethren at home; he knew that his companion, though black, yet for all that was a gentleman; and that was quite sufficient for him and vice versa.'[61] This observance of social above racial distinctions corresponded to the mid-Victorian view of racial justice. Yet the West African observer, who styled himself 'One of the Niggers', noted that during the 1860s a change had occurred in European racial attitudes. In West Africa 'the English gentleman has been to a certain extent superseded by the English GENT'. He observed that these whites were of inferior education and refinement to black gentlemen, and yet, 'affect to look down upon us as creatures beneath them by reason of the difference of colour.'[62] For the African commentator, the changed attitudes of the English were more a product of altered social position and outlook than a consequence of new opinions on the question of race.

The association of alien races with inferior status and the perception of race relations as a form of class relationship prepared the way for this transition in racial attitudes. Mid-Victorian attitudes to race rested upon assumptions about differences of class rather than upon a perception of the unique physical attributes of racial groups. The hardening of racial attitudes did not accompany the initial rise of an industrial class-oriented society, but occurred only after the mid-century when Britain was already a predominantly urban, industrial nation. This more strident racialism grew out of the identification of blacks with a slave past and the association of this servile status with the English lower orders. It can be best understood in the light of the new mid-Victorian cult of gentility, and the concurrent decline in what came to be known as 'Nigger Philanthropy'.

6

Mid-Victorian Gentlemen, 'Nigger Philanthropy', and the Growth of Racialism

Mid-Victorian England may seem an unlikely place for a transition in attitudes from ethnocentrism to racialism. In contrast to the turmoil of the 1830s and 1840s, the third quarter of the nineteenth century radiates a sense of prosperity and social harmony. It appears as an age of stability and balance, or in the phrase of W. L. Burn, an 'age of equipoise'. Recently a number of historians, most notably Geoffrey Best in *Mid-Victorian Britain, 1851–1875*, have taken a second look at this period. They have concluded that the stability and prosperity of the age have been exaggerated, and that a change in mood and temper had at least begun by the mid-1860s. W. L. Burn also suggests that a change occurred toward the end of this decade, for he concludes his period of mid-Victorian equipoise at 1867.[1] English attitudes toward the Negro were also changing at this time, and it would appear that the transition within the domestic society had a marked influence upon attitudes to race.

The mid-Victorian period began with a confident display of British technological leadership in the Great Exhibition of 1851. By the end of the 1860s, the mid-Victorians were less confident in their moral and material ascendency. Sir Robert Ensor argues that 1870 marked a 'watershed' in intellectual developments, for by that time one generation of prominent writers and thinkers including Dickens, Mill, Carlyle, Tennyson, Browning, and Darwin had accomplished their best works.[2] In economic development 1873, the beginning of the so-called 'Great Depression', marked a decisive change. The confidence of the business community had already suffered a serious shock seven years ealier when Overend and Gurney, and numerous other smaller banks and financial houses, collapsed. S. G. Checkland notes that 1866 was a particularly troublesome year. War between the German states, Fenian terrorism, an outbreak of cholera, a cattle plague, a poor crop due to bad weather, and the industrial advances of foreign rivals displayed a year later at the Paris Exhibition, all served to increase anxieties. The 1860s also shook middle-class confidence in its moral probity. Bankruptcies and financial scandals brought into question business integrity. Social surveys disclosed the extent of prostitution, and the public debate on the 'great social evil' brought into question the sexual mores of mid-Victorian gentlemen.[3]

A decisive political change also occurred between 1865 and 1868. Lord Palmerston, the last 'Whig' Prime Minister and favourite aristocrat of the middle class, died in 1865. The way was now open for new political leadership and a new style of politics. In the same year, Richard Cobden died and with him the old-style middle-class radicalism of the Anti-Corn Law League. Before his death, Cobden noted a change in the temper of English society:

> We have the spirit of feudalism rife and rampant in the midst of the antagonistic developments of the age of Watt, Arkwright, & Stephenson! Nay, feudalism is every day more & more in the ascendant in political and social life. So great is its power and prestige that it draws to it the support & homage of even those who are the natural leaders of the newer & better civilization. Manufacturers & merchants as a rule seem only to desire riches that they may be enabled to prostrate themselves at the feet of feudalism.[4]

To his distress, the middle class had not overwhelmed the aristocracy, but had succumbed to its charms. The passing of the Second Reform Act in 1867, accompanied by a short-lived revival of militant radicalism, the ascendancy of Gladstone and Disraeli, and the founding of the Liberal and modern Conservative parties all signified the emergence of a new era. Geoffrey Best has argued that the creation of two major political parties tended to polarize opinion. It tended to strengthen radical popular support for the Liberals, and propertied urban backing for the Tories. He concludes that 1873 may mark a definite break in economic trends, but in social and political terms, the mid-1860s mark a turning point.[5]

Following Palmerston and Bagehot as spokesmen for their age, Best suggests that the keys to mid-Victorian society were the attitude of 'deference' and the belief in 'removable inequalities'. The former implied an acceptance of the social hierarchy and respect for one's superiors. This 'deference' was not oppressive, for the inequalities were seen to be 'removable'. By self-improvement and industry, the individual could raise himself in the social scale. Just as alien races were expected to 'elevate' themselves by adopting the mores of middle-class philanthropists, so individuals in the lower orders could 'raise' themselves by adopting the manners and habits of their betters. As long as deferential attitudes persisted, and as long as individuals found the inequalities removable, the mid-Victorian scheme functioned smoothly.[6]

The predominance of calm over conflict did not mean there were no stresses in this social order. Best, together with Checkland and Perkin, argues that the mid-Victorian years were not as prosperous as they have been pictured. By the 1860s England held forth fewer opportunities for the self-made entrepreneur, yet mid-Victorian spokesmen still asserted that industry, thrift, and self-help brought salvation, success, and respectability. In the 1840s and in the last two decades of the nineteenth century, evidence exists for a large pauper class, dependent upon casual labour, poor relief, and private charity, and some upon mendicity and crime. Best, Perkin, and Checkland agree that no substantial evidence points to any diminution in this class in the 1850s and 1860s. This residuum, approximately the bottom third of the population, found that sermons on industry, thrift, and self-help offered no solution to the continuing problems of unemployment, poor health, bad housing, and subsistence living. In spite of the sense of social harmony between respectable workingmen and their social superiors, this bottom third was a constant reminder to wealthier mid-Victorians that savagery, violence, and brutality still lurked in the lowest depths of the English population.[7] In his comprehensive study of relations between the middle class and the London poor, Gareth Stedman Jones suggests that the very contrast middle-class observers saw between the 'improvement' of respectable working people in the 1860s and the continued poverty of the residuum led some observers to treat the poor as a collection of social outcasts morally and perhaps genetically incapable of self-sufficient labour.[8]

Above the residuum stood the respectable. According to Best, the cleavage between these two ranks was the deepest of all mid-Victorian social divisions. The respectable, a rank which included skilled workingmen as well as the more pretentious clerks and shopkeepers of the lower middle-class, lived in a manner above the reproach of their neighbours and cultivated frugal, industrious, and independent habits. They feared the residuum below and envied their wealthier superiors above. Respectability was not a distinction conferred by wealth, though it did exclude the residuum who had not the means to be independent of charity or poor relief. It was a description of character. The respectable were by definition independent, responsible citizens, the very backbone of society.[9]

They were not of the first rank of Englishmen. Those families more solidly within the ranks of the middle class, employing at least one household servant, sought to rise from respectable to gentle status. This elevated social station was within their reach only because notions of gentility had experienced a remarkable change. Gentlemen were no longer restricted to the ranks of the peerage and their near and distant relations in country society. Urban businessmen and professional men now considered themselves gentlemen and expected to be recognized as such. To be a gentleman, in its narrowest sense, an individual had to be free of working for his living. Anyone involved in the lowly and unseemly business of trade was clearly excluded, but by the 1860s, fewer manufacturers or merchants were self-made owner-managers. Ownership had passed from the self-made entrepreneur to his sons or grandsons, and professional managers now took charge of the day-to-day operation. The liberalization of laws governing joint-stock and limited liability between 1855 and 1862 hastened this divorce between ownership and management. The sons of merchants and manufacturers gained acceptance into the ranks of gentlemen by forsaking the family world of trade for education at the public schools and entrance into the learned professions. This rise of the professions into the ranks of gentility – particularly the established branches of law and medicine, rather than those new upstarts, engineering, architecture and accountancy – and the search by a more conservatively-orientated business community for gentle status created a new, self-conscious upper middle class.[10]

This creed of success, the search for respectability and the quest for gentility, rested upon the assumption that the evident inequalities within English society could be surmounted by individual effort and achievement. In this vision, opportunities were open for enterprising individuals to move upwards in the social scale. But at the same time this social mobility intensified class-consciousness by making all groups aware of their place on the social ladder.[11] This consciousness affected the skilled worker in his attitude toward the unskilled, no less than the clerk in his disdain for the manual labourer, or the lawyer in his contempt for the respectable merchant.

Harold Perkin suggests that there was from the 1860s a decline in social mobility. As a consequence, this striving for social status was intensified. Income tax statistics and the estimates of contemporary economic analysts point to an increased disparity between the incomes of the poorest and richest groups. Although the real wages of the more skilled workers, the labour aristocracy, were improving, the contraction of opportunities for the individual entrepreneur and the reduction of places for poor scholars at the better schools meant that fewer individuals could cross the divide between employees and owners. At the same time, fewer families from the middling ranks had opportunities to rise into landed society.[12] Within the middle class itself, J. A. Banks's research into family expenditure indicates that the number of families with sufficient income to afford a lower-middle-class living standard increased in the mid-century, while the expected requirements of conspicuous consumption for those seeking to enter the ranks of gentility grew at a much quicker rate. The increased cost of the paraphernalia of gentility, including new expenditures for the education and professional training of sons, coupled with the narrowing of opportunities for the self-made man and for the acquisition of land, intensified the search for gentility within the urban middle class.[13] Gentlemen, by definition, were leaders of the society in ability, character, and deportment, and therefore their ranks were restricted to the chosen few. In fact, this élitist group gained their prestige and respect as much by the exclusion of the unsuited as by the acceptance of the qualified. Certainly within the ranks of the newly prestigious professions competition for places was intense, and there was even some suggestion that the professions were rather overstocked with aspiring young gentlemen.[14]

In a society so dedicated to the task of getting-on, and so aware of the minutiae of social distinctions, a consciousness intensified by the obvious differences between classes in speech and dress, and by the increasing separation of classes by living areas in the cities, it is not surprising that a new significance should be assigned to racial characteristics. As we have seen, in behaviour as well as opinion, the mid-Victorians readily applied their conceptions of class differences to race relations overseas, and to the social distinctions between individual blacks in England. Some eminent Negro visitors were even admitted into the exalted ranks of gentlemen but, as the search for gentility intensified, men became more anxious to achieve acceptance and more concerned to exclude those of questionable status. Black gentlemen who visited England were usually professional men who gained acceptance with the urban upper middle class. As wealthy, respectable mid-Victorians became more competitive in the search for gentle positions in a new urban aristocracy, they also became more exclusive in their attitudes. Physical features identified even the most refined of black gentlemen with a savage heritage and a slave past. At the same time, the urban gentry found a convenient substitute for the family or blood relationship of the traditional aristocracy in a common identity as members of the Anglo-Saxon race.[15] A white skin became one essential quality of a gentleman. Blacks, regardless of the individual's social accomplishments, were lumped together in one category, excluded from the ranks of gentlemen, and identified with the residuum, the very social group respectable mid-Victorians most feared and the social stratum in which they most frequently encountered blacks within Britain.

This urban gentry included the best educated and most articulate members of society, and was therefore in a particularly advantageous position to spread its values and creed to those groups similarly conscious of their social position and striving to preserve their respectability. At the expanding public schools, the sons of country gentlemen and of wealthy urban businessmen learned, often at the expense of sentiment and intellectual achievement, the virtues of manliness and athleticism. They also learned how English gentlemen ruled an Empire, and they came to have pride in, and some actually to emulate, the achievements of these schoolboy heroes. The public schools disseminated both the creed of the gentleman and the ideals of Empire.[16]

These social changes, which had only commenced in the 1860s, eventually created the transformation in social attitudes which underlay the transition from ethnocentrism to racialism. One significant indication of this change was the shifting meaning of the words 'sentiment' and 'sentimentalist'. During the early nineteenth century, 'sentiment' conveyed a positive sense of a strong emotion which prompted the individual into action. Anti-slavery sentiment implied a positive commitment to abolition and active involvement in the campaign to end the slave trade and slavery. Gradually sentiment assumed a less positive sense, that of a morally uplifting opinion which satisfied the individual's conscience but did not call for action. Sentiment, therefore, became tinged with hypocrisy, a mere self-indulgence in the emotions; and a sentimentalist became a weak-kneed, impractical individual who, in the words of Carlyle, was particularly associated with the 'rosepink', 'spoutings, anti-spoutings, and interminable jangle and babble' of Exeter Hall.[17] By the 1860s, the public schools had begun to create a new breed of taciturn, manly, tough-minded, stiff-upper-lipped, young gentlemen who could no longer tolerate the emotional appeals which had moved an earlier generation. On the public platform, it was no longer acceptable, as it once had been, to see great men moved to tears by the power of their sentiments. As a consequence, the emotional appeals of evangelicals and abolitionists now savoured of bad taste, poor-breeding, and unmanly behaviour.[18]

Faced with these mid-century changes in attitude, the promoters of anti-slavery and overseas missions found their reputation and popularity were in decline. They also discovered that the new generation of Victorian gentlemen responded less favourably to appeals on behalf of the oppressed Negro. In the first half of the nineteenth century, philanthropic agencies for anti-slavery and missions, led by aristocrats and gentlemen, had an impressively large middle-class following. By the mid-century the social prestige of the Wilberforces and the Fowell Buxtons, and the intellectual brilliance and moral energy of the Clapham Sect, seemed to have seeped away, or at least to have been drawn off to other channels. 'Nigger Philanthropy', as it was now called, suffered in consequence, and the philanthropists themselves faced more frequent criticism. As their position and public reputation altered so did their attitude to the Negro. As a result, the black man's friends became more reserved in their affection, and his foes became more contemptuous in their criticism.

Those mid-Victorians who interested themselves in the welfare of blacks through missionary and anti-slavery charities were drawn from a broad spectrum of English society. In the most general terms, they were humanitarian or evangelical in outlook. Their origins were diverse, ranging from members of the aristocracy to working-class radicals, but, in the main, supporters of these charities came from the middle classes and were associated either with the Evangelical wing of the Established Church or with the various Nonconformist denominations.[19]

To participate in philanthropic labours one needed in the first place, money and the leisure which wealth afforded and, in the second, the commitment or interest which made the work of charity worthwhile. Besides Anglican clerics and Nonconformist ministers, who had a professional responsibility to participate in good causes, two groups played a particularly active part in the organization and administration of charitable works on behalf of blacks. These groups were middle-class women, who had the leisure and were attracted by the social prestige of anti-slavery and missionary works; and members of the Society of Friends, who had the money and the zeal to spend their time and wealth in acts of charity.[20]

The strength of the anti-slavery movement in the 1850s and 1860s was partly a result of its earlier success and ability in propaganda and organization. By the mid-century, abolitionists could still rely upon a widespread feeling that slavery was an intolerable evil. Abolitionists exercised their influence through a surviving, if weakened, network of local associations which they had established earlier in the century. The coordinating body for a great many of these local societies was the British and Foreign Anti-Slavery Society with its headquarters in London under the direction of the Broad Street Committee. Nonconformists, some Evangelicals, and a prominent group of wealthy Quaker families contributed largely to the financing and administration of the Society's activities. Other independent, and at times antagonistic, anti-slavery organizations existed in most large centres, with those in Bristol, Leeds, Dublin, Glasgow, and Edinburgh being particularly active. The British and Foreign Aborigines Protection Society was closely related to the anti-slavery movement and included some of the more active abolitionists. This group interested itself in the relationship between the incursions of British settlers and colonial officials and the rights and welfare of the various indigenous populations scattered throughout the Empire.[21]

Beyond those actively engaged in the work of anti-slavery, English abolitionists gained support from a large body of Nonconformist opinion. Quakers, Unitarians, Baptists, Congregationalists, some Methodists, and – in Scotland – Presbyterians, both established and free, all aided and sympathized with the abolitionist cause. Nonconformists made their chapels and halls available for anti-slavery meetings, and their preachers chaired these gatherings and sat as platform dignitaries.[22] In fact, the anti-slavery movement was part of a broader moral crusade which combined a number of widely supported causes that appealed to some of the middle classes, and especially to those belonging to the various Dissenting denominations. These good causes included free trade, temperance, peace, parliamentary reform, foreign and home missions, anti-church establishment, and women's rights. For example, Joseph Sturge combined his activities in the British and Foreign Anti-Slavery Society with the peace movement, free trade, parliamentary reform, the ballot, abolition of capital punishment, and disestablishment. Dr John Estlin (1785–1855), a Unitarian Bristol physician who was a leading supporter of Garrison in Britain, combined his anti-slavery interests with the treatment of eye diseases among the poor (52,000 patients in 36 years), religious toleration, temperance, the education of paupers, and the suppression of medical imposters. Another leading supporter of Garrison, George Thompson (1804–78), of a Northern lower-middle-class Wesleyan family, became something of a professional supporter of good causes. He lectured on anti-slavery and temperance, earned fees as a paid lecturer for the Anti-Corn Law League, was an active supporter of Joseph Hume's National Parliamentary Reform Association, sat as a Radical M.P. for Tower Hamlets from 1847 to 1852, and was a founding member of the British India Association, which aimed at encouraging Indian economic and political development in accordance with the principles of self-determination and free trade.[23] These various causes in no sense formed a coherent or organized unity. Some were mutually inconsistent, and led to conflicts of interest and principle.

The extensive appeal of anti-slavery sentiment and the surviving network of local associations gave the abolitionists a misleading appearance of strength. After the end of the apprenticeship system in the West Indies in 1838, British abolitionists directed their attentions toward eradicating the slave trade and slavery which were now solely in the hands of foreign powers. Under the aegis of the newly formed British and Foreign Anti-Slavery Society, the abolitionists hoped to use their propaganda and influence to encourage various national abolitionist societies, and thereby to persuade foreign governments, slave traders, and slave-owners to mend their ways.[24] With attentions now turning to the United States, at once the most powerful and the most vulnerable slave nation, the abolitionists initiated their new campaign with the World Anti-Slavery Convention in London in 1840. Here they found that serious differences, most notably over the admittance of women delegates to the Convention, arose between the cautious Quakers of the Broad Street Committee and William Garrison's American Anti-Slavery Society. These differences never healed, and the subsequent feuding among various British anti-slavery groups over relations with the differing sections of the American movement continued to plague British abolitionists into the 1860s.[25] Missionary and anti-slavery promoters suffered a further setback in 1841 with the disastrous failure of the Niger Expedition. This failure put the philanthropists on the defensive, for in the long memories of their critics it became the prime example of philanthropic folly.[26] Discouraged in their plans for an expansionist policy in West Africa, the humanitarians also found their achievements in the West Indies threatened. The demand by the new orthodoxy of free trade for a repeal of the protective duty on West Indian sugar confronted the abolitionists with a conflict of principle. Though committed to *laissez-faire* they realized that the sugar duty protected the produce of the emancipated slaves from the competition of foreign slave-grown crops. Once again the abolitionists found themselves divided, and exposed to public criticism.[27] Similarly between 1848 and 1850, the debate over the African Squadron forced the abolitionists to put aside their peace principles, and to support the government and the physical force of the Royal Navy in keeping down the slave trade. The abolitionists helped the government to defeat the proposals of the Hutt Committee, but this show of strength was more apparent than real, for it marked the last parliamentary victory for which the anti-slavery movement could claim some credit.[28]

By 1860 the abolitionists were an ageing group, and anti-slavery was a dying cause. At the same time, the anti-slavers' goals were in sight. The trans-Atlantic slave trade had been reduced to a trickle, and the largest and most powerful slave nation faced civil war over its peculiar institution. With the end of slavery in view, at least in the western hemisphere, British interest in abolition declined. Anti-slavery organizations had to rely upon trusted older members, for new recruits were not forthcoming. In its Annual Report for 1861, the Broad Street Committee expressed the hope that some new enthusiasts would come forward to replace the ranks which were being steadily depleted through the deaths of older members.[29] When L. A. Chamerovzow, the Society's Secretary, toured the country in 1862 to raise support for a campaign against the Cuban slave trade, he reported that 'the public [were] quite ready, even eager to respond to the appeal of the Society for a popular demonstration against the slave trade'. In spite of this expression of sympathy with the cause, Chamerovzow also reported that 'he found it most difficult to light upon persons willing to take the work in hand. Decease, & other causes, had removed from the scene, the Society's chief co-adjutors of past times. Many of those who remained, were incapacitated by age or infirmities, from taking part in a public movement'.[30] The abolitionists had been unable to attract or retain the support of a younger generation. In spite of their weakened condition, British anti-slavery groups, spearheaded by the Society of Friends, gave considerable financial and material aid to the American Freedman's-Aid movement at the close of the Civil War. But even in this achievement, the abolitionists did not revive their energies, but only exhausted their remaining and diminished resources.[31]

The 1860s were also a difficult time for the missionary movement. Internal divisions and disputes weakened this cause, just as disagreements and rivalries had frustrated the abolitionists. In the interests of peaceful and effective action, the Church of England had several societies devoted to missionary activities. Each body remained quite separate, and tended to draw support from a particular wing of the Church. High Churchmen supported the Society for the Propagation of the Gospel, and in 1859, under the inspiration of David Livingstone, they founded the Universities Mission to Central Africa. The Church Missionary Society, guided and supported by the Evangelicals, was the larger and more active agency of the Established Church.[32] During the 1850s, under the direction of the 'Palmerstonian Bishops', the Evangelicals attained their greatest period of influence within the English Church. At the same time, a religious revival – sometimes referred to as the second evangelical revival – commencing in 1859 and continuing into the 1870s added many new converts to the evangelical wings of the Established and Nonconformist denominations. In spite of these signs of vitality and strength, humanitarian and evangelical philanthropists received a growing barrage of public criticism.[33]

Changing attitudes toward missionary endeavour and philanthropic activities resulted in declining financial support. The African and West Indian missions were among the first victims of the disruption in Methodist ranks.[34] With the growth of the anti-state church movement, relations between the Evangelicals and their former allies in missionary endeavours, the Nonconformists, became severely strained. Within the Church of England, the growth of the ritualist movement further embittered relations between the Evangelicals and the Puseyites. The Evangelicals also became more strident in their puritanism, and their efforts to amend English society, particularly through the Sabbatarian campaign, made them far less popular in the 1860s than they had been 20 years earlier.[35] The missionaries also became embroiled in controversy. Through his experience in South Africa, Bishop Colenso became involved in disputes over his interpretation of the Pentateuch and his tolerance of polygamy among mission converts. In the face of these divisions and disagreements, and with growing commitments overseas, the missionary societies needed not only to maintain the level of contributions but to keep up the existing rate of growth in donations. The Wesleyan, London, Baptist, and Church Missionary societies each found their contributions ceasing to grow, or increasing at a diminished rate during the 1860s, and consequently each society faced a financial crisis which forced some curtailment of plans for expansion.[36] The Church Missionary Society further found that both the number and the quality of young candidates for mission work declined. Fewer university graduates entered the mission field. In 1872 Bishop R. Bickersteth complained that at the universities:

> There is a relaxation of discipline, an amount of luxury and self-indulgence, a disposition to countenance freethought, which is nothing better than a licence for unbelief; and these things are more than sufficient to explain the decay of that Christian life and zeal which underlie the missionary enterprise.[37]

This slump in missionary fortunes occurred at a time of religious revival within England. The revival did not have the whole-hearted support of either the Evangelical clergy or the Church Missionary Society, and therefore these groups did not immediately benefit from this new growth of religious enthusiasm. The immediate benefactors were home rather than foreign missions. Not until the 1870s did the mid-century revival provide a stimulus to missionary work overseas.[38]

The decline of interest in foreign missions coincided with changing attitudes toward charities for the English poor. During the 1860s philanthropists feared the growth of middle-class suburbs would sever the social bonds between rich and poor, and encourage the wealthy to be even more indifferent to the plight of their less fortunate brethren. In reaction to the over-confident predictions and outright failure of charitable organizations battling with urban poverty, respectable mid-Victorians, displaying some complacency in their own prosperity, showed less enthusiasm for visionary schemes promising to eliminate poverty. There was a revival of paternalistic language. The ranks of the social hierarchy seemed part of the natural order. The wealthy had a duty to participate in private charity to ameliorate intolerable suffering among the poor, but social reformers no longer hoped to re-order society by a victory of middle-class Anti-Corn Law Leaguers or by a social revolution of working-class Chartists.[39] New emphasis was put upon the demoralizing effect of wholesale charity. There was a new demand for more 'scientific' charity which did not give to the 'undeserving' poor indiscriminately, but rather attempted to induce habits of self-reliance through more measured alms-giving. From this movement of opinion against wasteful philanthropy, the Charity Organization Society was formed in 1869.[40]

As enthusiasm about visionary schemes for the radical reformation of English society diminished, many mid-Victorian observers also looked overseas, and in the West Indies and Africa they saw an even more disastrous example of philanthropic folly. Many observers felt that, despite years of toil, charities on behalf of the Negro were outright failures. Since emancipation the economic fortunes of the West Indies had continued to decline. In Africa the lives of a good many men and the money of still more had only managed to found a few isolated colonies of Christians in what seemed to be a vast continent of darkness and savagery.

During the 1850s and 1860s, criticism mounted against the philanthropists for their activities in encouraging Englishmen to spend their money and sympathies on an alien race of blacks. In 1852 Disraeli observed that the abolitionist cause demonstrated the limitations of its middle-class promoters.

The movement of the middle classes for the abolition of slavery was virtuous, but it was not wise. It was an ignorant movement. It showed a want of knowledge both of the laws of commerce and the stipulations of treaties; and it has alike ruined the colonies and aggravated the slave trade. But an enlightened aristocracy who placed themselves at the head of a movement which they did not originate, should have instructed, not sanctioned, the virtuous errors of a well-meaning but narrow-minded community.[41]

Dickens gave this supposed narrow-mindedness fuller treatment. In *Bleak House* Mrs Jellyby expended all her considerable energies caring for the poor black children of the remotest regions of the Niger, while her own family lived in a ruinous condition of squalor and neglect. To the critics of charities for the Negro, the sum of all philanthropic villainies was Exeter Hall, a large meeting hall off the Strand, where missionary and other religious and philanthropic organizations held their annual May meetings in order to review the year's past successes and to arouse their supporters to even greater achievement. In 1856 an article in the *Westminster Review* challenged the humbug of Exeter Hall. It claimed that the philanthropists spent money on a secretarial bureaucracy and central committees rather than in the field of endeavour, and that, in order to encourage support, they deliberately misguided sympathizers into believing disasters were miraculous successes.

The subscribing multitude assemble to hear of widows rescued from the pyre, children snatched from the Ganges, savages singing hymns, missionaries dying in the odour of sanctity, Jews extolling the cross, and infant converts from Romanism spitting out texts in priests' faces; and it would be a chilling disappointment to them to hear that widows still chose to burn; that the heathen are perishing out of their lands; that a dying missionary now and then hopes that no more brethren will come into the wilderness, and waste their lives as he has done; that some hypocrite has embezzled

funds; that a devoted member here and there has turned secular
and become devoted to Mammon in one form or another.[42]

This writer in the *Westminster Review* expressed the thoughts of a
growing number of the respectable classes for whom Exeter Hall
symbolized both hypocrisy and religious mania.

The abolitionists' enthusiasm and sentimentality gained only the
contempt of the new breed of manly, taciturn English gentlemen. A
series of disputes between various branches of the movement
strengthened this impression that anti-slavers were narrow-minded,
ill-bred, hysterical cranks.[43] Their involvement with multifarious
moral crusades further reduced their stature in the eyes of some
critics. In 1858 the *Statesman* observed that Joseph Sturge's ill-
mannered attacks on the army and the aristocracy in aid of peace
would reduce the effectiveness of his appeals against American
slavery.[44] By the mid-century, moreover, the abolitionists appeared
to be far more radical than they had been under the respectable
leadership of Wilberforce and Fowell Buxton in the 1830s. The
anti-slavers now looked upon the policy of apprenticeship and the
grant of 20 million pounds compensation to the slave-owners as
nothing less than a treaty with the devil. Their call was for nothing
short of immediate emancipation to rid the earth of the sin of
slavery.[45] This demand for immediate emancipation was not well
received. Many mid-Victorians looked back to 1833 with admiration
and pride, and thought all future emancipations should follow the
magnanimous British example.[46] In their new demand, abolitionists
and their friends at Exeter Hall appeared to follow a radical course,
and consequently critics and sympathizers alike dismissed them as
wrong-headed fanatics.

To contemporary observers abolitionist appeals seemed not only
fanatical but also hypocritical. As long as Britain's leading manufacturing industry depended upon slave-produced American cotton,
denunciations of Southern slavery had a hollow ring. In May 1852
at an anti-slavery meeting in Exeter Hall, Calvin Stowe, husband of
the famous novelist, made himself thoroughly unpopular by daring
to suggest that anti-slavery speeches would do little to bring down
American slavery. If Britain were sincere in her abolitionist principles, Professor Stowe argued, she would find sources of supply in
India or Africa, and thereby bring down American slavery through
removing its most important economic support. British abolitionists
and their supporters thought the professor's remarks impractical,
for America remained the sole economic supplier of raw cotton,
and the cotton industry was an essential cog in the machine of

mid-Victorian wealth and prosperity.[47] Although forced to concede Britain's dependence upon slave-grown cotton, the abolitionists did not hesitate to attack the cotton interests for putting profit before principle; and, in return, the anti-slavers received rebukes for hypocritical denunciations of American slavery, when they themselves benefited from the products and wealth of the cotton industry.[48] During the 1850s the *Anti-Slavery Advocate* frequently attacked Cobden, Bright, and the whole Manchester School. Having little or no success in winning over the cotton interests, the *Advocate* observed in 1859 that anti-slavery was a sentiment without much force or power. Once an Englishman went to America, it claimed, he soon supported slavery. The *Advocate* noted that at home *The Times* and the *Leader* openly expressed pro-slavery views; and that Cobden, Bright and the organ of the Manchester School, the *Manchester Examiner and Times*, refused to allow abolitionist principles to come before their economic interests.[49] To their contemporaries the abolitionists seemed fanatical in pursuit of their principles, but hypocritical in putting them into practice. Their appeals on behalf of the Negro often appeared to be nothing more than self-indulgent sentimentality.

The change in the philanthropists' standing and influence was partly a consequence of a broader change in the structure and temper of English society. Abolitionists and missionary supporters, like their critics, accepted the reality and propriety of social distinctions within England. In the abstract, they defended the rights of the black man; but they could rid neither themselves nor their countrymen of the idea that humanity was scaled according to a hierarchy. As the abolitionist movement declined and as enthusiasm for the missionary cause slackened, philanthropists found their contemporaries were less concerned about elevating the lowly to a high station and more with excluding the unacceptable from gentle status. They were therefore not enthused about visionary schemes for the training of black gentlemen. Within England itself, Samuel Smiles, the apostle of self-help, saw that the search for social respectability was destroying individualism, and his popular homily, *Self-Help* (1859), declared no new doctrine, but only enshrined conventional wisdom and encouraged the complacency of the successful.[50] In keeping with this quest for respectable and even gentle status, the philanthropists and their supporters now adopted a benevolent paternalism which claimed to care for the black man's welfare, but assumed he would remain a ward of his white guardians. The humanitarians and the evangelicals thereby became less confident in their vision of a capable race of black men raising themselves to equality with Englishmen by the tried panaceas of education and self-help.

This change in outlook was most evident in philanthropic attitudes toward the emancipated slaves of the West Indies.[51] Until 1870 at least, the history of the West India colonies since emancipation probably had a greater impact than British experience in Africa upon English attitudes to the Negro. After emancipation, British abolitionists and missionaries had hoped that the black population of the West Indies would elevate themselves through their new freedom to conform to the standards of their English benefactors. By the 1850s, it had become evident not only that the black population had failed to live up to these expectations but also that the sugar colonies had continued to decline economically. Critics of the abolitionists and defenders of the West India interest attributed these economic difficulties to emancipation. Under freedom, these commentators claimed, the ex-slaves sank into indolence, and therefore the sugar plantations ceased to be productive. *John Bull's* suggestion that the West Indian experience should be borne in mind by Americans, when they considered their peculiar institution, expressed a commonly held view of black indolence under freedom:

> There is no question, from what we have witnessed in the West Indies, but that the negro is disinclined to labour, and has not the disposition towards self-improvement manifested by the white man. Neither does this ineptitude result from the depressing effects of slavery, for never was it more seen than in the free blacks of our colonies.[52]

In a number of leaders during December 1857, *The Times* reassessed the wisdom of slave emancipation in light of the economic decline of the West Indies. The newspaper argued that the economic difficulties of the British Caribbean were a product of a shortage of labour brought about by the inherent laziness of the Negro race. The *Anti-Slavery Reporter* feared that *The Times* had taken up the case of the West India interest, and would push for a re-opening of the trade in labourers from West Africa. The abolitionist journal confidently predicted that *The Times* had miscalculated the mood of the country by falsely assuming that the anti-slavery spirit of England was dead. In this case, *The Times* was more in harmony with the changing mood of political circles at least than was the abolitionist journal.[53]

During the 1850s and 1860s, colonial administrators and politicians more readily accepted the view that the economic difficulties of tropical colonies were largely the result of the indolence of black labourers. These they deemed constitutionally incapable of steady and sufficient labour. In 1862, in his report on conditions in Gambia, Governor G. D'Arcy wrote to the Duke of Newcastle:

Viewing the African as a labourer, he is a good creature in his way, submissive and easily controlled by a strong mind; being however, without education, he acts from impulse, and has no control over his emotions and passions. . . . The West Indian and the Sierra Leone creole, on the contrary, has been taught from the force of circumstances to exercise some little judgement in ordinary affairs, and consequently weighs a little before he acts: but, again, his self-sufficiency is ridiculous, owing, I fancy, solely to want of example, and to that Spiritual education he receives from the good but scarcely practical missionaries.[54]

Governor D'Arcy combined his unfavourable, but by no means severe, view of black labourers with a low opinion of philanthropic efforts. Some administrators took a further step, reconsidering the institution of slavery itself and viewing it in a more favourable light. Governor Bayley reported from the Bahamas in 1862 that the idleness of liberated Africans and second-generation creoles has 'been twisted into an argument in favour of slavery. . . . The inference is, perhaps, more than plausible, if aptitude for labour is the only thing considered'.[55] In Britain politicians did not go so far as to revise their opinions about slavery, but they did question the assumption that Britain had a special responsibility to the black man. Lord Stanley observed in 1865 that 30 years had passed since Britain had abolished slavery, and in the meanwhile she had more than fulfilled her debt to the African. In a speech before Parliament he observed that the lives of European officers wasted on the West Coast of Africa 'measured by any rational standard of comparison [were] worth more than the merely animal existence of a whole African tribe'.[56] The Duke of Somerset, First Lord of the Admiralty, observed in 1862 that white men must command vessels on the West African coast and that therefore 'we must sacrifice brave white Christians to save doubtful black ones'.[57] Faced with the economic decline of the West Indies, and the problems of policing the slave trade, politicians and colonial officials assumed that the racial inheritance of blacks incapacitated them from aspiring to Anglo-Saxon standards of industrious labour and civilized conduct.[58]

This criticism from influential officials put the philanthropists on the defensive, but because of the limitations of their own vision they had difficulty answering their opponents. Like the critical journalists and officials, the humanitarians were distressed by the supposed failure of blacks to respond satisfactorily to freedom. The philanthropists had great difficulty in reconciling the apparent indolence of the freedmen with their former expectations that blacks would be assimilated to English norms. African religious practices had survived in contravention of Christian teaching; the sexual norms of a slave past had not adapted to Victorian ideas of rectitude; and, most importantly, blacks had not responded satisfactorily to the capitalist work-ethic. To prove that blacks were fit for freedom, the abolitionists felt it necessary to demonstrate that the emancipated slaves were an industrious, self-reliant, and self-improving class. The ex-slaves had not become respectable workingmen, and had shown even less inclination to develop their own middle-class élite. All too frequently, they seemed to cultivate the lazy profligate habits of the residuum in England. In the face of the 'evidence' from the West Indies, and their own attitudes toward labour, the philanthropists found it impossible to surmount the accusation that all Negroes were idle.

Unable to find proof of meritorious industry, the philanthropists sought some extenuating circumstances which would exonerate the freedmen from the charge of indolence. The *Juvenile Missionary Magazine* admitted that black Guianans were lazy, but claimed that 'all the Christian negroes are industrious'.[59] The *Wesleyan Methodist Magazine* agreed that Negroes lack industry but attributed this failing to tropical heat and humidity. Unlike the inclement North, the tropics did not provide the incentive or compulsion for continuous and industrious labour. This environmental influence, the magazine suggested, did not apply solely to blacks, for it was 'equally true of some of the Caucasian races in Southern Italy, Sicily, and in Southern Spain'.[60] Considering Anglo-Saxon attitudes toward southern Europeans, such a defence was, to say the least, faint-hearted.

Negrophobe and Negrophile alike measured black ability largely by the capacity of black labour, and they tended to accept the statistics of sugar production as the most appropriate yardstick. By the mid-century, sugar exports had fallen to about 75 per cent of the pre-1833 totals. The planters and their supporters assumed that this decline was a consequence of the inadequacy of free black labour. The emancipated slaves showed a preference for developing their own provision grounds rather than working for the low and irregular wages on the plantations.[61] Neither export statistics nor monetary wages indicated the value of labour on these small holdings. Therefore, English commentators believed black labour on the provision grounds to be less productive and less arduous, and thus less virtuous.

Consequently abolitionists were distressed by the freedmen's choice of their own small cultivations, and felt it necessary to find extenuating circumstances. The anti-slavers blamed the decline of sugar production on the mismanagement of the planters. They suggested that blacks, already disinclined to plantation work by memories of slavery, were driven by the low wages and hostile attitudes of the planters to cultivate the provision grounds.[62] Defenders of the Negro suggested that blacks were responding not to an innate love of idleness but to the same profit motives which influenced any English worker.[63]

In defence of their work on behalf of the ex-slaves, abolitionists also pointed to the planters' control of colonial politics. Supporters of black advancement criticized the heavy duties on consumer goods, the restrictions of trading privileges, and the importation of competing coolie labour, for these provisions damaged philanthropic hopes for the black community. The restrictions inhibited individual blacks from cultivating the entrepreneurial virtues of industry, thrift, and self-help. As a consequence, abolitionists feared that the West Indies would fail to create the black middle class which, in their vision, was required to elevate all groups in the islands. Abolitionists, planters, and officials in the Foreign and Colonial Offices all toyed with the idea of encouraging black American emigration to the British West Indies to supply this need for a middle class and a respectable working-class élite.[64]

In their attacks on the planting interest, in their hopes for the black community, and in their suggested remedies, the middle-class standards of the philanthropists were evident. They hoped to create the conditions which they felt pertained in English society for the upward mobility of individuals who followed the trusted values of the self-made entrepreneur. Yet by the 1850s and 1860s the avenues for the entrepreneur were narrowing, and men sought to raise their status through education at the public schools, entrance into the professions, and the cultivation of gentility. At the same time, philanthropists and their critics were less optimistic about the possibility of ex-slaves raising themselves to respectability by self-help.

The abolitionists, in particular, became less whole-hearted in their defence of the benefits of emancipation. In the early 1850s, they claimed that emancipation had benefited both the West Indian economy and the black population. Within a decade their assessment of the economic advantages of emancipation became more reserved. They now argued that the cost of emancipation, as seen in the economic decline of the West Indies, was more than repaid through the social and moral improvement of the ex-slaves since 1833.[65] An influential article of 1853 in the *Westminster Review* by W. E. Forster provided a measured defence of black Jamaicans in answer to Carlyle's outspoken 'Occasional Discourse on the Nigger Question':

> We do not say that the history of free Jamaica has proven how far the negro race is capable of the highest exploits of civilization, or how high is to be its rank among the races of the world, for these yet remain open questions, so far as Jamaica is concerned; but this much it has proved, that there has been found no people more quick to learn the lessons of freedom, and to forget those of slavery. Crimes and follies they commit, without doubt; but the question is, not how far they are absolutely vicious, nor even whether, comparatively with others, they are more or less foolish, or criminal, but whether they are more or less so as freemen than they were as slaves.[66]

Forster himself exemplified the changing position of many mid-Victorian spokesmen which led them to make this more reserved assessment of the ex-slaves. His father, a Bradford cotton manufacturer and a leading member of the Society of Friends, was an active abolitionist who died on an anti-slavery mission to the United States. His mother, Anna Buxton, was the eldest daughter of Thomas Fowell Buxton, who took up the lead of the British anti-slavery movement after the death of William Wilberforce. In 1850 William Forster married the daughter of Dr Thomas Arnold, and as a consequence was forced to leave the Society of Friends. During the mid-century, until they changed the Society's regulations in 1865, the Quakers suffered a considerable decline in membership from the drift of Friends into Anglicanism and conformity. This change weakened the active support of the anti-slavery movement, and even though W. E. Forster was the Liberal M.P. most outspoken in his defence of the Negro in the American Civil War, his commitment to the abolitionist cause was clearly not as whole-hearted or as enthusiastic as the life-long devotion of his grandfather and his parents.[67]

Even in making a more reserved defence of black West Indians, mid-Victorian abolitionists probably had some misgivings. In an Address to the Black and Coloured Population of Jamaica in 1866, the Committee of the British and Foreign Anti-Slavery Society admonished the Jamaicans to be honest, industrious, and peaceful lest they lose the sympathy of the English public.[68] The paternalistic tone and stern warning of the address indicated that the abolitionists found their own arguments in defence of the ex-slaves less than convincing. By 1868, the Anti-Slavery Society was in a position of appealing for aid from the black population of the West Indies. In a general letter to West Indian clergymen, the Society observed, 'we are painfully conscious that the black & coloured population appear to be unmindful of the claims our Society has on the negro race and its descendants'. The letter also stated that English support for the Society had greatly declined as older members had passed away and the younger generation had not stepped forward to take their place.[69] The abolitionists, unable to maintain their support in England and less certain about the success of emancipation, had little hope of influencing their critics who now denied that freedom had in any way improved the social or moral condition of black West Indians.

The mid-Victorians measured the success or failure of the emancipation policy in the West Indies by the standards of their own social background. Emancipated slaves failed to adjust to the established English pattern of wage-labour, therefore blacks appeared not only slothful but also culpably neglectful of their duty to work. The black community also failed to meet English expectations about the rise of a vigorous, self-reliant, industrious, and self-improving middle class which, in the abolitionist vision, would act as the salvation of the West Indies. As a consequence, English philanthropists became less sanguine about the ability of blacks to conform to this English model.

The approaching end of slavery in the New World, plus the apparent failures of emancipation in the West Indies and of missionary work in Africa, may in themselves provide a sufficient explanation for the decline in sympathy for blacks. Yet this explanation does contain one notable omission. It relies upon events external to the more immediate social context of mid-Victorian England, and tends to overlook changes taking place within the metropolitan community. Just as the evangelical revival of the late eighteenth and early nineteenth centuries gave birth to the anti-slavery and modern missionary movements, so too mid-century changes in values and attitudes contributed to the decline in humanitarian concern for blacks.

By the 1860s, philanthropic endeavour seemed to be failing at home as well as overseas, and, as in the case of the Negro, a reaction set in against the supposed benefactors of charitable enterprise. As noted earlier, decades of effort by voluntary agencies had failed to remedy the problem of urban poverty, and now mounting evidence indicated that this menace to the civilization of respectable society was growing ever greater. Respectable mid-Victorians saw the abject poverty and degeneracy of the residuum, like the indolence of black labour or idolatry of black heathens, as a matter of individual moral failure. Part of the blame for this menace within English society was put at the door of philanthropic agencies who by their sentimental proliferation of charities only demoralized the poor into dependant, dishonest beggars rather than converting them into industrious, self-reliant labourers. In response, the Charity Organization Society attempted to provide systematic relief which would remedy the corrupting generosity of the rich and reclaim the moral integrity of the poor.[70] While the active supporters of the Charity Organization Society undoubtedly believed in the merit of their campaign, there remains the suspicion that the wider opinion which gave vent to the denunciation of charitable activity did not share the moral idealism of the social reformers, and simply expressed a harsher, more arrogant attitude towards the poor which would culminate in the pessimistic social Darwinism of the 1880s.[71] The social reformers themselves were ambivalent in their attitudes towards the poor. On the one hand they still espoused the virtues of the industrious independent individual, but on the other hand, as members of the new urban gentry, they adopted a revived paternalism which aimed to recreate through rational charity a sense of obligation and deference between rich and poor in spite of their segregation into separate urban communities.[72] The social reformers, like the abolitionists, still believed that differences between rich and poor, or white and black, might be removed by self-help; but they also assumed that in most cases they would have to exercise a benevolent paternalism over less capable, and even potentially dangerous, dependants. Both sets of reformers also worked within a climate of opinion which was increasingly sceptical of the value of their efforts, and which adopted an attitude of bored indifference or haughty contempt towards the philanthropists and their charges.

The interrelationship between the domestic and colonial settings can be seen clearly in Thomas Carlyle's diatribes against black West Indians. The essayist's main object was to preach the duty to labour not only to blacks, but to whites as well. In his view, slavery itself would be good for members of both races if it could compel them to fulfil this God-given duty of meritorious industry.[73] Carlyle's remedy for the inadequacy of white and black labour was extreme. Many of his contemporaries shared his opinion about the necessity of labour, but they remained attached to the ideal of the industrious, self-reliant, self-improving individual. By the 1860s lip-service was still paid to this trusted model, but the social realities of middle-class competition for gentle status suggested that these entrepreneurial virtues were no longer sufficient.

The wealthy, respectable, and frequently Nonconformist, merchants and professional men to whom anti-slavery had an especial appeal now found that thrift, industry, and self-help gave them respectability, but still barred them from the first rank of Englishmen. These men, or at least their sons, now became attracted by the refinements and prestige of the English gentleman. Whereas the mid-Victorians could imagine, and even identify with, a black man improving himself to become a respected business or professional man, they found it more difficult to accept the notion of a black gentleman. By the 1860s, the young aspirants for the trappings of gentility found the very idea of a black gentleman absurd. These respectable and articulate commentators therefore placed less faith in philanthropic schemes for the social and moral elevation of Africans and black West Indians. Criteria of race and social origin had begun to replace the formerly ethnocentric standards of character and conduct.

With a new generation of articulate, educated, wealthy gentlemen, not self-made men, but men born into wealth; not denied power and privilege, but sharing in the political and social life of the nation; not seeking salvation through success alone, but gentility through graceful living, the enthusiasts for great causes, for the abolition of slavery, or the elimination of urban poverty, shrank both in numbers and in ardour. Groups which had formerly taken up these causes had now established their own place within society. Once this had been secured, they were less concerned to keep the door open to rival aspirants. And the lowly Negro what of him? His complexion and his history defined his place, and past visions of black gentlemen raised from slavery were only the naive notions of an old and tired generation.

7

Scientific Racism
and Mid-Victorian
Racial Attitudes

As a new confident group of gentlemanly scholars and professional men came to reject the sentimental notions of an older generation, mid-Victorian scientists took a fresh look at the question of race, and found compelling reasons for the rejection of philanthropic hopes for the moral and social 'improvement' of black societies. Historians of science have found this rise of scientific racist thought a perplexing and disturbing development, for it would appear scientists created a pseudo-science or new mythology of race.[1] In seeking reasons for the rise of scientific racism, scholars have concentrated upon the problems and limitations of the method, conceptual framework, and logic of mid-nineteenth-century biology and anthropology. As an explanation for the growth of a more strident racialism in the mid-nineteenth century, this history of science has its own limitations. It tends to exaggerate the influence of scientific thought and to overlook the social and political context in which these ideas developed.

In the late eighteenth century, when biologists sought to classify man by genus and species under the binomial system of Linnaeus, they struggled with two related problems. They attempted to find a satisfactory definition of racial types and sought in man's origin an explanation for these physical differences. Directly bearing on these questions was the thorny problem of the definition of species itself. The prevailing scientific opinion held that species were independent, immutable, and separately originating entities, although a minority thought that species were capable of change, development, or evolution through time. Most of those who thought all mankind had a common origin, the monogenists, also grouped all the races into one species, and were left with the difficult problem of accounting for the development of different races since creation. Those who argued that races had separate origins, the polygenists, classified races as distinct and usually immutable species. By making such a clear distinction between races, the polygenists provided a useful rationalization for the apparent historical subservience of non-whites to whites. The issues first set out in the late eighteenth century – the classification of racial types, the definition of species, and the origin of man's varieties – dominated the scientific study of race into the middle decades of the nineteenth century.[2]

From its inception, in the published treatises of John Hunter (d. 1809) and John Friedrich Blumenbach (1752–1840) in 1775, the theory of monogenesis gained greater support because it corresponded more closely to Scriptural orthodoxy, and the accepted tenets of biological science.[3] Hunter used Buffon's definition, that a species includes all organisms that can produce fertile offspring, to prove that all mankind belonged to the same biological family.[4] Hunter argued that environmental influences, especially climate and diet, produced racial differences.[5] Blumenbach, the more influential of the two writers, speculated that in origin man was white-skinned and at a fairly advanced level of development. Darker skins and barbarous cultures he attributed to the influence of environment which produced a degeneration from the primordial type. Blumenbach found the argument for separate species inadequate, since it compared only extreme types and failed to take into account the available zoological and physiological evidence for the many intermediate forms of man.[6]

Not all writers exercised the same reservation in their assessment of racial differences. In the *Sketches of the History of Man* published in 1774, Henry Home, Lord Kames (1692–1782), a Scottish jurist, denied that Buffon's criterion of the production of fertile offspring was an adequate definition of species. He claimed that racial differences could not be explained by climate or other environmental influences, and concluded that the races formed separate species. In 1799, Dr Charles White (1728–1813), an eminent English physician, in his *Account of the Regular Gradations in Man*, argued that the races formed distinct species and, more particularly, observed that the Negro had protruding jaws, and an offensive body odour, as well as a smaller brain and larger genitals than the European.[7] In his more popular and influential *History of Jamaica* (1774), Edward Long used the theories of the biologists to prove that blacks were like animals and a distinct species from the European. He claimed that in Jamaica mulattos were infertile. According to Buffon's definition, this proved that Negroes and Europeans were distinct creatures.[8] With Kames and White, Long saw a regular gradation in quality rising through the apes to the darker races until the height of intelligence and character was reached in those of fairest skin.

The belief that black men showed a sensual and animal nature much closer to brute creation than the civilized white races was not restricted to the polygenists. Blumenbach discussed the size of the Negro penis, and the libidinous nature of black women. On the same page he refuted the popular belief that the size of the Scotsman's genitals had anything to do with the wearing of the kilt.[9] He also took time to refute reports of 'centuars, sirens, cynoxephale, satyrs, pigmies, giants, hermaphrodites, and other creatures of that kind'.[10] The scientists' curiosity about the hypersexuality of strangers, black, white or imagined, reflected the widespread xenophobia of the age. The belief in the lasciviousness of the Negro, an impression shared by both polygenists and monogenists, was more a consequence of this xenophobia, and the association of the black man with the supposed sensual, animal nature of tropical, savage life than a result of empirical observations on the nature of species, the qualities of black skins, or the shapes of black skulls.[11]

The assumption by European of their own superiority over all other forms of humanity was partly a result of ethnocentrism, partly a consequence of scientific and philosophical thought, and partly a product of the hierarchical ordering of eighteenth-century society. Neither Hume nor Gibbon relied upon scientific studies or race to conclude that equatorial Africa was a region without history or civilization, and inhabited by a people notable only for their indolence, barbarism, and stupidity.[12] These ethnocentric assumptions were shared by scientific observers who used comparative anatomy, for example, to measure other races against the aesthetic and cultural standards of the European. Schooled in the logic of the Great Chain of Being, intellectuals ordered natural phenomena in a scale running from God to the lowest form of creation. This intellectual structure satisfied a desire for order in society as well as in nature. Just as the various forms of creation had their places in the Chain of Being, so society was properly ordered according to rank and status. It was therefore assumed that the Negro had a 'place' in nature and society, which scientific investigation could locate. The polygenists argued that the inferior place of the African was perpetual because of the distinct origin of the black and white races, whereas the monogenists thought this inferiority was conditional upon the distinct historical experiences of the various races since their common origin.[13]

In spite of increased English contact with the peoples of Africa and Asia, and the experience of multi-racial societies in the West Indies and America, the scientific debate on the races of man dealt with essentially the same issues from the 1770s to the 1860s. Philip Curtin has argued that increased British involvement in West Africa served only to create a greater distortion in English ideas about Africans.[14] Consequently, by the mid-nineteenth century the arguments of both schools of thought were increasingly out of touch with reality.

In the first half of the nineteenth century, monogenesis gained the ascendency, because it corresponded more closely to humanitarian interest in race relations. The work of Sir William Lawrence (1783–1867), and James Cowles Prichard (1786–1848) gave monogenesis the authoritative stamp of respected scientific opinion. These two eminent biologists recognized the weakness of environmental arguments, and in attempting a fresh explanation for the development of racial types, they accumulated an impressive range of evidence in favour of monogenesis. Although Lawrence thought Negroes resembled monkeys and were less intelligent than Europeans, he argued in favour of the unity of man. He concluded that racial differences were similar to variations in breeds of domestic animals.[15] James Cowles Prichard was more identified with monogenesis than Lawrence, and an authority more frequently cited by humanitarians. Contrary to Blumenbach, Prichard concluded that original man was black, and paled in colour as civilization progressed. This development, he conjectured, was the result of seemingly accidental and abrupt changes which occurred in the offspring due to some hidden characteristic in the parents.[16] Both Prichard and Lawrence anticipated Darwin's explanation of variations in type through accidental changes, but laymen tended to overlook the subtleties introduced by the two biologists. Commentators accepted the support that Lawrence and particularly Prichard gave to monogenesis, and thereby to humanitarian efforts, but continued to ascribe racial differences to the effect of climate.

Intent upon furthering the scientific study of race in accordance with humanitarian principles, a group of professional men founded the Ethnological Society in 1843. This association, an offshoot of the Aborigines Protection Society, was 'formed for the purpose of inquiring into the distinguishing characteristics, physical and moral, of the varieties of Mankind which inhabit, or have inhabited the

Earth; and to ascertain the causes of such characteristics'.[17] Meeting in the house of Dr Thomas Hodgkin, a Quaker physician and founder of the Aborigines Protection Society, the ethnologists had enrolled 157 members by May 1844. Under the leadership of prominent Quaker physicians, the Society's dominant tone was humanitarian and monogenetic.[18]

The ethnologists who became the leaders of the scientific study of man in Britain were not the only group of writers and thinkers with an interest in theories of race. Under the combined influence of nationalist feeling and the Romantic movement, historians looked with new interest upon the origin and character of modern nationalities. Most notably, Thomas Arnold's 1841 inaugural lecture as Regius Professor of Modern History at Oxford argued that the rise and fall of civilizations could best be explained by the racial character of various nationalities. In his view, the ascendency of the Germanic race, of which the English or Anglo-Saxon people were in the forefront, marked the most recent or modern period of history.[19] In contrast to the ethnologists, Arnold (and those historians who followed him in the study of Anglo-Saxons and Celts) showed less interest in explaining the physical variations of alien races than in describing the national character of the peoples of the British Isles. Thus these historians gave Englishmen a new awareness of their own racial identity. Certainly these historical studies had a greater influence than ethnological surveys upon the racist speculations of some leading writers and politicians such as Disraeli, Bulwer Lytton and Sir George Cornewall Lewis.[20]

The application of these racial theories to cultural, linguistic, and political, as well as physical, differences further confused the already ambiguous meanings given to the conception of race. Under Prichard's leadership, and under the influence of R. G. Latham, a prominent and energetic philologist, the Ethnological Society turned its attention away from physical classification towards linguistic affinities to prove the unity of mankind, and particularly the kinship of Indo-European peoples, or what came to be known as the Aryan race.[21] The ethnologists thereby made philology the dominant method of their science during the 1840s and 1850s, and in the process ethnology came to study much more than the origin and distribution of man's physical varieties. It now included the examination of national characteristics and cultural groupings. Researchers differed not over the all-encompassing nature of 'race', but rather over how far these cultural and physical traits were open to change and improvement, or how far they were fixed by biological inheritance. In the course of the century, race became more and more a physical category; but, at the same time, it became a determinant of intellectual, psychological and moral nature.[22] As this biological determinism became more pronounced the ethnocentrism of the scientists intensified into racism.

Working within a Biblical time scheme, the ethnologists used philology to push back the knowledge of human history ever closer to what seemed to be the date of the original appearance of man.[23] Eventually the monogenists simply ran out of time. In 1844 Samuel George Morton, the leading American anthropologist of his day, established that the modern races of man existed in ancient Egypt and further, that even then the Negro was bound in slavery. Since the monogenists placed man's origin only a millennium or two before the ancient Egyptians, Morton's evidence now left them only one or two thousand years to explain the diversity of man that developed after a common origin.[24]

Morton's telling rebuttal of monogenesis came at a propitious time in the development of English racial attitudes. By 1850 interest in the scientific and humanitarian defence of alien races was clearly on the decline. As a result, the Ethnological Society faced a reduction in membership and a financial crisis. In 1855 the Society was deeply in debt, and had only 32 paying members.[25] The ethnologists had also lost their lead in the scientific study of race, for interest turned from philology to follow the new methods in craniology.

Concerned with making the science of man more exact, craniologists devised a whole series of measurements of the skull to quantify the relationship which they assumed to exist between physical feature and intelligence or character. Although Blumenbach and Prichard, as well as earlier polygenists, had made use of craniology, the innovations of the mid-nineteenth century, including new standards of measurement such as Anders Retzius' cephalic index, resulted in a proliferation of 'racial' categories, and a strengthening of the polygenist case. Archaeological findings pointed to the existence of these varying skull types in the distant past, and seemed to deny the claims of Prichard and other monogenists that head shape altered with individual advance in education and civilization. The cult of phrenology, fashionable in the 1820s and 1830s, popularized the belief that skull shape and size provided an indication of mental character and development. By the 1850s, most who were interested in the scientific study of man had rejected the notion that ability and temperament could be read by measuring areas of the skull.

Nonetheless, they remained convinced that overall head shape and size indicated level of intelligence.[26]

The exacting calibrations of the craniologists readily incorporated the ethnocentric assumptions of mid-Victorian science. Since the European head shape was always the standard of comparison, any deviation from this ideal revealed degeneration in form or inferior development.[27] The only difficulty was that diversities in skull shape within racial groups invalidated many judgments about racial characteristics. Richard Owen, Hunterian Professor of Comparative Anatomy of the Royal College of Surgeons, observed that not all Negroes could be identified by skull shape. He had found skulls of non-European peoples no different than those of the 'uneducated and lowest classes of day-labourers in this country and in Ireland'.[28] In spite of these irregularities in skull shapes, a few scientific writers now used craniology to revive the polygenist thesis, and claimed with new certainty that race was the most powerful influence upon human history.

In the mid-nineteenth century, the outstanding British advocate of this revived polygenesis and of the place of race in determining man's past was Robert Knox, a Scottish anatomist. Knox had gained considerable notoriety for his connection with the body-snatchers and murderers Burke and Hare, and for his outspoken anti-religious and polygenetic opinions prior to the publication, in 1850, of *The Races of Man*, the fullest statement of his racist theory. In defence of his thesis that race was the sole determinant of human history, Knox rejected the 'superficial work' of Prichard, and revived Edward Long's erroneous observations about the infertility of hybrids.[29] A number of Knox's students became prominent physicians and anatomists, and in the 1860s his theories gained a considerable public hearing through the work and publications of Dr James Hunt (1833–69) and the Anthropological Society of London. C. Carter Blake, a leading member of that association, claimed that Knox 'revolutionised altogether the study of the races of man'. More recently, Philip Curtin has claimed that commentators have generally underestimated the Scottish anatomist's significance in the development of western racist thought. Knox himself accused *The Times* of plagiarizing his ideas.[30]

Interest in new archaeological discoveries about the age of man, and in the approaching crisis over American slavery, combined with the renewed support for polygenesis, revived the fortunes of the Ethnological Society. By 1860, the Society's growing list of new members included Sir George Grey, the Governor of the Cape of

Good Hope, and Sir James Kay Shuttleworth. Under a new president, John Crawfurd (1783–1868), an aged but energetic Highland Scot with extensive experience in South-East Asia, and James Hunt, the honorary foreign secretary, the Society had enrolled 211 members by 1863.[31] In that year, Hunt, dissatisfied with the lingering philanthropic links of the Ethnological Council and wanting to found a new and wider science of man, which included the racist speculations of Robert Knox, decided to break away from the older body.[32]

On 8 January 1863 Hunt, a medical doctor, expert in the treatment of speech impediments, and noted for his 'freedom of speech, quick temper, and skepticism in religion', called together his supporters to found the Anthropological Society of London.[33] Hunt described how in 1854 he had become a student of the writings of Robert Knox, 'the great modern British philosophical anatomist and physiologist'.[34] As Knox's disciple, the young doctor had plans to publish a journal dedicated to the science of man. Hunt, along with Robert Knox, Captain Richard F. Burton, and others, opposed the decision of the Ethnological Society to admit women, a step which limited the 'free and serious discussion of anatomical and physiological subjects', and thus they separated from the older association.[35]

As president of the Anthropological Society of London, Hunt became the leading British exponent of scientific racism in the 1860s. In his paper on acclimatization, read before the British Association in 1861 and before the Ethnological Society in 1862, Hunt argued that modern racial types had existed since the earliest times and that each race degenerated when it migrated from its own climatic region.[36] He made his fullest statement on the nature and status of the Negro in two papers he presented in 1863. At the British Association meeting in Newcastle, hisses and catcalls greeted the outspoken and unpopular views put forward in his paper 'On the Physical and Mental Characters of the Negro'. In the more friendly atmosphere of his own Anthropological Society, Hunt's paper, 'On the Negro's Place in Nature', occasioned such interest that discussion continued through another evening. The Society employed a special reporter to record the proceedings, and published 1,000 copies of Hunt's essay.[37] Hunt argued the same position in both papers, and drew the following conclusions:

1. That there is as good reason for classifying the Negro as a distinct species from the European, as there is for making the ass a distinct species from the zebra; and if, in classification, we take

intelligence into consideration, there is a far greater difference between the Negro and the European than between the gorilla and the chimpanzee. 2. That the analogies are more numerous between the Negro and the ape, than between the European and the ape. 3. That the Negro is inferior intellectually to the European. 4. That the Negro becomes more humanized when in his natural sub-ordination to the European than under any other circumstances. 5. That the Negro race can only be humanized and civilized by Europeans. 6. That European civilization is not suited to the Negro's requirements and character.[38]

Hunt's use of comparative anatomy and his attempt to assign specific divisions to racial groups belonged to the tradition of the polygenesis-monogenesis controversy which had dominated the scientific study of race since the late eighteenth century. Unfortunately for Hunt, discoveries in archaeology and the evolutionary synthesis in biology had already outmoded his polygenetic defence of white supremacy.

James Hunt and his followers rested their claim of black inferiority upon the old polygenist argument of Long and others that the races represented separate species incapable of producing fertile hybrid offspring. In order to correct the common view that racial crosses were fertile, the Anthropological Society published translations of recent works by two French scientists. In his work *On the Phenomena of Hybridity in the Genus Homo*, Paul Broca, President of the Anthropological Society of Paris, and a friend of James Hunt, argued that crosses of various races produced fertile offspring with varying degrees of success, and that 'there are human races the homogenesis of which is so obscure, that the results of first intermixture are still doubtful'.[39] After an extensive review of black-white intermixture, Broca concluded that their offspring were inferior in fecundity and longevity to either of the parent races, that they were less prolific in crossing with themselves than with parent stocks, and that the indefinite perpetuity of mulatto crosses remained doubtful. Broca claimed that the largeness of the Negro penis made unions between African men and European women less fertile than those between white men and black women.[40] In this adroit display of dubious but nonetheless compelling logic, the anthropologist confirmed the belief in the hypersexuality of the Negro, while he reassured European males that their virility did not suffer in comparison. Both Broca, and Georges Pouchet, another French anthropologist whose findings were translated by the Anthropological Society, refuted the Comte de Gobineau's theory that racial intermixture caused degeneration, for in their view such intermixture could not be sustained beyond one generation.[41]

As a result of these new, or rather revived racist theories, some contemporary observers claimed that scientific opinion on the racial question had undergone a significant change. In a paper 'On Fixity of Type', read before the British Association and before the Ethnological Society in 1864, the Rev. F. W. Farrar, novelist, classics master at Harrow, future Dean of Canterbury, and and an active member of both the Ethnological and Anthropological societies, claimed that 'the majority of scientific men' had now rejected the old opinion that racial variations could be 'accounted for from the effects of climate, custom, food, and manner of life', and that now evidence revealed 'an extraordinary *fixity of type* which, during every period of history from its earliest dawn, has characterised the races, and even the varieties of mankind.'[42] For James Hunt and his supporters, the argument for the infertility of racial hybrids and even the impossibility of lasting racial intermixture provided an essential claim in their theory of the specific division between the European and the Negro. In the 1860s, these ideas gained at least more extensive hearing if not broader support in the scientific community in spite of their contradiction of the available evidence of racial intermixture in Africa and the Americas.[43]

The scientific racist ideas promulgated by Hunt and the publications of the Anthropological Society did not go unchallenged, for their critics were sufficient both in number and in power of argument to make a loud and effective attack. James Africanus Horton, an African doctor educated in England, wondered if the scientific racists had ever seen a black man, for he could not recognize any of his countrymen from Hunt's 'prejudiced' and 'absurd' descriptions.[44] Thomas Huxley took an equally dim view of Hunt's anatomical studies. In a lecture before the Royal College of Surgeons, Huxley severely criticized Hunt for his paper, 'On the Negro's Place in Nature', and ridiculed, in particular, the comparison between the Negro and the ape. In Huxley's view, Hunt's study of the Negro was 'the most remarkable result of a modification of anatomical structure I had ever heard of. And the faculty for evolving nonsense displayed by its author.... I forbear to characterize, because the only appropriate phraseology would not be for me to utter or for you to hear.'[45] In spite of his support for the North during the American Civil War, and for the Jamaica Committee in the prosecution of Governor Eyre, Huxley was not a committed egalitarian in racial matters. Huxley did not think the 'average black' could equal the 'average white', and further doubted if when given an equal opportunity, the African

> will be able to compete successfully with his bigger-brained and smaller-jawed rival, in a contest which is to be carried on by thoughts and not by bites. The highest places in the hierarchy of civilization will be assuredly not be within reach of our dusky cousins, though it is by no means necessary that they should be restricted to the lowest.[46]

By implication, Huxley suggested that Hunt's hypothesis of Negro inferiority may have been exaggerated, but was sound; only the anthropologist's proof of that inferiority was inadequate. Alfred Russel Wallace, a scientist of moderate views on the racial question, observed that 'no one had denied – that the negro is very inferior in intellectual capacity to the European. The only question to be determined was, how far that inferiority extends'.[47] Most scientific men agreed with Huxley and Wallace. To these educated mid-Victorian gentlemen, the Negro was obviously the white man's inferior, but for what reasons and by how much remained the unanswered questions.

The anthropologists sought for a convincing scientific proof for their assumption of racial supremacy, but their quest brought them face to face with the perplexing difficulty of providing a satisfactory classification of racial types. Travellers pointed out differences between various African peoples, and therefore not all Africans could be 'real Negroes'. Hunt claimed he restricted his comments to the 'true Negro', the black-skinned, woolly-haired type of the Congo, and confidently predicted that refinements in craniology and psychology would provide more exact schemes of classification and conclusive proof of black inferiority.[48] In the meantime, the anthropologists and their ethnological cousins overlooked the problems of statistical averages and individual variation, and confirmed their belief in Negro inferiority by claiming that black brains were on the average smaller than white ones.[49]

In spite of their refinements in craniology and their researches into racial intermixture, the scientific racists failed to provide a convincing proof of the specific division of the races.[50] At the same time, critics of their schemes of racial classification also failed to provide a satisfactory explanation for man's racial differences, and for the assumed superiority of the Anglo-Saxon over all other varieties. John Crawfurd, the elderly President of the Ethnological Society, found all criteria for racial classification inadequate, and yet remained convinced that the races were separate and unequal.

He denied that skin, eye, and hair colour, hair texture, craniology, philology, and the infertility of hybrids could provide a measure of racial divisions, and yet he argued for the plurality of the human species as the only explanation for the differences in mental and cultural development.[51] While the scientific community generally accepted the validity of racial categories which described physical and mental traits in a hierarchical scale and in an interdependent relationship, only a few scientists accepted James Hunt's proofs of black inferiority. By the 1860s, a growing disenchantment with the inadequacies of the old polygenist-monogenist debate led the scientific community to look to evolutionary explanations in biology and in social theory to solve the riddle of the races of man and their significance.[52]

Ultimately Darwin solved the problems of the monogenesis-polygenesis argument simply by making them irrelevant. His theory of evolution greatly extended the time scheme in which the life processes operated, and thereby allowed for the development of the diverse types of men from a common origin. Before the British Association, Sir John Lubbock, a supporter of evolutionary theory, affirmed his belief in the unity of mankind, not from religious orthodoxy, but from his opinion that man was of much greater antiquity than most people assumed.[53] Darwin's theory of evolution described the origin of varieties by accidental or spontaneous changes in type, and the maintenance or elimination of these varieties by natural selection. It thus changed the conception of species, and thereby undermined the whole point of the polygenist argument. With the growing acceptance of an evolutionary framework, most biologists adopted the view that species were mutable and inter-related. Darwin had proved not only that the European was related to the Negro, but that all men were related to the ape.[54]

Alfred Russel Wallace presented one of the first attempts to adapt the theory of natural selection to the origin and development of the human races. Darwin and other notable scientists welcomed Wallace's paper, 'The Origin of the Human Races and the Antiquity of Man deduced from the Theory of Natural Selection', read before the Anthropological Society in 1864, and complimented its author on his significant contribution.[55] Wallace claimed that all men descended from one original type, but that the laws of natural selection operated to produce the different races according to regional variations. In time, through the development of social organization and the use of his mind, man adapted himself to his environment, and consequently freed himself from the operation of the laws of natural selection. Therefore, in the more recent period of human history, men ceased to change in physical form. According to Wallace, the validity of the rival theories of monogenesis or polygenesis depended upon the level of development of mankind's common parents. If the primeval ancestor was highly enough developed to be considered human, the monogenetic case was valid; if this original type was only a brute, then one could conclude for the separate origin of the races. Wallace also claimed that the trend was once more towards a more homogeneous race, for the superior races inevitably replaced the inferior.[56]

Wallace's paper met with a hostile reception from the Anthropological Society. Commentators criticized both the theory of evolution and the application Wallace made of it, but in spite of their objections the anthropologists realized that Wallace had undermined the foundation of their polygenetic theories.[57] Wallace had argued that the unity of varieties and species was an essential part of Darwin's theory. Hunt attempted to get round this awkward fact by incorporating his claim that the races represented specific divisions into an evolutionary scheme. Hunt accepted the view of Carl Vogt, a German anthropologist, that the races evolved not from one common ancestor, but from 'many parallel species of apes'.[58] Professor George Busk, a noted anatomist and close friend of Huxley, criticized Hunt's use of sources, and Wallace denied that Hunt's thesis could explain the similar mental characteristics of all races.[59] In *The Descent of Man* (1871), Darwin also argued that the similarity of mental characteristics of all races ruled out the possibility of separate ancestral pairs. Darwin founded his conclusion upon his experience in Tierra del Fuego and his acquaintance with a 'full-blooded' Negro, as well as upon the researches of E. B. Tylor and John Lubbock in social anthropology.[60] Even Carl Vogt, whom Hunt followed in arguing the consistency of evolution and separate origins, came round to Darwin's view. In a letter to Darwin, Wallace associated the theory of separate origins with 'the Anthropologists ... who make the red man descend from the Orang, the black man from the Chimpanzee, or rather the Malay & Orang one ancestor, the Negro & Chimpanzee another'.[61] Hunt had defended his case by maintaining that the question of the unity or plurality of man must remain an open one, and that, if anything, the theory of natural selection demonstrated a constant tendency to diversity and to an increasing number of racial varieties.[62] Darwin observed that once evolution was accepted, the whole attempt to differentiate species became meaningless, and as a consequence, he predicted that the dispute between the monogenists and polygenists 'will die a silent and unobserved death'.[63]

The supporters of Robert Knox and James Hunt had therefore failed to convince the scientific community that the races formed separate species. Their proof of Negro inferiority through comparative anatomy relied upon a conception of specific divisions derived from eighteenth-century biology. Their ideas became outmoded because they could not adjust to the discoveries of prehistoric archaeology, the known facts of racial intermixture in Africa and the Americas, and the synthesis of Darwinian evolution. Although Hunt had established the first learned society in England dedicated to the study of 'anthropology', even here he failed to establish a lead in the direction of research. As Huxley observed in 1878, scientists no longer thought the great question was the unity or multiplicity of the human species, rather they debated 'whether the ideas which Darwin has put forward in regard to the animal world are capable of being applied in the same sense and to the same extent to man. That question, I need not say, is not answered'.[64] The failure of Hunt and his colleagues to provide a satisfactory proof for their scientific racism did not mean that scientists no longer judged the black man to be inferior. On the contrary, men were still convinced that the races were distinct in nature and ability, only now they sought proof of Anglo-Saxon superiority in the application of natural selection to human societies.

In this quest, scientists and their educated friends found Charles Darwin of very little assistance. In 1864, Darwin, in a letter to Wallace, speculated that:

a sort of sexual selection has been the most powerful means of changing the races of man. I can shew that the difft. races had a widely difft. standard of beauty. Among savages the most powerful man will have the pick of women & they will generally have the most descendants. . . .

Our aristocracy is handsomer (more hideous to a Indian or Negro) than middle classes from pick of women.'[65]

In his *Descent of Man*, Darwin more fully explored this theory of sexual selection. He surmised that originally men had differed only slightly, but these slight differences were 'preserved and augmented during a long series of generations through natural selection'.[66] Darwin did not depict any trait as better or worse than any other. Racial characteristics were therefore not placed on a comparative scale of value, but left to the operation of natural selection to decide their survival or extinction.

For those wanting proof of the superiority of one race over another, Darwin's idea of sexual selection, and for that matter his description of the process of evolution, proved singularly unhelpful. John Crawfurd claimed that Darwin's theory was 'of no value to ethnology or the natural history of man', for it failed to clarify which of the races stood nearest to the ape and to distinguish the races and species of man in the evolutionary progression of human types.[67] The theory of natural selection described the mechanics of the origin and perpetuation of varieties, but it did not state which races were stronger, more fit or intelligent, or higher or lower in civilized development.

To find answers to these questions, scientists looked to the decline of the indigenous populations of New Zealand, Australia, southern Africa, and North America before the advance of European colonists. This retreat of the coloured races appeared to be the most immediate and forceful application of the principles of natural selection to mankind. In their discussions the anthropologists characteristically intermingled Malthusian observations on population growth and decline along with racist theories. Thomas Bendyshe claimed that 'promiscuous intercourse, artificial abortion, infanticide, wars, diseases, and poverty' caused the decline of the Australian Aborigine, while James Hunt, agreeing with Bendyshe and other commentators, concluded that the whole process revealed the law of race at work. Hunt observed: 'There could be no doubt that in the juxtaposition of the superior and inferior races, the latter will always become extinct if they attempt to compete with the civilized man. But when the savage is in subordination to the civilized, the extinction of the savage does not take place'.[68] Although the experience of the Australian Aborigine tended to be the model for these discussions of the disappearing races, mid-Victorian commentators saw the fate of the African in a similar light. In the narrative of his whirlwind tour of Africa, Winwood Reade concluded with the sobering thought that one day civilized persons would read of the 'Lost Race of Negroes'. Africa would undoubtedly be civilized but in the process the natural law that the 'weak must be devoured by the strong' could very well mean extermination for the Negro.[69] Reade's view was extreme, but even moderate men feared for the future of the savage races. In spite of his belief in the unity of man and the capacity of savages for improvement, Alfred Russel Wallace doubted if they could adapt to civilization with sufficient speed to avoid extinction.[70]

The theory of evolution provided an analogy for both man's

cultural as well as his physical development. Evolution described a progression of types from a lower and simpler form through intermediate stages to higher and more complex entities. The application of this progression to human societies gave Victorian commentators a ready scale on which to measure the 'simpler and primitive' against the 'complex and higher' forms of organization. This description of levels of development fitted into the hierarchical scale already applied to the races' distinctive physical features. The mid-Victorians assumed that Anglo-Saxon civilization and white skins were the culmination of this progressive evolution, and, in contrast, they assigned to African societies and to blackness a primitive and lowly, even degraded, status. Social Darwinism, it would seem, had a more pervasive influence in spreading racist assumptions than the comparative anatomy of the anthropologists. But even here a great deal was owed to patterns of thought quite outside and even hostile to the evolutionary trend of scientific inquiry.

Defenders of the Bible against the application of the God-less process of natural selection to man's development took a far dimmer view of savage life than did the social Darwinists. In his defence of missions before the Anthropological Society, James Reddie claimed that savages were a fallen and degraded people, and therefore it was impossible 'that Christianity had made people worse than they were; for he could not conceive men to be worse than the negroes were in their natural state'.[71] On a more scholarly level, in a well-known paper of 1855, Dr Richard Whately, Archbishop of Dublin, argued that no evidence existed that any savage people had raised themselves unaided from their lowly condition to a civilized way of life. Therefore, he concluded, Adam must have been created in a semi-civilized state, and must have had an 'Instructor' to help him in the initial steps towards civilization. Consequently savages were a fallen people living in a degraded existence far worse than the original state of the first man.[72] At the British Association meeting in 1867 Sir John Lubbock criticized Whateley's thesis, and argued that primeval man had lived in a state of 'utter barbarism', and had gradually evolved towards a civilized state. The Duke of Argyll responded with a series of articles in *Good Works*. He claimed that as much evidence existed for the degeneration of man from a higher state as for the progressive development of civilized life out of primeval savagery. Once again, before the British Association in 1869, Lubbock affirmed his position against Argyll's criticisms. Both E. B. Tylor and Lubbock denied that racial characteristics had a significant part in the rise of civilization, and eventually their researches into prehistoric archaeology and social anthropology convinced the educated public of the validity of the evolutionary thesis in the development of human societies.[73] Some clerics accepted this new evolutionary view, and assimilated it to the older evangelical tradition which denounced all facets of so-called savage life. The Rev. F. W. Farrar observed: 'The savage *might* have learnt many great and glorious lessons, he *has* learnt only what is vicious and degrading. Hence it is that these races – the lowest type of humanity and presenting its most hideous features of moral and intellectual degradation – are doomed to perish'.[74] Social Darwinism did not lead men to take any harsher view of savage life than that which the evangelicals had adopted earlier in the century, but by the 1860s many educated mid-Victorians had rejected all hope of alien peoples assimilating English ways, and even doubted if savages, including Africans, could survive the advance of white civilization.

As we have seen in an earlier chapter, the evangelicals managed to combine their total rejection of African customs and norms with a great optimism for the black man's conversion to English and Christian ways. By the 1860s the older philanthropic and philosophic 'idea that the savage is only an uncultured civilized man' who can be 'schooled into civilization' seemed to be erroneous.[75] In Farrar's view, the savage lived in

> Gross ignorance, total nudity, and promiscuous intercourse. . . ; in short, the savage is not a stately free, noble creature presenting the happy spectacle of unsophisticated innocence and primeval liberty, but too generally a wretch, depraved, hideous, and sanguinary; his body equally disgusting to the eye and to the nose.[76]

After observing to John Tyndall that he thought the Negro 'far below the level of the Englishman', and a savage in both Jamaica and Africa, Joseph Hooker noted a similar change in the accepted idea of savage life: 'It depends on the definition of the term "*Savage*". Johnson defined savage as "a man untaught, uncivilized"; in general parlance the world now superadds *cruelty* to the above. Now I hold the Negro in W. Africa and Jamaica is untaught, uncivilized and *cruel too*'.[77] By the 1860s, even moderate men, for example, Tylor and Lubbock, thought that visions of the noble savage belonged to the well-intentioned but outworn notions of sentimental philanthropists. This rejection of the religious enthusiasms of the evangelicals and the abstract rights of the philosophical radicals, was a characteristic feature of the professional intelligentsia of the 1860s.[78] This change in attitude owed more to the social and intellectual climate of the mid-nineteenth century than it did to the work of Darwin, and certainly it owed little to the comparative anatomy of Hunt and the scientific racists.

Although scientists by and large rejected past notions of the noble savage, they retained the image of the child-like innocence and simplicity of savage life. Commentators frequently made a comparison between the evolutionary stages of human development and the growth of the individual from infancy to maturity. Before the Anthropological Society, C. S. Wake used this analogy to prove the psychological unity of all men. At the level of the child, or selfish stage, stood the Australian Aborigine; next, the period of boyhood or wilful level typified the American Indian; the third stage of youth or emotional behaviour characterized the Negro; at the period of early manhood or empirical level stood the oriental; and finally, the position of maturity or rational state, typified the European. Wake argued that environmental conditions unfavourable to mental and physical development caused the 'inferiority' of the 'lower' races, and therefore these peoples could only progress with the aid of the more advanced European. The conception of the ages of man was only an analogy, however, and not an actual account of the line of descent. Oddly enough, the children of the human family, the Aborigines, were the oldest members in the evolutionary scale, and the mature Europeans were the new arrivals as more advanced off-shoots from the earlier varieties. James Hunt denounced Wake for adopting ideas 100 years out of date, and argued that no science of man could be founded upon the assumption of human unity. But he was the exception. Wallace and Lubbock, among others, used this parallel of the ages and races of man.[79]

This analogy of the ages of man looked back to the tradition of the noble savage living in primitive innocence, but introduced a new rigidity which barred the child-like savages from development. If savages were permanently children, it followed that the civilized were responsible guardians. Wallace argued that 'the relation of a civilized to an uncivilized race, over which it rules, is exactly that of parent to child, or generally adults to infants, and that a certain amount of despotic rule and guidance is essential in the one case as in the other'.[80] The idea of civilization developing through an evolutionary progression of simple to complex forms of social organization and culture relegated the savage to the position of the infant, and implied that civilized Europeans had a paternal relationship with the inferior coloured races. By the 1860s, that paternalism was no longer a trusteeship until maturity was reached, but a perpetual guardianship over ageless children.

This paternalism was not so much a product of scientific thought as an attitude of mind which infected the thinking of the scientists. In a direct line of descent, this pattern of thought owed much to evangelical and humanitarian attitudes toward alien and heathen peoples as it did to the logic of evolution. Sustaining both these influences were the habits of deference and authority ingrained by the social and political inequalities of mid-Victorian society itself.[81] During the 1860s, this paternalism became more rigid, for mid-Victorian commentators no longer saw much hope for the moral reclamation of the poor, or for the conversion of blacks to middle-class English norms. It would appear that science followed rather than led opinion on the racial question. Earlier in the nineteenth century, science acted as the servant of humanitarian orthodoxy. During the 1860s, scientists, in common with other educated gentlemen, experienced a change in social outlook which in turn resulted in a hardening of racial attitudes.

The proceedings of the Ethnological and Anthropological societies often revealed as much about this underlying political and social context as they did about the scientists' racial theories. Hunt and his followers tried to popularize their new science of anthropology by promoting discussions on current issues. The anthropologists attempted to capitalize upon contemporary interest in the 'Negro Question' occasioned by the American Civil War and the Jamaica Insurrection of 1865, and consequently their meetings often resembled a political debating union rather than a scientific gathering.

Under Hunt's direction, the Society clearly favoured the Southern cause in the American Civil War and Governor Eyre in the Jamaica controversy. During the American Civil War, the *Anthropological Review*, under Hunt's editorship, adopted the almost unique position among British journals of supporting not only the Confederacy, but also the institution of slavery. Professor George Rolleston, in a letter to Huxley, speculated that Hunt 'is paid by the Confederates to lie as he does.'[82] Some uncomplimentary remarks about himself in the *Anthropological Review* provoked Rolleston's anger, but his conjecture about the political affiliations of Hunt had some basis in fact. Henry Hotze, a Confederate agent in England and France, and editor of the London-based Southern propaganda sheet, the *Index*, served on the Council of the Anthropological Society from July 1863.[83] The Confederate agent apparently viewed the Society as a useful outlet for pro-Southern propaganda, for he included his donations to the anthropologists in his Secret Service Accounts for the Richmond Government. In the columns of the *Index*, Hotze and his staff favourably reviewed the discussions and publications of the Anthropological Society, reprinted extensive extracts from these sources, and gave special prominence and favourable comment to Hunt's views on the Negro.[84] The publications of the Anthropological Society included articles by defenders of slavery and supporters of the Confederacy, and even after the conclusion of the Civil War they reprinted a number of extracts from American sources arguing for a return of slavery in the South as the only condition under which blacks would do any productive work.[85]

It is not altogether clear if Hunt, and like-minded men, reached this conclusion as a consequence of their scientific notions about race. Certainly other commentators at the Anthropological Society meetings adopted a similar view on the American Civil War, and at the same time voiced hostile criticisms of Hunt and his new science. In an article on slavery in the *Anthropological Review*, James Reddie, a defender of the Bible and of missions against the attacks of the scientific racists, observed that Englishmen should not 'hamper the Southern States in their noble struggle for freedom', for 'the civilized races should have their inherited freedom and rights secured to them', before discussing the question of Negro emancipation.[86] He observed that the axiom that 'all men are created equal ... is untrue, and when we see the degradation of some of the *genus homo*, we instinctively feel that to make such a statement is to convey but a questionable appreciation of all that mankind implies'.[87] Hunt and his supporters among the anthropologists held similar ideas about the Negro and about egalitarianism, which, in their view, was an affront to the realities and ideals of human nature. Hunt and Reddie were in agreement not because they were both committed to the racist theories of Robert Knox, but because they shared similar political convictions.

During the Jamaica Insurrection and the ensuing Governor Eyre controversy, scientists freely expressed their opinions on the Negro, but once again political convictions more than specific scientific ideas seemed to shape attitudes. The Anthropological Society saw that it had a special task in removing popular delusions about the Negro, and in educating politicians and the public about the nature of racial antagonism. It therefore attempted to intervene directly in the political controversy surrounding Governor Eyre. Even the *Lancet*, the usually sober journal of the medical profession, thought that events in Jamaica called for a new look at the theory of Robert Knox on the inevitability of racial conflict. Knox's disciples in the

Anthropological Society were ready at hand to apply the Scottish anatomist's ideas to the Jamaican episode. James Hunt, in his anniversary presidential address for 1866, denounced Earl Russell for his ignorance of the anthropological truths about the Negro, and for his pandering to the pressures of deluded philanthropists. Contemporaries so closely identified the anthropologists with the defence of Eyre that in 1868 rumour had the ex-Governor nominated for the presidency of the Society.[88]

On 1 February 1866, as a public service, the Anthropological Society held an open meeting to hear Commander Bedford Pim (1826–86), a retired naval officer with interests in Nicaragua, read his paper, 'The Negro and Jamaica', in defence of Eyre's conduct.[89] To accommodate the large audience attracted to this public meeting, the anthropologists hired the more spacious quarters of St James Hall, Piccadilly, which ironically was the home of London's first permanent and most famous black and white minstrel company. The anthropologists were pleased with the large audience they attracted to their meeting. Banjo and Bones made a more lasting impact. The scientific gentlemen managed a rousing one-night stand; the minstrel variety show ran continuously until 1904.

Before his educated audience, Pim argued that the African and his New World descendant was 'little better than a brute, – in mental power a child, in ferocity a tiger, in moral degradation sunk to the lowest depths'. In slavery, the naval officer observed, 'a decidedly inferior race was rescued from a state of barbarism scarcely human, and compelled to take a useful position'.[90] The status of freedom and equality, in Pim's view, had caused black discontent in Jamaica. Haitian refugees and well-intentioned but misguided missionaries had stirred up this dissatisfaction until the insurrection had broken forth. He supported the prompt action of Governor Eyre, and concluded that only through the study of anthropology could statesmen learn the art of governing alien races.[91] The leaders of the Anthropological Society agreed with Commander Pim about the political benefits of anthropology, and in the practical application of their science to the American Civil War and the Jamaican crisis, they relegated the Negro to a subservient status, and supported the position of authority against humanitarian arguments and egalitarian principles.

Although Hunt and his fellow scientific racists claimed that racial divisions were of a different order than social divisions within English society, their attitudes towards race and towards class were often similar. Bedford Pim, for example, strengthened his case against the rebellious black peasantry of Jamaica by comparing them with the lower classes of Englishmen:

> We do not admit of equality even among our own race, as is proved by the state of the franchise at this hour in England!, and to suppose that two alien races can compose a political unity is simply ridiculous. One section *must* govern the others.

> I cannot see any hardship to the negro in deferring the claims of the negrophilists for equality on the part of their idol, until he has done what every man among us is obliged to do, viz. *prove his title* before he is admitted into fellowship.[92]

Pim was not alone in his use of English examples during scientific discussions of races.

By the mid-nineteenth century, scientists could rely upon a considerable body of ethnological literature, but the evidence of anatomists and travellers was often contradictory. To verify their conclusions about racial inequalities these armchair observers drew upon their experiences in English society.[93] Evangelicals and humanitarians favoured these comparisons of race and class, for these examples provided some justification for the philanthropists' feeling of superiority without denying their charitable concern for the 'improvement' of blacks. On the other hand, the scientific racists, intent upon proving the unique qualities of race, rejected any comparison of race and class.

In accordance with their biological determinism, the scientific racists criticized philanthropic efforts to educate or convert the 'inferior' races. From his African travels, Winwood Reade, who boasted of having been the first young man about town to make a *bona fide* tour in western Africa', described the 'absolute futility of Christian missions'. In a paper on the 'Efforts of Missionaries among Savages', presented before the Anthropological Society on 14 March 1865, Reade declared that his African, 'Christian servants made mental reservations about the eighth commandment; and their wives ... were equally willing to infringe the seventh. In plain words, I found that every Christian negress was a prostitute, and that every Christian negro was a thief.'[94] Reade thought missionaries could put their labours to better use in caring for Englishmen who suffered in worse misery and starvation in their own cities. Captain Richard Burton repeated Reade's charge, and observed that he would like to 'see a fair proportion of the half million now expended on missions amongst savages transferred to the Arabs of our own cities, and to others without natural black coats in a civilized land'.[95] In answer, the press sympathetic to the missionary cause blasted Reade, Burton, and the leaders of the Anthropological Society, and charged that the association preached atheism and infidelity, while contributing nothing of value to the scientific study of man.[96]

Defenders of philanthropic enterprise attempted to show that inequalities of race were of the same order as the differences of class.[97] In an extended comparison, the Right Rev. J. W. Colenso, Bishop of Natal, who also presented a paper on missions to the Anthropological Society, imagined that a visitor to London from another planet would not be greatly impressed by English standards of civilized life. Colenso claimed that this traveller

would probably find enough of drunkenness and prostitution – enough of all forms of vice and wretchedness – enough of selfish extravagance on the one hand, and of degraded ignorance and misery on the other – to make it just as reasonable for him to express strong doubts as to the effort, not merely of Christian ministry, but of all educational efforts, of all measures of social improvement, upon the inhabitants of the metropolis.[98]

In a direct comparison of the vices of blacks and whites, Joseph Hooker, who was no apologist for the Negro, similarly reflected upon the character of the lower classes, and reserved pride of place for Englishmen in both virtue and vice. In a letter to John Tyndall on the Jamaican outbreak, Hooker observed 'there are many Englishmen worse than the worst of any and all inferior races.'[99] Scientific gentlemen reserved for themselves the seat of enlightenment and virtue. They recognized that civilization in England itself was only a thin veneer, but they differed over how far beneath them the lower orders of Englishmen and the lower races of man stood in ignorance and vice.[100]

Intent upon proving that racial categories were fixed and immutable, the scientific racists felt obliged to reject comparisons of race and class, for such parallels implied that through time and education races like classes could change their station and character.[101] In spite of these claims, Hunt and his supporters did not adhere to this distinction between race and class with any consistency. The scientific racists acknowledged that their two bitterest enemies were the evangelical philanthropists, and the 'ultra-liberal and democratic party in politics'.[102] Hunt predicted that 'The age of revolution and anarchy is drawing to a close. Men are becoming weary of commotion, and ask everywhere for a strong government, adequate to the suppression of aimless insurrection'.[103] While Hunt had little use for the hereditary nobility, he did believe in the aristocratic principle. He looked forward to the day when English society would be further stratified and ruled by a superior caste based not on blood but upon intellect.[104] The scientific racists who preached that blacks were perpetually and innately inferior also thought that in England a new racial aristocracy should rule over the mass of their less able countrymen. These political convictions and authoritarian views did not rest upon erudite discussions of the nature of species, nor upon lengthy arguments about the significance of skull shapes. The scientific racism of James Hunt and his like-minded colleagues in the Anthropological Council was a product of their underlying assumptions about the nature of man and society.

The Anthropological Council, of course, represented the opinion of only a small, but particularly vocal part of the scientific community. After Pim's meeting on the Negro in Jamaica, Charles Buxton, M.P., a leading abolitionist, dissociated himself from the Anthropological Society. He objected to the Society's partisan stand on the Jamaica issue, and claimed that 'it is a fact among scientific men it [the Society] is spoken of with ridicule'. Thomas Huxley held a similar low opinion of Hunt and his colleagues, for he advised Dr Fayner of the Asiatic Society to avoid 'the quacks who are at the head of the "Anthropological Society" '.[105] Huxley denied that his pro-Federal stand during the American Civil War and his membership on the Jamaica Committee against Governor Eyre was derived from 'the smallest sentimental sympathy with the negro', or from ' "his peculiar views on the development of species" '.[106] Huxley viewed his own position on these issues, and that of other scientists, as an expression of 'their deepest political convictions'.[107] At least in Huxley's case, and probably in that of others, political beliefs, not scientific theories, lay behind attitudes toward racial conflict.

This interrelationship of racial and political attitudes was particularly evident in the thought of Charles Kingsley. In corresponding with the Anglican clergyman on the Governor Eyre controversy, Huxley identified Kingsley as one of the 'hero-worshippers' defending the Governor, recognized that they disagreed on 'fundamentals', and hoped that they could 'fight the question out as a matter of principle without bitterness'.[108] Kingsley's attitude in this case was partly a result of his own West Indian background, and partly a consequence of his political outlook and ideas on race. His mother was born in Barbados, the daughter of a judge, and Kingsley, acutely aware of his West Indian heritage, identified with the planters. While not a supporter of slavery, he once claimed that 'the negro has had all I ever possessed; for emancipation ruined me'.[109] In the

1860s, Kingsley, an honorary fellow of the Anthropological Society, took a keen interest in science. Politically, he supported the extension of the suffrage to the working class, but his support for the Southern Confederacy and for Eyre alienated his former Christian Socialist colleagues, J. M. Ludlow and Thomas Hughes.[110] Kingsley thought the vote could safely be given to the working man because in England the population formed a nearly homogeneous race, and therefore all shared to some degree in the capacity for self-government. He specifically denied the arguments of John Stuart Mill for basing the franchise on the abstract principle of equal rights, and for explaining human differences by environmental circumstance. In Kingsley's view, Mill and others like him overlooked 'the harsh school of facts' which meant they 'disparage, if not totally deny, the congenital differences of character in individuals, and still more in races'.[111] Kingsley's emphasis upon inherited characteristics enabled him to support an extension of the suffrage in England, while at the same time claiming that Irish Celts, the population of Romance countries, and blacks in the West Indies and America, lacked the historical experience and racial endowment for self-government.[112]

His use of racial explanations also had an application to English society. He disliked the implication of egalitarian and environmental arguments 'that inequality must be regarded as a wrong done by society to the less favoured'. Kingsley thought it more realistic to recognize 'congenital differences and hereditary tendencies', and then 'Society may pity those who are born fools or knaves, but she cannot, for her own sake, allow them power if she can help it'.[113] His Christian Socialist conscience pitied the poor in England, and he contrasted their 'short and stunted figures, the mesquin and scrofulous visages' with the 'health, strength and goodly stature' of blacks he saw on his travels in the West Indies.[114] At the same time he saw little difference between the intelligence of West Indian blacks and English paupers, for he reminded his readers that 'we have at home here tens of thousands of paupers, rogues, whatnot, who are not a whit more civilized, intellectual, virtuous, or spiritual than the Negro'.[115] For Kingsley, racial explanations enabled him to adopt one stance towards the political rights of subject colonial peoples, including the Irish, and another at home towards the respectable working class. These same arguments also allowed him to reconcile a greater measure of political equality in England with a defence of continued social inequalities, and provided a justification for his own sense of superiority of race and class.

Kingsley's racial theories gave legitimacy to his political preferences, and his case gives some weight to Huxley's observation that political convictions underlay differences of opinion about racial conflict. In the case of James Hunt and his fellow scientific racists it would also seem that their extreme racism was tied to a rejection of egalitarian values and a preference for an even greater degree of authoritarianism within English society. In view of the political values of the scientific racists, there is also a strong suspicion that these ultimate political convictions moulded their attitudes towards the Negro, and that scientific justifications of black subservience acted to reinforce these underlying and compelling assumptions.

The outcome of the anthropologists' attempts to persuade the educated public of the truths of scientific racism also owed less to the power of their ideas than to the political and social context in which they laboured. As one of the larger learned associations, the Anthropological Society may be taken as a representative group of the sort of persons interested in developments in science. More than a fifth of the approximately 500 Foundation Fellows belonged to other learned societies, with members of the Geological and Royal Geographical Societies being the most numerous. In the published list of Fellows for 1865, 60 out of the more than 450 members were doctors, and 23 were clergymen. Forty-five members, including some of the medical men, served with Her Majesty's Government in some naval, military or administrative capacity, and most commonly these officials served in colonial or foreign posts. In a recruitment drive, the Society gathered the names of 8,000 'gentlemen', and canvassed clergy and doctors in particular as prospective members.[116] Only a minority of members attended meetings, contributed papers, or offered their views in discussion These more active members were generally professional men on the uncertain threshold of acquiring or aspiring to upper-middle-class status. The simple judgment that blacks were inferior, which most of them held, was similar to the everyday distinction they made between themselves and the lower orders of their fellow Englishmen. The scientific racists therefore had fertile ground to work on, but their particular brand of racism only had a marginal influence upon the hardening of racial attitudes.

Through the Anthropological Society and its *Review*, popular meetings, inexpensive pamphlets, and paid lecturers, Hunt had hoped to popularize the lessons of his new science. While he failed to convince leading scientists of the truth of his racist theories, Hunt had greater success in attracting a substantial number of educated men to his Society. Joseph Hooker commented that he 'always regarded the Anthrop. Soc. as a sort of Haymarket to which the demi-monde of science gravitated on its establishment.'[117] Among this 'demi-monde', Hunt's best ally was ignorance. For most Englishmen, Africans remained an unknown people. Having at most only very limited contact with blacks in England, the mid-Victorians were ready to believe those who spoke with some authority on the subject of race. For example, a popularized version of learned opinion on the Negro, in *Chambers's Encyclopaedia* of 1864, compared Africans to apes and judged them inferior to Europeans.[118] For most educated persons, the anthropologists – and even more probably an encyclopaedia such as *Chambers's* – appeared to be authorities on the racial question, and therefore readers tended to accept racist conclusions as established scientific fact.

These readers of scientific works were few in number, and even for this select group science did not have the prestige and authority it came to have later in the century. Mid-Victorians frequently recalled examples of famous Negroes as readily as they remembered the results of craniology. In order to substantiate his belief that Africans were stronger than Hindus, Richard Cobden recalled that Molyneux, a West Indian boxer, had almost defeated Tom Cribb, the legendary English champion, in a series of bouts which had taken place as long ago as 1811.[119] Other commentators, like Cobden, intent upon substantiating an established viewpoint, used the anatomical measurements faithfully recorded by the scientists. The scientific racists thereby helped to spread popular notions about the distinctive thickness and shape of black heads, but even the acceptance of these supposed anatomical facts did not make people firm believers in the innate and perpetual inferiority of the Negro. Claims of the black man's distinctive physical properties – for example, the reported similarity to the ape – were probably only recalled because they seemed odd or peculiar. Such ideas were always open to correction from experience, or from the recollection of some other memorable incident or oddity – for example, the success of a black boxer.[120] The comparative anatomy of the scientific racists could only make their readers committed to theories of racial supremacy if those ideas fulfilled some intellectual or emotional need, and if the theorists themselves could gain the respect and confidence of their audience or readers as knowledgeable authorities on the subject. From the outset, the eccentricities of the leading scientific racists proved their undoing.

Since the conduct of Hunt and the Anthropological Society became a scandal to the scientific community, the scientific racists had little hope of gaining the confidence of the educated public. *The Times* had little respect for the scientific study of race under any form, and declared that 'ethnological generalizations, though very amusing, do not carry with them great weight'. The *Pall Mall Gazette* decided that anthropologists would add nothing to science or to social progress.[121] Huxley encountered much opposition to his science from his professed religious opinions, but his agnosticism was a pale shadow of the outspoken and provocative atheism of Knox, Hunt, Burton, and Reade. Leading scientists were also disturbed by the way the anthropologicals went about their business. Respectable learned societies did not publish their proceedings in a journal such as the *Anthropological Review*, a periodical of questionable scientific merit and under the editorial control of a man like James Hunt, a popularizer of equally dubious theories about race. Neither did respectable societies solicit membership from 8,000 'gentlemen', nor did they actively engage in political controversy. Professor Rolleston thought Hunt an 'ignorant and impertinent charlatan'.[122] Huxley resigned his honorory fellowship in the Anthropological Society, referring to its members as a 'nest of imposters'. He considered that the Society could do 'a good deal of harm if it went wrong'.[123] Huxley, Darwin, and Wallace thought a learned association devoted to the study of anthropology was worthwhile, but they objected to Hunt and his direction of the Society.[124]

From 1863 to 1871, the Anthropological and Ethnological societies, dedicated to what most considered to be the same subject under two different titles, carried on a futile and often bitter dispute over the control of the scientific study of man. There was less to choose between the two societies in the content of their interests and discussions than in the tone of their proceedings. John Beddoe, president of the Anthropological Society in 1869–70, observed: 'the prevailing temperament of the [Anthropological] Society was sanguine-choleric, and that of the Ethnological lymphatic'.[125] Huxley 'was thoroughly disgusted with the existing state of things', and from 1866 to 1871, along with Lubbock, Wallace and others, he worked for the union of the two groups. After the deaths of John Crawfurd in 1868, and Hunt in 1869, negotiation proved easier, but not until 1871, with both societies deeply in debt and flagging in membership, did necessity compel the former rivals to unite in the newly named Anthropological Institute of Great Britain and Ireland.[126] In 1873, some of Hunt's followers separated from the Institute to form their own society, for they saw their valued freedom of discussion and their study of the laws of race being turned into 'unearthing flint implements from the sewers of the metropolis'.[127] The new London Anthropological Society lasted for two years, but never gained much lasting support as serious students had turned from racial issues to prehistoric archaeology and the study of man's evolution.

The eccentricity of the leading anthropologicals destroyed their best hope for success, for they could only hope to influence the better-educated of the middle classes, who were the very people most concerned with conforming to standards of correct behaviour. In the 1860s professional men, educated at the public schools and universities and cultivating the attributes of gentility, sought social recognition by joining the growing ranks of learned societies.[128] As one of the enticements to encourage gentlemen to become 'Fellows' of the Anthropological Society, the Council gave members the privilege of adding the letters 'F.A.S.L.' after their names. Established scientists, for example Huxley and Rolleston, considered these titles meaningless appendages, and in fact Rolleston thought 'F.R.S.' –'Foolish Rebel Sympathizer' – would be a more appropriate title for the anthropologists.[129] But, to the 'demi-monde' of science, these honorary titles satisfied a desire for status. In a series of articles in criticism of the anthropologists which appeared in April and May 1865, the *Morning Star* claimed that the 'Society is the fussiest and most pretentious of the self-styled learned bodies', and 'having no solid claims to distinction, these gentlemen seek a substitute for it in notoriety'.[130] This search for notoriety endangered the anthropologists' position. The outspoken views and eccentricities of Hunt, Burton, and others on the Society's Council made it unlikely that they would gain the confidence of leading scientists, and therefore aspiring professional gentlemen seeking social recognition could not afford to give Hunt and his science their unstinting support.

At the same time, these educated men found the ideas of the scientific racists attractive. Lacking an aristocratic lineage, and yet seeking the trappings of gentility, pride of race formed one substitute. Unable to establish traces of aristocratic blue blood, all could share in a common inheritance as Anglo-Saxons.[131] Their conception of themselves as a superior race also implied an obligation toward the acknowledged inferior races. As superior men, they had a paternal duty, a sense of *noblesse oblige*, regarding the protection and governance of the childlike, savage races of man. During this period, even men of professedly liberal opinions were growing more sceptical about the efficacy of industry, thrift, and self-help to elevate the individual to a socially respectable status. Due to the growing physical separation of the classes with the rise of suburban living, the increased competition among professional men for gentle positions, and the growing social exclusiveness on their own part, educated men were less willing to advocate the elevation of those they considered beneath them. In the gospel of success, the successful were obviously the fittest and thereby survived, and deserved their place as a privileged élite against aspiring newcomers. In imperial affairs, philanthropic notions of civilizing subject peoples were now cast aside as sentiment. The improvement of savages, it was now believed, could only be achieved to a limited extent, and under the paternal and perpetual governance of the civilized English.[132] Many of Hunt's conclusions, if not his proofs of black inferiority, appealed to the new professional classes' desire for prestige and status. The doctrines of scientific racism in many case fell on believing ears.

Scientific racism gave some weight to the belief in black inferiority, but popular and literary sources were just as significant as scientific ones in the formation of the 'nigger' stereotype, and the concomitant conviction of English superiority. The mid-Victorians viewed the Negro as a happy-go-lucky, singing, dancing simpleton, who was perversely indolent, at times even deliberately and obstinately stupid, and on occasion ferociously cruel. This image, the *Daily News* noted, owed less to refinements in craniology or the definition of species, than to Thomas Carlyle, Charles Kingsley, and other less notable spokesmen for the West India interest.[133] In the spread of this image of Quashee or Sambo, these writers were unwittingly aided by the propaganda of philanthropic organizations which encouraged a contradictory picture of the Negro as a degenerate savage and as a naturally happy and naturally Christian Uncle Tom. Sir Joseph Hooker, John Tyndall, and Francis Galton, three sober and eminently respectable scientists, assigned the stereotyped qualities of laziness, stupidity, and perverse cruelty to all Africans. *Chambers's Encyclopaedia* also employed this stereotype.[134] Some of the scientific racists in an unguarded moment forgot about the Negro's head shape and species, and turned to the more evocative and popular image of the 'nigger minstrel'. In preparation for a meeting of the Anthropological Society, H. J. C. Beavan wrote to C. Carter Blake: 'So we have the irrepressible negro . . . Black yourself & play the banjo – I the bones Collingwood the tamborine!'[135] This image of Banjo and Bones thrived on literary and popular sources, not scientific ones, and was fostered by the values, inhibitions, and tensions of mid-Victorian society rather than by the realities of black communities in Africa or the New World.

Scientific racism, and for that matter the more widely accepted

Sambo stereotype, strengthened the English gentleman's sense of his racial superiority, but ultimately the professional and educated classes founded their assumptions about race upon their conception of themselves as civilized men in an uncivilized world, and as an enlightened intelligentsia in a largely barbarian England. As a self-conscious élite seeking to strengthen their own status by cultivating the habits of gentility, the professional gentlemen of the scientific community found pride of race was one way in which to satisfy both their desire for status and their own self-esteem as the able enlightened few above the stupidity and savagery of the mass of humanity. Scientific racism, then, was less important for the ideas it propounded than for its expression of the social and political undercurrents which led an articulate and influential minority of mid-Victorians – in Bagehot's phrase, the important ten thousand – to adopt a more rigidly racialist outlook.

8

English Opinion on the Negro in the American Civil War

To all appearances, the issues of race and slavery were far removed from the immediate concerns of most Englishmen. A few eccentric scientists spent long evenings in interminable disputes on the controversial subject of the Negro, while a diminished but dedicated band of philanthropists continued to plead the cause of the black man before enthusiastic but depleted audiences. These groups were clearly in a minority, and could be ignored by an indifferent public, and yet, during the 1860s, commentators talked and wrote with some impatience about the 'irrepressible' or 'inevitable' Negro Question.[1] It was in the engrossing realm of politics, not in science, nor in philanthropy, nor even in the popular amusements of black minstrels, that the mid-Victorians saw the Negro exercising this 'irrepressible' fascination.

With a prosperous economy and a period of relative social tranquility, mid-Victorians found their attentions drawn to the more dramatic political movements of Europe and the New World, and in the midst of the most violent of these distant conflicts stood the Negro. From 1861 to 1865, English politicians and journalists watched with passionate interest as America seemed to tear itself apart over black slavery. In four and a half years of commentary on the American Civil War, English public men, politicians, and writers of all qualities and degrees, gave an extensive airing to their views of the Negro, and thereby provided some measure of the nature of English racial attitudes.

From the disinterested distance of a century or more, the American Civil War takes on the appearance of a great morality play. Lincoln, the knight in shining armour, and his Federal Forces of Good fight for abolition, while a Satanic South vainly struggles for slavery, and justly falls because of its hellish institution. As interested spectators in this great moral drama, many mid-Victorians became confused, and ended up cheering for the South in flagrant violation of England's honoured anti-slavery tradition. In order to fathom this failure of English judgment, historians extended the moral drama to the United Kingdom, and aligned the villains, conservatives and reactionaries, with the South, and the virtuous, reformers and radicals, with the North.[2] More recent studies have found it difficult to substantiate these broad political generalizations. Tories and Liberals sat on both sides of the fence, and even radicals and the working class were less ardently pro-Northern than has often been assumed.[3] In fact the pro-Northern or pro-Southern proclivities of English spokesmen did not correspond to political and social divisions within England. Nor did pro-Northern or pro-Southern sympathies coincide with opposing views of slavery and the Negro.

The English expected the American struggle to be fought over slavery. When the North refused to take up an abolitionist crusade, many commentators, already suspicious of republican Washington, and dubious about the possibility of restoring the Union, thought the Northern cause had no moral sanction. This hostility to the North turned sympathies towards the South, for in English eyes, if the war was not fought to end slavery, the Confederacy had every right to self-determination. Expecting a morality play with good and evil clearly personified in the two protagonists, the mid-Victorians found that they were witnessing a great tragic drama in which the moral universe righted itself independently of the two warring factions. The Confederates and the Federals paid for their sins of slave-holding and slave-supporting on the battlefield, while the fates determined, so the English thought, that regardless of Northern conquest or Southern secession, the Negro would be free. Since they were convinced that the machinations of corrupt politicians and the enthusiasm of Nigger-hating Irishmen lay behind the Northern cause, many English observers thought that the slaves would more readily attain their freedom from an independent Confederacy than from a restored Union.

This distrust of Northern abolitionist claims and the belief in the moral and economic necessity of emancipation in an independent Confederacy influenced not only Southern propagandists and anti-Northern Cabinet Ministers, but also British abolitionists, religious leaders, and radical journalists.[4] As a result, the slavery question was never a serious obstacle to English sympathies with the South until

Lincoln declared emancipation a war aim on 22 September 1862. Although the extent of pro-Confederate sympathy seems to indicate a decline in mid-Victorian anti-slavery sentiment, it was the very strength of this abolitionist feeling which inclined English observers to expect, quite falsely, a Federal war of emancipation. When this Northern anti-slavery crusade failed to materialize, Englishmen of a broad range of social backgrounds and political viewpoints found it difficult to support a war fought for union and not freedom. Even after Lincoln's Preliminary Declaration of Emancipation, many Englishmen saw good reason for continued scepticism about Northern abolitionist pretensions, and they continued to place their trust in the inexorable laws of political economy and moral progress which in the long run, they thought, would force an independent South to free its slaves.

Lincoln's Emancipation Proclamation forced English abolitionists in the British and Foreign Anti-Slavery Society to end their neutral stance in the Civil War, and to declare support for the new Northern aim of emancipation. The President's proclamation also presented radical leaders with a rallying cry for popular agitation in favour of the North.[5] By making emancipation more clearly an issue in the Civil War, the Federal abolition policy created new and more revealing differences of opinion within England. Journalists and politicians now debated at length the wisdom of the Emancipation Proclamation, and uppermost in their thoughts was the possibility of a servile war breaking loose in the South. This discussion of a possible race war displayed differences in English opinion with greater clarity than the slavery issue, and revealed more about the interrelationship between mid-Victorian radical attitudes and the social and political cleavages within English society.

English critics of Lincoln's emancipation policy, encouraged to some extent by the statements of William Seward, the American Secretary of State, thought Washington had embarked upon the barbarous course of deliberately provoking servile war.[6] Englishmen most ardently in support of the Confederacy were also those most certain that the blacks would rise up and assault white women and children left behind on the plantations, and some went so far as to urge Her Majesty's Government to intervene to protect British lives and property in the South.[7] In contrast, the Confederates, including their London propaganda sheet the *Index*, expressed complete confidence in the loyalty of their slaves, and thought Lincoln's proclamation an idle threat.[8] English expectation of a servile war was therefore not a result of an intimate knowledge of race relations in the South. In spite of reassurances from Confederate sources, English commentators anxiously awaited news of a black insurrection, and as they waited, they predicted what form this slave rising would take. Some commentators predicted an insurrection of men degraded and made barbarous by slavery; others an uprising of black savages raging with the fearful passions of the African jungle.

While commentators of a broad political spectrum, including supporters of the North as well as the South, feared a servile insurrection, the prospect of rampaging African savages appeared most often in the rhetoric of pro-Confederate Tory journalists, and less frequently in the correspondence and speeches of politicians.[9] Though denying a general race war would take place, the *Index*, not surprisingly, played upon English fears of another Cawnpore or St Domingo. This organ of the Confederacy also had fewer reservations than the English press about appealing to racist arguments to defend black slavery and to arouse fears for the fate of white women and children confronted by 'a race naturally licentious, of weak intellect, and strong animal impulses'.[10] In November 1861 the *Standard*, a Tory paper and a strong defender of the Confederacy, contemplated the prospect of servile insurrection made particularly fearful for 'the negroes have kept in ignorance, taught to be unnatural, and steeped in crime' by their enslavement. By October 1862, after Lincoln's Preliminary Emancipation Proclamation, the *Standard* thought the North intended to provoke a slave insurrection, but predicted this dread plot would fail 'except where the presence of a Federal army has corrupted and maddened the ignorant, licentious, and excitable negro'.[11] The *Morning Herald*, another Tory and Evangelical paper, similarly declared that the Federals planned 'to rouse the passions of the negro', and *Evangelical Christendom* predicted 'the half savage African race would plunge to their worst excesses'.[12]

These descriptions of vengeful blacks on the rampage incorporated only one aspect of the multi-faceted stereotype of the Negro. An article of 4 January 1862 in the *Saturday Review*, a weekly appealing to a highly educated readership of both Conservative and Liberal leanings, revealed the paradoxical elements in the mid-Victorian caricature of the black man.

The negro, naturally a gentle and rather affectionate barbarian –
but still a barbarian, and even more a child than a barbarian –
would of a sudden feel all the savage, though latent, instincts of
his nature kindled into wild and unrelenting ferocity. The love of
mischief which characterizes the child, and the letch for blood

which characterizes the savage, would, under the promptings and goadings of superior power, find a rapid development in his untutored soul. Hitherto known only as humane, affectionate, tender, vain, garrulous, and sensual, he would of a sudden burst into the frenzy of a young tiger which now for the first time smells blood. Neither habit nor association would restrain him from gratifying the fell impulses of the new demon which possessed him. ... Pillage the most indiscriminate, havoc the most insatiate, carnage the most ruthless, would at once become the idols and the symbols of the new freeman's creed.[13]

From this paradoxical child-savage stereotype of the Negro, mid-Victorian commentators chose which features they thought appropriate for the particular situation. Fearful of a servile insurrection, and intent upon refuting the new humanitarian pleas of the North, these pro-Southern journalists found the African savage, rather than the child-like Uncle Tom, the more useful and appropriate representation of 'Negro Character' to present to their readers.

But even at this time of crisis, many English journalists avoided the stereotype of the vengeful black savage, and described Southern race relations in the more familiar language of English class conflict. On 11 October 1862 the *Saturday Review* declared that Lincoln attempted to bring white Southerners back into the Union through fear of having 'their throats cut by their domestics'.[14] The *Record*, an Evangelical paper critical of the Emancipation Proclamation, thought servile war threatened because 'the slaves have in so many plantations been so long kept down and treated as brutes'.[15] The *Daily Telegraph* with a large circulation and Liberal but pro-Southern sympathies viewed the Emancipation Proclamation as an illegal incitement to servile war, but did not dwell upon the fearful vengeance stored up in savage black hearts.[16] The *Economist* also avoided the use of racial stereotypes, criticized *The Times* for its violent tone, and, with English experience in mind, suggested that any slave revolts would occur in urban areas, but not in isolated agricultural districts.[17] In their appeal to race consciousness, then, pro-Confederate journalists had at hand the many-sided stereotype of the Negro, but in the use of this caricature they showed little consistency, and those of a more Liberal leaning often chose to depict the racial tensions within Southern society in the language of social rather than of racial conflict.

In spite of their fears of a servile or even a race war in the Southern States, English journalists claimed that their deepest concern was for the slaves. In the likely event of a servile insurrection these commentators claimed that they feared more for the fate of blacks than whites, for they conjectured that a slave rebellion would only result in a merciless reprisal from the slave-owners.[18] The pro-Southern press accused Lincoln of provoking the slaves into a futile rebellion. The Emancipation Proclamation, they argued, showed no principle, but only Northern hatred of the South, and Federal indifference to the fate of the blacks.[19] The conscription riots in New York in July 1863 soon confirmed the suspicion that Nigger-hating Yankees would neither fight for emancipation, nor care if the blacks were eliminated in an unsuccessful slave rebellion.[20] The English critics of the North neatly managed to reconcile prejudice and principle. Pro-Confederate journalists played upon their readers' fears of a black rebellion, while at the same time they accused the Federals of an unjustified, irrational hatred of the Negro.

As Lincoln's emancipation policy unfolded, the British public began to define the American conflict more sharply into a Southern struggle for slavery, and a Northern battle for freedom. In view of this change in opinion, some of the more committed supporters of the South made some tentative steps to defend slavery, or at least suggested that the Southern slave system should be gradually modified into some form of perpetual serfdom.[21] *The Times* attempted a defence of slavery from Holy Writ, as did the *Index* and a group of Confederate clergy. Both *The Times* and the Confederate advocates found their Biblical exegesis aroused more hostility than support.[22] Henry Hotze, the editor of the *Index*, actually paid periodicals for printing the address of the Confederate clergy, and *The Times* through the violence of its language and its vacillations on the issues of race and slavery, distressed some of its more respected and influential readers.[23] The newspaper's strong pro-Southern stand was partly due to the West Indian background and anti-abolitionist outlook of Mowbray Morris, its manager, and also to the racism of Charles Mackay, its New York correspondent.[24] Although provincial editors still tended to follow *The Times*'s leaders and reports, the rise of larger London rivals and of a vigorous provincial press meant that it no longer exercised so great an influence upon educated opinion as in earlier days.[25]

In order to substantiate its support of the South and slavery, the pro-Confederate press relied less upon the Bible than upon its readers' memories of recent British experience with subject races. Journalists prodded their readers' apprehensions of racial violence by recalling the distant horrors of St Domingo, or by conjuring up the more recent atrocities of the Indian Mutiny. At the same time, the economic ills of the British West Indies provided a ready illustration of the dangers of a sudden emancipation, and of the unfitness of the Negro for labour under free conditions.[26] With these precedents in mind, *The Times* and the Conservative press bolstered their defence of black servitude, but ultimately their acceptance of the perpetual inferiority of the Negro stemmed from their belief that not all men, and certainly not blacks, were fit for freedom.

In any society, England included, these pro-Southern advocates claimed, some were born to serve, and others were born to master. The *Index* stressed the paternalism of the white Southerner toward his slaves, and the gentility and conservative virtues of Southern life. The Tory press took up this theme, stressing the similarity of the South to aristocratic, Anglo-Saxon England.[27] In an effort to convince its readers that the Emancipation Proclamation meant servile, war, *The Times* not only depicted Lincoln appealing to 'the black blood of the African', seeking revenge on innocent women and children, but suggested that one can give 'an exhortation to the labouring class of any community to plunder and murder, and there will be some response. It might happen in London, or Paris, or New York'.[28] In another leader, *The Times* claimed; 'there is no society which cannot be destroyed by the process of setting loose those "dangerous classes" which are always to be found in every community whether urban or rural'.[29] In their defence of black subservience, and in their apprehensive discussions of black violence, these ardent supporters of the Confederacy, as their critics pointed out, had English social relations in mind.[30] Fully aware of the significance of divisions of opinion on the Civil War for the battle for parliamentary reform then taking shape, the Confederate backers reserved the full force of their invective for English radicals. The *Standard*, for example, poured forth its venom against pro-Northern radicals and abolitionists:

> They were Atheists, Socialists, advocates of 'free love', or universal licentiousness, of woman's rights, and every other abomination or absurdity which found favour in infidel France, in philosophical Germany, and in democratic America, but which religious and loyal Englishmen abhor and loathe.[31]

Among Tory newspapers, the *Standard* led the attack on the North and anti-slavery, but this firm stand for the South rested not upon the racial tensions of the United States, but upon the political perspectives of England, and this point of view appealed particularly – according to the *Daily News* – to 'a section of the upper classes and their imitators in other ranks'.[32]

English rather than American perspectives similarly moulded Liberal reactions to the Civil War. Liberal opinion, already fragmented over the question of support for the South or the North, did not find that the Emancipation Proclamation clarified the issue. Lincoln's hesitant approach to abolition, and in particular his advocacy of colonization, only strengthened the belief that Washington cared little for the fate of blacks and adopted an emancipation policy only as a measure designed to provoke servile war.[33] Liberal supporters of the North as well as those who defended the South feared a slave rebellion, and therefore the prospect of servile insurrection was not simply an idle argument conjured up by those wishing Washington ill. Richard Cobden, for example, expressed fear of a bloody servile insurrection breaking out in America as early as February 1861. Only in July 1863, after the blacks had proved quiescent in spite of Lincoln's provocations, did Cobden finally come to accept that no threat of servile war existed. He reassured himself by pointing to the supposed childlike attributes of the Negro:

I am not much afraid of any widespread acts of violence on the part of the Negroes. They are generally under religious impressions and are not naturally ferocious. They will grow unsettled, and some of them unmanageable, and there will be great confusion and swaying to and fro. But . . . I dont [*sic*] expect them to rise up and commit dreadful crimes.[34]

The Spectator, a Liberal weekly which held little hope for the restoration of the Union, but which supported the North, was equally aware of the horrors of a servile war 'where the insurgent race would be of the ignorant, degraded, brutal type, to which slavery has reduced the Africans in the Southern States'.[35] In an attempt to reassure its readers, the *Spectator* suggested that the violence of a servile insurrection was in direct proportion to the depth of the rebel's resentment. The most horrific rebellions were those in which the insurrectionaries were of the same race and intelligence as their rulers, but since 'the African temper, though exceedingly sensual, is also exceptionally placable', the *Spectator* suggested a black rebellion would not be a particularly violent one.[36] Similarly, E. V. Dicey, who wrote from the United States for the *Spectator* and *Macmillan's Magazine*, suggested that there was no reason to fear a servile uprising. He argued that the slaves were incapable of an insurrection without Northern assistance, and since Yankee troops had no love for blacks the soldiers would not 'look on and see a negro butchering a fellow white man without interfering on the side of the white'.[37] Even those who saw themselves as the special guardians of black rights and interests, the abolitionists, shared this fear of servile insurrection. For this reason Lord Brougham and Charles Buxton refused to support the British and Foreign Anti-slavery Society's decision to campaign for the North and emancipation.[38] The Society's address to Charles Francis Adams made the reassuring assertion that the Emancipation Proclamation would not lead to servile war, and approved of Lincoln's advice to Negroes to abstain from violence and to work peacefully for 'an equitable system of labour'.[39] By May 1863, Charles Buxton found he could lend his support to the abolitionists' pro-Northern stance, for to his surprise the slaves had not risen in revolt, but 'have shown still that patience, that wonderful forbearance and spirit of forgiveness, which has always characterized their race'.[40] The many-faceted stereotype of the Negro not only served to excite fear of racial violence in the South; it also served to ease the apprehensions of Liberal defenders of the North and abolitionists anxious to win English support for the Federal emancipation policy.

Fears of a servile war were partly a consequence of misconceptions about slavery encouraged by a lifetime of abolitionist propaganda. For some commentators, the prospect of servile insurrection appeared more terrifying simply because it would be a just rebellion. Firmly believing that slavery was an intolerable condition for the human spirit, commentators expected the slaves to be in a constant state of watchful rebellion awaiting the slightest opportunity to gain their liberty.[41] Apart from some Conservatives who expected social inferiors to be naturally servile and loyal, English observers had little conception of the social and psychological impact of slavery, and certainly they had little idea that the oppression of slavery could induce a kind of dependence which, as Harriet Martineau realized, might allow for individual acts of rebellion or escape, but which made a massive, organized slave revolt unlikely.[42]

Journalists and politicians who defended the South and white supremacy, and the publicists, political leaders, and philanthropists who defended the abolitionist intentions of the North, appealed to the race consciousness of their public, but the fears and anxieties upon which this racist rhetoric thrived were less a product of the distant confrontation of black and white in America than a consequence of the immediate realities of social life in England. For the defenders of a deferential society, whether Conservative or Liberal, classes lower in the social scale were expected to be loyal, obedient, and affectionate dependents, but experience had shown that on occasion these same social groups were given to outbursts of impetuous and even savage violence. Just as English observers expected and feared black violence in the South, so they prepared for riots and disturbances in distressed Lancashire. In both cases, the largely passive endurance of the labouring populations came as a pleasant surprise.

In their assessment of the Negro slaves of the Confederacy and of the distressed cotton operatives of Lancashire, English commentators applied similar standards. They denounced violence, and praised patient suffering. In the House of Commons, W. B. Ferrand, M.P. for Davenport and an outspoken critic of the cotton manufacturers, warned that the operatives 'are the same men as they were in 1841, 1842, and 1848. When the rebellion of the belly takes place no living man can control it; and you know that this is on the verge of taking place now'.[43] Expecting the cotton famine would produce violence, politicians found the long-suffering endurance of the Lancashire population remarkable. Lord Granville found the 'forbearance' of the cotton operatives showed 'an increased intelligence and intellectual improvement, as well as . . . great improvement in their moral character.'[44] Gladstone, greatly impressed by the physical and moral fortitude of the Lancashire populace, came round to the view that they were 'morally entitled to come within the pale of the Constitution'. In an address delivered in Cheshire on 27 December 1862, Gladstone praised the character of the cotton operatives:

Here is an affliction well and manfully endured by thousands, by masses of men, and women, of young and old. No murmuring against the dispensations of God: no complaining against men: no envious comparison of their case with the case of their employers: no discontent with the Government or with the laws: a universal and unbroken reverence for public order: under a homely and even rough exterior, a true delicacy, a true loftiness of sentiment: an unwillingness to be burdensome, a willingness to suffer patiently.[45]

For their silent, patient endurance, the Lancashire operatives were universally praised.

In March of 1863, riots did break out in Stalybridge. A dispute between the local population and the relief committee over the method of relief payments led to some violence. Crowds gathered in the streets. They smashed windows, stoned the police, and looted bakery and grocery shops. The authorities read the Riot Act and called in the troops to restore order. Sir James Kay-Shuttleworth, Vice-President of the Central Executive Relief Committee of Manchester, went to investigate the disturbances. In an address before a town meeting, he claimed that the rioters had damaged the high moral reputation earned by the Lancashire population, and observed that the crowd in behaving like undisciplined children had shown themselves unfit for the franchise.[46]

Other commentators, describing the working people in general during the cotton famine, and quite apart from the Stalybridge riots, thought that beneath a superficial appearance of industry and discipline lay inherent tendencies toward indolence and barbarism.[47] In his history of the cotton famine, written in 1866, John Watts was particularly concerned about the moral condition of the population. Faced with economic hardship, young men and women employed in the cotton industry could not afford to marry, and yet, Watts feared, they would not restrain their lusty natures.

Men of strong animal passions would probably abstain from the responsibilities of married life under circumstances of great penury, but they would not in consequence restrain themselves from the indulgence of sexual passion; and the girls, whose daily life is passed in the semi-tropical temperature of a cotton mill, with its tendency to early puberty, would, unless kept in good training, be likely to give way to temptation.[48]

Many English commentators described the Southern slaves as lazy, stupid, vicious animals. At other times, and in the eyes of other observers, blacks appeared capable of a saintly, silent endurance of oppression. Mid-Victorian attitudes to the distressed working people of Lancashire displayed a similar ambivalence. To most commentators, the working people seemed to endure their suffering as stoically as Uncle Tom himself. At other times, the operatives seemed lazy, profligate, immature, uncivilized, and over-sexed.

The parallels between attitudes to race and class were most striking in the organs of respectable opinion. The one significant exception occurred in the views of the popular radical weeklies. Looking at events in America out of a disparate social context and from a different political perspective, these journals shared none of the fears about black violence. *Lloyd's Weekly*, mystified by the apparent quiescence of the slaves during the early years of the Civil War, waited impatiently for them to rise up and win their own freedom.[49] *Reynolds's* welcomed the Emancipation Proclamation, for at long last the blacks would be given the opportunity to throw off their chains. If the slaves resorted to violence, *Reynolds's* declared, they would not be guilty of murder but of justifiable homicide: 'For our own parts, we shall hail a successful servile insurrection as one of the greatest blessings that could befall mankind. Moreover, we have no pity for the slave-master: all our sympathies are enlisted with the slave!'[50] *Reynolds's* mocked the delicate fears of the English ruling class for the lives of the women-folk of the hated slave-owner, and welcomed the prospect of a servile insurrection in the name of liberty.

The racial ideas and associations used by mid-Victorian commentators showed a remarkable flexibility in their application to the American Civil War, but in many cases, racial attitudes were consistent with attitudes toward social relations in England. The *Daily News* suggested that journalists who indulged in sensational descriptions of black violence evolved 'their images of horror from the depths of their own consciousness of the passions of the white towards the negro, of the oppressor towards the wronged and we may add, of the vindictive towards the generous'.[51] This Liberal pro-Northern daily also thought these fears more apparent than real. Apprehensive expectations of blacks assaulting white women and children thrived on a kind of voyeuristic fantasy, or as the *Daily News* suggested, English commentators were 'peeping out of their closets and asking when the ravishing is going to begin'.[52] Carried away with their descriptions of black sensuality and violence, English journalists indulged in a sensationalism which depended upon the repressed sexuality and guilt of their readers. At the same time, these fears and anxieties were less a product of the mid-Victorians' limited contact with alien races than a result of the social and psychological repressions within English society itself. In the language of the *Daily News*, they were a consequence of 'the passions of the white towards the negro', and 'of the oppressor towards the wronged'.

While English racial images and ideas displayed certain parallels to domestic social attitudes, the contradictions and inconsistencies in this racial rhetoric were far more apparent, and suggest that the sensationalism of press commentary gave an exaggerated impression of the intensity of racial prejudice. Certainly some strange twists in opinion occurred when English commentators dealt with the issue of racial discrimination in the Northern States. Defenders of the Confederacy, anxious to refute the sincerity of the Federal abolition policy, denounced racial prejudice and discrimination in the Free States, and claimed that in the South blacks and whites lived on friendly if not intimate terms.[53] In defence of the North, the *Spectator*, in contrast to the *Daily News* and other supporters of the Federal cause, attempted to justify the racial antipathies of the Northerners.[54] In a similar defence of Northern racism, E. V. Dicey, the *Spectator's* special correspondent in America, suggested that the prejudice against blacks in the North was no worse than anti-Irish feeling in England, and argued that this racial hostility was a light burden compared to the oppression of slavery.[55] The *Bee-Hive*, a trade unionist paper which had supported recognition of the Confederacy earlier in the war until Lincoln's Emancipation Proclamation forced a change in loyalties, drew a clear distinction between the oppression of slavery and the discrimination based on race prejudice: 'Englishmen will never believe that the instinctive feeling of superiority which the white man entertains toward the black man is to be viewed in the same light as a systematic legal right and property in the black man's person'.[56] 'BETA', the author of the article, admitted that 'Northerners despise the negroes', but by way of explanation he observed: 'It is hardly in nature that is should be otherwise, when we consider their position towards one another for so many years, together with that instinctive repugnance which exists between the two races'.[57] It would be foolish to suggest that 'BETA' represented the opinion of the 'labour aristocracy'. Nor should pro-Confederate criticisms of Northern racism be seen as evidence of racial tolerance, for these same critics reacted with shock and horror to a suggestion that a blending of the races might solve the racial problem in the United States. To the *Standard* and the *Saturday Review*, this prospect of miscegenation, invariably described as black males defiling white women, only demonstrated the absolute demoralization of extreme abolitionists and radical democrats.[58] Attitudes to racial discrimination showed as great a flexibility as the use of the stereotyped attributes of 'Negro' character. Critics of the North denounced Yankee racial hatred, while they themselves expressed the same feelings on the question of miscegenation; opponents of slavery and supporters of the Federal war effort, when faced with criticism of Northern racism, sought to justify racial prejudice and discrimination.

English commentators were equally inconsistent in their reaction to the enlistment of blacks in the Federal and Confederate armies. Of the two protagonists, the Federals were the first to employ black troops. For the North's English friends, this enlistment of blacks was reassuring, for here clearly was positive evidence that the Federals were sincerely conducting an anti-slavery war, and overcoming their sensibilities on the colour question.[59] Critics of the Washington Government thought the Federals planned to use blacks as the savage agents of Lincoln's servile war. At the same time these spokesmen suggested that blacks would not join the Northern forces only to be subject to the insults of Yankee soldiers. The Federals, relying on irresolute conscripts from lowly German and Irish immigrant stock, had now turned to the dishonourable stunt of enticing the childlike Negroes into the field, to be slaughtered by Southerners if they stood firm, or to be shot by Nigger-hating Yankees should they turn cowardly and run. For these opponents of the North, Washington had debased the military profession by this use of a servile race.[60] *Reynolds's Newspaper*, bemused by these criticisms of black troops, reminded readers that the British army had no scruples about enlisting black soldiers, and suggested that the objections of *The Times* and other like-minded journals were similar to the refusal of the Volunteer Movement to enlist Irish or English working men.[61]

The first rumours that the South planned to arm its slaves, circulated by Henry Hotze in the *Index*, reached England in September 1863. During that month and in late 1864, when the Confederates gave more serious consideration to this proposal, English attitudes to Negro soldiers experienced a sudden change. Supporters of the North were amazed at the Confederate proposal, yet sceptical about Southern intentions. Clearly, slavery was on its deathbed. The blacks would not fight for their masters, and the Southerners themselves could not stand by their promise of freedom for the soldier-slaves, for it would deny the whole reason for the existence of the Confederacy. To the critics of the South, the Confederates' arming of slaves was a last, desperate, disreputable tactic to prolong a futile cause. Since the blacks would fight for the free North, but not the slave South, the outcome of the Civil War would be decided neither by North nor South, but by the slaves themselves.[62]

A more dramatic reversal of opinion occurred in the ranks of the Confederacy's supporters. The rumour of the South arming its slaves seemed to vindicate all those pious hopes that the Confederates fought for independence not slavery. Concerning the character of these servile troops, the press, formerly critical of black soldiers in the Federal ranks, predicted that they would be loyal, disciplined and ferocious fighters under the steady command of the aristocratic officers of the Confederate army.[63] Clearly, a commentator's stand in favour of the North or the South was more influential than ideas about race in determining attitudes toward black soldiers in the Civil War.

Toward the end of the war and during its aftermath, English commentators considered the new freedmen's changed political and social status, and showed once again that they had no reservations about applying their experience of social divisions within England to the racial divisions of the South. English observers focussed their attentions upon the question of the freedmen's new social and economic role, and altered political status. Economically, the mid-Victorians saw a fundamental change taking place in the Negroes' condition. The blacks would be elevated from the status of slaves to that of wage-labourers, and thus have the opportunity to attain to the dignity of English working men.[64] *The Times* even suggested that the plantations established by the Federal Freedmen's Bureau was comparable to English workhouses, and the newspaper hoped that the freed slaves could be compelled like English paupers to learn the necessity of labour.[65] The question of the freedmen's political status presented a more perplexing difficulty. Some – for example, Lord John Russell and the *Standard* – rejected any notion of giving ignorant, landless ex-slaves the vote.[66] On the other hand, Sir Frederick Bruce (British ambassador in Washington), the *Saturday Review* and the *Record* favoured an 'English' solution to the problem. They suggested that blacks with education and property could be given the franchise, even though on these terms few blacks would qualify.[67] Those groups who were more in sympathy with radical agitation for the reform of Parliament, a movement now revived partly as a consequence of campaigning during the Civil War, or who belonged to abolitionist or freedmen's aid organizations looked upon the American situation as a special case. If political power remained solely in the hands of white Southerners, a danger remained that the blacks might be reduced to slavery once more. In the light of this special threat, English philanthropists and reforming Liberals argued that the freed blacks should be given the vote on an equal footing with whites. The more extreme radicals argued that the ex-slaves should have the vote not because of special circumstance, but as a matter of right.[68] Once again, political principles rather than specific attitudes to race seemed to determine the English response to the status of the emancipated blacks in America.

As distant witnesses to the American Civil War, English observers found the amorphous child-savage stereotype of the Negro could sustain many diverse and even contradictory viewpoints, and yet attitudes to race contained certain underlying and internal consistencies. Inherently full of ambiguities and contradictions, the racial stereotype was important for the way in which it was used, rather than for the specific racist ideas which it incorporated. The characteristics of the Negro altered according to their utility in substantiating the pro-Northern or pro-Southern position of the individual commentator. Friends of both Richmond and Washington

expressed fear of servile revolt and laid claim to paternalistic concern for the welfare of black Americans. In fact, mid-Victorians of a
wide range of political viewpoints assumed that blacks were less than
fully mature responsible adults, but within this common racist
assumption there was room for significant differences of opinion
about the likelihood of servile insurrection, the legitimacy of racial
discrimination, the use of black troops, and the social and political
standing of the freedmen. Underlying both this widespread
paternalism and the differences of opinion on these particular issues
were the political preoccupations and social habits of men familiar
with the racially homogeneous but rigidly stratified, and acutely
class conscious, society of England. Specific racist ideas added a
sensational appeal to the rhetoric of press comment, but these appeals
to race consciousness could not rely upon immediate personal
experience of encounters with blacks. The racial imagery may have
been that of the New World, but behind the rhetoric, giving form
and substance to mid-Victorian racial attitudes, lay the social
realities of England.

9

Governor Eyre, the Negro
and the
Honour of England

In late 1865, as the mid-Victorians paid their last respects to Lord Palmerston, and waited with mixed feelings for Russell and Gladstone to present plans for parliamentary reform, events in the distant Caribbean unexpectedly distracted their attention. A local rising among the Jamaican peasantry and its subsequent suppression by the colonial authorities provoked a violent controversy in the metropolis. Preachers, politicians, writers and journalists hotly disputed the question of the Negro and the Jamaica Insurrection. During November and December 1865 and throughout the early months of 1866, Victorian society drew up its battle-lines on this contentious issue, and for the following three years, the antagonists disputed the use or abuse of authority by Edward John Eyre, the Governor of Jamaica. In October 1866, the *Saturday Review*, growing weary of the whole affair, wondered if English society would be forever divided into two hostile camps:

> What have the English people done that the irrepressible negro should make an interruption into their daily press, disport himself at their dessert, chill their turtle, spoil their wine, and sour their pine-apple and their temper? ... Are we henceforth to be separated, as a nation, into negrophilites and anti-negroites? Is every dinner-party and every tea-party, every society of geographers and every society of social twaddlers, to be worried and wearied by prosy controversialists in the brutal inferiority or the angelic superiority of the sons of Ham?[1]

Following fast on the heels of the American Civil War, the Governor Eyre controversy prolonged the mid-Victorian debate about the Negro, but once again it was not so much the events in the distant

Caribbean as the temper of English society itself which shaped mid-Victorian attitudes. The supporters of Governor Eyre, as well as his prosecutors, defended the honour of England. They differed so passionately because they had two different Englands in mind.

On 11 October 1865, a crowd of black settlers had gathered before the court house of Morant Bay to protest against the harsh and – they felt – partial justice of the local magistracy. The magistrates, who happened to be prominent local planters, had recently pronounced severe sentences upon blacks accused of squatting upon uncultivated land. Four to five hundred demonstrators, led by Paul Bogle, a local black landowner and lay preacher in the Native Baptist Church, marched on the court house to present their grievances before the vestry meeting. The Custos, or chief magistrate, read the Riot Act, and advised the Volunteers to stand ready. As the crowd pushed forward and began hurling stones, the militia, upon order, fired, killing seven of the rioters and wounding several others. This action infuriated the crowd, who forced the Custos, the Volunteers, and the vestry officials back into the court house. After several hours of exchanging shots with the Volunteers, the mob set fire to the court house and the neighbouring fort-house, forcing the officials to flee. The crowd then set upon and murdered the Custos and 15 others. The rioters' victims included members of the black Volunteers as well as some white officials, and several of their captives, including two doctors, were set free. After the bloody events of 11 October, the black rebels – left in complete control of the remote parish of St Thomas-in-the-East – raided a number of estates, and killed two particularly hated white overseers.

In Kingston, the Governor, Edward John Eyre, declared martial law in the eastern region of Jamaica, and ordered troops to Morant Bay. Under the rule of martial law, the troops, aided by the Maroons shot or executed 439 blacks, flogged about 600 others, and burned over 1,000 huts and houses belonging to suspected rebels.[2] Eyre claimed that the military had quelled all signs of rebellion by 26 October, yet the reprisals continued for the full 30 days of martial law.[3] During this time, the troops met no resistance, and suffered no injuries apart from the discomfort of inclement weather and fatigue from their strenuous efforts.

In this tale of violence, the English public paid particular attention to one dramatic episode – the arrest and execution of George William Gordon, a prominent, though bankrupt, mulatto landowner, and a radical critic of Governor Eyre and the Country or Planters' Party. Gordon was the chief advocate of the interests of the black peasantry in the House of Assembly, and a lay preacher in the Native Baptist Church, an independent Jamaican sect closely associated with the black population. He had gained a reputation as a fiery, popular demagogue. When the riot broke out at Morant Bay, Eyre and his advisers suspected that Gordon had instigated a widespread conspiracy to overthrow white property and authority in the island. With this fearful prospect in mind, Eyre issued warrants for Gordon's arrest. After the political agitator had surrendered himself to the authorities, they transported him from Kingston, where martial law was not in effect, to Morant Bay. There military officers, acting with the approval of the Governor, and with scant regard for legal niceties, tried and executed Gordon before a makeshift court martial.[4]

In England, political reformers did not take long to see similarities between the Jamaican episode and their own struggle for parliamentary reform. In 1866 the Hyde Park riots and the suspension of the Habeas Corpus Acts in Ireland brought events in Jamaica nearer to home. The Government, recognizing the gravity of the crisis and the concern of the public, suspended Eyre and appointed a Royal Commission of Inquiry.[5] The Commission's Report, prepared by 9 April 1866, and presented to Parliament on 18 June, failed to satisfy a group of anti-slavery philanthropists and political radicals who had formed the Jamaica Committee. Unsuccessful in their attempt to gain a stronger official censure of the ex-governor, the Jamaica Committee initiated its own legal proceedings against Eyre for the murder of Gordon. To defend the ex-governor against his prosecutors, a group of sympathizers formed the Governor Eyre Defence and Aid Committee.

The controversy between the two warring factions prompted many of leaders of the Victorian intelligentsia to make public avowals of their sympathies. John Stuart Mill, Thomas Huxley, Herbert Spencer, Thomas Hughes, Frederic Harrison, Goldwin Smith, and John Bright served on the executive of the Jamaica Committee, and received the support of Leslie and James Fitzjames Stephen, Francis Newman, Sir Charles Lyell, and Charles Darwin.[6] The Earl of Shrewsbury, with landed interests in Jamaica, presided over the Eyre Defence and Aid Committee, while Thomas Carlyle led a group of hero-worshipping acolytes in praise of the ex-governor. Shrewsbury and Carlyle left the administrative details to John Ruskin and Sir Roderick Murchison, while Lord Cardigan, Lord Elcho, Lord John Manners, Professor John Tyndall, Sir Samuel Baker, Henry Kingsley, Alfred Lord Tennyson and Charles Dickens declared their support for the Committee's aims.[7] On 21 August 1866, at a banquet in Eyre's honour at Southampton, Charles Kingsley stoutly defended the ex-governor, but after receiving a thorough tongue-lashing in the radical press he refused to declare his support for the Eyre Committee. Kingsley's remarks at the dinner lost him the friendship of Thomas Hughes and J. M. Ludlow, two Christian Socialist colleagues who had joined the Jamaica Committee, while his silence thereafter offended Carlyle and Ruskin.[8] The Jamaica Committee took pride in its following of radical and ultra-Liberal M.P.s while the Eyre Committee had a much greater success in attracting support from leaders in the Church, the armed forces, and landed society. The Governor's defenders claimed to have the support of 71 peers, 6 bishops, 20 M.P.s, 40 generals, 26 admirals, 400 clergymen, and 30,000 others. The legal proceedings against Eyre began in 1866, and were finally concluded in 1869. Eyre was acquitted of all charges, but when as late as 1872 the Government proposed to pay the ex-governor's legal expenses the warring factions arose once again.[9]

When the news of the Jamaica Insurrection first burst upon the English public, and during the next few months when the controversy raged at its greatest intensity, the mid-Victorians gave free expression to their opinions of black West Indians. Michael St John Packe in his biography of John Stuart Mill has claimed that 'public opinion divided sharply along the line of preconceived ideas about the colour problem', whereas Leonard Huxley, son of Thomas Huxley, followed his father's opinion that the Eyre controversy 'became the touchstone of ultimate political convictions'.[10] The difference between these two opinions is more apparent than real, for the Eyre controversy demonstrated that the mid-Victorians' differences in racial attitudes were closely bound up with differences in political outlook.

For English observers, the violent events of Morant Bay in October 1865 created no new impressions about the Negro, but simply reconfirmed existing beliefs. During the previous 20 years, the economic decline of Jamaica had been a subject of dispute between the supporters of the planting interest and the friends of the ex-slaves. Spokesmen for the West India interest had argued that the decline in sugar production was the direct result of the indolence of free black labour. This assessment of the economic difficulties of the West Indies received a more favourable reception in respectable society in the mid-century, as it became more acceptable to deride the pious platitudes of the sentimental philanthropists.[11] The

Morant Bay uprising, the most violent result of the continuing economic problems of the island, sparked this old debate to life once more. During the mid-1860s, drought and the interruption in trade caused by the American Civil War aggravated Jamaica's long-term economic difficulties and created widespread distress. There was increased tension between the planting interest, backed by Governor Eyre and the Colonial Office, and the black peasantry, supported by Nonconformist missionaries and local radical leaders such as George William Gordon and Paul Bogle. In a prophetic moment in April 1865, the *Anti-Slavery Reporter* warned that unless some action were taken to provide a greater measure of social justice in Jamaica, the population would resort to violent action.[12]

On 3 November 1865, news reached London from Halifax by the new transatlantic telegraph that Governor Eyre had requested additional troops to crush a Negro uprising. Upon receiving this first scanty report, the London press, apart from ultra-Liberal or radical papers, depicted a race of black vagrants conspiring to massacre the whites, and asserted that this savage plot must be put down without mercy. On 4 November *The Times* declared that this latest news from Jamaica proved that blacks were unsuited to freedom. It advised that American legislators, when considering the political status of their recently liberated slaves, should keep in mind the sad past and present misery of Jamaica.[13] On 11 November the *Standard* admitting that little news had been received of the insurrection, surveyed previous slave revolts in Jamaica, and concluded that black rebellions were far worse than white ones. The indolent black savages of Jamaica, the *Standard* claimed, had no grievances, but sought only to satisfy their greed, hatred, and lust for white property, white lives, and white women.[14] The *Morning Herald* observed that 'the vagueness of the successive telegrams which we receive from Halifax throws a sort of mysterious horror over this negro rising'. Undeterred by the admitted inadequacy of reports, the *Herald* concluded that the blacks had shown themselves unsuited for freedom, and had demonstrated a monstrous ingratitude toward their British benefactors. As a consequence, this Conservative and Evangelical paper demanded that 'as a salutary lesson to the black race everywhere, ... the ringleaders in this wicked revolt ... be sternly and summarily dealt with as soon as they are caught'.[15] The *Daily Telegraph*, a Liberal paper, shared many of the fears of the Conservative press. Depicting the black population by the familiar child-savage stereotype, the *Telegraph* feared for the lives and honour of English men and women, and suggested that blacks, even those serving in the West India Regiment, could not be trusted. At the same time, it voiced fears that panic on the part of the Jamaican authorities might lead to an excessive repression which would disgrace the respected tradition of English justice.[16]

The *Daily News*, in contrast to other influential London dailies, emphasized the social and economic grievances of the black population, not the fears of the white planters. On 6 November, this Liberal paper forewarned that the black population had no confidence in either the colonial assembly or the island's judicial system, but at the same time it suggested that any assessment of the Jamaican news must await further reports from the West Indies. By 14 November, it expressed confidence in the authorities' ability to handle the local disturbance at Morant Bay, and rejected any conjectures that a massive conspiracy of blacks threatened to overrun the white population. This newspaper argued that the disturbance was indicative of discontent in the island, and recommended stronger metropolitan control to end the incompetent rule of the planters.[17]

The *Record*, an Evangelical paper, compared the response of *The Times* and the *Daily News*, rejecting the former's abuse of the black population, and the latter's claim of widespread discontent in the island. In the face of this conflict of opinion and the inadequacy of reports, the *Record* counselled its readers to withhold judgment about the Jamaican news, while at the same time admitting that Negro indolence had created many of the island's problems.[18] The *Methodist Recorder* adopted a similar attitude. It described in gruesome detail the reported murder of three Wesleyan ministers at Morant Bay, but rejected the *Standard*'s diatribes against the whole of the black population. This Methodist paper carefully distinguished the rioters, all of whom it described as Baptists, from the rest of the population, and urged the government to take strong action to end the planters' incompetent rule and to remedy Jamaica's social and economic distress.[19] Governor Eyre's report of the Jamaica Insurrection arrived in London on 17 November. By that time the fevered rumours from Jamaica, acting upon the preconceived notions of Englishmen about the condition of the island and the character of its black population, had already fixed the battle-lines for a lengthy and embittered controversy.

English journalists eagerly awaited the arrival of dispatches from Eyre and his military officers, and reports from the planter-orientated Jamaican press. When the first news of the outbreak reached Kingston, the authorities and the landed proprietors took fright, and as a result official dispatches and Jamaican news reports reflected this state of mind. Those commentators who anticipated race war found ample evidence to confirm their worst suspicions. At the same time, critics of the colonial government and the planting interest found reason to believe the white Jamaicans were back at their old slaveholding tricks.

Tales of atrocities committed by the Morant Bay rioters, and recipes for fiery Negro cocktails of rum and gunpowder, imbibed from the skulls of white victims, accompanied claims that several hundred whites had already met a violent death, and substantiated predictions that the remaining population of 13,000 whites awaited immediate extermination. The *Morning Herald* congratulated the authorities for their repression of this massive black conspiracy.

> The original nature of the African betokened itself in acts of horrible mutilation, and it is honourable to our countrymen that, when victorious, with the signs and recollections of recent atrocity about them, they displayed so much forbearance and discriminated so justly between the chiefs and vagrants of the seditious and homicidal mob. We are glad, indeed, that a good many were let off with a warm flogging, notwithstanding that they were accessories to the crime of deliberate murder; because after all, the executions were important as examples, and the rabble of this rebellion were in all likelihood drunken and worthless savages scarcely responsible for their misdeeds.[20]

Reports of racial strife in Jamaica reminded English commentators of the distant slave revolt in Haiti in 1791, and of the more recent violence of the Sepoys in India and the Fenians in Ireland. The *Record* declared: 'We assume without question for the present all the allegations of atrocities committed by the insurgents, and we fear that it was only the want of opportunity that prevented these atrocities from being more justly compared with those perpetrated in the Sepoy mutiny'.[21] By reference to precedents of the distant and recent past, journalists substantiated the exaggerated rumours reported from Jamaica, and confirmed their preconceived notions about the propensities of black savages.

Not all commentators shared these preconceptions. The observers who expressed some sympathy for the West Indian blacks found evidence in those Jamaican reports which refuted the existence of a black conspiracy against whites, and which indicated that the retaliation by the military had been out of all proportion to the severity of the uprising at Morant Bay. Journalists were quick to blame black indolence for the economic difficulties of Jamaica. They held a similarly low opinion of the white planters of the West Indies.

The Times and the *Saturday Review*, as well as the *Daily News*, suggested the white West Indians could not be wholly trusted to govern the colonies in a manner conducive to social harmony.[22] At a public meeting sponsored by the British and Foreign Anti-Slavery Society, G. W. Alexander, the treasurer of the Society and a recent visitor to Jamaica, stated that 'the persons in authority in Jamaica were in many cases the descendants of the slave-masters; and ... they were very different in character from the gentlemen of England. They had done little or nothing for the improvement of the poor people over whom they ruled.'[23] Approaching the reports from Jamaica in a critical frame of mind, English friends of black West Indians soon found evidence which confirmed their worst suspicions.

As the evidence accumulated, the copious dispatches from Eyre proved self-condemning, and the violence of the Jamaican press shocked many English readers.[24] *The Times* quoted a dispatch from Col. Francis J. Hobbs:

I have got Paul Bogle's valet for my guide, a little fellow of extraordinary intelligence. A light rope tied to the stirrup and a revolver now and then to his head caused us to understand each other, and he knows every single rebel in the island by name and face, and has just been selecting the prisoners just came in here, who I shall have to shoot tomorrow morning.

On the same page, *The Times* extracted a report from the *Jamaica Guardian* praising Captain Hale for his proceedings which were 'temperate, decided and judicious. All rebels captured, having been tried, he instantly executed'.[25] After congratulating Eyre for his vigorous and effective action, Edward Cardwell, the Colonial Secretary, perturbed by the reports from Jamaica, asked the Governor for more precise details about the nature and extent of the rebellion, and particularly requested a count of the numbers executed or punished by the military.[26] On 17 December, Gladstone, similarly disturbed by the Jamaican news and Eyre's dispatches, wrote to Cardwell:

I write as one who has no confidence whatever in Eyre's political judgement, exercised within the atmosphere of the so-called 'rebellion'. It is quite right to abstain from pre-judging him officially; but the papers he himself sent us, are so condemnatory as in their collateral effect to reduce his authority to *nil*.[27]

On 16 January 1866 John Delane, editor of *The Times*, forwarded a narrative of events and the minutes of Gordon's trial to Gladstone, and commented, 'I fear you will consider them as unsatisfactory as they appear to your very faithful servant'. Shortly thereafter, *The Times* reassessed its view of the Jamaica affair, and admitted, much to the delight of the *Anti-Slavery Reporter*, that Gordon's court martial had been irregular, and that there were undoubted excesses committed by the authorities.[28] The *Examiner* made an earlier and more complete reversal in its assessment. On 25 November 1865, this Liberal weekly declared that the Jamaica Insurrection proved that 'the negroes of our West Indies, free for a generation, ... are still, despite of generous hopes and vaticinations to the contrary, barbarians of Africa who have but changed their sky'. A week later, on 2 December, the *Examiner* began 'to disbelieve a great deal of what is said for and against that people, their capabilities and disposition'.[29] As the evidence grew that the authorities had met the Morant Bay rebellion with unusual severity, some moderation in opinion occurred, but, at the same time, these same reports confirmed the worst fears of the philanthropists and their radical friends.

For the defenders of the West Indian freedmen, the evidence pointed to the execution of 2,000 or even 3,000 blacks on the merest suspicion of conspiracy.[30] Missionary societies, receiving reports and letters from Jamaica, reassessed their view of events and called for a government inquiry. The Evangelicals and the Wesleyans proceeded cautiously, calling for an official investigation which they predicted would prove the stories of military atrocities unfounded and would vindicate the honoured name of British justice.[31] The Congregationalists in the London Missionary Society and the Baptists also demanded an inquiry, for they were convinced that the military had exacted a barbarous retaliation for the local disturbance at Morant Bay.[32] Eyre raised the anger of the Nonconformists to a still greater pitch by his speech to the Legislative Council in which he referred to 'the misapprehensions and misrepresentations of the pseudo-philanthropists in England'. The Governor blamed misguided dissenting missionaries and radical demagogues for stirring up the unrest which led to Morant Bay, and he added further insult to injury by introducing a bill into the Jamaica Assembly which sought to silence Nonconformist preachers.[33] At meetings throughout the British Isles, Nonconformists, abolitionists, and radicals denounced Eyre and urged the government to appoint a commission of inquiry. Delegations from Manchester, the Peace Society, the Society of Friends, the Baptists, and the British and Foreign Anti-Slavery Society went to Downing Street and petitioned Russell and Cardwell.[34] Abolitionists advertised a meeting in Exeter Hall with handbills proclaiming that eight miles of dead bodies lay slain in

Jamaica. At the meeting, organizers handed out suitably black-bordered copies of Gordon's last letter to his wife. Gordon had corresponded with Lord Brougham and L. A. Chamerovzow upon Jamaican problems, and now abolitionist spokesmen upheld the Jamaican radical as a model Christian gentleman and a martyr to the cause of British justice and liberty. In a letter to *The Times*, Charles Buxton disputed the claims of the Tory Press, and described Gordon as a man of property and wealth, a member of the Assembly, a devout Christian, and 'almost a white; the son of a Scotch gentleman; himself educated in Scotland; the husband of a white lady; . . . A man of such seeming character and of such standing would not have been lightly put to death'.[35] The Cabinet, influenced by the gravity of affairs in Jamaica, and not simply by the pressure of public opinion, recalled Governor Eyre, and appointed a Royal Commission of Inquiry. The Rev. Newman Hall wrote to Gladstone to express his approval of the government's decision. Hall observed that at public meetings of Dissenters and working men 'fullest confidence' was expressed in the government's handling of the Jamaican crisis.[36]

Angered by the suspension of their favourite, Eyre's defenders ridiculed the exaggerations of Exeter Hall, and denounced the government's ungrateful treatment of the 'saviour' of Jamaica. In the recall of the Governor, the *Morning Herald* claimed, the new Ministry had made its first concession to the democratic mob rule of dissenters and demagogues. The *Standard* feared for the safety of the whole of the British Empire, when persons in authority could be treated with such impunity.[37] The defenders of the ex-governor accused the Jamaica Committee and its philanthropic and radical associates of making exaggerated claims against the colonial authorities, and, at the same time, these spokesmen for imperial rule vindicated the heroic and humane character of Edward John Eyre. A recent article by Henry Kingsley, brother of Charles, had described Eyre's work among the Aborigines in Australia, and now, just as the philanthropists made Gordon a martyr, Eyre's defenders made the 'wronged' governor a virtual philanthropist.[38]

Partisans on either side of the controversy were quick to accuse their opponents of accepting only those reports which confirmed preconceived viewpoints.[39] Thomas Potter, a Manchester radical and a member of the Jamaica Committee, accused *The Times* of prejudiced reporting: 'However much the bigotry and intolerance of *The Times*' articles on the subject of the coloured people might please a certain section and small class of English society, they did not please the true heart of England'.[40] In answer to the claims of Potter and other critics, *The Times* retorted: 'When we are censured for not publishing the most absurdly extravagant details from the Jamaica papers, our critics, who adopt these fables, suppress important intelligence about which there can be no doubt'.[41] With each side diligently gathering more evidence to prove its case, events in Jamaica received a copious review in the press and at public meetings. As a consequence, when the Royal Commission presented its report to Parliament on 18 June 1866, it appeared to offer nothing new in the way of evidence, and even its conclusions seemed to confirm the contentions of both sides in the dispute.[42] The Commission concluded, on the one hand, that Governor Eyre was to be congratulated for his speedy and vigorous action in putting down the rebellion, but, on the other hand, he was censured for the duration and severity of the repression administered under martial law.[43] According to Gladstone, the *Spectator*, the *Daily News*, and the *Anti-Slavery Reporter*, the Commissioners had been far too mild in their criticism of Eyre. But for the public at large, the Jamaica Insurrection was a tired issue. Attention had turned to the more immediate and exciting prospect of the Prussian invasion of Austria, and the fall of Russell's Ministry over its ill-fated Bill for the reform of Parliament.[44] Faced with a violent conflict between white British authority and black rebellion in Jamaica, and inundated with endless reports on the events of October 1865, the mid-Victorians remained hopelessly divided over the character of the Negro and the significance of the uprising at Morant Bay. Neither a war between the races nor the needs of imperial authority could produce a consensus about the Negro, for beneath the mid-Victorians' disagreements about race lay conflicting views about their own domestic political and social order.

During the Governor Eyre controversy opinions upon the racial question corresponded roughly to differences in political outlook. Opinions varied from the considered denial or racial theories by John Stuart Mill and the *Westminster Review*; to the philanthropic paternalism of moderate liberal opinion expressed by Charles Buxton, W. E. Forster, the *Spectator* and the *Fortnightly Review*; and to the vehement racist invective of Thomas Carlyle, and Charles Mackay, a leader writer for *The Times* and contributor to the Tory *Blackwoods' Magazine*.[45] The longer the controversy continued, the more these political differences came to the forefront, and the racial question receded correspondingly into the background. As the litigation against Governor Eyre passed into 1867, then 1868, and on into 1869, public interest waned. Journalists, in their occasional reports, ignored the question of race altogether, and commented solely on the differing interpretations of martial law. Members of the Jamaica Committee and supporters of the Governor Eyre Defence and Aid Fund held differing views of the Negro, but these differences did not lead them into an examination of rival theories about race. Their differences in outlook led them into the courts, where they disputed the uses and abuses of martial law.[46]

By July 1866, the political implications of the Eyre controversy had, in the minds of the Jamaica Committee, taken precedence over philanthropic concern for the West Indian freedmen. At its first meeting, on 19 December 1865, the Committee brought together leaders in the British and Foreign Anti-Slavery Society, the Aborigines Protection Society, various missionary groups, and some interested Members of Parliament. The aims of the Committee were to demand a Parliamentary inquiry into the social and political condition of Jamaica, to act as a watchdog on the progress of the Royal Commission appointed to look into the insurrection, and to provide legal assistance to Mrs Gordon or other persons injured by the military reprisals. After the publication of the Royal Commission's findings and the fall of the Russell-Gladstone Ministry in June 1866, radical politicians took command. John Bright proposed that the Committee urge the government to lay charges against Eyre. John Stuart Mill replaced Charles Buxton as chairman, all M.P.s became members of the executive, and they decided to prosecute Eyre for the murder of Gordon.[47] Buxton, who had been the Anti-Slavery Society's chief spokesman in Parliament, resigned from the Jamaica Committee. The abolitionist society continued to support the Committee's legal proceedings, but clearly the radical politicians, particularly Bright and Mill, had taken over from the more cautious philanthropists in the prosecution of Governor Eyre.[48]

From the outset of the controversy, the Committee and its supporters argued that the racial conflict in Jamaica paralleled the social and political struggle in England, and that the actions of Governor Eyre endangered the liberties of Englishmen in the British Isles as well as the lives of British subjects in the Caribbean.[49] To substantiate this claim, Liberal and radical segments of opinion readily compared the racial strife in Jamaica to contemporary class conflicts in England. The *Daily News* persistently argued that black violence in Jamaica was no different from white violence in England. Recalling the disturbances of the 1840s, it observed that, if fired on by Volunteers, the London mob would not have spared the honour of women or the lives of infants. In the view of this Liberal paper, the Tories who supported Governor Eyre would be quite prepared to use the repressive tactics of the military in Jamaica against the working men in England. It suggested that 'The Tory journalists who denounce the English Reform agitation as illegal and seditious, have shown no readiness to discriminate between Hyde-park and Morant Bay'.[50]

In the radical press, journalists identified the social and political condition of the English working man with the circumstances of the Jamaican peasant. In a letter to the *Beehive*, Professor E. S. Beesly observed that the charge of laziness hurled at the Jamaican blacks was a familiar cry, for 'whenever a strike takes place in England we know how ready the press is to give tongue about "the laziness of the men" '.[51] The *Beehive* encouraged its trades unionist readers to support the Jamaica Committee, 'for the cause defended is the cause of labour, and the wrong-doers who are impeached are those who uphold the exactions and outrages of a class of employers'.[52] *Reynolds's Newspaper* suggested, on 26 November 1865, that the action of the military in Jamaica had been paralleled by the reprisals against the Fenians in Ireland, and predicted that the same excesses could be repeated in England against white working men. On 5 August 1866, *Reynolds's Newspaper* suggested that the English working classes had important lessons to learn from Jamaica.

They may learn that, without a sweeping measure of reform, justice is in abeyance, law a mockery, and judges the mere tools of the ruling classes in any serious contention between Government and the enslaved people; and that nothing hinders the Tories from doing to the working classes in London as Eyre did to the blacks in Jamaica, but the wholesome apprehension on the part of the Tories that it would be perilous to certain coroneted but incapable heads now entrusted with the government of the greatest empire on the face of the earth.[53]

In the charged atmosphere of the rising reform agitation, radicals and some of the more ardently reform-minded Liberals saw in Jamaica a foretaste of possible confrontations in England.

In spite of this tendency to identify the plight of black Jamaicans with the position of English working men, and the fate of Gordon with the situation of parliamentary reformers, some of Eyre's critics assumed that racial prejudice, not simply class hostility, lay behind much of the sympathy for the Jamaican authorities. The British and Foreign Anti-Slavery Society urged the government to lay charges against Eyre, to vindicate the principles of British justice

which did not permit a riot 'to be made the occasion for the indulgence of private revenge, and of the rancour of race'.[54] Estimating
that 2,000 blacks had been executed by the Jamaican authorities,
the *Methodist Recorder* observed that if a similar toll had been
taken in reprisal for recent rioting in Belfast, there would have been
no sympathy for the authorities, but a great public outcry against
their actions.[55] The *Spectator* from the end of 1865 through to 1868
argued that public reaction to Jamaican events demonstrated that
Englishmen had one standard of justice for whites and another for
blacks. This Liberal weekly claimed that Charles Buxton withdrew
his parliamentary resolutions demanding amnesty and compensation
for those who suffered from the military reprisals because the temper
of the Commons 'would have said that negroes are not entitled to
white man's justice'.[56] Justin McCarthy observed that although 'the
damned-nigger principle' was never expressed on the floor of the
House, it was prevalent in the Commons' smoking room.[57] After the
failure of legal proceedings against Eyre in 1868, the *Spectator* made
a broader generalization, claiming that nine-tenths of the English,
especially those of the upper and middle classes, had one law for
blacks and another for whites.[58] Somewhat inconsistently, the critics
of Eyre argued that the racial clashes in Jamaica were comparable
to class conflicts in England, and at the same time, observed that
sympathy for Eyre and the military was a product of racial prejudice
rather than class enmity.

Even some of the radicals and their Liberal friends admitted
feelings of racial prejudice. Professor Beesly, in a letter to the
Beehive, identified the plight of the Jamaican poor with the condition of the English working man, but at the same time he observed:

> I protest I am no negro-worshipper. I don't consider a black man
> a beautiful object, and I daresay he sings psalms more than is good
> for him. Some negroes may be men of ability and elevated
> character, but there can be no doubt that they belong to a lower
> type of the human race than we do, and I should not really like to
> live in a country where they formed a considerable part of the
> population. But there is no reason why the negro should work
> cheaper for us because he is ugly. If the white labourer has a right
> to put a price on his labour, so has the black labourer.[59]

In defending his support of the Jamaica Committee, Thomas Huxley
similarly declared that he had no love for the Negro nor any respect
for Gordon, but only a desire to defend the principle that 'English
law does not permit good persons, as such to strangle bad persons, as
such'.[60] In a more revealing statement, William Forster, Under-

Secretary of State for Colonies in Russell's Cabinet, confided to the House of Commons that 'he did not know that he or any Member of the House would have been free, from the race feeling – the feeling of contempt for what was regarded as an inferior race'.[61] Forster believed that Eyre should be dismissed from office, but he did not support the legal prosecution undertaken by the Jamaica Committee. Some of Eyre's critics shared the racial antipathies of the Governor's friends, but the priggish misgivings of the philanthropists and radicals were a pale shadow of the racist invective of Eyre's Tory defenders.

In defence of the Governor and the white military officers, Eyre's more extreme supporters claimed that blacks were responsible for the atrocities committed on both sides. W. F. Finlason (1818–95), a legal reporter for *The Times* and a pamphleteer for the Eyre Defence Committee, claimed not only that the black rioters committed butcheries at Morant Bay, but that the Maroons and Negro soldiers in the West India Regiment were solely responsible for the excesses committed by the military. Finlason concluded that Eyre and the white officers should be absolved of all responsibility for any atrocities committed during the repression of the rebellion.[62] Reporting on the first scant news of the outbreak, the *Daily Telegraph* expressed some fear that the black soldiery might commit acts of savagery, but, on the whole, journalists and politicians of all political complexions were not so blinded by race prejudice. The great majority of commentators assumed that military officers were responsible for acts committed by themselves and by the troops under their command.[63]

Eyre's sympathizers reacted as much to the sentimentality of the 'Nigger-philanthropists' and the radicalism of the Jamaica Committee as they did to the question of black violence. For many, the censure of the Royal Commission and the approval of Charles Buxton's resolution in Parliament was a sufficient vindication of the principles of British justice. The Jamaica Committee's legal prosecution of Eyre for the murder of Gordon seemed to be only an exercise in radical claptrap and rabble-rousing.[64] Professor John Tyndall joined the Eyre Defence and Aid Committee not because he whole-heartedly approved of the Governor's conduct, but because he thought the Jamaica Committee carried the case to an extreme.[65] The *Daily News* warned the Jamaica Committee that its persistence would only win Eyre friends and alienate many sympathizers with West Indian blacks.[66] On the other hand, some who expressed sympathy for Eyre thought the ex-governor had shown poor judgment in accepting the friendship of those Tory stalwarts given to outspoken attacks on Negroes, philanthropists, and political reformers.[67] In spite of this counsel of moderation, the antagonists persisted in their dispute in the name of honoured political principles.

Eyre's supporters rejected the claim that events in the Caribbean could be repeated in England. Mrs George Busk wrote to Professor John Tyndall: 'Let the execution of Gordon form a precedent and welcome. Meantime in our tolerably well-ordered society, it is absurd to speak of fear of such precedents'.[68] For the Rev. F. W. Farrar, W. F. Finlason, the *Morning Herald*, and the *Standard*, the Jamaica Committee erred in assuming that black and white could be treated as equal.[69] For the more ardent racists, including James Hunt and his friends in the Anthropological Society, events in Jamaica demonstrated that a natural antipathy of race existed not only between black and white, but between Anglo-Saxon and Celt. Two races could never live harmoniously as equals, but inevitably one type must dominate the other.[70] For those who supported Eyre and the actions of the military, the Jamaica Insurrection demonstrated the wilful indolence of the black labourer and the peculiar temperament of the child-savage Negro. These unique Negro traits and the Anglo-Saxon's inherent sense of superiority made it imperative that white dominion be upheld against black rebellion. This enforcement of British authority not only satisfied the racial pride of the white, but served the best interests of the dependent, imitative black.[71] To these critics of the Jamaica Committee, English comparisons were inappropriate. The insurrection at Morant Bay clearly demonstrated the unique qualities of racial strife.

Professor John Tyndall rested his defence of Eyre upon the belief that Negroes were a peculiarly indolent, savage race.[72] To reconfirm his view, Tyndall wrote to his scientific colleague and friend, Joseph Hooker, who had some limited acquaintance with blacks during visits to West Africa and Brazil. Having been repelled by the violence and bloodshed displayed by the rioters and the military in Jamaica, Hooker chose to remain neutral in the Eyre controversy. In his reply to Tyndall, he wrote that 'the Negro is . . . as a rule eminently fickle, impulsive and cruel', but 'under discipline or pressure whether artificial, of others, or engendered by the struggle for existence, he will work well, and I may doubt not, prove a good and useful member of any community'.[73] Anxious to cite Hooker as an authority in answer to those who seek 'to place Negroes and Englishmen on the same level', Tyndall wrote once again and received a more detailed reply from his friend. Hooker answered that he believed that blacks had been given too much liberty in Jamaica and West Africa, and that the Negro race was peculiarly savage, and only capable of steady labour under compulsion. Hooker further declred that 'I consider the Negro *far* below the level of the Englishman', but also affirmed: 'there are many Englishmen worse than the Negro, because the worst classes of the best races are worse than the worst of any and all the inferior races'.[74] At an Eyre Defence Committee meeting, Tyndall, citing Hooker as one authority, declared: 'I decline accepting the negro as the equal of an Englishman, nor will I commit myself to the position that a negro insurrection and an English insurrection ought to be treated in the same way'. In Tyndall's view, a black rebellion would be a sexual assault on white women. Faced with a riotous mob of blacks, Englishmen would be forced to follow the precedent of British officers in India. They would have to shoot their wives to save them from a fate worse than death itself. During an insurrection in England, Tyndall observed, 'I should not approve of the shooting of wives through the fear of prospective insult'. Because a race war endangered the honour of white women, the Jamaican authorities, the professor concluded, were justified in acting with a vigour and severity which would have seemed out of place in suppressing an English riot.[75] In Tyndall's mind, then, the difference between a racial and a class conflict was not in the likelihood of violence and bloodshed, but in the sexual, and therefore savage, threat dark-skinned males posed to civilized white females.

Among journalists and spokesmen sympathetic to Eyre, few drew so clear a distinction between the propensities of black Jamaicans and the character of an English mob. The *Saturday Review* suggested that the Negro 'is neither ferociously cruel nor habitually malignant. He often does cruel and barbarous things; but so do our draymen and hackney-coachmen and grooms and farm-servants through want either of thought or power of thinking'.[76] *The Times* similarly justified the swift severe justice of the military in Jamaica, since 'for the lower classes of minds death loses all its terrors if it is seen at a considerable interval'.[77] The *Standard* observed that 'the tendency to falsehood increases just as the complexion darkens', and therefore 'the negro only tells the truth by accident'. Citing no less an authority that John Stuart Mill, the *Morning Herald* was equally certain that in England 'the working men are mostly liars'.[78] The *Pall Mall Gazette* suggested that the single difference between the English working class and Negroes was that in England the masses were content with atheism, while the blacks must have religion, if only a corrupted Christianity which they convert to 'the hereditary Fetichism of their race'.[79] Edwin Paxton Hood, a Jamaican resident and defender of the planting interest, claimed that there were savages quite capable of the atrocities of Morant Bay in France, Spain, Italy, Austria, and England. The Negro, Hood observed, 'is in Jamaica as the costermonger is in Whitechapel; he is very likely often nearly a savage with the mind of a child'.[80] English working-class rebels, like Jamaican blacks, were also a sexual threat to respectable women. Speaking to Cambridge undergraduates in 1862, and not having in mind the comparison to black rioters, Charles Kingsley reflected upon the violence of class conflicts earlier in the nineteenth century. He remarked that in his generation students quite rightly believed 'that "the masses" were their natural enemies, and that they might have to fight any year, or any day, for the safety of their property and the honour of their sisters'.[81]

The *Daily Telegraph* was convinced that riotous blacks with white skins lived in English cities. Hearing reports that the Jamaica Committee planned a counter-rally to the banquet in Eyre's honour at Southampton, the newspaper feared the radicals might incite a riot. It asserted: 'There are a good many negroes in Southampton, who have the taste of their tribe for any disturbance that appears safe, and who are probably imbued with the conviction that it is a proper thing to hoot and yell at a number of gentlemen going to a dinner party'.[82] The *Daily Telegraph*'s 'Negroes' were in fact the very English and very white Southampton mob who thronged the streets outside the banquet hall, while their more respectable working-class colleagues attended the largest popular meeting in the city's history to protest against the official reception given to Governor Eyre. Further large meetings of working men were held in London at Bartholomew Close on 30 August 1866, and on 3 September a crowd at Clerkenwell Green burned the ex-governor in effigy for his crimes in Jamaica.[83] Governor Eyre's friends asserted that hostilities between racial groups were of a different order from conflicts between social classes. Yet as they witnessed popular agitation over the Eyre controversy and for the reform of Parliament, they reacted to the protests of English working men in much the same language as they did to the rebellion of black Jamaicans. In spite of their protestations to the contrary, these defenders of British authority did not adhere to their rigid distinction between race and class relations.

Thus differing attitudes to the social, not the racial, dimensions of the Jamaican conflict account for the marked disagreement in

English opinion about the bloody events of October 1865. Yet, in spite of these differences in social attitude, there was one area of universal agreement. Both the champions and the denigrators of Governor Eyre thought that the conduct of the military authorities vitally affected the honour and reputation of Englishmen. The two sides in the dispute differed so greatly not because they held conflicting opinions about the Negro, but because they held contrasting views about themselves.

Critics of Governor Eyre claimed that the authorities had violated the honoured tradition of English justice. The *Daily News* asserted that 'From the Queen down to the humblest subject, we are all dishonoured men and women', and *Reynolds's Newspaper*, a radical journal not always looked upon as a source of patriotic zeal, claimed the Jamaican authorities 'have exposed us even to the scorn and derision of the blood-stained minions of the murderous despots of continental Europe'.[84] The *Fortnightly Review* also worried lest events in Jamaica had stained the fair name of England before the despotic Continentals.[85] Appeals to England's reputation for just treatment of her subject peoples was a common rallying cry used by philanthropists and politicians. During an Anti-Slavery delegation to Cardwell on 9 December 1865, the Rev. William Arthur, a secretary of the Wesleyan Missionary Society, argued that the Jamaican affair endangered the 'moral influence' of England. He suggested that an attempt was now afoot 'to destroy the old British sentiment of kindness and generosity towards the black', and to replace it with a new kind of racial contempt.[86] According to the *Spectator*, 'the Englishman is at bottom good-natured, is at home a law-abiding man, credits himself justly enough with an instinctive preference for fair play'. Even so, the Liberal weekly continued, 'Deep down in the Anglo-Saxon heart . . . lies the instinct of masterfulness'. Eyre made his gravest mistake when he allowed this Anglo-Saxon lust for dominion to get out of control.[87] Just as the Negro was both a savage and a child, so the Anglo-Saxon was both a lover of justice and a vengeful master. Eyre's critics hoped to uphold English humanitarian traditions against a new call for more authoritarian rule.

Governor Eyre's defenders recognized that English opinion was strongly influenced by the philanthropic appeals of an earlier decade, but they sought to cast this old-fashioned sentiment aside. They saw a new need for a sterner hand in human affairs. Charles Lever, in his novel 'Cornelius O'Dowd', serialized in *Blackwood's Magazine*, derisively described English philanthropic traditions:

The appeal of white sympathy for the black man, is, however, never made in vain. It is like one of those great national airs, to beat a few bars of which is alone enough to call forth a perfect thunder of applause. Next to our roast beef and bitter beer, I believe we like our nigger, – and he is as much a national institution as either of them.[88]

Quite contrary to this institutionalized philanthropy, the *Standard* accused the Jamaica Committee of being 'all avowedly of foreign sympathies with alien hearts and affections'. Eyre exemplified the true manly English spirit in his quick, vigorous action. Without this ability to apply a speedy, stern discipline, the *Standard* claimed, the name of England would be neither respected nor feared, and English rule could not continue over the barbarous races.[89] *Punch* argued that the Jamaica Committee, in attacking Governor Eyre and British authority, wished to rid England of her colonies.[90] The *Daily Telegraph* complained that England disgraced her heroes rather than honoured them, while *The Times* and the *Pall Mall Gazette* asserted that Jamaica's problems could only be solved by the imposition of strong government.[91] It was this growing spirit of hero-worship and mindless support of authority regardless of the law which led Thomas Huxley to join the Jamaica Committee.[92] It was also these contrary conceptions of English rule which aroused the prolonged dispute over the actions of Governor Eyre.

The Jamaica controversy occurred at a critical time in the changing political and social life of mid-nineteenth century England. To the mid-Victorians, Governor Eyre and George William Gordon were less important for what they did than for what they symbolized. The debate over the Negro disguised the real issue of contention – the role of authority and the rule of law in the face of social turmoil and violence. Already apprehensive about an extension of the franchise at home, trade union radicalism, and unrest in Ireland, Governor Eyre's supporters rose to the defence of the authority of gentlemen at home and abroad.[93] Since they believed the ex-governor had acted to the best dictates of his conscience and without malice of intent, Eyre's sympathizers could spare no patience for the legal prosecution of their hero. The ex-governor had suffered enough in his suspension from office. According to the *Morning Herald*, the legal prosecution of the Jamaica Committee led to Eyre being ostracized in good society.

A man who in England is placed on his trial on a criminal charge may be acquitted or condemned, but he is thenceforth a disgraced man. He cannot be admitted into society; he cannot succeed in any profession or employment; he is incapable of discharging the duties of any public office.[94]

Since this was the prospect that faced Eyre, the sympathies of those who valued social propriety went out to the condemned ex-governor.

In many ways, this very problem of acquiring and maintaining the position of a gentleman plagued the whole of the ex-governor's career. Eyre, the third son of a vicar, sought fame and fortune in the colonies. Earning a measure of both in Australia, he entered the Colonial Service which opened up new avenues for advancement. After climbing to the position of Lieutenant-Governor in New Zealand, and marrying a socially ambitious woman, Eyre found he could never quite attain social or financial security. In New Zealand, and later in St Vincent, he found that he lacked the established wealth at home which was expected of high-ranking colonial officials, and as a consequence his income proved inadequate for the expenditures of his office. His circumstances in no way improved in Jamaica, and once the news of the dreadful events of October 1865 had reached England, his predicament went from bad to worse.[95] Eyre could only maintain his financial and social standing by continued employment in the Colonial Service. After many entreaties, often to the annoyance of his closest supporters, the ex-governor finally accepted the fact that the Colonial Office had no opening for him. He then sought a position as a gentleman farmer. Since his wife refused to settle in Ireland, Eyre limited his search to England where he found there were more gentlemen seeking farms than there were farms for gentlemen.[96] Eyre was simply one of many who sought a gentle life in the ranks of landed society. To the defenders and admirers of this way of life, who still placed a higher value upon social position than upon mere wealth or learning, an attack by radicals upon the gentleman who defended white lives and property against riotous black savages seemed to violate all standards of patronism and morality. Governor Eyre won the admiration of gentle society not simply because the Morant Bay rioters were black, but because he defended the rule of the propertied, gentlemanly, and therefore responsible elements in society.

To many observers, this passionate defence of Eyre's use of authority and the contemptuous dismissal of 'Nigger-philanthropy' represented the new trend in English opinion. The *Morning Herald* remarked that a great change had come over English opinion, for 'the world-renowned question, once thought so convincing, of "Am I not a man and brother?" would nowadays be answered with some hesitation by many – with a flat negative to its latter half by those

who regard the blacks as an inferior race'.[97] The *Saturday Review*
contrasted contemporary conceptions of the inferiority of blacks with
the sentimental notions of an older generation, and suggested:
'There is too much disposition in English society so far to share the
Colonial prejudice as to assume ... that all acts committed by
authority were justifiable'.[98] For the *Spectator*, this reticence about
forming an opinion and speaking out against abuses particularly
affected the young, for 'the new generation always wants reasons
for *not thinking* and acting'.[99] Distressed by the reaction in English
society to the Jamaican news, the Duke of Argyll wrote to Gladstone,

> I grieve to think also that some anti-religous feeling is at the
> bottom of the military desire to slay a Preacher – Hatred of what
> they call 'cant' ... is very well in its way – but it is hardly a good
> reason for hanging a man!
>
> Nevertheless I have heard the hanging of Gordon defended
> and rejoiced over ... ![100]

This new contempt for sentimental 'cant' applied not only to subject
races in the Empire, but to domestic social relations as well.

The Eyre controversy uncovered the feelings of class antagonism
which still existed in mid-Victorian society beneath the confidence
in working-class respectability and greater social harmony.[101] Professor E. S. Beesly, managing to make himself an object of press
abuse, remarked on 'the savage feeling of the upper and middle
classes towards the lower'.[102] John Stuart Mill, the object of abusive
letters and assassination threats for his part in the prosecution of
Eyre, thought his correspondents' sentiments were indicative of 'the
spirit of our higher classes and a considerable portion of the
public'.[103] The widespread support of Eyre and the authorities in
Jamaica, Mill attributed to:

> the sympathy of officials with officials, and of the classes from
> whom officials are selected with officials of all sorts. I ascribe it to
> the sympathy with authority and power, generated in our higher
> and upper middle classes by the feeling of being especially
> privileged to exercise them, and by living in a constant dread of
> the encroachment of the class beneath, which makes it one of their
> strongest feelings that resistance to authority must be put down.[104]

At the time of the Governor Eyre controversy, popular pressure for
parliamentary reform made commentators hypersensitive to the
similarities between the imperial and the domestic situation. The
Record warned: 'It is well for Mr BRIGHT that in this free country
a man can go to such lengths without being judged by the rules
which Mr EYRE and Dr BOWERBANK carried out when they sent

poor GORDON to execution'.[105] On the reform question itself, the *Record* advised: 'the middle classes should put on one side the unhappy jealousies which during the early part of the century separated them from the upper classes, and should unite with one heart and hand in defence of all that is dear in our liberties and sacred in our religion'.[106] The change in English racial attitudes and the widespread support for Governor Eyre were a measure of how far this transition had already taken place.

The Jamaica Insurrection and the Governor Eyre controversy acted like a mirror in which Englishmen saw themselves and their own society reflected. All the discussion, debate, and controversy did not so much change English opinions about the Negro, as make the mid-Victorians aware of how far their attitudes to race had already altered. This change had taken place unseen, because it was not the blacks in Jamaica, nor the subject races in other parts of the Empire, who had changed in the eyes of the mid-Victorians, but rather it was Englishmen themselves who had altered. The growth in racialism occurred when wealthier mid-Victorians lost interest in the ethnocentric self-improving enthusiasms of the earlier part of the century. This articulate minority became more complacent in their respectability, and as they strove for gentility they became more contemptuous of those beyond the pale of respectability. Within or even beneath this residuum, and beyond all hope of improvement, they classified the Negro. By the late 1860s this process was still incomplete, and consequently, Governor Eyre landed himself in the midst of a domestic crisis. Changes within English society gave events in Jamaica a larger dimension and, as a result, disputes about the Negro became a jousting ground for rival social and political philosophies. The transformation in English racial attitudes was not simply a response to the demands of imperial rule, but an extension into the Empire of social and political attitudes moulded within the changing environment of mid-Victorian England.

10

The Growth of
Racialism in
Mid-Victorian England

The reasons for the growth of racialism in mid-nineteenth century England must be looked for not so much in mid-Victorian opinions about blacks or other alien groups as in the forces changing the assumptions which underlay racial attitudes. The available source materials are often a hindrance rather than an aid to this task. Most commentators upon the racial question had axes to grind. Frequently they drew from personal experience in the colonies, or had some personal connection or interest which led them to identify with their countrymen overseas who were in face-to-face confrontation with alien races. As a consequence, they were untypical of their more insular countrymen. Certainly politicians, journalists, philanthropists, scientists, officials, and other spokesmen tended to come from a select group, and their comments incorporate the values and assumptions of their largely middle-class background. These limitations upon the value of the opinions of our select group could be overcome if more were known about English conduct toward blacks. From the little that has been gleaned, it would appear that opinion, and press reports in particular, exaggerate and distort the degree of racial antipathy in mid-Victorian England.

Many mid-Victorian spokesmen expressed opinions repugnant to their grandchildren and great-grandchildren, and if prejudice simply means a 'prejudgment' based on erroneous information, then these people were prejudiced. But the historian who makes such an assessment has clearly become as stuffy a moralist as the most God-fearing Victorian preacher. If prejudice is used in the more specific sense of a projection of pent-up feelings of guilt or frustration upon a convenient scapegoat, it cannot be applied as a blanket generalization regarding nineteenth-century Englishmen. Undoubtedly prejudiced individuals existed – James Hunt and Captain Richard Burton among them. The mechanics of projection can be seen at work, but what is more apparent in mid-Victorian judgments about race is the insouciant assumption of Anglo-Saxon superiority by Negrophobe and Negrophile alike. This supposition was not a prejudiced projection of guilt or frustration, but an entirely conventional assumption resting upon social attitudes shaped by the evident and accepted inequalities of class within England. Belief the superiority of one race over another was a consistent part of mid-Victorian attitudes toward man and society in general.

The compatibility of assumptions of racial supremacy with existing attitudes to class differences suggests that the growth of racialism in the mid-nineteenth century was not merely the work of historians and anthropologists who formulated a new racist ideology, but also the product of a multitude of sources embedded within the very framework of the society as a whole. In its nineteenth-century English context, racism as an ideology was unique not for its rejection of egalitarianism, but first of all for its denial of individual variation within groups, and thus for its rejection of the liberal notions of individual improvement through industry, thrift, and self-help. This classification of individuals into rigidly defined groups was in itself a product of the perception of human beings as belonging to classes which were separate, unequal, and different in potential. The second distinguishing feature about the ideology of racism at this time was its combination of a more pessimistic view of man's potential with a new determinism. This declared that biological inheritance governed the individual's physical, intellectual, and psychological attributes, and thus fixed at birth a person's place in the natural and social order. By providing a defence of racial and social inequality, and by giving expression to a new pessimism about human nature and capacity, this racism caught hold of one trend in well educated, respectable opinion in the 1860s. On the other hand, the ideology of race met with stern emotional and intellectual resistance insofar as its materialism and determinism challenged established religious beliefs and entrenched liberal assumptions about individual self-improvement through upward social mobility.

More significant in the growth of racialism than this racist ideology was the ease with which the personal experience of class relations within England could be translated into racial terms. This consistency in attitude, first explored in the pioneering study of Kenneth Little, was particularly evident in the manner in which mid-Victorians perceived the black man.[1] They rarely depicted the Negro solely by his distinguishing physical features. Invariably, they perceived him in a particular social or cultural context: as the African savage, the suffering slave, the West Indian plantation labourer, or the black minstrel. The attitudes of most mid-Victorian observers, who were remote from the racial tensions of the Empire, and who rarely, if ever, encountered blacks in Britain, were as much responses to social and cultural attributes as to the physical distinctions of race. This response to the black man's social status, as shown in the extensive commentary on the American Civil War and the Jamaica Insurrection, accounts for the obvious inconsistencies in the mid-Victorian stereotype of the Negro. The physical characteristics of the black man remained constant, but his attributes altered according to changes of social and cultural context. The Negro was at once the obedient, humble servant, and the lazy, profligate, worthless worker; the natural Christian and the unredeemable sinner; the patient, suffering slave, and the cruel, vengeful savage. It was not simply a case of Negrophile emphasizing the positive attributes, and Negrophobe the negative ones. Evangelicals thought Africans were natural Christians and unredeemable savages; the advocates of the planting interest thought Negroes were lazy and profligate, yet particularly suited to vigorous physical labour in tropical climates. Racial attitudes were thus the result of the interaction between English social values and the particular context in which Victorians pictured the black man.

In their behaviour, at least until the 1860s, Englishmen responded to the social rather than to the physical attributes of black residents and visitors. They identified blacks with lowly social status and servile origins, yet they were prepared to accept black gentlemen as gentlemen, and sought to educate and 'elevate' West Indians and Africans to become an élite, black middle class. A change in attitude occurred when the quest for gentle status within English society intensified, and the aspirants for gentility became more concerned about excluding those of questionable status. Blacks were identified by their race and history with servitude and savagery. For those mid-Victorians who placed increased emphasis upon the visible signs of gentility, and who perceived race relations as a particular form of class relationship, blacks could no longer qualify as gentlemen. As a consequence all Negroes were classed in a common category of the brutish and perpetually inferior lower orders. In this vision even success through self-help could not secure acceptance for respectable black men. Gentlemen could not be directly involved with trade, and therefore could not be self-made men. More important, gentlemen were now seen to share a common nobility of character which was learned at the public schools, but which they liked to think they inherited. Lacking the common inheritance of aristocratic birth, the seekers of gentility founded a new racial aristocracy. Henceforth, only Anglo-Saxons could be gentlemen.

This growth of a more racialist attitude originated with the new ethos of gentility in mid-Victorian society, and was reinforced by the rise of a popular, derogatory stereotype of the Negro. This stereotype, which began with philanthropic propaganda and was made into a comic caricature by the popular minstrel shows, encouraged a greater number of people to look upon blacks with contempt, and to ascribe to them a common, uniform set of attributes. At the same time, West Indian experience appeared to confirm the growing belief in the Negro's inability to conform to middle-class standards under freedom, and thereby prompted the identification of black attributes with the vices of the residuum in England. The decline in the influence of 'Nigger-philanthropists' meant that black West Indians had fewer defenders, and the diminished reputation of these humanitarians signified the rise of a more tough-minded attitude toward charity and moral crusades in general.

The emergence of scientific racist thought and the attempt of its theorists to spread their doctrine were also symptomatic of the changing values within English society. The more ardent scientific racists – the exponents of polygenesis, the infertility of racial crosses, and the lessons of comparative anatomy – attracted only a limited following, failed to meet the tests of mid-Victorian science, and were not a significant cause of the change in racial attitudes. The urban, professional gentlemen interested in science began with a presumption in favour of inequality based upon their personal experience of English class divisions. They were interested in the 'Negro Question' partly because they saw it as a test case of how far biological inheritance determined an individual's character and potential. In the 1860s, this issue had domestic as well as colonial applications. Select members of the working class were about to be given the franchise. Means were needed to ascertain if this class had the capacity for self-government and, more importantly, some measure of discrimination was needed to separate the trustworthy respectable working class from the degenerate residuum. If it could be conclusively proven that blacks were inferior by reason of their biological endowment, then there might be grounds for limiting the rights of others having white skins but inappropriately-shaped skulls. This class application of biological determinism also took on a more specifically racial form, as historians and anthropologists investigated the make-up of the British population, and speculated about the dangers of urban degeneracy leading to conditions where inferior, swarthy Celts might outbreed their superior, tall, blond-haired, blue-eyed Anglo-Saxon cousins. This division of the British population into competing races had its most concrete application to the Irish question, and involved not simply the Home Rule issue but also the immigration of the Irish into industrial centres in England. Toward the end of the century, Jewish immigration aroused similar racial phobias.[2] The 'Negro Question', then, engaged the attentions of the mid-Victorians because it had implications for the direction of political and social change in their own society. Some scientists, for example T. H. Huxley, recognized these implications, and observed that their responses to racial conflict were a product of their political convictions rather than their scientific ideas.

The racist assumptions within mid-Victorian science cannot be traced to the influence of any single theory or theorist. Scientists and their educated public formed their impressions about racial groups in much the same way as did those outside the scientific community. In addition to the anatomical data provided by biologists and anthropologists, they incorporated impressions from travellers' accounts, newspaper reports, philanthropic propaganda, and even the antics of black minstrels in their composite stereotype of the Negro. As the 1860s advanced the tired debate between monogenists and polygenists gradually petered out, and attention focussed upon the application of Darwin's evolutionary synthesis to man's racial groups. The evolutionary scheme strengthened the case for the unity of man without necessitating a belief in racial equality. It also reconciled a belief in progress with a more pessimistic view of human nature, for advance came from the elimination of the unfit rather than from the self-improvement of the inferior. It is doubtful if these ideas were simply a by-product of Darwin's theory of evolution by natural selection, for they owed a great deal to habits of thought ingrained within the intellectual and social fabric of the age. Neither the radical defenders of black rights nor the extreme exponents of scientific racism won the debate of the Negro Question. Rather a middle of the road position materialized which accepted the black man's humanity but assumed he would remain the perpetual ward of his superior white guardians. This new rigid paternalism was often expressed in social Darwinian terms, but it had links to the evangelical tradition of the past, and appealed to the aristocratic pretensions of a wealthy middle class seeking the attributes of gentility.

The debate about blacks also had a significance for the Empire, but here a clear distinction should be maintained between attitudes shaped by the metropolitan setting and those formed by the racial tensions within colonial societies.[3] Clearly the more spectacular conflicts within the Empire, for example the Indian Mutiny and the Jamaica Insurrection, excited an intense interest and discussion within England. In particular these events made Englishmen aware of the potential for violent strife, and led many to question the wisdom of applying English liberal standards and institutions to subject alien peoples. Events outside the Empire also influenced Victorian views of race. The popular stereotype of the Negro in the mid-nineteenth century owed more to the New World than to Africa. Even then American rather than West Indian images predominated in anti-slavery rhetoric, in the popular fiction of Harriet Beecher Stowe, and in the minstrel shows. The mid-Victorians had become so familiar with the Negro is these contexts that when an imperial crisis did impinge upon their consciousness, as from Jamaica in 1865, the event made few new impressions and simply confirmed existing viewpoints. Racial conflicts overseas did make those who identified with white settlers and colonial officials more ready to sanction the imposition of tougher authoritarian rule. The characteristic form of that new authoritarian emphasis was a paternalism which reconciled humanitarian traditions and conscience with imperial needs. As we have seen, this paternalism was not simply imperial in origin. In the outlook of the liberal intelligentsia and in class relations within England, a more paternalistic outlook reconciled a growing pessimism about the rationality of the common man with a perceived need for more authority in human affairs.[4]

This mid-nineteenth-century growth in racial arrogance was not limited to mid-Victorian Englishmen, but was a general phenomenon within Europe. The reasons of its rise may therefore be found more generally within European social and intellectual developments rather than within the particular features of English society. Historians have tended to focus upon ideas about race in this period in order to trace the origins of the virulent racism of twentieth-century fascism. One must be careful to distinguish the horrendous long-term consequences of these doctrines from their immediate impact upon contemporaries. While the ideology of race had its origins in the mid-nineteenth century, its embodiment in a political programme receiving mass popular acclaim had to await the emergence of a profound social and political crisis suitable to the spread and transformation of these ideas. Racist assumptions were common in the mid-nineteenth century, and yet systematic works on race had a limited readership among a well-educated minority. Among this intelligentsia, treatises on race had even less influence in Britain than in France or Germany.[5]

Although the history of nineteenth-century thought on race is fairly well-known, the process by which these ideas became part of the general climate of opinion is less thoroughly studied. Exponents of the ideology of race began with popular xenophobias and folk myths and gave them a more elaborate and systematic form. Whether these treatises in turn intensified existing superstitions remains unclear. We need to know more about which social groups responded most enthusiastically to the call of race. It has been suggested that the appeal of nationalism first developed among well-educated lesser gentry and middle-class professionals and functionaries who were literate in the national language, interested in its cultural traditions, and came to espouse the ideal of the nation-state.[6] To assess the appeal of a racist ideology we also need to know to what degree race consciousness affected behaviour towards racial and ethnic minorities. This study of nineteenth-century English attitudes toward the Negro has attempted to show that the influence of racist ideas can only be tested by measuring opinion against behaviour. Furthermore in this instance, out of the long, tragic, and at times heroic, history of relations between Englishmen and blacks, there had emerged a multifarious assortment of positive and negative associations with the Negro in the popular culture. The historical recollection of slavery and the struggle for its abolition plus the awareness of the continuing subordination of blacks to whites provided abundant, graphic parallels to class relations within English society. Racial attitudes were a product of the conjunction between the individual's awareness of this historic and continuing relationship, and of his own particular consciousness of his place within the class hierarchy. Insofar as the historic links and associations with the Negro were particularly abundant, so too specific racist writers had a less decisive role in moulding racial stereotypes and attitudes. From this perspective, it is no accident that the Jews, the ethnic minority having the most abundant historic associations within the popular culture, and a group readily identified with particular social and economic roles, should become the chief victims of European racism.

Anti-semitism is the one form of European racism which has been examined most thoroughly from the standpoint of the social historian. It developed in the last half of the nineteenth century earlier and more stridently in Germany and Austria than in France, while in Britain hostility to Jews was less intense. On the Continent anti-semitism gained its greatest strength among the middle class who were in competition with Jews in business and the professions. Pulzer's study of anti-semitic movements in Germany and Austria suggests that the middle class, experiencing a sudden and recent industrial revolution, was less imbued than the British with liberal values, was more inclined to distrust the free competition of *laissez-faire* capitalism, and more willing to rely upon the state for security and protection.[7] Here the British case appears to vary from the European experience. The mid-Victorian middle class faced intense competition for social status among themselves, but no alien ethnic group played a significant part in that rivalry. Irish immigrants and, later in the century, European Jews competed not with the middle class, but with workers for jobs and housing. The appeal of free trade and distrust of state intervention remained strong, as the Liberal Party in particular attracted middle-class reformers still seeking the liberation of individuals from outworn privilege and state restriction.

In spite of differences in the intensity of anti-semitism, English and European racism shared important similarities. The rise of a more strident racialism in both cases dates from the 1850s and 1860s, though as a widespread phenomenon – whether in the form of white supremacy, intense national chauvinism, or anti-semitism – it did not materialize until the 1870s and 1880s. The striking feature about this development was the apparent need to create races out of folk myths. Once rediscovered, these folk groups were assigned uniform physical characteristics, the historic intermixture of these remote peoples was either denied as a biological impossibility, or seen to be a source of degeneration, and studious efforts were then made to trace the distribution of these physical types within populations which defied any clear division on the basis of readily visible physical characteristics.

The complex variety within European society and the present state of knowledge about the spread and intensity of race consciousness beyond the ranks of the intelligentsia make it impossible to pinpoint the precise intellectual and social conditions which gave rise to this race-thinking. Nonetheless some tentative observations may be made about English racism in comparison to the European variety. Ruth Benedict in an early and perceptive study suggested that racism began as a justification for inequalities of class, but shortly changed into a defence of national rivalry.[8] In his study of Count Gobineau, Michael Biddiss convincingly demonstrates that this father of modern racist ideology developed his ideas out of a profound pessimism generated by his aristocratic reaction to a bourgeois world in a state of degeneration due to the forces of materialism, industrialism, urbanization, and democracy.[9] Gobineau's aristocratic background made him exceptional, but his adoption of racism as a defensive reaction to threatening social and political changes made him fairly representative. In France, Germany, and Austria, a middle class troubled by the economic uncertainties of the last three decades of the nineteenth century, anxious about the advance of democracy, and frightened by the militant left, came to identify Jews as the source of their anxieties. At the same time the climate of mounting international rivalry plus the quest for social respectability prompted a more intense loyalty to the nation-state, and a need to proclaim one's aversion from its internal and external enemies. It is difficult, perhaps impossible, to know how far this identification with the nation was spontaneous. E. J. Hobsbawm makes the interesting observation that possibly the most potent force for creating national loyalty was the spread of compulsory state education.[10] It would seem that the rise of intense nationalism and with it a determinist racial exclusiveness, was a common reaction to the increasingly antagonistic international climate and to the threatening political and social environment posed by the advance towards a more fully industrial, urban, and democratic order.

While these forces posed a threat to political and social stability in western Europe, in eastern and southern Europe a crisis of a different order gave rise to a militant nationalism and in the case of the Jews, an extreme racial hatred and political persecution. Whether these outpourings of popular animosity and resentment have much in common with the racist ideologies of the west is open to question. The animosities were fired in part by traditional peasant reactions against the forces of modernization, and these resentments were given free play by outworn autocracies hoping to deflect hostility away from their own political inadequacies. Nor were these ethnic hatreds the prerogative of the defenders of the old order. They also served to intensify a righteous anger against alien political oppression and an allegiance to the ethnic ideal among the educated minority who spearheaded the drive for national self-determination. Until a more thorough comparison of the forms of nationalism and racism in Europe is undertaken, and until more is known about the dissemination of racist ideas in the popular culture, we can make at best the rather general and hardly satisfactory observation that race-thinking in the last half of the nineteenth century was a common response to disparate social and political crises.

More specific conclusions can be made about English racism. The tendency toward a more pessimistic and determinist view of human nature and social groups developed during the same decades in England and on the Continent. English racism, like the Continental variety, rested upon established attitudes toward distinctions of class. The typical Anglo-Saxon was an upper-middle-class gentleman, and this same social group often perceived members of the residuum as belonging to an innately different and inferior race. At the same time English racial attitudes were not as affected by intense national rivalries and ethnic competition. Rather, imperial experience including relations with the Irish became the focal point of English racial sentiments. This imperial orientation also meant that apart from the contrast of Anglo-Saxon and Celt, mid-Victorian commentators on race focused upon the highly visible distinctions of skin colour.

In the particular case of attitudes toward the Negro, the historical experience of slavery and the continued servile status of blacks meant that the colour question became a matter of class. The growth of mid-Victorian racialism rests upon the dynamics of this class-colour dichotomy. It is important to realize that there are two sets of historical agents at work in this situation. On the one hand, in the coloured world of the Empire, the racially distinct subject peoples showed an increasing tendency toward militant resistance to British imperial authority, prompting in response a stronger imposition of military and political control.[11] On the other hand, within the white world of England, the forces of change were also at work. The mid-Victorians were not simply spectators passively reacting to the racial conflicts of the Empire. Social and intellectual developments within the metropolitan society altered their perception of race relations abroad. Behind the growth in mid-Victorian racialism lay the experience of class relations at home, and in particular among the articulate, influential wealthy middle class the cult of gentility encouraged a greater social exclusiveness and arrogance.

It was once thought that racism was a gross intellectual error which could be corrected by reasoned argument. In the past half-century the intellectual defences for racial inequality have been pretty thoroughly smashed, yet racism persists. This persistence may be accounted for, in part, by the fact that in its nineteenth-century origins race-thinking was not simply an intellectual error. It was a habit of mind deeply embedded within the social and political fabric of the age. The Victorians made many foolish and mistaken judgments about race but at least they had the good sense to recognize that racial inequality was similar to and directly related to other forms of social subordination. Consequently they viewed the racial question as one of the great ethical and political issues of their time. We have eliminated some of the Victorians' grosser errors about the nature of racial differences but, like them, we still need to face up to the historical and sociological foundations of racial inequality.

Appendix

Negroes in Britain
1750–1880

In the absence of quantitative data on the numbers and experience of Negroes in Britain during the eighteenth and nineteenth centuries, one is forced to rely on a variety of sources which record incidents and episodes, and from these to gain an impression of the lives and experiences of individual blacks in English society. Some of these individual cases have been included in the text to illustrate aspects of English reactions to the Negro. An effort has been made to ensure that the examples are not exceptional by comparing them to other reports of Negroes in Britain. Although the following is by no means a complete list of black residents and visitors in Britain, the additional examples may substantiate the claim that the recorded cases reflected typical rather than exceptional incidents.

1. NEGROES IN BRITAIN IN THE EIGHTEENTH CENTURY

Although estimates of the number of black slaves in England varied as widely as from 10,000 to 30,000, J. J. Hecht, 'Continental and Colonial servants in eighteenth-century England', *Smith College Studies in History*, XL (1954), 34, states that the figure of 15,000 is most often cited; see also H. T. Catterall (ed.), *Judicial Cases Concerning American Slavery and the Negro* (Washington, 1926–37), I, 18; K. L. Little, *Negroes in Britain* (1948), 170; and M. Dorothy George, *London Life in the XVIIIth Century* (1925), 134–5. The higher estimates of 20,000 in London alone by *Gentleman's Magazine*, XXXIV (1756), 493, and 30,000 for the whole of England by *London Chronicle*, XVIII (1756), 387b, were probably exaggerations. Dorothy George (*op. cit.*, 24–5, 329) estimates the population of London in 1750 at 676,250 and growing to about 900,000 by 1801.

The population of London represented about a tenth of the total population of England. At a population of 700,000 for London, 14,000 Negroes would represent 2 per cent, about the same proportion as the present coloured community in Britain represents in relation to the total population of the country. Although not a complete list, the following examples of distinguished Negroes in eighteenth-century England may be cited:

Francis Barber Dr Johnson's famous servant, who after the doctor's death became a schoolmaster. Barber's son by his English wife preached as a Methodist minister. (Eva Dykes, *The Negro in English Romantic Thought*, or *A Study of Sympathy for the Oppressed* (Washington, D.C., 1942), 38.)

Francis Williams Born in Jamaica at the beginning of the eighteenth century, he came to the attention of the Duke of Montagu, the governor of the island. The duke sent Williams to England where he went to a private school and then to Cambridge where he studied science and mathematics. After spending several years in England, he returned to Jamaica and opened his own school. Williams was also known as the author of Latin poetry. (A. Mott, *Biographical Sketches and Interesting Anecdotes of Persons of Colour* (1826), 1–2.)

Philip Quaque A native of the Cape Coast, Quaque was brought to England by the Society for the Propagation of the Gospel in 1756 and received there his training and ordination as an Anglican priest. On his return to Cape Coast Castle, with his English wife, he served as a missionary living in the European manner. He corresponded regularly with the Society for the Propagation of the Gospel throughout his long ministry which he continued until his death in 1816. (F. L. Bartels, 'Philip Quaque, 1741–1816', *Transactions of the Gold Coast and Togoland Historical Society*, 1 (1952–5), 153–74); and Margaret Priestly, 'Philip Quaque: Introduction', in *Africa Remembered*, ed. Philip D. Curtin (Madison, Wisc., 1967), 99–112.)

Aula Suleiman Diallo of Bondu (Job Ben Solomon) An African Moslem of high social standing, Diallo was sold into slavery by his trading rivals. He was brought to England when his Arabic letter from slavery in the United States attracted the attention of Thomas Bluett. He translated an Arabic manuscript for Sir Hans Sloane, and transcribed the Koran from memory. During his 14 months' stay in England, Hans Sloane introduced the distinguished African to the king and the royal family, the queen presented him with a gold watch, and he met the Duke of Montagu and other members of the nobility. (Thomas Bluett, *Some Memoirs of the Life of Job, the Son of Solomon, the High Priest of Boonda in Africa* (1734), *passim.*,

Philip D. Curtin, 'Introduction: Ayula Suleiman of Bondu', in *Africa Remembered, op. cit.,* 17–34.

Olaudah Equiano or Gustavus Vasa Escaping from slavery in the West Indies, Equiano led an adventuresome and widely travelled existence as a sailor. He visited England on many occasions and expressed a particular liking for London. Although the Bishop of London rejected him as a missionary to Africa, he did serve as commissary to the government on the project to send black poor to Sierra Leone. He was dismissed when he objected to the mismanagement of funds for the expedition, but was later exonerated by the government. He was active in the anti-slavery movement, presenting a petition against the slave trade to the queen in 1788. In the same year, he received a friendly reception in Birmingham when he visited the city to advocate the abolitionist cause and sell the narrative of his life. (Olaudah Equiano, *The Interesting Narrative of the Life of Olaudah Equiano, or Gustavus Vasa, the African* (1814), 400–39; John A. Langford, *A Century of Birmingham Life, from 1741 to 1841* (1868), I, 6–8.)

2. CENSUS OF 1871: ALIENS AND COLONIALS IN ENGLAND AND WALES

Nineteenth-century censuses never classified residents by race, but they did enumerate the number, distribution and sex of aliens and colonials in the United Kingdom. These statistics are of limited use, for place of origin or nationality does not give an indication of race. For example there are listings for the British West Indies, but there is no way of determining the ethnic origin of persons included in this category. Therefore, no generalizations about the number of blacks in Britain can be made from these figures, but the proportion of these groups to the total population and their concentration in London and the seaports is of interest. *Census of England and Wales in 1871,* IV, *Censuses,* 70, lists the following:

Date	Total population	Indian or colonial born	Foreign born
1841	15,906,741	17,248	39,446
1851	17,927,609	33,688	61,708
1861	20,066,224	51,572	101,832
1871	22,712,266	70,812	139,445

As well as the rapid rise in the number of foreign and colonial born, it should be noted that of those foreign born the vast majority were European, with the French and Germans alone accounting for about one-half. Those from Africa other than Egypt counted for only 0.24 per cent of the foreign population (table 94, p. 63). The largest concentrations of those groups were in London with 20,324 colonial and Indian born, and 66,101 foreign born. Other than London, only seaports, with the exception of Bath, had over 1,000 Indian and colonial born; Liverpool (over 2,000), Portsmouth, Plymouth, and Bristol, as well as Bath, were included in this group: see table 85, p. 70 and table 93, p. 76. Interestingly enough, the number of colonial or Indian born women over 20 years in age exceeded the number of men in the same grouping by 21,146 to 13,714 (tables 89 and 90, p. 73). Of course the accuracy of these figures is suspect, especially as aliens and colonials would be among the most difficult segment of the population about which to collect accurate information.

3. Negro Students in Nineteenth-Century England

Philanthropists and missionaries have recorded some details of Africans whose education they sponsored in Britain. Less is known about students who were sent to Britain by their parents or came through some other private means. This applies especially to West Indian students who undoubtedly received higher education and professional training in Britain, but left little record of their experiences. Part of the difficulty is that registers of university graduates or of admissions to professional institutions, for example the Inns of Court, list only the student's place of origin, and in some cases his father's profession. These registers contain many references to students coming from the West Indies, but no indication of racial origin. Therefore, one has to know something about the background of the individual students before these registers are of much help. Until the 1870s, the Scottish universities and the University of London attracted most black students, but once the religious qualification had been removed from Oxford and Cambridge, black students also attended these senior institutions in increasing numbers. Medical schools and the Inns of Court also received black students. Although we need to know much more about the reaction of the Victorians to these students, the entrance of blacks into these prestigious institutions, usually considered the preserve of the upper middle classes, is in itself indicative of a certain tolerance toward Negroes of respectable social standing. One interesting case is that of Thomas Jenkins, reported to be the son of an African king brought to Scotland for his education. Jenkins was left stranded when his benefactor died. He worked as a labourer and educated himself until sufficiently qualified to apply for a school-teaching post in Teviot-head. Although Jenkins was the best qualified applicant, the Jedburgh Presbytery refused to hire him because of his colour. Jenkins was vindicated when provided with his own school and stipend by the Duke of Buccleuch. After continuing his education at Edinburgh University, Jenkins went to Mauritius as a missionary to the slaves. (Therefore the incident probably occurred before 1833, and at least before 1838). Whether read as a moral tract on the ability of the Negro or on the virtues of self-help, or as an accurate narrative – and only the specific details give it credibility – the account of the objections of the Jedburgh Presbytery recognized both that racial discrimination existed, and that it was unjustified. (See H. G. Adams, *God's Image in Ebony* (1854), 70–80; W. Armistead, *A Tribute for the Negro* (1848), 317–23.)

A. *Some black West Indians educated in Britain*

Richard Hill of Spanish Town, Jamaica His father, a Yorkshireman, married a Jamaican woman of African and East Indian extraction. In the early years of the nineteenth century, Hill was sent to England where he stayed from the age of 5 to 14. He lived with his English relatives and attended the Elizabethan Grammar School, Hornscastle. He returned to Jamaica, but then came back to England in 1827 and stayed until 1830. During this time he worked with Macaulay, Clarkson, Wilberforce, and T. F. Buxton on the anti-slavery campaign. He last visited England in 1832. From that date until his death in 1872, Hill lived in Jamaica serving as a stipendary magistrate and as a member of the legislative assembly. He belonged to various learned societies including the Smithsonian Institute and the Zoological Society of London, and was an authority on natural science and Jamaican history. (Frank Cundall, 'Richard Hill', *Journal of Negro History*, v (1920), 37–44.)

Other, less notable, examples include the following: The Hon. Peter Moncrieffe, a 'quadroon', educated at Oxford and Middle Temple, became a judge in the Supreme Court of Jamaica ('Jamaican worthies', *Anti-Slavery Reporter*, 3rd ser., xiv (1866), 208–10). Hon. Alexander Heslop, also a 'quadroon', received his B.A. from Queen's College, Oxford, in 1835, and rose to the position of member of the Legislative Assembly and Attorney-General of Jamaica

(*Anti-Slavery Reporter*, 3rd ser., xiv (1866), 208–10, and *Alumni Oxonienses, 1715–1886*, ed. Joseph Foster (1888), II, 650). London Bourne, described as a pure Negro, and a wealthy Barbadian merchant, sent his son to be educated in Edinburgh (Armistead, *op. cit.*, 552–60). Dr Thornton, a black Trinidadian, was also educated at Edinburgh (Sir George Stephen, *The Niger Trade* (1849), 64). John Minns, an Englishman born in Clerkenwell, married a Negro woman in Barbados. Their two sons were educated in England (Armistead, *op. cit.*, 399–404). Lambert Mackenzie, whom the *Anti-Slavery Reporter* claimed to be the first black West Indian ordained in the Church of England, was educated at a grammar school in Demerara. In 1852, he came to England and attended St Augustine's Missionary College, Canterbury, and gained the Hebrew prize. The Society for the Propagation of the Gospel recommended him for the priesthood (*Anti-Slavery Reporter*, 3rd ser., xvii (1855), 186–7). Dr Davis, a Negro from Barbados, was trained at Aberdeen and served as house-physician at St Bartholomew's. He died of smallpox in London in 1871 at the age of 28 (*Anti-Slavery Reporter*, 3rd ser., xvii (Oct. 1871), 191). Although he was not educated in England, Sir Edward Jordan was the first Negro to receive a knighthood, and therefore his background is of some interest. As a journalist who advocated the rights of the black population of Jamaica, he was tried for treason in 1830, but was acquitted. In 1851, he was appointed to the Upper House (Council) of Jamaica, and in 1854, he served as premier of the island and president of the Privy Council. In spite of opposition, he became mayor of Kingston in 1859, and in 1861 Queen Victoria elevated him to Companion of the Bath (*Anti-Slavery Reporter*, 3rd ser., ix (1861), 19–22).

B. *African students*

At the beginning of the nineteenth century the African Institution actively promoted the education of African children in England. The Institution reported an expenditure of £3,500–£4,000 to further this programme. In 1799, 25 youngsters were brought to England, and 1801–2 about eight more, who remained in England about six years. The plan was discontinued as the frequency of consumption and chest complaints, including several deaths among the students made it unwise to continue (*Special Report of the African Institution*, 12 Apr. 1815, 23–4). The Institution continued to bring over a few children and placed them in schools run along the Lancastrian-

Bell monitor system (*2nd Report*, 23 Mar. 1814, 24). Other agencies and interested individuals brought African children to England for their education. Simeon Wilhelm, an African boy under the care of the Church Missionary Society and attending the National School, Shoe Lane, died in London in 1817 at the age of 17 (Edward Bicker-steth, *Memoir of Simeon Wilhelm. A Native of Susoo Country, West Africa* (New Haven, 1819); Mott, *op. cit.*, 118–24; Armistead, *op. cit.*, 382–7). William Singleton of Sheffield brought back two African youths whom he taught to read and write. They returned to Africa as teachers (*The Negro's Friend, or Sheffield Anti-Slavery Album*, 1826, 185–190). The Rev. N. Denton returned from Sierra Leone in 1848 with two African girls whom he planned to train as teachers, but in 1850, Mary Smart, one of the girls, died in Reading, a model of Christian devotion according to the *Church Missionary Intelligencer*, 1 (1850), 144.

A more extensive record of African students exists in the Church Missionary Society archives for those students receiving either a missionary or practical training during the 1850s and 1860s. A perusal of the Church Missionary Society archives uncovered no reported incident of discrimination during these students' stay in England: G/ATm 1/2, Committee of Visitors C. M. College, Islington, Vol. III–V (1843–93); C.A1/023 Misc. Letters to Home Secretaries, 1825–80; C.A2/032 S. Crowther, jun., Letters and Reports, 1851–62; C.A1/080 Henry Robbin, *Letters*, 1856–74; Rev. Thomas B. Macaulay, *Letters*, 1852–77, C.A2–065a; Venn Papers, Diaries and Accounts. *C.M.S. Register of Missionaries and Native Clergy, 1804–1904, in Two Parts*, printed for private circulation, listed 23 West Africans who received some higher education or missionary training in England, or had visited Britain between 1840 and 1883. Other students, of course, went to England for their education independent of the Church Missionary Society. John Thorpe, from Sierra Leone, entered the new University College, London, in 1832. He returned to England in 1846 and entered the Inner Temple, and remained until his death ten years later (Christopher Fyfe, *A History of Sierra Leone* (1962), 188–9, 261). Joseph Wright, an ex-slave, received two years' training in London before returning to Africa in 1844, and in 1848 became one of the first African ministers in the Wesleyan Church in Sierra Leone (P. D. Curtin, 'Introduction: Joseph Wright of the Egba', in *Africa Remembered, op. cit.*, 317–22). Sir Samuel Lewis, the first African knight, studied law at University College, London, from 1866 to 1868, graduating in the first division. He then continued to study law at Middle Temple receiving the two-guinea law prize in 1870, and passing his bar examinations in 1871 (Frederick W. Hooke, *The Life Story of a Negro Knight* (Freetown, 1915), *passim*). Christian Frederick Cole described himself as the first Negro graduate of Oxford, and a student at the Inner Temple (Cole to Lord Derby, Colonial Secretary, Inner Temple, 27 July 1883, Anti-Slavery Papers, Brit. Emp. S18. C163/82–82a; *Alumni Oxonienses*, I, 274, lists Cole as matriculating at the age of 21 in 1873, receiving his B.A. in 1876, and barrister at the Inner Temple in 1883). For extensive reference to Sierra Leoneans educated in England see the index of C. Fyfe, *A History of Sierra Leone*.

With the patronage of British abolitionists, Alexander Crummell, an American Negro of the Episcopalian Church, attended Queens' College, Cambridge, and received his B.A. in 1853. During his stay in England, Crummell preached in various Anglican churches before crowded congregations. Feeling the pull of his ancestral home, he went to Liberia, and became tutor in theology at Monrovia (J. A. Venn, compiler, *Alumni Cantabrigienses* (1944), pt ii, 1952–1900, II, 193; Alexander Crummell, *Hope for Africa. A Sermon on behalf of the Ladies' Negro Education Society* (1853), 47–8; J. A. B. Horton, *West African Countries and Peoples* (1868), 176; Armistead, *op. cit.*, 486–7). Queen Victoria herself took an active interest in an African girl in England providing for her education as a royal protege, and and introducing her several times at Court. The African princess, Sarah Forbes Bonetta, married an African merchant in a Brighton Church, and the couple received the honour of having the Queen as godmother by proxy for their first child (W. Knight, *Memoir of Rev. H. Venn. The Missionary Secretariat of Henry Venn, B. D.* (1880), 133; *Anti-Slavery Reporter*, 3rd ser., x (1862), 194, and xii (1864), 268). Some African children lived in England with the families of missionaries on leave, (E. Hammond to L. A. Chamerovzow, F. O., 17 Sept. 1856, ASP. C161/135, answered an inquiry about two Africans staying with Dr Schoen of the Christian Missionary Society. Henry Venn reported that the two boys were 'as home-sick as any Swiss': Knight, *op. cit.*, 133). Some English schools prided themselves on the cosmopolitan origin of their students. The Wesleyan Grammar School in Sheffield reported that it had students from Egypt, Malta, Rome, the East and West Indies, South America, and Australasia (*The First Report of the Sheffield Wesleyan Proprietary Grammar School* (1841), cited in F. C. Pritchard, *Methodist Secondary Education* (1949), 140).

4. American Negroes in Victorian England

The following reported favourably of their treatment in Britain (any who offered critical comments were discussed in the body of chapters 2 and 3).

Moses Roper A very fair-skinned ex-slave who left the North to cross to England in 1835. He received some education and religious instruction in England, and after eight years in Britain, in 1844, he claimed to have lectured in over 2,000 towns and villages. He married an English woman from Bristol. He appealed to the British and Foreign Anti-Slavery Society for funds to go to the Cape of Good Hope to raise cotton. In 1854, Wilson Armistead noted that Roper had reappeared in England, and asked the Anti-Slavery Society what they knew of him, for 'I remember hearing unsatisfactory rumours of him some time ago – & his present appearance seems like a resurrection' (Wilson Armistead to L. A. Chamerovzow, Leeds, 11 Oct. 1854, Anti-Slavery Papers, Brit. Emp. S18 C27–60). In a letter to the same society in 1844, Roper himself claimed to have sold 25,000 English copies of his narrative and 5,000 copies in Welsh. (Moses Roper to the Committee of the British and Foreign Anti-Slavery Society, Daventry, 9 May 1844, Anti-Slavery Papers, Brit. Emp. S18. C27/60; and Moses Roper, *A Narrative of the Adventures and Escape of Moses Roper from American Slavery* (1837), *passim.*)

The Rev. Josiah Henson Claimed to be the real Uncle Tom on whom H. B. Stowe had based her famous hero. Henson represented the Dawn Institute of fugitive American slaves in Upper Canada at the Great Exhibition in 1851, exhibiting some polished black walnut boards manufactured at the Institute. He addressed the mammoth Exeter Hall meeting in May, and many smaller ones. He took a special interest in ragged schools, had an interview with Sumner, the Archbishop of Canterbury, and along with some Sabbath School teachers dined as the guest of Lord John Russell, then the Prime Minister (June 1852). In his third and last visit to England in 1876–7, he was the guest of the Queen, who had always taken an interest in anti-slavery, and especially in the work of H. B. Stowe. (Josiah Henson, *The Autobiography of the Rev. Josiah Henson* ('*Uncle Tom*'), *from 1789 to 1883*, ed. J. Lobb (1890); J. L. Beattie, *Black Moses. The Real Uncle Tom* (Toronto), 1957).)

Francis Federic Fled to Canada from slavery, where he met and married an English woman from Devon. They then came to England, and Federic set up a lodging house in Manchester. The 'cotton famine' during the American Civil War forced him to close down. As he was crippled with arthritis, he could not find work except for the occasional anti-slavery lecture when his health permitted. He contrasted discrimination in Canada with its absence in England. In Liverpool, he could get a haircut without fear of objections to his colour. (Francis Federic, *Slave Life in Virginia and Kentucky; or Fifty Years of Slavery* (1863).)

Henry Watson   A destitute slave in New England, he was advised by William Garrison to go to Britain. Putting himself in the service of Mr Hodges, Watson travelled over a large area of England without experiencing any abuse because of his colour. After a few months in England he returned to America. (Henry Watson, *Narrative of Henry Watson, A Fugitive Slave* (3rd edn, Boston, 1850).)

The Rev. J. Asher   A Negro Baptist clergyman, toured England around 1850 to collect funds for his church in Philadelphia. After encountering discrimination on board the transatlantic ship, he successfully toured Britain raising £500 for his church. He preached to many Independent and Baptist congregations and stayed at the homes of preachers and prominent lay people. He contrasted his freedom of movement in England with discrimination in America, and said he was everywhere warmly received. On enquiry, he was assured that Baptist institutions of learning in London, Bristol and Bradford had no prohibition against black students. (Rev. J. Asher, *Incidents in the Life of Rev. J. Asher, Pastor of Shiloh (Coloured) Baptist Church, Philadelphia, U.S.* (1850).)

Linda Brent   An ex-slave who became a servant to an English family in America. Upon the death of the mother of this family, the Negro nurse went to England to care for the daughter. During her ten months in England, Linda Brent found she was treated as a white servant, and in fact treated according to 'my deportment without reference to my complexion'. (Linda Brent, *The Deeper Wrong; or, Incidents in the Life of a Slave Girl*. (ed. L. M. Child) (1862), 265.)

Some lesser known American Negro anti-slavery lecturers in England included the following: J. D. C. A. Smith, a worker on the underground railroad who fled to England when things got too hot for him in the States. He found that his audiences began to decline after the *Anti-Slavery Reporter*'s warnings against coloured imposters, but he received the requested testimonial (*Anti-Slavery Reporter*, 3rd ser., II (1854), 93–4, 107–8). John Bull, *alias* Dimmock Charlton, described himself as a fugitive needing aid, and William Lindsay applied for employment as a lecturer for the Anti-Slavery

Society in 1866 (Letter of amanuensis for Bull to L. A. Chamerovzow, 15 Jan. 1859, C28/125–6; and James W. Massie to A. Hamp-
ton, 20 Jan. 1866, C119/51 (Anti-Slavery Papers, Brit. Emp. S18).
Some better-known Negro abolitionists who visited Britain were
Charles L. Remond, who in 1840 was the first prominent American
Negro abolitionist to visit Britain; the Rev. Henry Highland Garnett
who came for the World Peace Conference in 1850 and stayed in
Europe for three years; the Rev. James W. C. Pennington, who lec-
tured in Britain and particularly Scotland from 1849–51, and was in
great demand as a preacher to Nonconformist congregations (Armis-
tead, *op. cit.*, 408); Martin R. Delany, a Negro doctor from
Chatham, Ontario, who, returning from the Niger, lectured upon
Africa, and aided in the formation of the African Aid Society, in-
terested in the regeneration of Africa through the self-help of the
Negro race. Delaney advocated voluntary emigration of American
Negroes to Africa. He also created quite a stir at the International
Statistical Congress in July 1860, when Lord Brougham, before
Dallas, the American minister in London, made reference to
Delaney's presence in the distinguished assembly. Much to Dallas's
embarrassment, Delaney was loudly cheered by the sedate statisti-
cians. In the House of Lords, Brougham, commenting on this inci-
dent, said the American delegates left the Congress as a result.
Delaney also delivered a paper before the Royal Geographical Society, and spent seven months touring England and Scotland speaking on Africa (see Martin R. Delaney, *Official Report of the Niger
Valley Exploring Party* (1861); *The Times*, 17 July 1860, 5c; *Parliamentary Debates*, 3rd ser., CLXXI (22 June 1863), col. 1227–8;
Lancet, 13 Oct. 1860, 373, reviewed Delaney's lecture on Africa
which he gave in Glasgow). With the outbreak of the American Civil
War, Negro abolitionists increased their activities in Britain to encourage support of the North. H. H. Garnett returned in 1861, and
was joined by William H. Day, and J. Sella Martin, a particularly
effective campaigner. At this time, the most active Negro abolitionist
in Britain was Sarah Remond, who in 1859 began as agent for the
Leeds Anti-Slavery Society, and continued her work until 1867
advocating the cause of the freedman in America. More excitement
was added to the campaign when in 1862, William Andrew Jackson,
Jefferson Davis's escaped coachman, arrived in Britain. All these
speakers were enthusiastically welcomed in Britain and received hos-
pital treatment throughout their travels (see Dorothy B. Parker,
'Sarah Parker Remond, abolitionist and physician', *Journal of Negro
History*, XX (1935), 287–93; see especially for work and influence of

these speakers B. Quarles, 'Ministers without portfolio', *Journal of Negro History*, XXXIX (1954), 27–42).

Outside the abolitionists, the most notable Negro American to visit Britain during the mid-Victorian period was Ira Aldridge, a tragic actor. As early as the 1830s, Aldridge had established a reputation as an actor playing at Covent Garden in 1833. It took the London critics some time before they could accept the idea of a Negro actor in the respectable theatre. He returned to London in 1848, but not to the West End, and when in 1858 he performed at the Lyceum the critics admired the courage of the theatre manager in combating colour prejudice. After completing three successful European tours, he returned to the West End in 1865, and played at the Haymarket to favourable reviews. He married Margaret Gill, the daughter of a Yorkshire stocking weaver, and apparently there was no opposition to this match. Aldridge was most famous for his Othello, but also played European roles: W. W. Brown admired the Negro tragedian's Hamlet as his best part (Herbert Marshall and Mildred Stock, *Ira Aldridge, The Negro Tragedian* (1958), *passim*; W. W. Brown, *The Black Man, His Antecedents, His Genius, and His Achievements* (Boston, 1863), 118–24).

Abbreviations

AR	*Anthropological Review*
ASP	Anti-Slavery Papers, Rhodes House, Oxford
BL Add. MSS.	British Library, Additional Manuscripts
CMS	Church Missionary Society
DNB	*Dictionary of National Biography*
JASL	*Journal of the Anthropological Society of London*
JESL	*Journal of the Ethnological Society of London*
OED	*Oxford English Dictionary*
Parl. Deb.	*Parliamentary Debates*
P.P.	*Parliamentary Papers*
P.R.O.	Public Record Office
TESL	*Transactions of the Ethnological Society of London*

In addition, the following abbreviations have been used in all references to periodicals:

Bull.	*Bulletin*
J.	*Journal*
Mag.	*Magazine*
Procs.	*Proceedings*
Q.	*Quarterly*
Rev.	*Review*
Soc.	*Society*
Trans.	*Transactions*

Notes

CHAPTER ONE

1. W. H. Flower, 'Comparative anatomy of man', *Nature*, XXII (27 May 1880), 79.

2. *Daily Telegraph*, 17 Aug. 1866, 4e–f; see also Philip D. Curtin, *The Image of Africa, British Ideas and Action, 1780–1850* (1965), vi–vii; H. A. C. Cairns, *Prelude to Imperialism. British Reactions to Central African Society, 1840–1890* (1965), 53, 76; Christine Bolt, *Victorian Attitudes to Race* (1971), 133–4, 142–3, 209–11; and review of Livingstone's *Missionary Travels and Researches in South Africa* (1857), *Westminster Rev.*, n.s., XIII (Jan. 1858), 1–28.

3. Mid-Victorian commentators were themselves aware of this change: *Anti-Slavery Reporter*, 3rd ser., XI (May 1863), 112; *Saturday Rev.*, 9 Dec. 1865, 726b.

4. T. Shibutani and K. M. Kwan, *Ethnic Stratification, A Comparative Approach* (New York, 1965), 242–3; Michael Banton, *Race Relations* (1967), 45–50; Louis L. Snyder, *Race. A History of Modern Ethnic Theories* (New York, 1939), 210; J. W. Burrow, *Evolution and Society. A Study in Victorian Social Theory* (1966), 75–6; Kenneth Little, 'Race and society', in *Race and Science* (UNESCO, 1961), 93–4; Oliver Cromwell Cox, *Caste, Class and Race. A Study in Social Dynamics* (New York, 1959), 483–4; Isacque Graeber, 'An examination of theories of race prejudice', *Social Research*, XX (1953), 273.

5. C. C. Eldridge, *England's Mission: the Imperial Idea in the Age of Gladstone and Disraeli, 1868–1880* (1973), 39–49, 238–44, 251–5; W. P. Morrell, *British Colonial Policy in the Mid-Victorian Age* (1969), 40–1; R. Robinson and J. Gallagher, 'The partition of Africa', *New Cambridge Modern History*, XI (1962), 594.

6. For studies stressing the colonial setting see Curtin, *op. cit.*, and Cairns, *op cit.*; for attitudes assessed from press and travellers' accounts see Bolt, *op. cit.*; see also H. S. Deighton, 'History and the study of race relations', *Race*, I (1959), 15–25.

7. For concept of attitude see Milton Roeack, 'Attitude', *International Encyclopaedia of Social Science* (New York, 1968), 457; G. W. Allport, 'Attitudes in the history of social psychology', T. M. Newcomb, 'On the definition of attitude', J. B. Cooper and J. L. McCargh, 'Attitudes as cognitive structures', in *Attitudes*, ed. M. Jahoda and N. Warren (1966), 15–39; W. D. Jordan, *White over Black. American Attitudes towards the Negro, 1550–1812* (Chapel Hill, N.C., 1968), viii.

8. Pierre L. van den Berghe, *Race and Racism. A Comparative Perspective* (New York, 1967), 9.

9. Richard D. Altick, 'The sociology of authorship. The social origins, education, and occupation of 1,100 British writers, 1800–1935', *Bull. New York Public Library*, LXVI (June 1962), 389–404.

10. van den Berghe, *op. cit.*, 12; see also M. Banton, 'The concept of racism', in *Race and Racialism*, ed. S. Zubaida (1970), 17–34.

11. Both Maoris and Indians were referred to as 'niggers': *Parl. Deb.*, 3rd ser., CLXXIX (26 Apr. 1864), 1641, and CLXXV (30 May 1864), 793–4; [W. H. Russell], 'The sahib and the nigger', *The Times*, 20 Oct. 1858, 10a–b, and leader, 20 Oct. 1858, 8c–d; *Aborigines' Friend and Colonial Intelligencer*, I (Sept.–Oct. 1858), 486–90, and n.s., II (July–Dec. 1859), 67–74; *Anti-Slavery Reporter*, 3rd ser., VI (1858), 263–4; see also P. D. Curtin, ' "Scientific" Racism and the British theory of Empire', *J. Historical Soc. of Nigeria*, II (1960), 43; Eric Partridge, *A Dictionary of Slang and Unconventional English*, I (5th edn, 1961).

12. Charles Lamb, 'Imperfect sympathies', *Essays of Elia* (Everyman edn, 1954), 73.

13. M. Banton, *White and Coloured* (1959), 31, and *Race Relations*, 8; G. E. Simpson, and J. Milton Singer, *Race and Cultural Minorities* (New York, 3rd edn, 1965), 82–3; Bruno Bettleheim and Morris Janowitz, *Social Change and Prejudice, including the Dynamics of Prejudice* (Glencoe, Ill., 1964), *passim*; James Martin, *The Tolerant Personality* (Detroit, 1964), *passim*.

14. Shibutani and Kwan, *op. cit.*, 92–3; van den Berghe, *op. cit.*, 20–1.

15. Banton, *White and Coloured*, 31.

16. van den Berghe, *op. cit.*, 20–1.

17. Rev. John Cunningham, *God in History* (1849), 60–1.

18. *Parl. Deb.*, 3rd ser., CLXV (13 Mar. 1862), 1449.

19. *Parl. Deb.*, 3rd ser., CLXXVI (26 July 1864), 2103; 'Case of A. Fitzjames', *P.P.* 1863, XXXVIII, 407.

20. Palmerston to Russell, 12 Apr. 1861, Russell Papers, P.R.O. 30/22/21.

21. van den Berghe, *op. cit.*, 149; Deighton, *op. cit.*, 24–5.

CHAPTER TWO

1. Eldred Jones, *Othello's Countrymen. The African in English Renaissance Drama* (1965), *passim*; Winthrop D. Jordan, *White Over Black. American Attitudes Toward the Negro, 1550–1812* (Chapel Hill, N.C., 1968), 3–43; David B. Davis, *The Problem of Slavery in Western Culture* (Ithaca, N.Y., 1966), 281–2; Katherine George, 'The civilized world looks at primitive Africa: 1400–1800; a study in ethnocentrism', *Isis*, XLIX (March 1958), 62–72.

2. Jordan, *op. cit.*, 3–43; James Walvin, *The Black Presence: A Documentary History of the Negro in England, 1555–1860* (New York, 1972), 12; *idem*, *Black and White: The Negro and English Society, 1555–1945* (1973), *passim*.

3. Pierre L. van den Berghe, *Race and Racism. A Comparative Perspective* (New York, 1967), 1–41; H. Hoetink, *Slavery and Race Relations in the Americas: Comparative Notes on their Nature and Nexus* (New York, 1973), 192–210.

4. Asa Briggs, 'The language of "class" in early nineteenth-century England', *Essays in Labour History*, ed. A. Briggs and J. Saville (1967), 43–73; Harold Perkin, *The Origin of Modern English Society*,

1780–1880 (1969), 17–38; E. P. Thompson, *The Making of the English Working Class* (1968), *passim*.

5. George, *op. cit.*, 62–72; H. N. Fairchild, *The Noble Savage. A Study in Romantic Naturalism* (New York, 1928), *passim*; W. Sypher, *Guinea's Captive Kings: British Anti-Slavery Literature of the XVIIIth Century* (Chapel Hill, N.C., 1942), 5, 103–4, 229–30; Davis, *op. cit.*, 181–2, 474–82; Jordan, *op. cit.*, 9–10, 27; Philip D. Curtin, *The Image of Africa, British Ideas and Action, 1780–1850* (1965), 48–51; R. Anstey, *The Atlantic Slave Trade and British Abolition, 1760–1810* (1975), 91–183.

6. Eva B. Dykes, *The Negro in English Romantic Thought, or A Study of Sympathy for the Oppressed* (Washington, D.C., 1942), 154; Davis, *op. cit.*, 481; Anstey, *op. cit.*, 145–51.

7. Mrs A. Behn, *Oroonoko: or, the Royal Slave. A True History* (1688), 21.

8. Curtin, *op. cit.*, 327–8.

9. Thomas F. Gossett, *Race. The History of an Idea in America* (Dallas, 1963), 16, 31; Eric Williams, *Capitalism and Slavery* (Chapel Hill, N.C., 1944), 19–21; see also chapter 8 below.

10. Edward Long, *The History of Jamaica*, II (1774), 383; see also Davis, *op. cit.*, 460–4; Walvin, *Black and White*, 168–9; F. O. Shyllon, *Black Slaves in Britain* (1974), 148–53, 162–4.

11. Curtin, *op. cit.*, *passim*; Davis, *op. cit.*, *passim*.

12. Philip D. Curtin, 'Foreword to Part I, African travellers of the eighteenth century', *Africa Remembered* (Madison, Wis., 1967), 13; Kenneth Little, *Negroes in Britain* (1948), 164–7.

13. Appendix, 212–13; J. Jean Hecht, 'Continental and colonial servants in 18th century England', *Smith College Studies in History*, XL (1954), 33–49; Walvin, *Black and White*, 46–8.

14. V. Sackville West, *Knole and the Sackvilles* (1922), 191–2.

15. Hecht, *op. cit.*, 40–2; Shyllon, *op. cit.*, 3–16.

16. Henry Angelo, *Reminiscences of Henry Angelo*, I (1828), 446–53.

17. Letter XIV to Mr S——e, 11 Oct. 1772, *Letters and Memories of the late Ignatius Sancho, An African*, ed. J. Jekyll (5th edn, 1803), 31–2; see also Jekyll's life of Sancho, *ibid.*, i–xvi, and Paul Edwards, 'Introduction', *Letters of Ignatius Sancho* (1968), i–xv.

18. For examples of other prominent blacks in eighteenth-century England see Appendix, 213–14.

19. Shyllon, *op. cit.*, 162–3; Walvin, *Black and White*, 52–5.

20. *Gentleman's Mag.*, Dec. 1731, 542.

21. Hecht, *op. cit.*, 46–8.

22. Comment of William Eden, Irish Chief Secretary to Edmund Burke, in *Correspondence of Edmund Burke*, ed. Charles Williams *et al.*, II (1844), 459.

23. Hecht, *op. cit.*, 46; M. Dorothy George, *London Life in the XVIIIth Century* (1925), 135–7; Walvin, *Black and White*, 57.

24. Mary Beth Norton, 'The fate of some black loyalists of the American Revolution', *J. Negro History*, LVIII (1973), 416.

25. James Albert Ukawsaw Gronniosaw, *A Narrative of the most remarkable Particulars in the Life of James Albert Ukawsaw Gronniosaw, An African Prince* [?1770], 39–49.

26. H. T. Catterall (ed.), *Judicial Cases concerning American Slavery and the Negro* (Washington, D.C., 1926–37), I, 14–18; Edward Fiddes, 'Lord Mansfield and the Somerset Case', *Law Q. Rev.*, L (Oct. 1934), 499–511; Jerome Nadelhaft, 'The Somerset Case and slavery: myth, reality, and repercussions', *J. Negro History*, LI (1966), 193–9; Shyllon, *op. cit.*, 77–176; Walvin, *Black and White*, 105–31; David Brion Davis, *The Problem of Slavery in the Age of Revolution, 1770–1823* (Ithaca, N.Y., 1975), 471–501.

27. Thomas Day, *The Dying Negro* (1773); John Latimer, *The Annals of Bristol in the Eighteenth Century* (1893), 492; *5th Report of the African Institution*, 27 March 1811, 87–95, and *9th Report*, 12 April 1815, 68–72; Walvin, *Black and White*, 127–9, 132–41.

28. Shyllon, *op. cit.*, 120–1; Davis, *Slavery in the Age of Revolution*, 497.

29. Shyllon, *op. cit.*, 206–7.

30. Eric Williams, *op. cit.*, *passim*; R. A. Austen and W. D. Smith, 'Images of Africa and British slave-trade abolition: The transition to an imperialist ideology, 1787–1807', *African Historical Studies*, II (1969), 69–83; R. Anstey, 'Capitalism and slavery: A critique', *Economic History Rev.*, 2nd ser., XXI (1968), 307–20, and 'A reinterpretation of the abolition of the British slave trade, 1806–1807', *English Historical Rev.*, LXXXVII (1972), 304–32; *ibid.*, *The Atlantic Slave Trade and British Abolition, 1760–1810* (1975), 406–9, and *passim*; Davis, *Slavery in the Age of Revolution*, 427–53.

31. Henry Smeathman, *Plan of a Settlement to be made near Sierra Leone* (1786), 16–17, 23–4; C. B. Wadstrom, *An Essay on Colonization*, II (1795), 220, 227–8; Prince Hoare, *Memoirs of Granville Sharp* (1820), 259–61; Christopher Fyfe, *A History of Sierra Leone* (1962), 13–19; Hecht, *op. cit.*, 44–5; Little, *op. cit.*, 183; E. C. P. Lascelles, *Granville Sharp and the Freedom of the Slaves in England* (1928), 81; Walvin, *Black and White*, 144–56; Report of the Select Committee on the State of Mendicity in the Metropolis, *P.P.* 1816, V, 15–16.

32. Hecht, *op. cit.*, 48–9; Walvin, *Black and White*, 46–79; Shyllon, *op. cit.*, 110–11.

33. O. Cugoano, *Thoughts and Sentiments on the Evil and Wicked Traffic of the Slavery and Commerce of the Human Species* (1787), 138–42; O. Equiano [Gustavus Vasa], *The Interesting Narrative of the Life of Olaudah Equiano, or Gustavus Vasa, The African* (1814), 416–28.

34. *Cobbett's Annual Register*, V (Jan.–June 1804), 935, 937.

35. *Ibid.*, I (Jan.–June 1802), 701, and V (Jan.–June 1804), 937.

36. Excerpt of letter from Hester Piozzi to P. Pennington, 19 June 1802, in Oswald G. Knapp (ed.), *The Intimate Letters of Hester Piozzi and Penelope Pennington, 1788–1821* (1914), 243–4.

37. Maria Edgeworth to Mrs Barbauld, 18 Jan. 1810, in Anna L. Le Breton, *Memoir of Mrs Barbauld* (1874), 136. The first edition of *Belinda* appeared in 1802; the edited version in 1810.

38. Henry Noble Sherwood, 'Paul Cuffee', *J. Negro History*, VIII (1923), 174–81, which includes excerpts from Cuffee's journal in Cuffee MSS., Public Library, New Bradford, Mass., from 12 July to 20 Sept. 1811, while Cuffee was in England; *6th Report of the African Institution*, 25 Mar. 1813, 32–3; *Memoir of Captain Paul Cuffee, a Man of Colour*

(1811), 21–7; Peter Williams, *A Discourse delivered on the Death of Captain Paul Cuffee* (New York, 1818).

39. Hecht, *op. cit.*, 56; Little, *op. cit.*, 198–203; George, *op. cit.*, 137.

40. John Matthews, James Penny, Robert Norris, to John Tarleton, Liverpool, 16 Apr. 1788, No. 4, Letter from the Delegates from Liverpool in answer to an Enquiry made by the Committee respecting the Natives of Africa who have been sent to England for Education, *Part I of the Report of the Lords Committee of the Privy Council . . . Relating to Trade and Plantations; Concerning the Present State of Trade to Africa* (1789).

41. Wadstrom, *op. cit.*, II (1795), 124.

42. M. Knutsford, *Life and Letters of Zachary Macaulay* (1900), 35–8; Anna Falconbridge, *Narrative of Two Voyages to the River Sierra Leone, During the Years 1791–2–3* (2nd edn, 1802), 126–7.

43. *Cobbett's Annual Register*, v (Jan.–June 1804), 937; Z. Macaulay to Miss Selina Mills, 16 June 1798, in Knutsford, *op. cit.*, 223–4.

44. W. Innes Addison, *The Matriculation Album for the University of Glasgow, from 1728 to 1858* (1913).

45. See Appendix, 216–17; Walvin, *Black and White*, 194–6.

46. 'The Negro Boy', Religious Tract Society [1830].

47. W. B. Pope (ed.), *The Diary of Benjamin Robert Haydon*, V (Cambridge, Mass., 1960), 42–3, entry for 8 Apr. 1841.

48. William Wilberforce to Mrs Clarkson, 11 Mar. 1822, letter 56, in E. L. Griggs and C. N. Prater, *Henry Christophe and Thomas Clarkson, A Correspondence* (Berkeley, 1952), 246, 254n.; see also E. L. Griggs, *Thomas Clarkson, The Friend of the Slaves* (1936), 146–7.

49. Z. Macaulay to Mrs Macaulay, 20 Sept. 1821, in Knutsford, *op. cit.*, 368.

50. T. Clarkson to Z. Macaulay, 19 Nov. 1821, *ibid.*, 373.

51. Mrs Wilkins, 'Introduction', *The Slave Son* (1854), 6.

52. Hannah Kilham, *Memoirs of Hannah Kilham*, ed. S. Biller (1837), 221–2.

53. *Ibid.*, 294–5.

54. For example, the case of Thomas Jenkins, a black schoolmaster in Scotland. See H. G. Adams, *God's Image in Ebony* (1854), 70–80; W. Armistead, *A Tribute for the Negro* (1848), 317–23; Appendix, 215–16.

55. W. B. Pope (ed.), *op. cit.*, IV, 644, entry for 29 June 1840.

56. *Loc. cit.*, entry for 30 June 1840.

57. Zilpha Elaw, *Memories of the Life, Religious Experience, Ministerial Travels and Labours of Mrs Zilpha Elaw* (1846), 140–1; see also Zilpha Elaw to J. Tredgold, 1840, ASP, Brit. Emp. S18 C6/127.

58. For some census returns on the numbers of colonial and foreign born see Appendix, 214–15.

59. F. D. Walker, *Thomas Birch Freeman, The Son of An African* (1929), 11–14, 24; J. F. Ade Ajayi, *Christian Missions in Nigeria: The Making of a New Elite, 1841–91* (1965), 257.

60. Maurice E. Kenealy, *The Tichborne Tragedy* (1913), 219–23.

61. *All the Year Round*, n.s., XIII (6 Nov. 1875), 492–3.

62. Linda Brent, *The Deeper Wrong; or, Incidents in the Life of a Slave Girl*, ed. L. M. Child (1862), 278.

63. 'Abstract of two orders in Council of 16th March 1808', in *4th Report of the African Institution*, 28 Mar. 1810 (2nd edn, 1814), 49–50, 59–60, and *Special Report of the African Institution*, 12 Apr. 1815, 114–15; Maj. Alex. M. Tullock, Statistical Report on Sickness, Mortality and Invaliding Troops in the Western Coast of Africa, *P.P.* 1840, XXX, 15.

64. *Cobbett's Annual Register*, v (Jan.–June 1804), 936–7; *10th Report of the African Institution*, 27 Mar. 1816, 37.

65. Kilham, *op. cit.*, 132–3; Sir George Stephen, *The Niger Trade* (1849), 29; *Anti-Slavery Reporter*, 3rd ser., 1 (Feb. 1853), 25–8.

66. P.R.O., F.O. 5/579, (printed) Correspondence relative to the Prohibition of Free persons of Colour into Certain Ports of the United States, 1823–1851, *passim*.

67. P.R.O., F.O. 5/579, Correspondence between Millian Mure, H.M. Consul, New Orleans, and Palmerston, 7 June 1850 to 24 Dec. 1851; John Brown, *Slave Life in Georgia; Narrative of the Life, Sufferings, and Escape of John Brown, Fugitive Slave now in England*, ed. L. A. Chamerovzow (1855), 31–44; E. Hammond to L. A. Chamerovzow, P.R.O., F.O., 24 May 1855, ASP, C 161/120; Rev. J. Asher, *Incidents in the Life of Rev. J. Asher, Pastor of Shiloh (Coloured) Baptist Church, Philadelphia, U.S.* (1850), 79–80.

68. Correspondence relating to these cases is scattered in P.R.O., F.O. 5 America, 710–98, 1859–61: see especially P.R.O., F.O. 5/720, Consul R. Bunch to Russell, Charleston, 24 Dec. 1859; P.R.O., F.O. 5/729, James Booth of the Committee of the Privy Council for Trade to E. Hammond, 21 June 1859, enclosing Circular No. 114, Board of Trade, 14 June 1859; P.R.O., F.O. 5/891, No. 657, Lord Lyons to Russell, 20 July 1863, and No. 666, Lyons to Russell, 24 July 1863.

69. *Liverpool Mercury*, 21 Jan. 1857, 4e–f, and 23 Jan. 1857, 3d–e.

70. Convocation of Canterbury, *Church Work Amongst the Sailors in 64 Home Ports* (1878), 2–3; Lt Col. R. M. Hughes, *The Laws relating to Lascars and Asiatic Seamen employed in the British Merchants' Service, or Brought to the United Kingdom in Foreign Vessels* (1855), 5–9; J. Salter, *The Asiatic in England; Sketches of Sixteen Years' Work among Orientals* (1873), 25–6.

71. Salter, *op. cit., passim*; J. M. Weylland, *These Fifty Years, Being the Jubilee Volume of the London City Mission* (1884), 183–4; 'Wapping, Shadwell, and Poplar', *London City Mission Mag.*, xxii (Aug. 1857), 213–36.

72. For fullest discussion of middle class attitudes toward the 'residuum' see Gareth Stedman Jones, *Outcast London: A Study of the Relationship between Classes in Victorian Society* (1971), *passim*.

73. *London City Mission Mag.*, xxii (Aug. 1857), 217.

74. Henry Mayhew, *London Labour and London Poor*, IV (1862), 229, 366.

75. *Ibid.*, I, 224; IV, 425–6; III, 190–4.

76. *Ibid.*, IV, 245.

77. Report of *Ladies' Society to Aid Fugitives from Slavery* (1855), (printed), in ASP C84.

78. John Hawkins Simpson, *Horrors of the Virginia Slave Trade. . . The True Story of Dinah, an Escaped Virginia Slave now in London* (1863), 58.

79. *African Times*, II (23 Dec. 1862), 68–9; *Colonial Intelligencer and Aborigines' Friend*, n.s., II (Jan.–Dec. 1862), 297–8.
80. Mayhew, *op. cit.*, II, 493.
81. *Ibid.*, IV, 425–6.
82. Michael Banton, *The Coloured Quarter. Negro Immigrants in an English City* (1955), 22–38; J. A. Jackson, *The Irish in Britain* (1963), 153–6; John Garrard, *The English and Immigration, 1880–1910* (1971), 51–81; B. Gainer, *The Alien Invasion: The Origins of the Aliens Act of 1905* (1972), 118–28.

CHAPTER THREE

1. Wilson Armistead to L. A. Chamerovzow, 9 June 1853, ASP C27/54; activities of more prominent black abolitionists in Britain described in Benjamin Quarles, 'Ministers without portfolio', *J. Negro History*, XXXIX (1954), 27–42.
2. William Wells Brown, *The American Fugitive in Europe. Sketches of Places and People Abroad* (Boston, 1855), 32; press reports from the *Sutherland Herald* cited in the *Anti-Slavery Reporter*, n.s., V (1850), 175 on Rev. Pennington and Rev. H. H. Garnett, and the *British Banner* (28 May 1851, 359) on Pennington, Garnett, and Josiah Henson.
3. Thomas J. Brewin to L. A. Chamerovzow, 18 Nov. 1854, ASP C28; *Anti-Slavery Reporter*, 3rd ser., I (1853), 82–3, and II (1854), 60, 94–5; *Anti-Slavery Advocate* (Aug. 1853), 85.
4. B. Quarles, 'Introduction', *Narrative of the Life of Frederick Douglass* (Cambridge, Mass., 1960), xiii; William Wells Brown, *Narrative of William Wells Brown, A Fugitive Slave* (1850).
5. Charles H. Nichols, *Many Thousand Gone: The Ex-Slaves' Account of Their Bondage and Freedom* (Leyden, 1963), xiii–v; report of S. R. Ward's speeches, *Nonconformist* 18 May 1853, 392–4; remarks of W. L. Garrison and Charles Remond in Glasgow Emancipation Society, *Reports of Speeches and Reception of American Delegates* (1840), 12, 19–20; case of Sarah Remond denied passport by U.S. Embassy in London in the *Morning Star*, 10 Dec. 1859, 4d–e, and the *Anti-Slavery Advocate*, II (2 Jan. 1860), 294.
6. Mrs E. L. Follen to Mary Estlin, 7 Jan. 1852, Estlin Papers, Dr Williams's Library, London, 24.123.10; Mrs E. L. Follen to Mary Estlin, n.d., *ibid.*, 24.123.12; William G. Allen, *American Prejudice against Colour* (1853), *passim*; 'Colour prejudice', *Anti-Slavery Reporter*, 3rd ser., I (1853), 121–3, and XI (1863), 154; Quarles, 'Ministers without portfolio', *op. cit.*, 35–6; *Anthropological Rev.*, VI (1868), 224.
7. William Craft, *Running a Thousand Miles for Freedom; or, the Escape of William and Ellen Craft from Slavery* (1860), *passim*; *Anthropological Rev.*, I (1863), 388–9.
8. Craft, *op. cit.*, 100–8; W. W. Brown, *Three Years in Europe* (1852), 7; Samuel R. Ward, *Autobiography of a Fugitive Negro; his anti-slavery labours in the United States, Canada, and England* (1855), 38–9, 235.
9. *Anti-Slavery Advocate* (Dec. 1852), 20.

10. Frederick Douglass, *My Bondage and My Freedom* (New York, 1855), 366–7, 372, 391; *The Times*, 8 Apr. 1847, 4e–f; following Douglass's letter in *The Times*, 6 Apr. 1847, 7c, Cunard's apology appeared 13 Apr. 1847, 6d.

11. Douglass, *op. cit.*, 391; observation repeated in letter to W. L. Garrison, Belfast, 1 Jan. 1846, reprinted from the *Liberator* in 'Documents', *J. Negro History*, VIII (1923), 103–7; *Report of Proceedings at a Soiree given to Frederick Douglass* (1847), 27–8.

12. George Shepperson, 'Frederick Douglass and Scotland', *J. Negro History*, XXXVIII (1953), 318; Philip S. Foner, *Frederick Douglass, a Biography* (New York, 1964), 62–75, 182–3; Margaret Howith (ed.), *Mary Howith. An Autobiography* (1889), II, 33–4; William Lovett, *The Life and Struggles of William Lovett* (1876), 321.

13. Brown, *Three Years in Europe*, 7–8; Brown repeated his observations in *The Negro in the American Rebellion* (Boston, 1867), 364.

14. Brown, *Three Years in Europe*, 313–14.

15. *Ibid.*, 17, and xxiv, 138–41, 210, 221; *idem, American Fugitive in Europe*, 284–95.

16. See Appendix, 220–3.

17. Ward, *op. cit.*, 39–40.

18. *Ibid.*, 150–1.

19. *Ibid.*, 335–7, 370–83, 392–6, 189–90, 233–4.

20. *Ibid.*, 311.

21. *Ibid.*, 284, and 245, 311–26.

22. *Anti-Slavery Reporter*, 3rd ser., XII (May 1864), 112.

23. *Loc. cit.* Ward ran into disfavour both from his handling of money gained on his tour, and out of personal squabbles in abolitionist circles in Canada (Robin W. Winks, *The Blacks in Canada: a History* (1971), 227, 265–6).

24. W. W. Brown, *The Black Man: His Antecedents, His Genius, and His Achievements* (Boston, 1863), 47; Palmerston's praise of the entrepreneurial virtues in his Don Pacifico speech (1850) is quoted in H. Perkin, *The Origins of Modern English Society, 1780–1880* (1969), 408–9.

25. *The Times*, 30 July 1852, 6e–f.

26. John Brown, *Slave Life in Georgia, Narrative of the Life, Suffering, and Escape of John Brown, Fugitive Now in England*, ed. L. A. Chamerovzow (1855), 170.

27. *Ibid.*, 206–9, 249–50; Thomas E. Binns to L. A. Chamerovzow, 16 Sept. 1854, ASP C28/51.

28. H. T. Catterall (ed.), *Judicial Cases concerning American Slavery and the Negro* (Washington, D.C., 1926–37), V, 340–8; Frederick Rogers to E. Hammond, 16 Jan. 1861, enclosing copy of Duke of Newcastle to officer administering the Government of Canada, 9 Jan. 1861, P.R.O., F.O.5/795; *Parl. Deb.*, 3rd ser., CLXI (8 Feb. 1861), 218–24; Winks, *op. cit.*, 175–6.

29. *Anti-Slavery Reporter*, 3rd ser., IX (1861), 109, 164.

30. Remarks of John Noble, jr., in Harper Twelvetrees (ed.), *The Story of John Anderson, the Fugitive Slave* (1863), 159, also 118, 142–3, 149, 163, 172, 179.

31. *Aborigines' Friend and Colonial Intelligencer* (Feb., Sept. 1858),

437–8; L. A. Chamerovzow to Lord Brougham, 20 May 1862, Brougham Papers, University College, London.

32. David Kimble, *The Political History of Ghana. The Rise of Gold Coast Nationalism, 1850–1928* (1963), 63–93.

33. See Appendix, 215–19.

34. Brown, *Three Years in Europe*, 233.

35. *Ibid.*, 310.

36. Rev. William Knight, *Memoir of Rev. H. Venn. The Missionary Secretariat of Henry Venn, B.D.* (1880), 377; J. F. Ade Ajayi, *Christian Missions in Nigeria: The Making of a New Elite, 1841–91* (1965), 145–6; see Appendix, 218.

37. Kimble, *op. cit.*, 65–7.

38. *Anti-Slavery Reporter*, 3rd ser., 1 (Aug. 1853), 175–6.

39. *Ibid.*, 176–7; Haliburton (1796–1865) moved from Nova Scotia to England, and later became Conservative M.P. for Launceston, 1859–65 (*DNB*).

40. Ward, *op. cit.*, 261.

41. Sir George Stephen, *The Niger Trade* (1849), 63–4; see also 58–65.

42. A. P. Eardly Wilmot to H. Venn, Fernando Po, 16 May 1865, CMS Archives, C.A.1/023.

43. Duke of Somerset to Russell, 13 Sept. 1865, Russell Papers, P.R.O. 30/22/24.

44. Henry Venn, 'Letter to the Bishop of Kingston, Jamaica', Jan. 1867, and 'Missionary Secretariat: II. On Nationality (Instructions to the Committee of the CMS, 30 June 1868)', in Knight, *op. cit.*, 214–15, 284–5; J. F. Ade Ajayi, 'Henry Venn and the policy of development', *J. Historical Soc. of Nigeria*, 1 (1958–9), 331–42, and *idem*, *Christian Missions*, 14–19; Kimble, *op. cit.*, 63–125; H. S. Scott, 'The development of education of the African in relation to Western contact', *The Year Book of Education* (1938), 693–739.

45. Memorandum by Rev. S. Crowther, Windsor, 18 Nov. 1851, and extracts from private journal of Henry Venn, in Knight, *op. cit.*, 379–82, 119–22; Ajayi, *Christian Missions*, 20–1, 26–7, 72–4; Jessie Page, *Samuel Crowther, the Slave Boy of the Niger* (1932), 74–5, 83–4, 102–3.

46. Ajayi, *Christian Missions*, 165.

47. *Ibid.*, 180–9, 240–1, 250–3.

48. *Church Missionary Intelligencer*, xv (1864), 97–8; *African Times*, III (23 Apr. 1864), 126; E. A. Ayandele, 'An assessment of James Johnson and his place in Nigerian history, 1874–1917, Part II, 1890–1917', *J. Historical Soc. of Nigeria*, IV (Dec. 1964), 75; *Church Missionary Intelligencer*, n.s., XVII (1892), 546–8.

49. J. A. B. Horton, *West African Countries and Peoples* (1868), 136; see also letter of 'One of the Niggers', probably Horton, to the editor, *African Times*, v (23 Jan. 1866), 72–3; and George Shepperson (ed.), 'Introduction', *West African Countries and Peoples* (1969), viii–xii; Christopher Fyfe, *Africanus Horton, 1835–1883: West African Scientist and Patriot* (1972), *passim*.

50. J. B. Marsh, *The Story of the Jubilee Singers* (3rd edn, 1876, and rev. edn, 1900), *passim*.

51. Ellen Craft to Mrs E. E. Nichols, 31 Mar. 1882, ASP C156/136.

52. Amanda Smith, *Amanda Smith, An Autobiography* (1897), 156–7, 243.

53. W. G. Allen to Miss Edwards, 21 Apr. 1869, and Allen to A. Peckover, 12 Apr. 1869, ASP C105/113–13a, and 115–15b.

54. Douglass's remark quoted in Foner, *op. cit.*, 343–4.

55. J. R. Maxwell, *The Negro Question, or Hints for the Physical Improvement of the Negro Race* (1892), 54–5; J. Foster (ed.), *Alumni Oxonienses, 1715–1886*, III (1888), 934.

56. Maxwell, *op. cit.*, 110; see also 41, 55–6.

57. J. R. Maxwell to Earl of Derby, Secretary of State for Colonies, 23 Aug. 1883, ASP C159/77; J. R. Maxwell to F. W. Chesson, 21 July 1885, ASP C142/139.

58. Edward W. Blyden to Sir Thomas Fowell Buxton, 22 June 1878, ASP C109/10; see also *idem, Africa and Africans* (1903), 24; Hollis R. Lynch, *Edward Wilmot Blyden, Pan-Negro Patriot, 1832–1912* (1967), *passim*.

59. Christopher Fyfe, *Sierra Leone Inheritance* (1964), 213; J. A. Venn, *Alumni Cantabrigienses, Part II, 1752–1900*, IV (1944), 550.

60. James H. Minns to G. William Allen, treasurer of the *Anti-Slavery Reporter*, Nassau, 20 Sept. 1879, ASP C105/107.

61. D. G. Garraway to Charles H. Allen, St Georges, Grenada, 7 Feb. 1882, ASP C58/23–23a.

62. L. A. Chamerovzow to Lord Brougham, 3 Oct. 1860, Brougham Papers.

63. W. C. Berwick Sayers, *Samuel Coleridge-Taylor, Musician. His Life and Letters* (1915), 1–3.

64. *Ibid.*, 255–81; Jessie S. F. C. Taylor, *A Memory Sketch of my Husband, Genius and Musician, Samuel Coleridge-Taylor* (1943), 13–14, 20.

65. A. B. C. Merriman Labor, *Britons through Negro Spectacles* (1909), *passim.*

CHAPTER FOUR

1. In a reference to Philip and the Ethiopian, *Acts*, VIII. 26–40, in the *Wesleyan-Methodist Magazine*, 5th ser., LXXXIX, pt II (July 1866), 590.

2. Ford K. Brown, *Fathers of the Victorians* (1961), 326–40; Sampson Low, *The Charities of London in 1861* (1862), xi, 288–301.

3. For example, *British Banner*, 15 Dec. 1852, 858c.

4. CMS, *The Slave Trade of East Africa: is it to continue or be suppressed?* (1868), 27–32; J. F. Ade Ajayi, *Christian Missions in Nigeria: The Making of a New Elite, 1841–1891* (1965), 9–10, 14–19; Reginald Coupland, *The Exploitation of East Africa, 1856–90. The Slave Trade and the Scramble* (1939), 115–16.

5. For example, *Juvenile Missionary Magazine*, XVII (July 1860), 154–8.

6. 'Constitution of the British and Foreign Anti-Slavery Society', *Anti-Slavery Reporter*, 3rd ser., 1 (1853), frontispiece; Memorial to Evangelical Alliance from British and Foreign Anti-Slavery Society (1846), ASP E2/20, 307–10; Address of the Com^e. of the British and Foreign Anti-Slavery Society to the Moderator, Office Bearers,

and Members of the General Assembly of the Free Church of Scotland on American Slavery (1846?), ASP E2/20, 311–26.

7. David B. Davis, 'The emergence of immediatism in British and American anti-slavery', *Mississippi Valley Historical Rev.*, XLIX (Sept. 1962), 227–30; *idem, The Problem of Slavery in Western Culture*, 292–4, 363–4.

8. Ajayi, *op. cit.*, 9–10.

9. Philip D. Curtin, *The Image of Africa* (1965), vi, 292.

10. Frank Thistlewaite, *The Anglo–American Connection in the Early Nineteenth Century* (Philadelphia, 1959), *passim*; A. H. Abel and F. J. Klingberg, *A Side-light on Anglo–American Relations* (1927), 24–8.

11. *The Times*, 18 Dec. 1856, 6e.

12. Howard Temperley, *British Antislavery, 1833–1870* (1972), 229.

13. *Anti-Slavery Advocate*, II (May 1858), 129–30.

14. The following newspapers are some of those which extracted material: *Empire* (ed. George Thompson); *Morning Advertiser*; *Nonconformist*; *Patriot*; *British Banner*.

15. For example, the British and Foreign Anti-Slavery Society, *Tracts on Slavery in America, No. 1 – What the South is fighting for* (3rd edn, 1862), states 30,000 published.

16. Sir James Picton, *Memorials of Liverpool*, I (1863), 520.

17. *Anti-Slavery Reporter*, 3rd ser., XI (1863), 169–70.

18. *The Uncle Tom's Cabin Almanack, or Abolitionist Memento for 1853* (1852), 56.

19. George Thompson, *American Slavery* (1853), 17.

20. The general remarks on missionary periodicals follow from a reading of the following: *Church Missionary Intelligencer* (1859–68); *Church Missionary Record*, n.s., V–XIV (1860–8); *Wesleyan Methodist Magazine*, 5th ser., LXXX–XCII (July 1857–June 1869); *Wesleyan Missionary Notices*, 3rd ser., IV–XV (1857–68); *Evangelical Alliance Intelligencer*, nos. XV–XLVIII (1861–8); *Baptist Magazine* (including the *Missionary Herald*), LII–LIX (1860–7); *The Mission Field, a Monthly Record of the Society for the Propagation of the Gospel*, V–XIII (1860–8); *Missionary Reporter, relating chiefly to missions of the United Brethren of Moravians*, I–V (1861–5); *Missionary Magazine and Chronicle* (London Missionary Society), XXIII–XXX (1857–66).

21. CMS, *Conference on missions held in 1860 at Liverpool* (1860), 69.

22. *Ibid.*, 61.

23. Curtin, *op. cit.*, 325–9; Ajayi, *op. cit.*, 261–2; H. A. C. Cairns, *Prelude to Imperialism. British Reactions to Central African Society, 1840–1890* (1965), 101.

24. The following juvenile missionary magazines were consulted: *Church Missionary Juvenile Instructor*, n.s., IX–XIII (1860–4), and n.s., I–IV (1865–8); *Wesleyan Juvenile Offering: a Miscellany of Missionary Information for Young Persons*, XVII–XXIII (1860–6); *Juvenile Missionary Mag.* (London Missionary Society), XVI–XXIII (1859–66).

25. CMS, *Talks on Africa* (1906), 2.

26. Edith M. A. Baring-Gould, *A Missionary Alphabet for Children*, (CMS), n.d.

27. William Fox, *A Brief History of the Wesleyan Missions on the*

Western Coast of Africa (1851), 623; on race prejudice and colour symbolism see also Cairns, *op. cit.*, 75; Christine Bolt, *Victorian Attitudes to Race* (1971), 131–4.

28. For example, *Church Missionary Juvenile Instructor*, n.s., IX (1860), 91, 112–14; *Missionary Mag. and Chronicle*, XXIV (1860), 210–11, and XXIX (1865), 290–2.

29. Alexander Crummell, *Hope for Africa* (1853), 41.

30. CMS, *Conference on Missions*, 59.

31. J.B. of Upper Holloway, 'The highest motive to missionary enterprise', *Wesleyan–Methodist Mag.*, 5th ser., LXXXI pt i (Jan.–June 1858), 433.

32. Bruno Bettleheim and Morris Janowitz, *Social Change and Prejudice, including the Dynamics of Prejudice* (Glencoe, Ill., 1964), 146; Marie Jahoda, 'Race relations and mental health', in *Race and Science* (New York, 1961), 462–73; G. E. Simpson and J. M. Singer, *Race and Cultural Minorities* (3rd edn, New York, 1965), 49–53; M. Banton, *Race Relations* (1967), 307–11; Philip Mason, *Prospero's Magic. Some Thoughts on Class and Race* (1962), 52–7.

33. CMS, *Conference on Misisons*, 29; 'The Irish Church considered in its missionary aspect – the past and present', *Church Missionary Intelligencer*, n.s., IV (Nov. 1868), 337–48.

34. 'Minute on native churches', CMS, *Conference on Missions*, 310.

35. M., 'Civilization and pauperism in large towns', *Wesleyan–Methodist Mag.*, 5th ser., LXLII, pt I (Mar. 1869), 248; see also Asa Briggs, *Victorian Cities* (1968), 62, 64, 313, 315, 316, 362.

36. *Record*, 12 Dec. 1859, 2b.

37. K. Inglis, *Churches and the Working Classes in Victorian England* (1963), *passim*; Owen Chadwick, *The Victorian Church, Part I* (1966), *passim*; G. Kitson Clark, *The Making of Victorian England* (1965), 147–205.

38. On mid-Victorian ideas about charity, and similarly between attitudes toward home and foreign missions see: Gareth Stedman Jones, *Outcast London: A Study of the Relationship between Classes in Victorian Society* (1971), 239–70; David Owen, *English Philanthropy, 1660–1960* (Harvard, 1965), 103–4; Charles Loch Mowat, *The Charity Organization Society, 1869–1913. Its Ideas and Works* (1961), 7–8.

39. For more detailed discussion of the popular stereotype of the Negro see D. A. Lorimer, 'Bibles, banjoes, and bones: images of the Negro in the popular culture of Victorian England', in *In Search of the Visible Past*, ed. B. Gough (Waterloo, 1975), 31–50.

40. R. K. Webb, *The British Working Class Reader, 1790–1848* (1955), 160–3; Margaret Dalziel, *Popular Fiction 100 Years Ago* (1957), 72–4; Louis James, *Fiction for the Working Man, 1830–50* (1974), *passim*.

41. Anne Eaton, 'Widening horizons, 1840–1890: 10. Magazines for Children in the 19th century', in *A Critical History of Children's Literature*, ed. Cornelias Meigs *et al.* (New York, 1953), 270–85; Louis James, 'Tom Brown's imperialist sons', *Victorian Studies*, XVII (Sept, 1973), 89–99.

42. Martha Vicinus, *The Industrial Muse: A study of nineteenth-century British working class literature* (New York, 1974), 238–54.

43. Clarence Gohdes, *American Literature in Nineteenth-Century England*

(New York, 1944), 29–31; R. D. Altick, *The English Common Reader, A Social History of the Mass Reading Public, 1800–1900* (Chicago, 1957), 301.

44. H. B. Stowe, *Sunny Memories of Foreign Lands* (1854), 20; Charles Edward Stowe, *The Life of Harriet Beecher Stowe compiled from her letters and journals* (1889), 205–7.

45. Margaret Howith (ed.), *Mary Howith. An Autobiography*, (1889), II, 91–3, 102–3; *Christian Times*, 3 Dec. 1853, 769; C. E. Stowe, *op. cit.*, 232–4.

46. *Morning Chronicle*, 16 Sept. 1852, 3a–c.

47. H. B. Stowe, *The Key to Uncle Tom's Cabin* (1853), 41.

48. *Christian Observer*, LII (Oct. 1852), 708–9; *Eclectic Review*, n.s., IV (Dec. 1852), 734–5; *Nonconformist*, 8 Sept. 1852, 708.

49. 'School children at Belize', *Wesleyan Juvenile Offering*, XVIII (Nov. 1861), 174; *Punch*, XXIII (July–Dec. 1852), 179.

50. *Nonconformist* (8 Sept. 1852), 708.

51. *Westminster Rev.*, n.s., VI (July–Oct. 1854), 617; *Morning Chronicle*, 16 Sept. 1852, 3a–c.

52. *English Rev.*, XVIII (Oct. 1852), 96.

53. *Weekly Dispatch*, 23 May 1852, 326a–b.

54. 'Uncle Tom's Cabin and its opponents', *Eclectic Rev.*, n.s., IV (Dec. 1852), 735.

55. *Morning Post*, 10 Sept. 1852, 8b.

56. Charles Dickens to Mrs Stowe, 17 July 1852, in 'The author's introduction of 1878', reprinted in *Uncle Tom's Cabin*, ed. John Woods (1965), xxxviii.

57. *Morning Chronicle*, 16 Sept. 1852, 3a–c.

58. *Christian Observer*, LII (Oct. 1852), 708–9.

59. Charles Kingsley to Mrs Stowe, 12 Aug. 1852, reprinted in *Uncle Tom's Cabin*, ed. John Woods (1965), xliii; see also Charles Nichols, 'The origin of *Uncle Tom's Cabin*', *Phylon Q.* XIX (July 1958), 328–34; and George M. Frederickson, *The Black Image in the White Mind: The Debate on Afro-American Character and Destiny, 1817– 1914* (New York, 1972), 110–12, 117–18.

60. *Morning Chronicle*, 16 Sept. 1852, 3a–c.

61. H. B. Stowe, *The Key*, 17.

62. For example, Richard Hildreth, *The White Slave. Another Picture of Slave Life in America* (1852); F. C. Adams, *Manuel Periera: or, The Sovereign Rule of South Carolina* (1853); Sir George Stephen, an essay on slavery reprinted in Lord Denman, *Uncle Tom's Cabin and Its Reviewers* (1853), 42–3; see also H. B. Stowe, *The Key*, 364.

63. Harry Birdoff, *The World's Greatest Hit – Uncle Tom's Cabin* (New York, 1947), 144–65.

64. On the history of minstrelsy see: Carl Wittke, *Tambo and Bones. A History of the American Minstrel Stage* (Durham, N.C., 1930); Hans Nathan, *Dan Emmett and the Rise of Early Negro Minstrelsy* (Norman, Okla., 1962), Harry Reynolds, *Minstrel Memories. The Story of Burnt Cork Minstrelsy in Great Britain from 1836 to 1927* (1928); George F. Rehin, 'Harlequin Jim Crow: continuity and convergence in blackface clowning', *J. Popular Culture*, IX (1975/76), 682–701.

65. Reynolds, *op. cit., passim.*
66. *Ibid.,* 88–9, 164.
67. J. B. T. Marsh, *The Story of the Jubilee Singers* (3rd edn, 1876), *passim.*
68. W. A. Barratt, 'Negro hymnology', *Musical Times,* xv (1 Aug. 1872), 559–61; Edmund Wilson, *To the Finland Station* (1960), 223.
69. Henry Mayhew, *London Labour and London Poor,* iii (1861), 190–4; see also *Illustrated London News,* 12 Sept. 1885, 266.
70. 'Wandering Negro Minstrels', *Leisure Hour,* xx (23 Sept. 1871), 600, 602; see also Reynolds, *op. cit.,* 47, 103–4.
71. G. W. Moore, *Bones: His Anecdotes and Goaks* (1870), 4–8.
72. 'Negro minstrelsy', *Chambers's Encyclopaedia,* iv (1864), 698–9.
73. Charles Dilke to Joseph Knight, 23 Aug. 1866, Dilke Papers, BL. Add.MSS. 43, 909, fos. 83–4.
74. Reynolds, *op. cit.,* 162–5, 201–12.
75. *Ibid., passim.*
76. 'Banjo and bones', *Saturday Rev.,* lviii (7 June 1884), 740; Reynolds, *op. cit.,* 206–7.
77. For example, *ibid.,* 172–5, described the court minstrels who wore Georgian dress; and G. H. Chirgwin, *Chirgwin's Chirrup, Being the Life and Reminiscences of George Chirgwin, the 'White-eyed Musical Kaffir'* (1912).
78. *Illustrated London News,* 16 Feb. 1867, 152.
79. Philip S. Foner, *Frederick Douglass, a Biography* (New York, 1964), 343–4.
80. Maj. A. B. Ellis, *The History of the First West India Regiment* (1885), 19.
81. See chapter 3.
82. Advertisements illustrated in Leonard de Vries, *Victorian Advertisements* (Philadelphia, 1968), *passim.*
83. George F. Rehin, 'Harlequin Jim Crow', 689–96.
84. *Illustrated London News,* 27 July 1889, 120.

CHAPTER FIVE

1. H. B. Stowe, *Uncle Tom's Cabin, or Life Among the Lowly* (author's edn, 1852), 232; see also 242–3, 249–51.
2. Richard Oastler, *Slavery in Yorkshire. Monstrous Barbarity!!!* (1835); *Yorkshire Slavery. The 'Devil-to-Do' Amongst the Dissenters in Huddersfield. A Letter to Edward Baines, M.P.* (1835); Cecil Driver, *Tory Radical. The Life of Richard Oastler* (1946), 19–20; see also D. B. Davis, *The Problem of Slavery in the Age of Revolution, 1770–1823* (Ithaca, N.Y., 1975), 453–68.
3. Lord Carlisle to H. B. Stowe, 8 July 1852, in *Autographs for Freedom,* by H. B. Stowe and 39 eminent writers (1853), 39.
4. Nassau Senior, *American Slavery: Reprint of article on 'Uncle Tom's Cabin',* ... *published in the 'Edinburgh Review'* (1862), 39.
5. Frank J. Klingsberg, 'Harriet Beecher Stowe and social reform in England', *American Historical Rev.,* xlviii (Apr. 1938), 542–52.

6. Klingberg, *op. cit.*, 548; A. H. Abel and F. J. Klingberg, *A Side-Light on Anglo-American Relations* (1927), 319–24.

7. *The Times*, 18 May 1853, 6b; H. B. Stowe, *Sunny Memories of Foreign Lands* (1854), 169–70.

8. For example, Warren Asham, *The Mud Cabin; or, the Character and Tendency of British Institutions* (New York, 1853); J. Thornton Randolph, *The Cabin and the Parlour; or, Slaves and Masters* (1852); W. L. G. Smith, *Uncle Tom's Cabin as it is; or, Life at the South* (1952); for more recent comparisons of standard of life of slave and free labour see R. W. Fogel and S. L. Engerman, *Time on the Cross: The Economics of American Negro Slavery* (Boston, 1974), 109–26; E. D. Genovese, *Roll, Jordan, Roll: The World the Slaves Made* (New York, 1974), 56–64, 503–4.

9. *Reynolds's Newspaper*, 10 Apr. 1853, 8c. In 1870, *Reynolds's* had a circulation of 200,000.

10. George W. M. Reynolds, 'Black slavery abroad and white slavery at home', *Reynolds's Newspaper*, 15 May 1853, 1a.

11. *Ibid.*

12. *Ibid.*, 19 Dec 1852, 7c; 20 Feb. 1853, 9a–b; 1 May 1853, 8b–c; 12 Dec. 1852, 16d; 24 Apr. 1853, 2b–d; 20 Feb. 1853, 2a–b; 25 Dec. 1859, 7a.

13. *Northern Ensign and Weekly Gazette for the Counties of Caithness, Ross, Sutherland, Orkney, and Zetland*, 25 Sept. 2, 9, 16 Oct., 1853); *Reynolds's Newspaper*, 1 May 1853, 8b–c; 19 Dec. 1852, 7c; 16 Jan. 1853, 7b–c.

14. *Leader*, 18 Sept. 1852, 900; 13 Nov. 1852, 1090–1; 18 Jan. 1853, 39–40.

15. *Star of Freedom*, 24 Sept. 1852, 105.

16. 'The Stafford House Address', *Anti-Slavery Reporter*, 3rd ser., 1 (Feb. 1853), 38; H. R. Temperley, *British Antislavery, 1833–1870* (1972), 70–3.

17. *Reynolds's Newspaper*, 15 May 1853, 1a; *Christian Times*, 21 Jan. 1853, 40; 28 Jan. 1853, 58.

18. *Q. Rev.* CI (Jan.–Apr. 1857), 324.

19. 'American slavery and European revolutions', *Englishman's Mag.*, 1 (Sept. 1852), 125–8.

20. E. E., 'A few words about *Uncle Tom's Cabin*', *British Mother's Mag.*, IX (1 Apr. 1853), 79.

21. *Ibid.*, 80.

22. *Ibid.*, 80–1.

23. *Uncle Tom's Cabin in England: or, a Proof that Black's White* (1852), 206.

24. 'The Stafford House Address', *Anti-Slavery Reporter*, 3rd ser., 1 (Feb. 1853), 37–8; for similar arguments see *English Rev.*, XVIII (Oct. 1852), 114–15; *Morning Advertiser*, 14 Jan. 1853, 4a–b; *Christian Times*, 29 Oct. 1852, 696; *Eclectic Rev.*, n.s., IV (Dec. 1852), 739.

25. *Anti-Slavery Reporter*, 3rd ser., 1 (Feb. 1953), 37.

26. For example, *Empire*, 26 May 1855, 413–14; *Anti-Slavery Advocate*, II (Jan. 1859), 194; J. B. Estlin to L. A. Chamerovzow, 21 May 1851, ASP C156/37; see also Howard Temperley, *British Antislavery, 1833–1870* (1972), 74–5.

240

240

27. George Thompson, *American Slavery* (1853), 17, see also 14–17.
28. Mrs M. W. Chapman to Mrs Wigham, 11 Feb. 1859, Estlin Papers, 24.122.26.
29. *Anti-Slavery Reporter*, 3rd ser., x (1862), 114–15.
30. *Anti-Slavery Reporter*, 3rd ser., xiii (1865), 197–8.
31. Sarah Pugh to Mary Estlin, 31 Jan. 1869, Estlin Papers, 24.121.76 fos. 131–2; Millicent Fawcett, 'The medical and general education of women', *Fortnightly Rev.*, n.s., iv (Nov. 1868), 555; J. S. Mill, *The Subjection of Women* (2nd edn, 1869), 16–18.
32. D. B. Davis, *The Problem of Slavery in Western Culture* (Ithaca, N.Y., 1966), 292–4, 363–4; Temperley, *op. cit.*, 75–6.
33. *The Colonial Intelligencer: or Aborigines' Friend*, i (Dec. 1847), 170–1; ii (Sept.–Oct. 1848), 67–70; ii (Nov.–Dec. 1848), 99–103; ii (Jan.–Feb. 1849), 131–3; and *Aborigines' Friend, or Colonial Intelligencer*, n.s., i (Jan.–Mar. 1856), 63–5.
34. For example, J. F. Ade Ajayi, *Christian Missions in Nigeria 1841–91: The Making of a New Elite* (1965), 14–19.
35. *Saturday Rev.*, xvii (16 Jan. 1864), 72a. I have been unable to trace the author. It is not Lord Robert Cecil (J. F. A. Mason, 'The Third Marquis of Salisbury and the *Saturday Review*', *Bulletin of the Institute of Historical Research*, xxxiv (1961), 41–54). M. Bevington, *Saturday Review, 1855–1868* (New York, 1966), cites the article (p. 59), but does not identify the author. Among Bevington's list of contributors two who wrote on American politics and slavery and who had a similar viewpoint are Sir Henry Maine, a distinguished jurist and author, and George S. Venables, a friend of Carlyle and prominent leader writer.
36. *Ibid.*, 72b.
37. A. Ellegard, *The Readership of the Periodical Press in mid-Victorian Britain* (Gotenborg, 1957), 24.
38. On comparison of factory and slave labour see Genovese, *op. cit.*, 290–2.
39. For example, see Frederick Engels, *The Condition of the Working Class in England* (Panther edn, 1969), 154.
40. G. Kitson Clark, *The Making of Victorian England* (1965), 113, 115–18; comparison of depressed state of agricultural labourers and condition of Negro slaves in E. J. Hobsbawm and G. Rudé, *Captain Swing* (1973), 241, also 18–33.
41. W. Ferguson to the editor, *Patriot*, 4 Apr. 1853, 214d–e.
42. Charles Kingsley, *Alton Locke* (Everyman edn, 1970), 251–2.
43. Anthony Trollope, *North America*, ii (1862), 117.
44. Cobden to Bright, 31 Dec. 1863, Bright Papers, BL Add.MS. 43, 652 f. 136.
45. *Spectator*, 30 Sept. 1869, 1423a.
46. *Empire*, 30 Sept. 1854, 759.
47. F. M. L. Thompson, *English Landed Society in the Nineteenth Century* (1963), 184–6, discusses rural deferential attitudes.
48. On domestic servants, see Dorothy Marshall, *The English Domestic Servant in History* (1948); Pamela Horn, *The Rise and Fall of the Victorian Servant* (1975); J. A. Banks, *Prosperity and Parenthood: a study of family planning among the Victorian middle classes* (1954);

John Burnett, *Useful Toil: Autobiographies of Working People from the 1820s to the 1920s* (1974), 135–74; W. L. Burn, *The Age of Equipoise* (1968), 269–70.

49. For discussion of relations in the 'Big House' see Genovese, *op. cit.*, 328–65.
50. H. Taine, *Notes on England* (1872), 49; Burnett, *op. cit.*, 148–9.
51. Genovese, *op. cit.*, 332–40; Marshall, *op. cit.*, 10–16; Burnett, *op. cit.*, 164–74.
52. Burnett, *op. cit.*, 174.
53. Mrs J. Bakewell, *Friendly Hints to Female Servants* (1841), 44–6; Horn, *op. cit.*, 133–8; Steven Marcus, *The Other Victorians. A Study of Sexuality and Pornography in Mid-Nineteenth-Century England* (1966), 128–60.
54. Horn, *op. cit.*, 111–13.
55. J. H. Friswell, *The Gentle Life. Essays in Aid of the Formation of Character* (5th edn, 1865), 15–21.
56. *Ibid.*, 174 and 166.
57. *Saturday Rev.*, IX (18 Feb. 1860), 205–6.
58. *Church Missionary Juvenile Instructor*, n.s., IX (1860), 63.
59. Burnett, *op. cit.*, 165 and 164–74; Marshall, *op. cit.*, 28.
60. Hobsbawm and Rudé, *op. cit.*, 18–33.
61. 'One of the Niggers' to the editor, *African Times*, V (23 Jan. 1865), 72. [The writer could be Dr James Africanus Horton.] See also Chapter 3 above.
62. *Ibid.*

CHAPTER SIX

1. Geoffrey Best, *Mid-Victorian Britain, 1851–1875* (1971), 228–33; W. L. Burn, *The Age of Equipoise* (1968), 15–16.
2. R. C. K. Ensor, *England, 1870–1914* (1936), 136.
3. Best, *op. cit.*, 283; S. G. Checkland, *The Rise of Industrial Society in England, 1815–1885* (1964), 44–6; Harold Perkin, *The Origins of Modern English Society, 1780–1880* (1969), 442–4.
4. Cobden to William Hargreaves, 10 Apr. 1863, BL Add.MS.43,655 f. 320; Best, *op. cit.*, 238–42.
5. Best, *op. cit.*, 284–6.
6. *Ibid.*, 233–8; also Checkland, *op. cit.*, 284–5; Asa Briggs, 'The language of "class" in early nineteenth-century England', *Essays in Labour History*, ed. A. Briggs and J. Saville (1967), 69–73; T. R. Tholfsen, 'The intellectual origins of mid-Victorian stability', *Political Science Q.*, LXXXVI (1971), 61–7.
7. Best, *op. cit.*, 92–9, 122–4, 230, 266–70; Perkin, *op. cit.*, 423; Checkland, *op. cit.*, 219–22, 229, 277–9.
8. Gareth Stedman Jones, *Outcast London: A Study of the Relationship Between Classes in Victorian Society* (1971), 1–16 and *passim*.
9. Checkland, *op. cit.*, 228–30, 237–8; Best, *op. cit.*, 256–63; David Lockwood, *The Blackcoated Worker. A Study in Class Consciousness* (1958), *passim.*; Tholfsen, *op. cit.*, 61–91.
10. Best, *op. cit.*, 81–90, 245–56; Checkland, *op. cit.*, 107–8, 114,

129–30, 296–301; Perkin, *op. cit.*, 428–53; Burn, *op. cit.*, 255–70; G. D. H. Cole, *Studies in Class Structure* (1955), 63–8; G. Kitson Clark, *An Expanding Society. Britain, 1830–1900* (1966), 31–6; W. J. Reader, *Professional Men. The Rise of the Professional Classes in Nineteenth-Century England* (1966), *passim*.

11. Checkland, *op. cit.*, 280–1.

12. Perkin, *op. cit.*, 410–28.

13. J. A. Banks, *Prosperity and Parenthood: a study of family planning among the Victorian middle classes* (1954), 48–112, 129–38, 173–94.

14. Best, *op. cit.*, 260; Reader, *op. cit.*, 185; F. Musgrove, 'Middle class education and employment in the nineteenth century', *Economic History Rev.*, 2nd ser., XII (1959), 99–111; H. J. Perkin, 'Middle class education and employment in the nineteenth century: a critical note', *ibid.*, XIV (1961), 122–30; F. Musgrove, 'Middle class education and employment in the nineteenth century: a rejoinder', *ibid.*, XIV (1961), 320–9.

15. Hannah Arendt, *The Origins of Totalitarianism* (1958), 180.

16. D. Newsome, *Godliness and Good Learning. Four Studies on a Victorian Ideal* (1961), *passim*; Kitson Clark, *op. cit.*, 32–5; and *The Making of Victorian England* (1965), 267–74; Reader, *op. cit.*, 203–5; Best, *op. cit.*, 149–51, 164–6, 253–4; H.A.C. Cairns, *Prelude to Imperialism. British Reactions to Central African Society, 1840–1890* (1965) 92–3; Louis James, 'Tom Brown's imperialist sons', *Victorian Studies*, XVII (Sept. 1973), 89–99.

17. *OED;* Thomas Carlyle, 'Occasional discourse on the Nigger Question', *Fraser's Mag.*, XL (July–Dec. 1849), 671.

18. Newsome, *op. cit.*, *passim*.

19. Howard Temperley, *British Antislavery, 1833–1870* (1972), 68–70, 73; David Owen, *English Philanthropy, 1660–1960*, (Harvard, 1965), 3–5; for general discussion of Victorian philanthropy see Brian Harrison, 'Philanthropy and the Victorians', *Victorian Studies*, IX (1966), 353–74.

20. For activities of women see correspondence of Sarah Alexander, ASP C114/1–161; also K. Heasman, *Evangelicals in Action* (1962), 23; G. C. Findlay and W. W. Holdsworth, *The History of the Wesleyan Methodist Missionary Society* (1921–4), III, 15–41.

21. The most thorough study of mid-Victorian anti-slavery is Temperley, *op. cit.*, see especially 72–84, 212–15, 237–9, 271–2; see also the *Anti-Slavery Reporter*, 3rd ser., I (1853), 115–16, 163–5, 188–9, 212; *Morning Advertiser* 31 July 1851, 3b–c; Minute Book of the Bristol and Clifton Ladies' Anti-Slavery Society, 11 Feb. [1854], Estlin Papers, 24.120; William Smeal to L. A. Chamerovzow, 16 Apr. 1853, ASP C36/52; *Anti-Slavery Reporter*, 3rd ser., III (1854), 156–7.

22. *Morning Advertiser*, 31 July 1851, 3b–c; Temperley, *op. cit.*, 68–74.

23. *DNB;* Temperley, *op. cit.*, 72–5, 212–13, 237–9; William James, *Memoir of John Bishop Estlin* (1855); *Anti-Slavery Reporter*, 3rd ser., III (1855), 156–7; *Annual Register* (1878), iii, 175–6; *Empire*, ed. George Thompson, 2 Dec. 1854, 4a–b; Sir James Picton, *Memorials of Liverpool* (1873), I, 520; C. Duncan Rice, 'The anti-slavery mission of George Thompson to the United States, 1834–5', *J. American Studies* II (Apr. 1968), 13–41.

24. 'Constitution of the British and Foreign Anti-Slavery Society',
Anti-Slavery Reporter, 3rd ser., I (1853), frontispiece; Temperley,
op. cit., 62–8.
25. Margaret Howith (ed.), *Mary Howith, An Autobiography* (1889), I,
291–2; Temperley, *op. cit.*, 85–92, 209–17.
26. 'Christian missions: their principle and practice', *Westminster Rev.*,
n.s., x (July–Oct. 1856), 48; Temperley, *op. cit.*, 56–61; Philip D.
Curtin, *The Image of Africa, British Ideas and Action, 1780–1850*
(1965), 298–310; J. Gallagher, 'Fowell Buxton and the new Africa
policy', *Cambridge Historical J.*, x (1950), 36–58.
27. Cobden to Sturge, 11 Mar. 1845, Cobden Papers, BL Add.MSS.
43,656 fos. 3–4, and *ibid.*, 13 Jan. 1845, fos. 9–10; Bright to Sturge,
I Sept. 1843, Sturge Papers, BL Add.MSS. 43,845 fos. 12–15;
Temperley, *op. cit.*, 137–67.
28. Cobden to Sturge, 18 Dec. 1850, Cobden Papers, BL Add.MSS.
43,656 fos. 170–1; and following letters of 31 Dec. 1850, *ibid.*,
fos. 174–6; 25 Jan. 1851, *ibid.*, f. 184; 4 July 1851, *ibid.*, fos. 207–8;
16 July 1851, *ibid.*, fos. 211–12; Cobden to Sturge, 25 July 1854,
Sturge Papers, BL Add.MSS. 43,722 fos. 28–30; Cobden to Sturge,
11 Oct. 1850, BL Add.MSS. 50,131 fos. 211–14; Report of the
presentation of memorial to Lord Palmerston opposing the slave
squadron, Minute Book III, Minute 165, 27 Oct. 1848, 165, ASP E2/8;
Minute Book II, Minute 933, 18 Sept. 1846, 442–3, ASP E2/7;
Minute Book III, Minute 354, 22 Feb. 1850, and Minute 370, 4 Apr.
1850, ASP E2/8; see also Temperley, *op. cit.*, 176–83; Curtin, *op. cit.*,
iv, 315–17; 444–8; G. R. Mellor, *British Imperial Trusteeship,
1783–1850* (1951), 27–8.
29. 'Twenty-second annual report of the British and Foreign Anti-Slavery
Society', 20 May 1861, 21, at back of *Anti-Slavery Reporter*, 3rd ser.,
IX (1861); Temperley, *op. cit.*, 228–31.
30. Minute Book IV, Minute 323, 17 Feb. 1862, ASP E2/9.
31. Christine Bolt, *The Anti-Slavery Movement and Reconstruction: A
Study in Anglo-American Co-operation, 1833–1877* (1969), 54–113;
Temperley, *op. cit.*, 258–61.
32. Eugene Stock, *The History of the Church Missionary Society*, II
(1899), 17–19, 26–9.
33. Owen Chadwick, *The Victorian Church, Part I* (1966), 447–52;
J. Edwin Orr, *The Second Evangelical Awakening* (1949), *passim*.
34. Chadwick, *op. cit.*, 384–6; Findlay and Holdsworth, *The History of
the Wesleyan Methodist Society*, I, 191, II, 360.
35. Chadwick, *op. cit.*, 441–5.
36. R. Lovett, *The History of the London Missionary Society, 1795–1895*,
(1899), II, 689–707, 752; Findlay and Holdsworth, *op. cit.*, I, 128–33,
191–4 (the Wesleyans' missionary support declined from 1871–1894);
Stock, *op. cit.*, II, 325–54, 387; Baptist Missionary Society, *Annual
Reports*, 1861–1866.
37. Quoted in Stock, *op. cit.*, II, 392.
38. *Ibid.*, 30–4, 336–8.
39. Briggs, *op. cit.*, 69–73; Perkin, *op. cit.*, 445–6; Stedman Jones, *op. cit.*,
I–16, 241–61, 268–70.
40. Charles Loch Mowat, *The Charity Organization Society, 1869–1913*.

Its Ideas and Works (1961), 1–18; Best, *op. cit.*, 137–8; Owen, *English Philanthropy*, 215–46; Stedman Jones, *op. cit.*, 241–61.

41. B. Disraeli, *Lord George Bentinck, a Political Biography* (1852), 324.
42. 'Christian missions: their principle and practice', *Westminster Rev.*, n.s., x (July–Oct. 1856), 47.
43. Minute Book of the Bristol and Clifton Ladies' Auxiliary Anti-Slavery Society, Minutes for 13 Nov. 1851, and 11 Feb. [1854?], Estlin Papers, 24.120; J. B. Estlin to L. A. Chamerovzow, 21 May 1855, ASP C/57/37; *Anti-Slavery Advocate*, Jan. 1855, 225–6; Feb. 1855, 238–40; 2 July 1855, 282; 1 July 1856, 379–80; *Morning Advertiser*, 19 Jan 1851, 4b–c; 19 Feb. 1851, 3c–e; 22 July 1851, 4e–f; 24 July 1851, 6a–b; 25 July 1851, 4b–d; 28 July 1851, 4b–d; 31 July 1851, 3b–c; 5 Nov. 1851, 2a–b; 11 Jan 1853, 2c–d; *Bristol Examiner and Bath Record*, 30 Aug. 1851, 5c–e; Temperley, *op. cit.*, 209–20, 241–7.
44. *Statesman*, 11 Dec. 1851, 853–4.
45. L. A. Chamerovzow to Brougham, 5 Oct. 1861, Brougham Papers; also *Anti-Slavery Advocate*, Feb. 1853, 34; *Anti-Slavery Reporter*, 3rd ser., vi (1858), 76.
46. For example, *Sunday Times*, 22 May 1853, 2d.
47. C. E. Stowe to L. A. Chamerovzow, 28 Nov. 1853, ASP C36/123; *Sunday Times*, 22 May 1853, 2d; *Anti-Slavery Advocate*, June 1853, 68; *Anti-Slavery Reporter*, 3rd ser., 1 (Oct. 1853), 227.
48. For example, *The Times*, 30 Jan. 1857, 6c–d.
49. *Anti-Slavery Advocate*, 11 Jan. 1859, 193–4, and Feb. 1853, 36, 1 Sept. 1856, 389–90; see also *Manchester Examiner and Times*, 9 Aug. 1856, supplement.
50. Kenneth Fielden, 'Samuel Smiles and self-help', *Victorian Studies*, xii (Dec. 1968), 170–6.
51. For economic and social changes in Jamaica, 1838–65, I have relied on Douglas Hall, *Free Jamaica, 1838–1865. An Economic History* (New Haven, 1959), and Philip D. Curtin, *Two Jamaicas. The Role of Ideas in a Tropical Colony, 1830–1865* (1955).
52. *John Bull and Britannia*, 24 Dec. 1859, 825a.
53. *The Times*, 19 Dec. 1857, 8c–d; and 29 Dec. 1857, 6e–f; *Anti-Slavery Reporter*, 3rd ser., vi (1858), 9.
54. Gov. G. D'Arcy to Newcastle, Bathurst, Gambia, 25 Sept 1863, in *PP.* 1864, lx, Reports for 1863 on the State of H.M. Colonial Possessions, Part II, The African Settlements and St Helena, 29.
55. Gov. G. J. Bayley to Newcastle, No. 3, Nassau, 30 Aug. 1862, in *P.P.* 1863 xxxix, Reports on the State of H.M.Col. Possessions, Pt I, West Indies and Mauritius, 9; similarly Lt. Gov. A. Musgrove to Gov. J. Walker, St Vincent, 7 July 1862, in *P.P.* 1862, xl 61–2; and Swinburne Ward to Sir Henry Barkly, Gov. of Mauritius, Seychelles, 16 Feb. 1864, in *P.P.* 1865, xxxvii, 126.
56. *Parl. Deb.*, 3rd ser., clxxvii (21 Feb. 1865), 550–1.
57. Somerset to Russell, private, 20 June 1862, Russell Papers, P.R.O. 30/22/24.
58. W. L. Burn, *The Age of Equipoise*, 69–71.
59. *Juvenile Missionary Mag.*, xvi (1 Apr. 1859), 85.
60. *Wesleyan Methodist Mag.*, 5th ser., lxxxix, pt II (Nov. 1866), 1010; cf. *Anti-Slavery Reporter*, 3rd ser., ii (1854), 52–4.

61. As well as Curtin, *Two Jamaicas*, and Hall, *Free Jamaica*, a lengthy and informative letter from H. H. Garnett, a black American clergyman resident in Jamaica, to L. A. Chamerovzow, 2 Oct. 1854, ASP C31/65.

62. *Anti-Slavery Reporter*, n.s., IV (Apr. 1851), 60–2; 3rd ser., II (1854), 38–40; also *Melioria*, I (Oct. 1858), 261–76; III (1861), 105–15.

63. [W. E. Forster], 'British philanthropy and Jamaican distress', *Westminster Rev.*, n.s., III (Apr. 1853), 348–9, 355–6.

64. *Anti-Slavery Reporter*, n.s., V (Nov. 1850), 174, and 3rd ser., XIII (Sept. 1865), 221–2; [W. E. Forster], *op. cit.*, 359–60; P.R.O., F.O.5/934, Case of Free Negro Emigration, 1862–5; Sir F. Bruce to Earl of Clarendon, no. 209, 25 June 1866, F.O.5/1065.

65. National Association for the Promotion of Social Science, *Transactions* (1858), 699–701; (1859), 703–5; *Anti-Slavery Reporter*, 3rd ser., V (1857), 102–3; Temperley, *op. cit.*, 113–16, 120–37; John Stuart Mill, *Principles of Political Economy* (1848), I, 297.

66. [W. E. Forster], *op. cit.*, 356.

67. *DNB*; 'Memoir of W. Forster', *Anti-Slavery Reporter*, 3rd ser., II (1854), 84–5, 97; T. Wemyss Reid, *Life of Right Honourable William Edward Forster* (1888), I, 293; O. Chadwick, *The Victorian Church, Part I* (1966), 429–35.

68. The Committee of the British and Foreign Anti-Slavery Society Address to the Black and Coloured Population of Jamaica, 15 Aug. 1866, in *Anti-Slavery Reporter*, 3rd ser., XIV (1866), 226–7.

69. Enclosure in L. A. Chamerovzow to Chesson, 15 July 1868, ASP C137/152.

70. See especially Jones, *op. cit.*, 1–16, 241–315; Owen *op. cit.*, 134–62, 215–46; Mowat, *op. cit.*, 1–18.

71. Owen, *op. cit.*, 167–9, 213–18; Helen M. Lynd, *England in the Eighteen Eighties* (1945), 85–98; Jones, *op. cit.*, 127–51, 286–7, 308–12, 328–9.

72. *Ibid.*, 268–70.

73. Carlyle, 'Occasional discourse on the Nigger Question', *op. cit.*, and 'Shooting Niagara and after?', *Macmillan's Mag.*, XVI (Aug. 1867); Moncure D. Conway, *Autobiography. Memories and Experiences* (1904), I, 357; Eric Williams, *British Historians and the West Indies* (1966), 59–75.

CHAPTER SEVEN

1. Frank H. Hankins, *The Racial Basis of Civilization* (New York, 1926); Jacques Barzun, *Race: a Study in Superstition* (rev. edn, New York, 1965); A. C. Haddon and A. H. Quiggin, *History of Anthropology* (1910); R. H. Lowie, *The History of Ethnological Theory* (1937); T. K. Penniman, *A Hundred Years of Anthropology* (3rd rev. edn, 1965); M. T. Hodgen, *Early Anthropology in the 16th and 17th Centuries* (Philadelphia, 1964); G. M. Stocking, *Race, Culture, and Evolution: Essays in the History of Anthropology* (New York, 1968); E. W. Count, 'The evolution of the race idea in modern western culture during the period of the pre-Darwinian nineteenth century',

Trans. New York Academy of Sciences, 2nd ser., VIII (1946), 137–65; Louis L. Snyder, *Race. A History of Modern Ethnic Theories* (New York, 1939); Thomas F. Gossett, *Race. The History of an Idea in America* (Dallas, 1963); William Stanton, *The Leopard's Spots: Scientific Attitudes toward Race in America, 1815–1859* (Chicago, 1960); Herbert H. Odom, 'Generalizations on race in nineteenth-century physical anthropology', *Isis*, LVIII (Spring 1967), 5–18; Philip D. Curtin, *The Image of Africa British Ideas and Action, 1780–1850* (1965); Christine Bolt, *Victorian Attitudes to Race* (1971), 1–28; M. Banton, 'The concept of racism', in *Race and Racialism*, ed. S. Zubaida, (1970), 17–34; Leon Poliakov, *The Aryan Myth: a History of Racist and Nationalist Ideas in Europe* (1974).

2. Penniman, *op. cit.*, 47–8; Count, *op. cit.*, 158–9. Odom, *op. cit.*, 6–13; B. Willey, 'Darwin's place in the history of thought', in *Darwinism and the Study of Society*, ed. M. Banton (1961), 8–10.

3. *DNB;* Thomas Bendyshe (ed. and trans.), *The Anthropological Treatises of Johan Friedrich Blumenbach, with memoirs of him by K. Marx and M. Flourens; and the Inaugural Dissertation of John Hunter, M.D., on the varieties of Man*, pub. for the Anthropological Society of London (1865).

4. *Ibid.*, 363.

5. *Ibid.*, 369–77.

6. Blumenbach, ed. Bendyshe, *op. cit.*, 264–76, 297–8; also Hunter, *op. cit.*, 363, 393–4.

7. Henry Home, Lord Kames, *Sketches on the History of Man*, (1774), I, 11–15, 32; Charles White, *An Account of the Regular Gradations in Man, and in different Animals and Vegetables* (1799), 61–2, 83–5, 124–9, 136–7; *DNB*; see also Curtin, *op. cit.*, 43–6; Gossett, *op. cit.*, 45–51; Penniman, *op. cit.*, 46; Stanton, *op. cit.*, 15–17.

8. Edward Long, *The History of Jamaica* (1774), II, 335–7, 371, 374–5, 383; Curtin, *op. cit.*, 43–5.

9. Blumenbach, ed. Bendyshe *op. cit.*, 249–50.

10. *Ibid.*, 141; also reports of tailed men, 258–9, and of Wild Peter, the supposed natural man, 329–39.

11. W. D. Jordan, *White over Black, American Attitudes toward the Negro, 1550–1812* (Chapel Hill, N.C., 1968) 238–9.

12. David Hume, 'Essay XXI: of national characters', *Essays Moral, Political, and Literary* (1963 edn), 202–20, especially 202, 213, 218; Edward Gibbon, *The History of the Decline and Fall of the Roman Empire*, ed. J. B. Bury (1909), III, 53–5.

13. Jordan, *op. cit.*, 216–28, 509–11; Odom, *op. cit.*, *Isis*, LVIII (1967), 6–7; A. O. Lovejoy, *The Great Chain of Being; A Study in the History of an Idea* (Cambridge, Mass., 1936), 227–41.

14. Curtin, *op. cit.*, *passim*.

15. Sir William Lawrence, *Lectures on Physiology, Zoology, and the Natural History of Man* (1819), 363, 446, 548; *DNB*.

16. James Cowles Prichard, *Researches into the Physical History of Man* (1813), 230–9; 2nd ed, (1826), II, 548–9, 581–2; Thomas Hodgkin, 'Obituary of Dr Pritchard', *JESL*, II, (1850), 182–207; *DNB*; Gossett, *op. cit.*, 54–5; Penniman, *op. cit.*, 61–4.

17. Regulations of the Society, *JESL*, I (1848), 3. Richard King, 'Address

to the Ethnological Society of London delivered at the anniversary
meeting, 25 May 1844', *ibid.*, II (1850), 14–16.

18. Thomas Hodgkin to Lord Brougham, 11 Mar. 1843, Brougham Papers;
G. B. Greenough, MS. account of first anniversary meeting of the
Ethnological Society of London, 29 May 1844, pasted in back of
JESL, I (1848), Archives of the Royal Anthropological Institute; E.
Dieffenbach, 'The study of ethnology', *ibid.*, I (1848), 16–17.

19. Thomas Arnold, *An Inaugural Lecture on the Study of Modern
History* (1841), 27–41; Curtin, *op. cit.*, 375–7, Reginald Horsman,
'Origins of racial Anglo-Saxonism in Great Britain before 1850', *J.
History of Ideas*, XXXVII (1976), 381–410.

20. B. Disraeli, *Lord George Bentinck: A Political Biography* (1852),
496–8; E. Bulwer Lytton, 'Speech at Leeds Mechanics Institution,
Jan. 25, 1854', *Speeches of Edward Lord Lytton* (1874), I, 172–89;
George Cornewall Lewis, *A Treatise on the Methods of Observation
and Reasoning in Politics* (1852), I, 140; II, 432–5; see also L. P.
Curtis jr, *Anglo-Saxons and Celts; A Study of Anti-Irish Prejudice
in Victorian England* (Bridgeport, Conn., 1968), 42–3, 74–89.

21. J. C. Prichard, 'Abstract of a comparative review of philological and
physical researches as applied to the history of the human species',
Report of the British Association (1831–2), 543–4; 'On the relations
of ethnology to other branches of knowledge', *JESL*, I (1848), 301–29;
'On the various methods of research which contribute to the
advancement of ethnology, and relations of that science to other
branches of knowledge', *British Association Reports* (1847), 230–53;
R. G. Latham, 'On the present state of philological evidence as to the
unity of the human race', *Report of the British Association* (1845), 78;
see also Joan Leopold, 'British applications of the Aryan theory of race
to India, 1850–1870', *English Historical Rev.*, LXXXIX (July 1974),
578–603; Poliakov, *op. cit.*, 209–14.

22. Thomas Hodgkin, 'The progress of ethnology', *JESL*, I (1848), 28;
Richard Cull, 'Remarks on the nature, objects, and evidences of
ethnological science', *ibid.*, III (1854); J. C. Prichard, 'On the relation
of ethnology to other branches of knowledge', *ibid.*, I (1848), 329;
Curtin, *op. cit.*, 363–5.

23. J. C. Prichard, 'Abstract of a comparative review of philological and
physical researches', *Report of the British Association* (1831–2), 544.

24. Curtin, *op. cit.*, 386–7; Stanton, *op. cit.*, 51–2; J. B. Davis, 'On the
forms of crania of Ancient Britons', *Report of British Association*
(1854), 127–8.

25. Minutes of the Ethnological Society of London Council, 17 May
1849, 27 May 1853, 28 May 1856, Archives of the Royal
Anthropological Institute.

26. Blumenbach, ed. Bendyshe *op. cit.*, 237–43; Prichard, *Researches into
the Physical History of Man* (2nd edn, 1826), I, 160–2, 166–72, and
The Natural History of Man, ed. Edwin Norris, (4th edn, 1855), I,
113–14; Robert Dunn, 'Some observations on the various forms of the
human cranium, considered in relation to outward circumstances,
social state, and intellectual condition of man', *JESL*, IV (1856), 36,
49; Richard Cull, 'Remarks on three Naloo Negro skulls', *ibid.*, II
(1850), 241; Gossett, *op. cit.*, 69–70; 75–6; Stanton, *op. cit.*, 25;

Penniman, *op. cit.*, 61; Curtin, *op. cit.*, 232–5, David de Giustino, *Conquest of Mind: Phrenology and Victorian Social Thought* (1975), *passim*.

27. Richard Owen, 'Observations on three skulls of Naloo Africans', *JESL*, II (1850), 236–7.

28. Richard Owen, 'Report on a series of skulls of various tribes of mankind inhabiting Nepal', *Report of British Association* (1859), 101–2.

29. Robert Knox, *The Races of Man: A Philosophical Enquiry into the Influence of Race over the Destinies of Nations* (2nd edn, with supp. chs., 1862), preface to 1st edn (1850), v, and 89–90, 106–20, 503, 588–600; Curtin, *op. cit.*, 368–9; Sir A. Keith, 'Presidential address'. *J. Royal Anthropological Institute*, XLVII (1917), 16; Knox, 'Ethnological inquiries and observations', *AR*, I, (1863), 246–7.

30. C. Carter Blake, 'Review of Henry Lonsdale's *The Life of Robert Knox, the Anatomist*', *J. Anthropology* (1870), 334; Henry Lonsdale, *Sketch of the Life and Writings of Robert Knox* (1870); Curtin, *op. cit.*, 377–81; Knox, *The Races of Man*, 565; M. D. Biddiss, 'The politics of anatomy: Dr. Robert Knox and Victorian Racism', *Procs. Royal Society of Medicine*, LXIX (1976), 245–50.

31. *DNB*; Minutes of the Ethnological Society of London Council, 15 Mar. 1860; 24 May, 1860; Sir A. Keith, 'How can the Institute best serve the needs of Anthropology?', *J. Royal Anthropological Institute*, XLVII (1917), 16–18; Membership list in *TESL*, n.s., II (1861–2), 1–10; *Spectator*, 7 Dec. 1861, 1338a–1339b.

32. For various interpretations of the reasons for the formation of the Anthropological Society of London see Keith, *op. cit.*, 19–22; John L. Myers, 'The influence of anthropology on political science', *University of California Publications in History*, IV (1916), 74; Michael Banton, 'Race as a social category', *Race*, VIII (1966), 6; J. W. Burrow, 'Evolution and anthropology in the 1860's: The Anthropological Society of London, 1863–71', *Victorian Studies*, VII (1963), 137–54, and *Evolution and Society: A Study in Victorian Social Theory* (1966), 118–35; George M. Stocking, 'What's in a name? The origins of the Royal Anthropological Institute (1837–71)', *Man*, n.s., VI (1971), 369–90.

33. John Beddoe, *Memories of Eighty Years* (1910), 211; *DNB*; [James Hunt], 'On the origin of the *Anthropological Review* and its connection with the Anthropological Society', *AR*, VI (1868), 431–42; E. Dally, 'Écologe de James Hunt', *Mémoires de la Société d'Anthropologie de Paris*, 2nd ser., I (1873), xxvi–xxxvi; J. Beddoe, 'President's Annual Address: Remarks on Dr. James Hunt', *JASL*, VII (1870), lxxviii–lxxxxiii.

34. [James Hunt], 'On the origin of the Anthropological Review and its connection with the Anthropological Society', *AR*, VI (1868), 432–3.

35. Hunt in his dedication to Paul Broca, translator of Carl Vogt, *Lectures on Man: his Place in Creation, and in the History of the Earth* (1864), viii.

36. James Hunt, 'On ethnoclimatology; or, the acclimatization of man', *Report of the British Association* (1861), 147, and 129–50; *TESL*, n.s., II (1861–2), 50–79.

37. Council Minutes of the *Anthropological Society of London*, 1 Dec. 1863, p. 39, Archives of Royal Anthropological Institute.

38. James Hunt, 'On the Negro's place in nature', *Memoirs of the Anthropological Society of London*, 1 (1863–4), 51–2; see also *JASL*, II (1864), xv–lvi, for discussion of the paper; and Hunt's 'On the physical and mental characters of the Negro', abstracted in *AR*, 1 (1863), 386–91.

39. Paul Broca, *On the Phenomena of Hybridity in the Genus Homo*, ed. and trans. C. Carter Blake (1864), 15, and translator's preface.

40. Broca, *op. cit.*, 28–9, 160.

41. *Ibid.*, 1; Georges Pouchet, *The Plurality of the Human Race*, ed. and trans. H. J. C. Beavan (1864), 100, 105–6.

42. Rev. F. W. Farrar, 'Fixity of type', *TESL*, n.s., III (1863–4), 394; see also *AR*, II (1864), 302.

43. R. B. N. Walker, 'On the alleged sterility of the union of women of savage races with native males after having children by a white man', *Memoirs of the Anthropological Society of London*, II (1865–6), 283–7; John Crawfurd, 'On the supposed infertility of human hybrids and crosses', *TESL*, n.s., III (1863–4), 356–62; and discussion of Crawfurd's paper at the British Association, 'On the commixture of races of man as affecting the progress of civilization', *AR*, 1 (1863), 405–10; John Lubbock, *The Origin of Civilization and the Primitive Condition of Man* (1870), 354; on Hunt's wilful ignorance see Spencer St John to A. R. Wallace, Port au Prince, 9 May 1864, Wallace Papers, BL Add.MSS.46,435 fos. 11–12 (unbound). In defence of the infertility of racial crosses: discussion of W. Bollaret, 'Population of the New World', *AR*, 1 (1863), iii–viii, 410; Hunt's review of the pamphlet, by an 'American white man' (D. G. Croly, C. Wakeman, and E. C. Haswell), *Miscegenation, the theory of the blending of the races, applied to the American white man and the negro* (New York, 1864) in *AR*, II (1864), 116–21; [Hunt], 'Knox and the Saxon Race', *AR*, VI (1868), 263; John Bowden, 'The history of ancient slavery', *Memoirs of the Anthropological Society of London*, II (1865–6), 401.

44. J. A. B. Horton, *West African Countries and Peoples* (1868), 37, and 35–6, 43; see also letter to the editor of the *African Times*, V (Apr. 23, 1866), 113–14.

45. T. H. Huxley, 'Structure and classification of mammalia', quoted in the *Reader*, III (27 Feb. 1864), 267–8.

46. T. H. Huxley, 'Emancipation – Black and White', *Reader*, V (20 May 1865), 561.

47. Wallace's comments on the paper of Henry F. Guppy, 'Notes on the capabilities of the Negro for civilization', *JASL*, II (1864), ccxiii.

48. 'Anthropology at the British Association', *AR*, 1 (1863), 388; discussion of 'On the Negro's place in nature', *JASL*, II (1864), xviii–xxii, xlvi–xlviii; James Hunt on Congo type, *ibid.*, lvi.

49. James Hunt, 'On physio-anthropology, its aim and method', *JASL*, V (1868), ccxxxix–ccxl; report of Hunt's paper 'On anthropological classification' at the British Association, *AR*, 1 (1863), 382–3; Vogt, *op. cit.*, 81, 177–80.

50. Theodore Waitz, *Introduction to Anthropology*, ed. and trans. J. F. Collingwood (1863), 53, 90, 143, 190, 213, 229–30, 266–7, 327–8,

380, extensively reviewed schemes of racial classification and found them all wanting; Charles Darwin, *The Descent of Man and Selection in Relation to Sex* (1871), I, 226, cited Waitz with favour on this subject.

51. John Crawfurd, 'Of the effects of commixture, locality, climate, and food on the races of man', *TESL*, n.s., I (1861), 76–92; 'On the Aryan or Indo-Germanic theory', *ibid.*, 268–86; 'On the connection between ethnology and physical geography', *ibid.*, n.s., II (1862–3), 4–19; 'On the early migrations of man', *ibid.*, n.s., III (1863–4), 335–50; 'On the supposed infecundity of human hybrids or crosses', *ibid.*, 352–62; 'On the physical and mental characteristics of the Negro', *ibid.*, n.s., IV (1864–5), 212–39; 'On the plurality of the races of man', *ibid.*, n.s., VI (1867), 49–58; 'On the classification of the races of man according to the form of the skull', *ibid.*, 144–9.

52. Burrow, *Evolution and Society*, ix–xiii, 118–35.

53. J. Lubbock, comments reported in *AR*, II (1864), 308.

54. J. Barzun, *op. cit.*, 47–8; Odom, *op. cit.*, *Isis*, LVIII (1967), 13; Burrow, *Evolution and Society*, 114–16.

55. C. Darwin to Wallace, 28 May [1864], Wallace Papers, BL Add.MSS. 46,434 fos. 39–42; Charles Lyell to Wallace, 22 May 1864, *ibid.*, 46, 435 f. 13; J. S. Hooker to Wallace [1864], *ibid.*, 46, 435 fos. 118–119.

56. Alfred Russel Wallace, 'The origin of the human race and the antiquity of man deduced from the theory of natural selection', *JASL*, II (1864), clvii–clxx; also 'Varieties of man in the Malay Archipelago', read at the British Association and reported *AR*, I (1863), 443–4; 'Letter to the editor of the *Anthropological Review*: natural selection applied to anthropology', *AR*, V (1865), 103–5.

57. Wallace to Darwin, 10 May 1864 (unbound typed copy), Wallace Papers, BL Add.MS. 46,434 f. 38; discussion of Wallace, 'The origin of the human race...', *JASL*, II (1864), clxx–clxxxi.

58. Vogt, *op. cit.*, 147; see also Hunt's editorial preface.

59. James Hunt, 'On the application of the principle of natural selection to anthropology', *AR*, IV (1866), 320–40; also report of Hunt's comments at British Association, *AR*, IV (1866), 395–8.

60. Darwin, *op. cit.*, I, 231–3.

61. Wallace to Darwin, 30 Aug. [1868?] (unbound typed copy), Wallace Papers, BL Add.MSS. 46,434 f. 17.

62. James Hunt, 'On the application of the principle of natural selection to anthropology', *AR*, IV (1866), 320–40; also Hunt's comments *AR*, IV (1866), 395–8; Hunt, 'On the doctrine of continuity applied to anthropology', *AR*, V (1867), 110–20.

63. Darwin, *op. cit.*, I, 235.

64. T. H. Huxley, 'Address to the Anthropological Department of the British Association, Dublin, 1878, informal remarks on the conclusions of anthropology', from *Nature*, XVIII (1878), 445–8, in *The Scientific Memoirs of Thomas Henry Huxley*, ed. M. Forster and E. R. Lankester (1902), IV, 270–1.

65. Darwin to Wallace, 29 May [1864?] (unbound), Wallace Papers, BL Add.MSS. 46,434 fos. 41–2; see also fos. 43–6.

66. Darwin, *op. cit.*, I, 248–51.

67. John Crawfurd, 'On the theory of the origin of species by natural selection in the struggle for life', *TESL*, n.s., VIII (1868), 37–8.
68. Richard Lee, 'The extinction of races', *JASL*, II (1864), xcviii; Thomas Bendyshe, 'On the extinction of races', *JASL*, II (1864), xcix; Hunt's comments, cix–x.
69. W. Winwood Reade, *Savage Africa* (1863), 587.
70. Alfred Russel Wallace in discussion of Lee's and Bendyshe's papers on the extinction of races, *JASL*, II (1864), xv.
71. J. Reddie, comments on Reade's paper on missions and savages, *JASL*, II (1865), clxxvii; see also ccxxii–xxxiv.
72. Richard Whately, 'On the origin of civilization', *Lectures delivered before the Young Men's Christian Association* (1855), 1–36.
73. John Lubbock, 'On the origin of civilization and the early condition of man', *Report of the British Association* (1867), 118–25; G. D. Campbell, Duke of Argyll, *Primeval Man, An Examination of some Recent Speculations* (1869), 1–6, 198–200; Lubbock, 'On the origin of civilization and the primitive condition of man', *TESL*, n.s., VI (1867), 328–41; see also Lubbock, *Pre-Historic Times* (1865), 466, 464–80, and *The Origin of Civilization and the Primitive Condition of Man* (1870), 7, 322–3, 337–62; E. B. Tylor, *Researches into the Early History of Mankind and the Development of Civilization* (1865), 160–3, 182–90, 361, 364–71, and *Primitive Culture* (1871), I, 6–7, 27–38, 61–2.
74. Rev. F. W. Farrar, 'Aptitudes of races', *TESL*, n.s., V (1866), 122–3.
75. [James Hunt], 'Aboriginal and savage races of man', *Popular Mag. of Anthropology* (1866), 59.
76. Farrar, 'Aptitudes of races', 119.
77. Joseph Hooker to John Tyndall, 15 Feb. 1867 (typed copy), Huxley Papers, Imperial College, 10.340.
78. Lubbock, *The Origin of Civilization and the Primitive Condition of Man*, 303, 484; Tylor, *Primitive Culture*, I, 27–8; see also Burrow, *Evolution and Society*, 97–100, 134–6, 176–8.
79. C. S. Wake, 'The psychological unity of mankind', *Memoirs of the Anthropological Society of London* III (1867–9), 134–47; also discussion, *JASL*, VI (1868), clxviii–clxx, including Hunt's comment, clxx; see also: C. S. Wake, *Chapters on Man* (1868), 115–49, 287–90; Lubbock, 'On the origin of civilization and the primitive condition of man', 150–1; A. R. Wallace, 'On the progress of civilization in Northern Celebes', *AR*, II (1864), 332–4; H. A. C. Cairns, *Prelude to Imperialism: British Reactions to Central African Society, 1840–1890* (1965) 91–2; Burrow, *Evolution and Society*, 132.
80. A. R. Wallace, 'On the progress of civilization in Northern Celebes', as reported in *AR*, II (1864), 333.
81. Asa Briggs, 'The language of "class" in early nineteenth-century England', *Essays in Labour History*, ed. A. Briggs and J. Saville (1967), 69–73; H. Perkin, *The Origins of Modern English Society, 1780–1880* (1969), 445–7.
82. George Rolleston to Huxley, 1 Jan 1865, Huxley Papers, 25.168.
83. MS. Minutes of Anthropological Society of London General Meeting, 7 July 1863, Archives of Royal Anthropological Institute; Stanton,

op. cit., 174; E. D. Adams, *Great Britain and the American Civil War* (1925) I, 154n.1.

84. J. F. Jameson, 'London expenditure of the Confederate Secret Service', *American Historical Rev.*, xxxv (July 1930), 818; *Index*, 23 July 1863, 204–205a; 26 Nov 1863, 486–7; Dec. 1863, 501–3.

85. For example, Count Oscar Reichenbach, 'On the vitality of the black races, of coloured people in the United States, according to the census', *JASL*, II (1864), lxx–lxxiii; 'McHenry on the Negro as a freedman', *Popular Mag. of Anthropology* (1866), 36–9; 'The Negro race', *ibid.*, 102–18; 'Negro emancipation in America', *ibid.*, 136–40; and Samuel Phillips Day, 'On the power of rearing children among savage tribes', *JASL*, v (1867), cc–cci.

86. James Reddie, 'Slavery', *AR*, II (1864), 291–2.

87. *Ibid.*, 280.

88. James Hunt, 'Anniversary Address', *JASL*, IV (1866), lxxvii–ix, also comments cix–cx; 'On the Negro Revolt in Jamaica', *Popular Mag. of Anthropology* (1866), 14–20; *Lancet*, 2 Dec. 1866, 626–7, reprinted as 'Race antagonism', *Popular Mag. of Anthropology* (1866), 24–6; *AR*, VI (1866), 461.

89. *DNB.*

90. Commander Bedford Pim, *The Negro and Jamaica*, a special number of the *Popular Magazine of Anthropology* (1866), 15–16.

91. *Ibid.*, 40–50.

92. *Ibid.*, 35.

93. *AR*, I (1863), 388–90; *JASL*, II (1864), xx–xli.

94. Winwood Reade, 'Efforts of missionaries among savages', *JASL*, III (1865), clxiv–v; Reade's boast in preface to his *Savage Africa* (1863).

95. Winwood Reade, 'Efforts of missionaries among savages', *JASL*, III (1865), clxxix, ccix.

96. *Morning Star*, 20 Apr. 1865, 4d–f; 18 May 1865, 4e–f; *Evangelical Christendom*, n.s., VI (1 May 1865), 245–6 (1 July 1865), 321–5, VII (1 Jan. 1866), 34–5; *Church Missionary Intelligencer*, n.s., I (July 1865), 193–7; *African Times*, IV, 24 Apr. 1865, 128; 23 June 1866, 78–9; *Patriot*, 20 Apr. 1865, 248b–d; 4 May 1865, 275c–d; 26 Oct. 1865, 689c.

97. *JASL*, III (1865), ccx–ccxii, ccxviii, ccxxxvii.

98. J. W. Colenso, 'On the efforts of missionaries among savages', *JASL*, III (1865), cclxvi.

99. J. Hooker to J. Tyndall, 15 Feb. 1867 (typed copy), Huxley Papers, 10.340.

100. J. Reddie, 'On Anthropological Desiderata considered with reference to the various theories of man's origin and existing condition, savage and civilized', *JASL*, II (1864), cxxi; also *idem.*, 'On the various theories of man's past and present condition', *J. Trans. of Victoria Institute*, I (1866–7), 174–220; J. Lubbock, 'On the origin of civilization and primitive condition of man', *TESL*, n.s., VI (1867), 341; also Lubbock's *Pre-Historic Times*, 489, and *The Origin of Civilization and the Primitive Condition of Man*, 118.

101. *JASL*, II (1864), xxii–xxix, xxxiv–xxxix, xliv–xlv, liv–lv.

102. [James Hunt], 'Race in legislation and political economy', *AR*, IV

(1866), 114; see also Hunt's address to the Manchester Anthropological Society, *AR*, v (1867), 17–18.

103. [James Hunt], 'Race in religion', *AR*, iv (1866), 291.

104. *Ibid.*, 315; see also Hunt's Presidential Address, *JASL*, v (1867), xi.

105. Charles Buxton to the Secretary of the Anthropological Society of London, 3 Feb. 1866, and 6 Feb. 1866, Collected Letters of the Anthropological Society of London, A–D, 1865–6, Royal Anthropological Institute Archives; Leonard Huxley, *Life and Letters of T. H. Huxley*, (1903), i, 396.

106. Huxley to his sister in Tennessee, in L. Huxley, *op. cit.*, i, 363, and Huxley to editor of *Pall Mall Gazette*, 30 Oct. 1866, in *ibid.*, 404.

107. Huxley to Tyndall, 9 Nov. 1866, Huxley Papers, 9.27–8; 'Professor Huxley's lecture on "The Structure and Classification of Mammalia" ', *Reader*, iii (27 Feb. 1864), 266–8; 'Emancipation – Black and White', *Reader*, v (20 May 1865), 561; also 'Huxley on the Negro Question', *Reader*, iii (5 Mar. 1864), 387–8; William Irvine, *Apes, Angels and Victorians* (New York, 1955), 238–43.

108. Huxley to Charles Kingsley, 8 Nov. 1866, in Huxley, *op. cit.*, i, 406–8.

109. R. B. Martin, *The Dust of Combat. A Life of Charles Kingsley* (1956), 258; Mrs C. Kingsley, *Charles Kingsley: His Letters and Memories of his Life* (1877), I, 3–6, and letter to his mother from the West Indies, Dec. 1869, *ibid.*, II, 308; Susan Chitty, *The Beast and the Monk: a life of Charles Kingsley* (New York, 1975), 241–2. I am also in debt to Professor Michael Banton for a copy of his article 'Kingsley's racial philosophy', *Theology*, LXXVIII (Jan. 1975), 22–30.

110. Martin, *op. cit.*, 257–61; Chitty, *op. cit.*, 242.

111. Kingsley to J. Lorimer, 17 Dec. 1866, Mrs C. Kingsley, *op. cit.*, II, 242; see also Kingsley, *Alton Locke* (Everyman edn, 1970), 344; 'Preface to the Ancient Regime', 138; and 'The first discovery of America', 251–2, of *Historical Essays and Lectures* (1880).

112. Kingsley to J. Lorimer, 17 Dec. 1866, Mrs C. Kingsley, *op. cit.*, II, 242–3.

113. *Ibid.*, 242.

114. Charles Kingsley, *At Last* (1871), i, 51.

115. *Ibid.*, 51–2.

116. 12th List of Foundation Fellows in Blumenbach, ed. Bendyshe; J. W. Burrow, 'Evolution and anthropology in the 1860s', *VS*, vii (1963), 146–7 (Burrow claimed the Anthropological Society of London listed 66 doctors); MS. note of J. S. Collingwood and C. Carter Blake, 1 Feb. 1866, Correspondence of the Anthropological Society of London, A–D, 1865–6; 'Report of General Meeting, 2 Dept. 1868', *JASL*, vi (1868), clxxxv–ix; 'Letters of Hyde Clark to the editor of *The Athenaeum*', *Athenaeum*, 15 Aug. 1868, 210; 29 Aug. 1868, 271–2; 29 Oct. 1868, 569.

117. Hooker to Huxley, 8 Jan. 186?, Huxley Papers, 3.85.

118. 'Negroes', *Chambers's Encyclopaedia*, vi (1864), 699–701.

119. Cobden to Charles Sumner, 8 Oct. 1863 (typed copy), Cobden Papers, BL Add.MSS. 43,676 f. 241.

120. For example, Benjamin Haydon, a painter, rejected polygenesis after meeting an ex-slave from Jamaica: W. Pope (ed.), *The Diary of Benjamin Haydon* (Harvard, 1960), 208–10, 210 n2.

121. *The Times*, 5 Sept. 1863, 8c–d; *Pall Mall Gazette*, 20 Oct. 1865, 10b–11a.

122. Rolleston to Huxley, 1 Jan. 1865, Huxley Papers, 25.166.

123. Huxley to John Lubbock, n.d. [Apr.–May 1863], Avebury Papers, BL Add.MSS. 46,639 f. 103; draft of Huxley to Hunt, n.d., Huxley Papers, 18.349–50 [C. Carter Blake], 'Man and beast', *AR*, 1 (1863), 157–9, 162.

124. Wallace to Huxley, 21 Feb. 1864, Huxley Papers, 28.91–2; see also Darwin to Wallace, 22 Sept. 1865(?), Wallace Papers, BL Add.MSS. 46,434 f. 58, and Wallace to Darwin, 21 Oct. 1865, *ibid.*, f. 59; Huxley to Sir Joseph Norman Lockyer, 22 Aug. 1865[?], Huxley Papers, 21.242–3; Thomas Bendyshe to the Anthropological Society of London, 19 Feb. 1866, Collected Letters, A–D, Archives of the Royal Anthropological Institute.

125. J. Beddoe, *Memories of Eighty Years* (1910), 210.

126. Huxley to Lubbock, 24 Sept. 1866, Avebury Papers, BL Add.MSS. 49,640 f. 133; Huxley to Lubbock, 18 Oct. 1867, *ibid.*, fos. 24–5; Huxley to Lubbock, 1 Aug. 1866, *ibid.*, f. 137; Huxley to Lubbock, 22 Jan. 1871, *ibid.*, 49,642 f. 5; Huxley Papers 33.1–58 contains drafts, correspondence and resolutions of Huxley and Hunt for union of the two societies in 1868.

127. R. S. Charnock, 'President's Address before the London Anthropological Society', *Anthropologia*, 1 (1873–5), 6–7.

128. W. J. Reader, *Professional Men. The Rise of the Professional Classes in Nineteenth-Century England* (1966), 23–4, 68; G. D. H. Cole, *Studies in Class Structure* (1955), 65–8; W. L. Burn, *The Age of Equipoise* (1964), 255; Leone Levi, 'On the progress of learned societies, illustrating the advancement of science in the United Kingdom during the last thirty years', *Report of the British Association* (1868), 169–97.

129. Rolleston to Huxley, 1 Jan. 1865, Huxley Papers, 25.168.

130. *Morning Star*, 20 Apr. 1865, 4c; 18 May 1865, 4e; *Evangelical Christendom*, VI (1 May 1865), 245; H. J. C. Beavan to C. Carter Blake, n.d., A.5, Collection of Letters, Anthropological Society of London, Archives of the Royal Anthropological Institute.

131. Hannah Arendt, *Origins of Totalitarianism* (2nd enlarged edn, 1958), 178–84.

132. Burn, *op. cit.*, 267–70; Reader, *op. cit.*, 98–9; 185, 203–5; F. Musgrove, 'Middle class education and employment in the nineteenth century', *Economic History Rev.*, 2nd ser., XII (Aug. 1959), 99–111; H. J. Perkin, 'Middle class education and employment in the nineteenth century: a critical note', *ibid.*, 2nd ser., XIV (Aug. 1961), 122–30; F. Musgrove, 'A rejoinder', *ibid.*, 2nd ser., XIV (Dec. 1961), 320–9; E. Stokes, *The English Utilitarians and India* (1959), 78; John Roach, 'Liberalism and the Victorian intelligentsia', *Cambridge Historical J.*, XIII (1959), 58–81.

133. *Daily News*, 21 Sept. 1867, 4b–d; see also Thomas Carlyle, 'Occasional discourse on the Nigger Question', *Frasers' Mag.*, XL (July–Dec. 1849), 670–97; Charles Kingsley, *At Last: A Christmas in the West Indies* (1871), II, 149–51, and *passim*.

134. Hooker to Tyndall, n.d. (typed copy), Huxley Papers, 10.337; Hooker

to Tyndall, 15 Feb. 1867 (typed copy), *ibid.*, 10.340; Professor
Tyndall's reply to the Jamaica Committee, 7 Nov. 1866 (printed),
ibid., 10.316–17; Francis Galton, 'Hereditary talents and character',
Macmillan's Mag., xii (May–Oct. 1865), 321, 327; 'Negroes',
Chambers's Encyclopaedia, vi (1864), 700.

135. H. J. C. Beavan to C. Carter Blake, n.d., Anthropological Society of
London Collection of Letters, 1865–6, Archives of the Royal
Anthropological Institute.

CHAPTER EIGHT

1. For references to the 'eternal', 'inevitable', 'everlasting', or
   'irrepressible' Negro, see W. W. Clarke to J. Parkes, 22 Aug. 1864,
   Russell Papers, P.R.O. 30/22/15c; J. Bright to R. Cobden, 13 Jan.
   1862, Bright Papers, BL Add.MSS. 43,384 f. 292; *The Times*, 21
   Mar. 1862, 8e, and 19 Nov. 1862, 9b; *Saturday Rev.*, 4 Jan. 1862,
   6a, and 13 Oct. 1866, 446b.
2. See particularly E. D. Adams, *Great Britain and the American Civil
   War*, (1925); B. Villiers and W. H. Chesson, *Anglo-American
   Relations, 1861–1865* (1919); D. Jordan and E. J. Pratt, *Europe and
   the Civil War* (Boston and New York, 1931); Joseph H. Park, 'English
   working Men and the American Civil War', *Political Science Q.*,
   xxxix (1924), 432–57.
3. For recent studies, see Joseph M. Hernon, 'British sympathies in the
   American Civil War: a reconsideration', *J. Southern History*, xxxiii
   (1967); 356–67; Mary Ellison, *Support for Secession: Lancashire and
   the American Civil War* (Chicago, 1972), including Peter d'A. Jones,
   'The history of a myth: British workers and the American Civil War',
   199–219; W. D. Jones, 'British Conservatives and the American
   Civil War', *American Historical Rev.* lviii (1953), 527–43; Arnold
   Whitridge, 'British Liberals and the American Civil War', *History
   Today*, xii (1962), 688–95; Royden Harrison, 'British labour and the
   Confederacy', *International Rev. of Social History*, ii (1957), 78–105,
   and 'British labour and American slavery', *Science and Society*, xxv
   (1961), 291–319; D. P. Crook, 'Portents of war: English opinion on
   Secession', *J. American Studies*, iv (1970), 163–79.
4. For fuller discussion of English opinion on the slavery issue see D. A.
   Lorimer, 'The role of anti-slavery sentiment in English reactions to the
   American Civil War', *Historical J.*, xix (June 1976), 405–20.
5. ASP, Minute 424, 7 Nov. 1862, Minute Book IV, E2/9; see also
   Lorimer, *op. cit.*, 412–14, 417–19.
6. Seward to Adams, 28 May 1862, North America no. 12, Further
   correspondence relating to the civil war in the U.S.A., *P.P.* 1862,
   xlix pt 1; Russell to Stuart, 28 July 1862, P.R.O., F.O.5/820; Stuart
   to Russell, no. 87, 21 July 1862, F.O.5/834; Russell to Stuart, 7 Aug.
   1862, F.O.5/820; Russell to Lyons, no. 30, 17 Jan. 1863, F.O.5/868;
   Lyons to Russell, 2 Jan. 1863, Russell Papers, P.R.O. 30/22/37.
7. Lyons to Russell, no. 46, 19 Jan. 1863, P.R.O. F.O.5/865; The
   Admiralty to the Foreign Office, 28 Jan. 1863, enclosing letter of Sir
   A. Milne, 1 Jan. 1863, F.O.5/916; Commander W. Hewett to Sir A.

Milne, 1 Jan. 1863, enclosing Admiralty to Foreign Office, 17 Feb. 1863, F.O.5/917; copied extract of Ellice to Sir G. Grey, 21 Aug. 1862, Russell Papers, P.R.O. 30/22/25; a magistrate of the County of Somerset to Russell, 14 Oct. 1862, F.O.5/865.

8. Consul R. Bunch to Russell, 21 Oct. 1862, P.R.O. F.O. 5/844; Bunch to Russell, no. 10, 24 Jan. 1863, F.O. 5/906; Acting Consul F. J. Cridland to Russell, no. 23, 29 Oct. 1862, F.O. 5/846; *Index*, 7 Aug. 1862, 233–4, 19 Oct. 1862, 366–7a, 3 Sept. 1863, 298–9.

9. For the most violent anti-Negro speech in Parliament see remarks of E. Horsman, *Parl. Deb.*, 3rd ser., CLXX (24 Apr. 1863), 241–3.

10. *Index*, 7 Aug. 1862, 234; see also 9 Oct. 1862, 376–7; 3 Sept. 1863, 298–9.

11. *Standard*, 4 Nov. 1861, 4d, 8 Oct. 1862, 4c.

12. *Morning Herald*, 16 Jan. 1863, 4c; and similarly, 7 Oct. 1862, 4b; *Evangelical Christendom*, n.s., III (Nov. 1861), 630.

13. *Saturday Rev.*, 4 Jan. 1862, 5b.

14. *Saturday Rev.*, 11 Oct. 1862, 426a.

15. *Record*, 14 Jan. 1863, 2a; also 25 Mar. 1863, 2a–b, 8 Oct. 1862, 2a; a similar view in the *Methodist Recorder*, 23 Jan. 1863, 25d, and the *Baptist Mag.*, LIII (Aug. 1861), 470.

16. *Daily Telegraph*, 7 Oct. 1862, 4a–c, 14 Jan. 1863, 4a–b.

17. *Economist*, 25 Oct. 1862, 1177b–9a; see also 11 Oct. 1862, 1122b–3a.

18. *Standard*, 8 Oct. 1862, 4b–c; *Methodist Recorder*, 23 Dec. 1863, 25c–d; *The Times*, 7 Oct. 1862, 8b–d, 5 Dec. 1862, 8b–c.

19. *Standard*, 10 Aug. 1861, 4b–c, 3 Oct. 1862, 4b–d; *Saturday Rev.*, 2 Feb. 1861, 106a–b, 4 Jan. 1862, 5a–b; *Morning Herald*, 16 Jan. 1863, 4c–d; *Index*, 20 Oct. 1864, 657–8; *The Times*, 6 Oct. 1862, 8b–d, 5 Dec. 1862, 8b–c, 15 Jan. 1863, 8c–d; see also Lyons to Russell, 19 June 1863, Russell Papers, P.R.O. 30/22/37; Lyons to Russell, no. 434, 24 June 1864, P.R.O. F.O. 5/953; Lyons to Russell, no. 562, 5 Aug. 1864, enclosed in F.O. 5/957.

20. *Standard*, 30 July 1863, 4b–c, 31 July 1863, 4c–d; *Anti-Slavery Reporter*, 3rd ser., XI (Nov. 1863), 243–4.

21. *Saturday Rev.*, 16 Feb. 1861, 160b–161c, 4 May 1861, 454a–455a, 20 June 1863, 773a–774a; *Standard*, 22 Mar. 1862, 4d–e; *Morning Herald*, 9 Jan. 1863, 4a–b; *The Times*, 26 Mar. 1862, 10e–f.

22. *The Times*, 6 Jan. 1862, 3b–c; Goldwin Smith, *Does the Bible Sanction American slavery?* (1863); *A brief reply to an important question: being a letter to Professor Goldwin Smith from an implicit believer in Holy Scripture* (1863); *Standard*, 10 Nov. 1863, 4c–d; *An address of the Confederate clergy* (1863); *Index*, 11 June 1863, 104a–c, 13 July 1863, 249–50, 5 Nov. 1863, 439a, 441c–442b; *Evangelical Christendom*, n.s., IV (Aug. 1863), 1–8, *ibid.*, (Sept. 1863), 411–15; *Church Missionary Intelligencer*, XIV (Aug. 1863), 188–93; *Anti-Slavery Reporter*, 3rd ser., XI (Oct. 1863), 237–8.

23. J. F. Jameson, 'London expenditures of the Confederate secret service', *American Historical Rev.*, XXXV (July 1930), 816–17; on *The Times*, see Leslie Stephen, *The 'Times' and the American Civil War. A Historical Study* (1865), *passim*; Argyll to Gladstone, 1 Jan. 1862, Gladstone Papers, BL Add.MSS. 44,099 f. 102; Gladstone to Brougham, 10 Jan. 1862, Brougham Papers.

24. *The History of the Times. II: Their tradition established, 1841–1884* (1939), 63–4, 366, 377, 384, 387; Charles Mackay, *Through the Long Day, or Memorials of a Literary Life During Half a Century* (1887), II, 215–16, 219–20, 251–2.

25. John Vincent, *The Formation of the Liberal Party, 1858–1868* (1966), 62–5.

26. Lord Campbell, *Parl. Deb.*, 3rd ser., CLXIX (23 Mar. 1863), H/L, 1626; *Index*, 7 Aug. 1862, 233–4, 9 Oct. 1862, 376–7c, 3 Sept. 1863, 298–9; *Morning Herald*, 7 Oct. 1862, 4a–b; *Saturday Rev.*, 18 Jan. 1862, 62b–64a; *Standard*, 22 Mar. 1862, 4d–e; *Aris's Birmingham Gazette*, 1 Feb. 1862, 4c–d; *Record*, 14 Jan. 1863, 29; *The Times*, 15 Jan. 1863, 8c–d, 26 Mar. 1863, 10e–f, 5 Sept. 1863, 8c–d.

27. *Index*, 12 Feb. 1863, 249–50b, 14 Jan. 1864, 24, 23 Mar. 1865, 185–6; *Standard*, 6 May 1861, 4d–e, 19 Oct. 1863, 4d–e; *Morning Herald*, 9 Jan. 1863, 4a–b.

28. *The Times*, 7 Oct. 1862, 8c.

29. *The Times*, 5 Dec. 1862, 8c.

30. C. F. Adams to C. F. Adams jr, 27 Feb. 1863, in W. C. Ford (ed.), *A Cycle of Adams Letters, 1861–1865* (1921), I, 254; *Spectator*, 23 Nov. 1861, 1278–9; *Lloyd's Weekly London Newspaper*, 27 July 1862, 6c.

31. *Standard*, 3 Oct. 1862, 4c; see also *Standard*, 21 Jan. 1863, 4b–c, 22 Oct. 1863 4d–e; *Saturday Rev.*, 7 Feb. 1863, 163–4b, 20 June 1863, 773a–4a; *Record*, 26 Oct. 1863, 2a–b.

32. *Daily News*, 21 Oct. 1863, 4b–c.

33. Extract of article, 'Colonization of Negroes – views of the President', *National Intelligencer*, 18 Aug. 1862, enclosed in Stuart to Russell, no. 164, 18 Aug. 1862, P.R.O. F.O. 5/835; *Standard*, 9 Sept 1862, 4b–c; *Saturday Rev.*, 21 Dec. 1861, 629a–b, 4 Jan. 1862, 5a–6b, 10 May, 1862, 519–20b; *Record*, 10 Sept. 1862, 2b–c, 1 Oct. 1862, 2b–c, 8 Oct. 1862, 2a; *Birmingham Daily Post*, 8 Oct. 1862, 2c–d; *Spectator*, 1 Dec. 1860, 1144, 5 Jan. 1861, 11, 7 Sept. 1861, 970–1, 21 Dec. 1861, 1388–9, 11 Oct. 1862, 1125–6; *Anti-Slavery Reporter*, 3rd ser., x (1862), 261–3; *Daily News*, 2 Sept. 1862, 4c–d.

34. Cobden to A. W. Paulton, 18 July 1863, Cobden Papers, BL Add.MSS. 43,662 fos 258–9; see also Cobden to John Slagg, 4 Feb. 1861, 43,676 f. 71; Cobden to Bright, 19 May 1861, 43,651 f. 239; Cobden to Bright, 8 Aug. 1861, 43,651 fos. 246–9; Cobden to Joseph Parkes, 3 Nov. 1861, 43,644 fos. 98–101; Cobden to Bright, 6 Oct. 1862, 43,652 fos. 49–53; Cobden to Bright, 29 Dec. 1862, 43,652 fos. 65–7.

35. *Spectator*, 21 Sept. 1861, 1031a.

36. *Loc. cit.*

37. E. V. Dicey, 'The outbreak of the war', *Macmillan's Mag.*, VI (July–Oct. 1862), 415.

38. Brougham to Gladstone, 2 Feb. 1863, Gladstone Papers, BL Add.MSS. 44,114 fos. 315–16; Brougham Papers: Brougham to Joseph Parkes, n.d. [1863]; Brougham to Clarendon, 4 Feb. 1863; Brougham to Parkes, 30 Mar. 1863; L. A. Chamerovzow to Brougham, 10 Feb. 1863, 5 July 1863, 23 Oct. 1863. On Buxton, see the *Spectator*, 8 Nov. 1862, 1237–8; *Daily News*, 27 Dec. 1862, 4d–f; George Thompson to L. A. Chamerovzow, 9 Nov. 1862, ASP C37/9; C. Buxton to the editor, *The Times*, 26 Dec. 1862, 9e–f.

39. *Anti-Slavery Reporter*, 3rd ser., XI (Feb. 1863), 36–7.
40. Charles Buxton's remarks at the Anti-Slavery Society's Annual Meeting, 22 May 1863, in the *Anti-Slavery Reporter*, 3rd ser., XI (June 1863), 136; L. A. Chamerovzow to Brougham, 15 May 1863, Brougham Papers.
41. *Anti-Slavery Reporter*, 3rd ser., XI (Aug. 1863), 184; *Saturday Rev.*, 3 Jan. 1863, 16b–17b; *Spectator*, 13 July 1861, 749b.
42. Harriet Martineau, 'The Negro race in America', *Edinburgh Rev.*, CXIX (Jan. 1864), 203–20.
43. *Parl. Deb.*, 3rd ser., CLXX (27 Apr. 1863), 790.
44. *Parl. Deb.*, 3rd ser., CLXVI (12 May 1862), 1538; see also Lord Derby's remarks, *Parl. Deb.*, 3rd ser., CLXIX (5 Feb. 1862), 27–8.
45. MS. of address on Lancashire distress delivered in Cheshire, 27 Dec. 1862, Gladstone Papers, BL Add.MSS. 44,690 fos. 73–4; see also Phillip Magnus, *Gladstone, A Biography* (1963), 160–4.
46. Sir James Kay-Shuttleworth's speech quoted in John Watts, *The Facts of the Cotton Famine* (facsimile reprint, 1968), 279.
47. See remarks of Charles Gilpin, Secretary to the Poor Law Commissioners, *Parl. Deb.*, 3rd ser., CLXXII (14 July 1863), 762.
48. Watts, *op. cit.*, 350.
49. *Lloyd's Weekly London Newspaper*, 21 Sept. 1862, 6c.
50. *Reynolds's Newspaper*, 18 Jan. 1863, 4c.
51. *Daily News*, 10 Oct. 1862, 4a.
52. *Ibid.*, 4b.
53. *Standard*, 31 July 1863, 4c–d; *Morning Herald*, 9 Jan. 1863, 4a–b; *The Times*, 26 Apr. 1862, 8c–d, 2 Sept. 1862, 8e–f, 2 Jan. 1863, 6d, 26 Mar. 1863, 10e–f.
54. *Spectator*, 26 Apr. 1862, 460–1, 6 Sept. 1862, 986–7, 15 Aug. 1863, 2364–5, 26 Aug. 1865, 947–8a, 2 Sept. 1865, 968a–9a, 977b–8b. In contrast, see *Daily News*, 2 Sept. 1862, 4c–d; *Lloyd's Weekly Newspaper* 1 Feb. 1863, 6c–d; *Anti-Slavery Reporter*, 3rd ser., X (1862), 261–3.
55. E. V. Dicey, 'The outlook of the War', *Macmillan's Mag.*, VI (May–Oct. 1862), 414–15.
56. *Bee-Hive*, 6 June 1863, 4c; see also Royden Harrison, 'British labour and American slavery', *Science and Society*, XXV (1961), 299–304. Stephen Coltham, 'The *Bee-Hive* Newspaper: its origin and early struggles', in *Essays in Labour History*, ed. A. Briggs and J. Saville (1967), 198–201.
57. *Bee-Hive*, 6 June 1863, 4d.
58. *Saturday Rev.*, 12 Mar. 1864, 311b–12b; *Standard*, 3 Nov. 1864, 4d–e; American White Man, [D. G. Croly, C. Wakeman, and E. C. Howell], *Miscegenation: the Theory of the Blending of the Races, applied to the American White Man and the Negro* (1864).
59. Cobden to Sumner, 8 Oct. 1863, Cobden Papers, BL Add.MSS. 43,676 fos. 241–2, and 7 Jan. 1863, *ibid.*, fos. 243–4; Cobden to A. W. Paulton, 8 July 1863, 43,662 fos. 254–6; Cobden to J. Slagg, 11 Nov. 1863, 43,676 f. 136; *Daily News*, 7 Oct. 1862, 4b–c; *Spectator*, 5 Mar. 1862, 294–5, 13 Dec. 1862, 1377–8.
60. Stuart to Russell, 18 Aug. 1862, and Russell's minute of 13 Sept. 1862, P.R.O. F.O. 5/866; Lyons to Russell, no. 266, 18 Mar. 1862,

F.O. 5/869; Consul Walker to Russell, no. 77, 5 June 1863, F.O.
5/906; Memorial of the executive committee of the Manchester
Southern Club to Russell, 16 Sept. 1863, F.O. 5/929; *Standard*, 23
Oct. 1862, 4c, 26 Oct. 1864, 4c–d; *Saturday Rev.*, 13 Sept. 1862,
298a–b, 27 June 1863, 813b–14a; *Index*, 20 Oct. 1864, 656–8; *The
Times*, 29 Jan. 1864, 9b–d.

61. *Reynolds's Newspaper*, 28 June 1863, 4c.
62. Argyll to Russell, 9 Sept. 1863, Russell Papers, P.R.O. 30/22/26;
Lyons to Russell, 26 July 1864, 30/22/38; Bright to Cobden, 8 Nov.
1864, BL Add. MSS. 43,384 f. 321; Cobden to W. Hargreaves, 12
Nov. 1864, BL Add.MSS. 43,655 fos. 372–3; Argyll to Gladstone, 13
Nov. 1864, BL Add.MSS. 44,099 f. 304; *Daily News*, 8 Sept. 1863,
4a–b, 8 Nov. 1864, 4b–c; *Bee-Hive*, 19 Sept. 1863, 4c–d; *Reynolds's
Newspaper*, 13 Sept. 1863, 1a–b.
63. J. Hume Burnley to Russell, no. 168, 16 Mar. 1865, P.R.O. F.O.
5/1016; Newcastle to Russell, 19 Sept. 1863, Russell Papers, P.R.O.
30/22/26; Joseph Parkes to Brougham, 8 Sept. 1863, Brougham
Papers; *Index*, 10 Sept. 1863, 312–13, 3 Nov. 1864, 698a–b, 10 Nov.
1864, 713c–14a, 19 Jan. 1865, 40c–1a; *Saturday Rev.*, 12 Nov. 1864,
583a–4a; *Standard*, 12 Nov. 1864, 4c–e, 10 Jan. 1865, 4b–c; *The
Times*, 7 Nov. 1864, 7b–c.
64. There are extensive reports on the condition of the freedom and
discussion on Negro suffrage in P.R.O. F.O. 5/959–1068; Russell to
Sir F. Bruce, 5 Aug. 1865, Russell Papers, P.R.O. 30/22/97; Petition
of Freedman's Aid Association to Russell, 4 July 1865, P.R.O. F.O.
5/1042; National Committee of British Freedman's Aid Societies,
Speech of the Duke of Argyll (1865); *Patriot*, 25 May 1865, 322d–3b;
Anti-Slavery Reporter, 3rd ser., xi (May 1863), 117, (1 June 1863),
137, xiii (July 1865), 162, xiv (1 May 1866), 133–4; *Spectator*, 13
July 1861, 749–50, 4 Mar. 1864, 258–9, 4 Dec. 1869, 1422a–3a;
Daily News, 28 May 1862, 5a–b, 21 Sept. 1867, 4c. For extensive
treatment of the Freedman's Aid Movement in Britain and of British
attitudes to Reconstruction see Christine Bolt, *The Anti-Slavery
Movement and Reconstruction: A Study in Anglo-American
Co-operation, 1833–77* (1969), *passim*.
65. *The Times*, 29 July 1865, 8b–d; also 4 Aug. 1865, 8b–c, 20 Oct.
1865, 6e–f.
66. Russell to Sir F. Bruce, 8 July 1865, Russell Papers, P.R.O. 30/22/97;
Standard, 16 Oct. 1865, 4c–d; for more extensive treatment of the
suffrage question see Bolt, *op. cit.*, 163–9, and *idem.*, *Victorian
Attitudes to Race* (1971), 60–9.
67. Sir F. Bruce to Russell, 18 June 1865, Russell Papers, P.R.O.
30/22/38; *Record*, 30 Oct. 1865, 2b; *Saturday Rev.*, 30 Sept. 1865,
410–11b, 20 Oct. 1865, 536a–7b.
68. J. E. Cairnes, 'The Negro suffrage', *Macmillan's Mag.*, xii (May–Oct.
1865), 334–5; *Anti-Slavery Reporter*, 3rd ser., xiii (July 1865), 162;
Spectator, 10 June 1865, 630–1, 1 July 1865, 715, 2 Sept. 1865,
968a–9a; *Patriot*, 19 Oct. 1865, 678d–9a; *Daily News*, 1 Nov. 1865,
4c–d; *Morning Star*, 3 Feb. 1865, 4c–d; *Lloyd's Weekly Newspaper*,
5 Mar. 1865, 6d.

CHAPTER NINE

1. *Saturday Rev.*, 13 Oct. 1866, 446.
2. The above account drawn from Report of the Royal Commission, *P.P.* 1866, xxx; and S. Olivier, *The Myth of Governor Eyre* (1935); William Law Mathieson, *The Sugar Colonies and Governor Eyre* (1936); Avrel B. Erickson, 'Empire or anarchy: the Jamaica rebellion of 1865', *J. Negro History*, XLIV (Apr. 1959), 99–122; George H. Ford, 'The Governor Eyre case in England', *University of Toronto Q.* XVII (Apr. 1948), 219–33; Bernard Semmel, *The Governor Eyre Controversy* (1962); Geoffrey Dutton, *The Hero as Murderer. The Life of Edward John Eyre* (1967); W. P. Morrell, *British Colonial Policy in the Mid-Victorian Age* (1969), 399–432; Christine Bolt, *Victorian Attitudes to Race* (1971), 75–108.
3. Eyre to Cardwell, 26 Oct. 1865, Cardwell Papers, P.R.O. 30/48/42.
4. Eyre to Henry Taylor, 23 Feb. [1866], (copy), Russell Papers, P.R.O. 30/22/16A.
5. Jamaica, 1 Dec. 1865, Gladstone Papers, BL Add.MSS. 44,754 fos. 136–7; Gladstone to Argyll, 1 Dec. 1865, BL Add.MSS. 44,535 fos. 154–5; Gladstone to Cardwell, 17 Dec. 1865, 44,535 fos. 161–2; Gladstone to Cardwell, 28 Feb. 1866, 44,536 f. 29; Milner-Gibson to Bright, 7 Dec. 1865, Bright Papers, BL Add.MSS. 43,388 f. 110; Henry Taylor to Eyre, 31 Jan. 1866, Russell Papers, P.R.O. 30/22/16A.
6. *Jamaica Papers, No. 1* (1866), 94–7; Frederic Harrison, *Martial Law* (*Jamaica Papers, No. 5*) (1866), i–iii; Ford, *op. cit.*, 219–33.
7. W. F. Finlason, *The History of the Jamaica Case* (2nd enlarged ed, 1869), 368 pp-vv; Ford, *op. cit.*, 219–33, Semmel, *op. cit.*, 105–17; see also correspondence *re* Eyre in Murchison Papers, BL Add.MSS. 46,125–28; and Gillian Workman, 'Thomas Carlyle and the Governor Eyre controversy: an account with some new material', *Victorian Studies*, XVIII (1974), 77–102.
8. Semmel, *op. cit.*, 99–101; Susan Chitty, *The Beast and the Monk: a life of Charles Kingsley* (New York, 1975), 241–3.
9. Debate on Eyre's legal expenses, Dilke Papers, BL Add.MSS. 43,909 fos. 284–5; *Parl. Deb.*, 3rd ser., CXCII (22 June 1868), 1850–2; Dutton, *op. cit.*, 324–5.
10. Michael St John Packe, *The Life of John Stuart Mill* (1954), 468; Huxley to Tyndall, 19 Nov 1866, Huxley Papers, 9:28–9, and Huxley to Charles Kingsley, 8 Nov. 1866, *ibid.*, 19:243–6; both letters reprinted in Leonard Huxley, *Life and letters of T. H. Huxley* (1903), I, 406–9; see also Semmel, *op. cit.*, 14.
11. Philip D. Curtin, *Two Jamaicas. The Role of Ideas in a Tropical Colony* (Cambridge, Mass., 1955), *passim*; see also ch. 6 above.
12. *Anti-Slavery Reporter*, 3rd ser., XIII (Apr. 1865), 86.
13. *The Times*, 4 Nov. 1865, 9; see also 13 Nov. 1865, 8.
14. *Standard*, 11 Nov. 1865, 4d–e.
15. *Morning Herald*, 11 Nov. 1865, 4b–c.
16. *Daily Telegraph*, 14 Nov. 1865, 4c–d.
17. *Daily News*, 6 Nov. 1865, 4c–d; 14 Nov. 1865, 4b–c.
18. *Record*, 13 Nov. 1865, 2a.

19. *Methodist Recorder*, 17 Nov. 1865, 396b.
20. *Morning Herald*, 18 Nov. 1865, 4f; see also *Daily Telegraph*, 20 Nov. 1865, 4e; *Methodist Recorder*, 17 Nov. 1865, 306b; *African Times*, v (23 Nov. 1865), 52, and v (23 Dec. 1865), 62–3; *Juvenile Missionary Mag.*, xxiii (Jan. 1866), 3–7; *Patriot*, 16 Nov. 1865, 746a–c; *Lloyds' Weekly London Newspaper*, 26 Nov. 1865, 6c–d; *The Times* 16 Dec. 1865, 9.
21. *Record*, 20 Nov. 1865, 2b; also *Standard*, 17 Nov. 1865, 5a–b; *Pall Mall Gazette*, 17 Nov. 1865, 1a–b; *The Times*, 26 Dec. 1865, 7; *Morning Herald*, 29 Nov. 1865, 4a–b.
22. *The Times*, 13 Jan. 1866, 8; *Saturday Rev.*, 9 Dec. 1865, 726–727a; *Daily News*, 5 Dec. 1865, 4d–e.
23. *The Times*, 13 Dec. 1865, 13.
24. *Saturday Rev.*, 25 Nov. 1865, 656a–7a, 2 Dec. 1865, 687a–8b; *Pall Mall Gazette*, 20 Nov. 1865, 1a–2a; *Spectator*, 25 Nov. 1865, 1303–4.
25. *The Times*, 17 Nov. 1865, 9.
26. Cardwell to Eyre, 17 Nov. 1865, Cardwell Papers, P.R.O. 30/48/42; also minutes of Henry Taylor to Sir F. Rogers, 4 Apr. 1866, on Jamaica (2549), P.R.O. C.O. 136/400.
27. Gladstone to Cardwell, 17 Dec. 1866, Gladstone Papers, BL Add.MSS. 44,535 fos. 161–2; also memorandum of 1 Dec. 1865, 44,754 f. 137; similarly, Sir C. Phipps to Cardwell, 18 Nov. 1865, and Brougham to Cardwell, 25 Nov. 1865, Cardwell Papers, P.R.O. 30/48/42.
28. John T. Delane to Gladstone, Gladstone Papers, BL Add.MSS. 44,409 f. 86; *The Times*, 25 Jan. 1866, 8, 27 Jan. 1866, 8; *Anti-Slavery Reporter*, 3rd ser., xiv (16 Apr. 1866), 98–100.
29. *Examiner*, 25 Nov. 1865, 742, 2 Dec. 1865, 757.
30. *Daily News*, 1 Jan. 1866, 4c–d; *Methodist Recorder*, 1 Dec. 1865, 412a–b; *Anti-Slavery Reporter*, 3rd ser., xiii (1 Dec. 1865), 288, 300, 306, and xiv (15 Jan. 1866), 8; *Saturday Rev.*, 2 Dec. 1865, 687a–8a.
31. *Evangelical Christendom*, n.s., vi (1 Dec. 1865), 599–601, vii (1 Jan. 1866), 36–8; *African Times*, v (23 Mar. 1866), 103–4, and v (23 May 1866), 122–3; *Record*, 29 Nov. 1865, 2a–b, 6 Dec. 1865, 2a–b, 16 Feb. 1866, 2a–b; *Wesleyan Missionary Notices*, 3rd ser., xiii (Jan. 1866), 1–8, (Feb. 1866), 17–20.
32. *Missionary Mag. and Chronicle*, xxix (Dec. 1865), 326–30, xxx (Jan. 1866), 1–2, (Mar. 1866), 49–50; *Patriot*, 23 Nov. 1865, 762a–c, 30 Nov. 1865, 778c–d, 14 Dec. 1865, 810b–d, 27 Dec. 1868, 826c–d; *Annual Report of the Baptist Missionary Society for 1866* (1866), 20–2.
33. *The Times*, 29 Nov. 1865, 9, speech extracted from the *Jamaica Guardian*; also Eyre to Cardwell, 24 Dec. 1865 (private), P.R.O. C.O. 137/396; minutes of Henry Taylor and Sir F. Rogers, 19–20 July 1866, on Sir H. Storks to Cardwell, no. 130, 20 June 1866, C.O. 137/406; *Spectator*, 10 Feb. 1866, 151a–b.
34. *The Times*, 28 Nov. 1865, 5, 7, 1 Dec. 1865, 8, 9 Dec. 1865, 12, 11 Dec. 1865, 12, 12 Dec. 1865, 7, 13 Dec. 1865, 12, 14 Dec. 1865, 12, 15 Dec. 1865, 5, 8; and *Patriot*, 7 Dec. 1865, 798–9a, 14 Dec. 1865, 814c–d; *Spectator*, 16 Dec. 1865, 1394e–5a; *Anti-Slavery Reporter*, n.s., xiii (Dec. 1865), 304–5, and xiv (15 Jan. 1866), 1.
35. Charles Buxton to the editor, *The Times*, 13 Dec. 1865, 12; on

Gordon, see Brougham Papers: L. A. Chamerovzow to Brougham, 2
Oct. 1865; George W. Gordon to Brougham, 22 July 1862; L. A.
Chamerovzow to Brougham, 16 Aug. 1862; L. A. Chamerovzow to
Brougham, 18 Nov. 1865; also John Brown to Chamerovzow, 18 Jan.
1866, ASP C28/103; *Anti-Slavery Reporter*, 3rd ser., xv (15 Aug.
1867), 192, and xvi (Jan. 1868), 22.

36. Rev. Newman Hall to Gladstone, 21 Dec. 1865, BL Add.MSS. 44,188
fos. 55–6; Cabinet memorandum on Jamaica, 1 Dec. 1865, 44,754
fos. 136–7; Gladstone to Argyll, 1 Dec. 1865, 44,535 fos. 154–5;
Milner-Gibson to Bright, 7 Dec. 1865, Bright Papers, BL Add.MSS.
43,388 f. 110; Henry Taylor to Eyre, 31 Jan. 1866, Russell Papers,
P.R.O. 30/22/16A, and Cardwell to Russell, 30 Apr. 1866,
30/22/16B.

37. *Morning Herald*, 13 Dec. 1865, 4a–b; *Standard*, 14 Dec. 1865, 4d–e.

38. *Ibid.*, 30 Nov. 1865, 5e–f, 19 Dec. 1865, 4c–d; *Morning Herald*, 13
Dec. 1865, 4a–b, 18 Jan. 1866, 4b–c; *Daily Telegraph*, 31 Mar. 1866,
4d–e; *The Times*, 2 Dec. 1865, 8–9, 29 Nov. 1864, 8, and numerous
letters to *The Times* from Eyre's defenders, 30 Nov. to 12 Dec. 1865;
Henry Kingsley, 'Eyre, the South Australian Explorer', *Macmillan's
Mag.*, xii (May–Oct. 1865), 501–10, and xiii (Nov. 1865–Apr. 1866),
55–63.

39. *Spectator*, 9 Dec. 1865, 1362–3; *Saturday Rev.*, 9 Dec. 1865, 719a,
17 Feb. 1866, 186a–7a, 24 Mar. 1866, 342a–3a; *The Times*, 12 Dec.
1865, 5; *Standard*, 19 Dec. 1865, 4c–e; *Morning Herald*, 18 Jan. 1866,
4b–c.

40. *The Times*, 28 Nov. 1865, 7.

41. *Ibid.*, 21 Dec. 1865, 8.

42. Justin McCarthy, *A History of Our own Times* (1880), iv, 29–30.

43. Report of the Jamaica Royal Commission, *P.P.* (1866), xxx, 489–531.

44. Gladstone to Cardwell, 13 June 1866, Gladstone Papers, BL Add.MSS.
44,536, f. 60; *Spectator*, 23 June 1866, 683–4; *Daily News*, 20 June
1866, 4e–f; *Anti-Slavery Reporter*, 3rd ser., xiv (2 July 1866), 163;
Record, 22 June 1866, 2b–c; *Morning Herald*, 20 June 1866, 4c–d.

45. *Westminster Review*, n.s., xxxii (1867), 189–206; Thomas Carlyle,
'Shooting Niagara and after?', *Macmillan's Mag.*, xvi (May–Oct.
1867), 319–36; [Charles Mackay], 'The negro and the negrophilists',
Blackwood's Mag., xcix (Jan.–June 1866), 581–97; *Fortnightly Rev.*,
vi (15 Aug. 1866), 106–7; *Spectator*, 27 Jan. 1866, 90, 24 Mar. 1866,
322; *Anti-Slavery Reporter*, 3rd ser., xiv (1866), 202–3, 273–6.

46. *Standard*, 23 Oct. 1866, 4d–e; 9 Feb. 1867, 4g–5a; 28 May 1868,
4f–g; *Daily News*, 15 Oct. 1866, 4b–c.

47. ASP E5/6(a) Minute Book of the Executive Committee (Dec. 1865–72),
E2/9 Minute Book IV, Special Meeting of the Committee, 20 Nov.
1865 and 24 Nov. 1865. Frederic Harrison, *Autobiographic Memoirs*
1911), i, 305; *Jamaica Papers, No. 1* (1866), 97.

48. *Anti-Slavery Reporter*, xiv (1 Aug. 1866), 202–3; *African Times*, vi
(23 July 1866), 10; ASP E2/9 Minute Book IV, 9 Nov. 1866; L. A.
Chamerovzow to Carnarvon, 9 Nov. 1866, P.R.O. C.O. 137/409;
Anti-Slavery Reporter, 3rd ser., xiv (Dec. 1866), 285–7.

49. See Goldwin Smith to L. A. Chamerovzow, 4 Dec. 1865, ASP C36/63;
Frederic Harrison, 'Governor Eyre to be tried at home', *Beehive*,

9 Dec. 1865, 4d–e; *Fortnightly Review*, III (1 Dec. 1865), 244–5; reports of philanthropic delegations to Downing Street in *The Times*, 9 Dec. 1865, 12, 11 Dec. 1865, 12.

50. *Daily News*, 12 Sept. 1866, 4b; see also 23 Nov. 1865, 4b–c, 29 Jan. 1866, 4c–d, 30 Jan. 1866, 4b–c, 16 Feb. 1866, 4c–d, 12 Feb. 1866, 4b–c.

51. *Beehive*, 25 Nov. 1865, 4f.

52. *Beehive*, 20 Oct. 1866, 4c.

53. *Reynolds's Newspaper*, 5 Aug. 1866, 4c–f, 26 Nov. 1865, 1a–b; also 17 Dec. 1865, 1b.

54. ASP E2/9 Minute Book IV, Minute 937, 9 Nov. 1866, Declaration of the British and Foreign Anti-Slavery Society on the Prosecution of Governor Eyre.

55. *Methodist Recorder*, 1 Dec. 1865, 412 a–b.

56. *Spectator*, 4 Aug. 1866, 849–50a; see also 25 Nov, 1865, 1303–4, 15 Sept. 1866, 1024–5.

57. McCarthy, *op. cit.*, IV, 44–5.

58. *Spectator*, 6 June 1868, 666.

59. E. S. Beesly to the editor, *Beehive*, 25 Nov. 1865, 4f.

60. T. H. Huxley to editor of the *Pall Mall Gazette*, 30 Oct. 1866, Huxley Papers, 10:47–8, reprinted in L. Huxley, *op. cit.*, I, 404–5; see also Huxley to Charles Kingsley, 8 Nov. 1866, Huxley Papers, 19:242–6, also reprinted in L. Huxley, *op. cit.*, I, 406–8.

61. *Parl. Deb.*, 3rd ser., CLXXXIV (31 July 1866), 1812–13.

62. Finlason, *op. cit.*, 361, 368k–l, 368e, 510.

63. *Daily Telegraph*, 14 Nov. 1865, 4c–d.

64. Thomas Carlyle, 'Shooting Niagara and after?', *Macmillan's Mag.*, XVI (May–Oct. 1867), 324–5; [Charles Mackay], 'The negro and the negrophilists', *Blackwood's Mag.*, XCIX (1866), 581–97; *Standard*, 17 Dec. 1865, 4d–e, 26 Dec. 1866, 4c, 31 Jan. 1866, 4c–d, 3 Feb. 1866, 4f–g, 30 June 1866, 4e–f; *Illustrated London News*, XLVIII (3 Feb. 1866, 103; *Pall Mall Gazette*, 13 Dec. 1865, 40, 22 June 1866, 9b–10a; *Record* 26 Oct. 1866, 2b–c; *Daily Telegraph*, 21 Aug. 1866, 4c–d; *Lloyd's Weekly Newspaper*, 12 Aug 1866, 6d–e.

65. John Tyndall to Joseph Hooker, n.d. [?Nov. 1866], (copy), Huxley Papers, 10:341.

66. *Daily News*, 15 Oct. 1866, 4b–c, 3 June 1868, 4b–c.

67. *Pall Mall Gazette*, 23 Aug. 1866, 1a–b; *Record*, 27 Aug. 1866, 2c–d; *The Times*, 23 Aug. 1866, 6b–d; McCarthy, *op. cit.*, IV, 44–7.

68. Elda (Mrs) Busk to Tyndall, n.d., Huxley Papers, 10:327.

69. F. W. Farrar to Tyndall, n.d., (copy), Huxley Papers, 10:342, also (10:334), Warren de la Rue to Tyndall, 11 Mar. 1867; Finlason, *op. cit.*, lxxv–vi, 225–31, 650–1, 282; *Morning Herald*, 15 Jan. 1866, 4d–e, 11 Nov. 1865, 4b–c; *Standard*, 3 Sept, 1866, 4c.

70. James Hunt, 'Anniversary Address', *JASL*, IV (1866), lxxviii–lxxix; *Lancet*, 2 Dec. 1865, 627; W. Finlason, *Justice to a Colonial Governor; or Some Considerations in the Case of Mr. Eyre* (1869), cxxxi; [Charles Mackay], *op. cit.*, 583, 590; [C. J. Bayley], 'Jamaica, its disturbance and its prospects', *Q. Rev.*, CXX (July–Oct. 1866), 222; *The Times*, 20 Nov. 1865, 8.

71. Commander Bedford Pim, 'The Negro and Jamaica', *Popular Mag.*

of *Anthropology* (1866), *passim*; Hamilton Hume, *The Life of Edward John Eyre, late governor of Jamaica* (1867), 113–14, 217; *African Times*, v (23 Dec. 1865), 63; 'Jamaica and the recent insurrection there', *Fraser's Mag.*, LXXIII (1866), 161–79, and 'The Jamaica Problem', *ibid.*, 277–305; *Pall Mall Gazette*, 17 Nov. 1865, 1a–b; 24 Nov. 1865, 1a–2a.

72. 'Professor Tyndall's reply to the Jamaica Committee, 7 Nov. 1866', Huxley Papers, 10:316–16; reprinted in Hume, *op. cit.*, Appendix B, 268–76.

73. Copies of letters in Huxley Papers: J. D. Hooker to J. Tyndall, 13 Nov. 1866, (10:318); Tyndall to Hooker, n.d. [1867], (10:336); Hooker to Tyndall, n.d., (10:337).

74. J. Tyndall to Hooker, n.d., Huxley Papers, 10.338; J. Hooker to Tyndall, 15 Feb. 1867 (10:340).

75. Hume, *op. cit.*, Appendix C, 'Report of a meeting of the Eyre Defence Committee held at Willis's Rooms', 283–4.

76. *Saturday Review*, 13 Oct. 1866, 447b; see also *Morning Herald*, 14 Nov. 1865, 4c; *The Times*, 17 Nov. 1865, 6; 'On the Negro revolt in Jamaica', *Popular Mag. of Anthropology* (1866), 19–20; [Free Labour Registration Society], *Jamaica: its State and Prospects* (1867), 6–7.

77. *The Times*, 18 Nov. 1865), 8.

78. *Standard*, 22 Mar. 1866, 4c; *Morning Herald*, 13 Dec. 1865, 4b.

79. *Pall Mall Gazette*, 7 Mar. 1866, 10a.

80. [Edwin Paxton Hood], A Thirty Years' Resident, *Jamaica: Who is to Blame?* (1866), x.

81. Charles Kingsley, 'Preface to undergraduates at Cambridge', *Alton Locke* (Everyman edn, 1970), 3.

82. *Daily Telegraph*, 21 Aug. 1866, 4d.

83. Semmel, *op. cit.*, 94–8; Dutton, *op. cit.*, 339–41.

84. *Daily News*, 18 Nov. 1865, 4d; *Reynolds's Newspaper*, 26 Nov. 1865, 1b.

85. *Fortnightly Rev.*, III (15 Dec. 1865), 362.

86. *Anti-Slavery Reporter*, n.s., XIII (1 Dec. 1865), 306–7; see also extensive reports of public speeches and meetings in *Anti-Slavery Reporter*, n.s., XIII (Dec. 1865) and XIV (Jan. 1866).

87. *Spectator*, 24 Mar. 1866, 321–2.

88. [Charles Lever], 'Cornelius O'Dowd', *Blackwood's Mag.*, CIX (Jan.–June 1868), 101.

89. *Standard*, 26 Dec. 1866, 4d, 13 Dec. 1865, 4d–e, 23 Aug. 1866, 4d–e.

90. *Punch*, LII (26 Jan. 1867), 37.

91. *Daily Telegraph*, 17 Aug. 1866, 4e–f; *The Times*, 17 Nov. 1865, 8; *Pall Mall Gazette*, 24 Nov. 1865, 1a–2a, 28 Dec. 1865, 1b.

92. Huxley to C. Kingsley, Nov. 8, 1866, Huxley Papers, 19:243–6, reprinted in L. Huxley, *op. cit.*, I, 406–8.

93. Royden Harrison, *Before the Socialists: Studies in Labour and Politics, 1861–1881* (1965), 85–6.

94. *Morning Herald*, 2 Jan, 1866, 4a.

95. Dutton, *op. cit.*, *passim*.

96. Sir H. Storks to Cardwell, 9 July 1866; Cardwell Papers, P.R.O. 30/48/45; Murchison Papers, BL Add.MSS. 46,126. fos. 112–57; there is an extensive correspondence between Eyre and Murchison in which Eyre discusses his difficulties in securing employment.

97. *Morning Herald*, 23 Nov. 1865, 4a–b.
98. *Saturday Review*, 9 Dec. 1865, 726–7, 16 Dec. 1865, 746.
99. *Spectator*, 9 Dec. 1865, 1363.
100. Argyll to Gladstone, 2 Dec. 1865, Gladstone Papers, BL Add.MSS. 44, 100 f. 82.
101. For discussion of class antagonism underlying the reform issue see Royden Harrison, 'The 10th April of Spencer Walpole: the problem of revolution in relation to reform', *International Rev. of Social History*, VII (1962), 369–85.
102. E. S. Beesly to Frederic Harrison, 6 July 1867, Beesly Papers, University College, London.
103. J. S. Mill to Goldwin Smith, 28 May 1868, in Hugh S. R. Elliott (ed.), *The Letters of John Stuart Mill*, (1910), II, 111.
104. J. S. Mill to David Urquart, 26 Oct. 1866, in Elliot, *op. cit.*, II, 69–70.
105. *Record*, 28 Mar. 1866, 2a.
106. *Record*, 5 Sept. 1866, 2c.

CHAPTER TEN

1. Kenneth Little, *Negroes in Britain* (1948).
2. J. A. Jackson, *The Irish in Britain* (1963); L. P. Curtis jr., *Anglo-Saxons and Celts: A Study of Anti-Irish Prejudice in Victorian England* (Bridgeport, Conn., 1968), 24–5, and *passim*; John Garrard, *The English and Immigration, 1880–1910* (1971); Bernard Gainer, *The Alien Invasion: The Origins of the Aliens Act of 1905* (1972).
3. For the situation in colonies of white settlement see R. A. Huttenbach, *Racism and Empire: White Settlers and Colored Immigrants in the British Self-Governing Colonies, 1830–1910* (1976).
4. Thomas R. Metcalf, *The Aftermath of Revolt in India, 1857–1870* (Princeton, N.J., 1964), 75, 145, 169–70, 277–89, 304–5, 309–10, 317, 325–6; George C. Bearce, *British Attitudes towards India, 1784–1858*, (1961), 233–4, 296–306; Eric Stokes, *The English Utilitarians and India* (1959), ix, 268–9; C. C. Eldridge, *England's Mission: The Imperial Idea in the Age of Gladstone and Disraeli, 1868–1880* (1973), 238–44, 251–5; John Roach, 'Liberalism and the Victorian intelligentsia', *Cambridge Historical J.*, XIII (1957), 58–81; J. W. Burrow, *Evolution and Society: A Study in Victorian Social Theory* (1966), 176–8.
5. Michael Biddiss, 'Gobineau and the origins of European racism', *Race*, VII (1966), 255–70, and *Father of Racist Ideology: the Social and Political Thought of Count Gobineau* (1970); Leon Poliakov, *The Aryan Myth: a History of Racist and Nationalist Ideas in Europe* (1974), 215–54; J. Barzun, *Race: a Study in Superstition* (New York, 1965), 70–7.
6. E. J. Hobsbawm, *The Age of Revolution, 1789–1848* (1962), 133–7.
7. P. G. Pulzer, *The Rise of Political Anti-semitism in Germany and Austria* (New York, 1964), 18–27, 44–59, 279–87; Michael R. Marrus, *The Politics of Assimilation: A Study of the French Jewish Community at the Time of the Dreyfus Affair* (1971), 49–50, 124–5.
8. Ruth Benedict, *Race: Science and Politics* (New York, 1940), 174–99.

266

9. M. D. Biddiss, *Father of Racist Ideology*, 266–70, and *passim*.
10. E. J. Hobsbawm, *The Age of Capital* (1975), 94–7.
11. Ronald Robinson, 'Non-European foundations of European imperialism: a sketch of a theory of collaboration, in *Imperialism: The Robinson and Gallagher Controversy*, ed. W. R. Louis (New York, 1976), 128–51.

Bibliography

I. PRIMARY SOURCES

A. MANUSCRIPT SOURCES

British Library, London
Avebury Papers, Add.MSS. 49638–42
Bright Papers, Add.MSS. 43384–92
Cobden Papers, Add.MSS. 43651–52, 43655–56, 43659, 43662,
    43664–65, 43676–78
Dilke Papers, Add.MSS. 43899, 43900, 43909
Gladstone Papers, Add.MSS. 44099, 44100, 44107, 44112, 44118, 44121,
    44127, 44133, 44136, 44140, 44141, 44156–57, 44165, 44170,
    44183–84, 44186, 44188, 44196, 44213, 44236, 44263, 44270, 44272,
    44282, 44292–93, 44300, 44303–4, 44318, 44330, 44336, 44344–45,
    44369–71, 44384–85, 44388, 44392–99, 44400–14, 44416–17,
    44420–22, 4427–28, 44439, 44441, 44450, 44511, 44531–36, 44571,
    44593–99, 44606, 44616–17, 44636, 44649, 44656–59, 44689–90,
    44701, 44724, 44726–27, 44729, 44732, 44734, 44752, 44754,
    44777, 44790–91, 44793
Layard Papers, Add.MSS. 38951–54, 38959, 38987–91, 39103
Murchison Papers, Add.MSS. 46125–28
Ripon Papers, Add.MSS. 43512–13, 43520, 43533, 43536, 43551
Sturge Papers, Add.MSS. 43722–23, 43845, 50131
Wallace Papers, Add.MSS. 46434–35, 46441

Church Missionary Society Archives, London
Records of Committee of Visitors, C.M. College, Islington, III–V
    (1843–93)
Miscellaneous Letters to Home Secretaries, 1825–80
S. Crowther, jr, Letters and Reports, 1851–62
Rev. Thomas B. Macaulay, Letters, 1852–77
Henry Robbin, Letters, 1856–74
Venn Papers:
    Diaries and Accounts
    Correspondence, 1813–77

Dr Williams's Library, London
Estlin Papers:
    Minute Book of the Bristol and Clifton Ladies Anti-Slavery Society
    Correspondence of the Estlin Family with British and American
        abolitionists

Imperial College of Science and Technology, London
T. H. Huxley Papers

Hooker Correspondence (typed copies of correspondence of Sir Joseph
Dalton Hooker and John Tyndall, 1856–93, included in Huxley
Papers)

Public Record Office, London
Cardwell Papers, P.R.O. 30/48/7, 8, 40, 42–45
Colonial Office, C.O.137/387–421, Jamaica, 1865–66
Foreign Office, F.O.5/708–1068, America, 1859–66
F.O.5/579, America (British Claims of the United States),
Free Blacks, 1823–53
Hammond Papers, F.O.391/5–17
Russell Papers, P.R.O. 30/22/14–39, 96–97

Rhodes House, Oxford
Anti-Slavery Papers: Papers of the British and Foreign Anti-Slavery
Society and the Aborigines Protection Society
E2/6–9, Minute Books of the British and Foreign Anti-Slavery
Society, 1839–68
E2/19–20, Memorials and Petitions, 1839–53
E5/6, Miscellaneous Minute Book, Dec. 1865–April 1872 (Minutes
of the Jamaica Committee)
C1–166, Correspondence

Royal Anthropological Institute, Archives, London
Ethnological Society of London:
Council Minutes, 2 Jan. 1844–9 Feb. 1869
Record of Members Elected, 1844
Anthropological Society of London:
Council Minutes, 1863–71
Ordinary Meeting Minutes, 24 Jan. 1863–31 Jan. 1871
Minutes of Annual General Meetings, 6 Jan. 1864–14 Feb. 1871
Collection of Letters, A–D, 1865–66

University College, London
E. S. Beesly Papers
John Bright Letters
Brougham Papers

B. PRINTED SOURCES

Official Publications
Hansard's Parliamentary Debates
Parliamentary Papers:
Report from the Select Committee on the State of Mendicity in the
Metropolis, V (1816), 15.
Statistical Report on the Sickness, Mortality, and Invaliding among
the Troops on the Western Coast of Africa, XXX (1840), 135.
The Reports for the year 1860 of the Past and Present State of Her
Majesty's Colonial Possessions, Part I, West Indies, Mauritius and
Ceylon, XXXVI (1861).

The Report for 1859, Past and Present State of Her Majesty's Colonial
Possessions. Presented 1861, XL (1861).

Case of fugitive slave, Anderson, LXIV (1861), 293.

Copy of 'Mr Farnall's Reports to the Poor Law Commissioners on the
Distress in the Cotton Manufacturing Districts', XLIX (1862), 89.

State Papers. United States of North America, LXII (1862).

Abbeokuta. 'Copy of Letters from Rev. H. Venn respecting conduct of
missionaries at Abbeokuta with enclosures', XXXVIII (1863), 45.

Case of A. Fitzjames, XXXVIII (1863), 407.

Island of St Vincent. 'Copy of Extracts of Correspondence between
Secretary of State for Colonies and Governor in Chief of the
Windward Islands, relating to recent Riots and St. Vincent's',
XXXVIII (1863), 563.

Reports for 1861 on Past and Present State of Her Majesty's Colonial
Possessions, Part I, West Indies and Mauritius, XXXIX (1863).

State Papers. North America, LXXII (1863).

Copy of Quarterly Medical Reports that have been received in the years
1863 and 1864, from the Troops serving on the Gold Coast, XXXV
(1864).

Army Medical Department. Statistical, Sanitary and Medical Reports
for 1862, XXXVI (1864).

Reports for 1862 on the Past and Present State of Her Majesty's Colonial
Possessions, XL (1864).

Report of the Select Committee appointed to consider the State of the
British Establishment on the Western Coast of Africa, V (1865).

Army Medical Department. Statistical, Sanitary and Medical Reports of
the Army Medical Department for 1863, XXXIII (1865), 323.

Papers relating to the war among the Native Tribes in the
Neighbourhood of Lagos, XXXVII (1865), 11.

Copy of the Report of Colonel Ord, the Commissioner appointed to
Inquire into the Condition of the British Settlements on the West
Coast of Africa, XXXVII (1865), 287.

The Reports for 1863 for the Past and Present State of Her Majesty's
Colonial Possessions, Part I, West Indies and Mauritius, XXXVII
(1865).

Report of the Jamaica Royal Commission, Part I, XXX (1866).

Report of the Jamaica Royal Commission, Part II, Minutes of Evidence,
XXXI (1866).

Papers on Disturbances in Jamaica, LI (1866).

Report from the Select Committee on Emigration and Immigration
(Foreigners), XI (1888).

Published Autobiographies, Diaries, Letters, Memoirs, Narratives

Adams, Henry. 'Diary of a visit to Manchester', ed. A. W. Silver,
American Historical Rev., LI (Oct. 1945).

Adams, H. G., ed. *God's Image in Ebony: Being a series of Biographical
Sketches, Facts, Anecdotes, etc., demonstrative of the Mental Powers
and Intellectual Capacities of the Negro Race* (1854).

Allen, William G. *American Prejudice against Colour* (1853).

Anderson, John. *The Story of the Life of John Anderson, the Fugitive
Slave*, ed. Harper Twelvetrees (1863).

Angelo, Henry Charles William. *Reminiscences of Henry Angelo, with Memories of his Late Father and Friends*, 2 vols, (1828).

Armistead, Wilson. *A Tribute for the Negro* (1848).

Asher, Rev. Jeremiah. *Incidents in the Life of Rev. J. Asher, Pastor of Shiloh (Coloured) Baptist Church, Philadelphia, U.S.* (1850).

Ball, Charles. *The Life of a Negro Slave; the Narrative of Charles Ball*, ed. Mrs Alfred Barnard (1846).

Basset, Josiah. *Life of a Vagrant. . . . To which is added a Brief Account of Andreas Stoffles, the African Witness* (1850).

Beddoe, John. *Memories of Eighty Years* (1910).

Bickersteth, Edward. *Memoir of Simeon Wilhelm. A Native of Susoo Country, West Africa* (New Haven, 1819).

Bluett, Thomas. *Some Memories of the Life of Job, the son of Solomon, the high priest of Boonda in Africa* (1734).

Brent, Linda. *The Deeper Wrong; or, Incidents in the Life of a Slave Girl*, ed. L. Maria Child (1862).

Brown, John. *Slave Life in Georgia: Narrative of the Life, Sufferings and Escape of John Brown, Fugitive Slave now in England*, ed. L. A. Chamerovzow (1855).

Brown, William Wells. *The American Fugitive in Europe. Sketches of Places and People Abroad* (Boston, 1855).

—*Narrative of William Wells Brown, A Fugitive Slave* (1850).

—*Three Years in Europe; or Places I have Seen and People I have Met* (1852).

Burke, Edmund. *Correspondence of Edmund Burke*, ed. Charles Williams et al., (1844), 11.

Burnett, John, ed. *Useful Toil: Autobiographies of Working People from the 1820s to the 1920s* (1974).

Campbell, Robert. *A Pilgrimage to My Motherland; or Reminiscences of a Sojourn among the Egbas and Yorubas of Central Africa in 1859–1860* (1861).

Catterall, Helen Tunnicliff (ed.). *Judicial Cases concerning American Slavery and the Negro*, I–V (Washington, D.C., Carnegie Institution, 1926–1937).

Chirgwin, George H. *Chirgwin's Chirrup, Being the Life and Reminiscences of George Chirgwin, the 'White Eyed Musical Kaffir'* (1912).

Coffin, Levi. *The Simeon Holiday of Uncle Tom's Cabin, Reminiscences of an Abolitionist* (1876).

Conway, Moncure Daniel. *Autobiography. Memories and Experiences*, 2 vols (1904).

Craft, William. *Running a Thousand Miles for Freedom; or, the Escape of William and Ellen Craft from Slavery* (1860).

Crowther, Samuel A. *The African Slave Boy. A Memoir of Rev. Samuel Crowther* (1852).

—*Letters from the Rev. Samuel Crowther and the Rev. Henry Townsend (CMS), extracted from 'The Colonial Magazine' for December 1850* (1850).

Cuffee, Paul. *Memoir of Captain Paul Cuffee, a Man of Colour: to which is subjoined the epistle of the society of Sierra Leone, in Africa* (1811).

Cugoano, Ottobah. *Thoughts and Sentiments on the Evil and Wicked Traffic of the Slavery and Commerce of the Human Species* (1787).

Darwin, Francis. *The Life and Letters of Charles Darwin*, 3 vols, (New York, 1887).

Delaney, Martin Robinson. *Official Report of the Niger Valley Exploring Party* (1861).

Douglass, Frederick. *The Life and times of Frederick Douglass, from 1817 to 1882* (1882).

—*My Bondage and My Freedom* (New York, 1855).

—*Narrative of the Life of Frederick Douglass, An American Slave* (1846).

Edwards, Paul, ed. *Letters of Ignatius Sancho* (1968).

Elaw, Zilpha. *Memories of the Life, Religious Experience, Ministerial Travels and Labours of Mrs Zilpha Elaw, an American Female of Colour* (1846).

Elliot, Hugh S. R., ed. *The Letters of John Stuart Mill*, 2 vols (1910).

Equiano, Olaudah. *The Interesting Narrative of the Life of Olaudah Equiano, or Gustavus Vasa, the African* (1814).

Frederic, Francis. *Slave Life in Virginia and Kentucky* (1863).

Ford, Worthington Chauncey (ed.). *A Cycle of Adams Letters, 1861–1865*, 2 vols (1921).

Freeman, T. B. *Journal of Various Visits to the Kingdoms of Ashantee, Aku, and Dahomi* (1844).

Gooch, G. P., ed. *The Later Correspondence of Lord John Russell*, 2 vols (1925).

Grandy, Moses. *Narrative of the Life of Moses Grandy, late a Slave*, ed. George Thompson (Boston, 1844).

Griggs, Earl Leslie and Prator, Clifford N. (eds.). *Henry Christophe and Thomas Clarkson, A Correspondence* (Berkeley, Cal., 1952).

Gronniosaw, James Albert Ukawsaw. *A Narrative of the most remarkable Particulars in the Life of James Albert Ukawsaw Gronniosaw, an African Prince* (Bath, [?1770]).

Hare, A. J. C., ed. *The Life and Letters of Maria Edgeworth* (1894), 1.

Harrison, Frederic. *Autobiographic Memoirs*, 2 vols (1911).

Haydon, Benjamin Robert. *The Diary of Benjamin Robert Haydon*, ed. W. B. Pope, 5 vols (Cambridge, Mass., 1960).

Henson, Josiah. *The Autobiography of the Rev. Josiah Henson ('Uncle Tom'), from 1789 to 1883*, ed. John Lobb (1890).

Hoare, Prince. *Memoirs of Granville Sharp* (1820).

Holyoake, George Jacob. *Sixty Years of An Agitator's Life*, 2 vols (1892).

Howith, Margaret, ed. *Mary Howith, an Autobiography*, 2 vols (1899).

Huxley, Leonard. *Life and Letters of Thomas Henry Huxley*, 3 vols, (1903).

Jekyll, Joseph, ed. *Letters and Memories of the late Ignatio Sancho, An African* (5th edn, 1803).

Kilham, Hannah. *Memoirs of Hannah Kilham* (1837).

Kingsley, Charles. *At Last: A Christmas in the West Indies*, 2 vols (1871).

Kingsley, Mrs Charles. *Charles Kingsley: His Letters and Memories of His Life*, 2 vols (2nd edn., 1877).

Knapp, Oswald G., ed. *The Intimate Letters of Hester Piozzi and Penelope Pennington, 1788–1821* (1914).

Knight, Rev. William. *Memoir of Rev. H. Venn. The Missionary Secretariat of Henry Venn, B.D.* (1880).

Knutsford, Viscountess of. *Life and Letters of Zachary Macaulay* (1900).

Le Breton, Anna L. *Memoir of Mrs. Barbauld, including Letters and Notices of her Family and Friends* (1874).

Lovett, William. *The Life and Struggles of William Lovett* (1876).

Lucas, William. *A Quaker Journal. Being the Diary and Reminiscences of William Lucas of Hitchin*, ed. G. E. Bryant and G. P. Baker, 2 vols (1934).

Mackay, Charles. *Through the Long Day, or Memorials of a Literary Life During Half a Century*, 2 vols (1887).

Moore, Archy. *The Slave: or, Memoirs of Archy Moore*, ed. F. R. Lees (1848).

Mott, A. *Biographical Sketches and Interesting Anecdotes of Persons of Colour* (1826).

Prance, R. Sharpe, ed. 'The Diary of John Warde of Clitheroe, Weaver, 1860–1864', *Trans. Historical Soc. of Lancashire and Cheshire* (1953).

Prince, Mary. *The History of Mary Prince, A West Indian Slave, to which is added the Narrative of Asa-Asa, a Captured Slave*, ed. Thomas Pringle (1831).

Reynolds, Harry. *Minstrel Memories. The story of Burnt Cork Minstrelsy in Great Britain from 1836 to 1927* (1928).

Roper, Moses. *A Narrative of the Adventures and Escape of Moses Roper, from American Slavery* (1837).

Sancho, Ignatius. *Letters of the late Ignatius Sancho, an African*, 2 vols (1782).

Sayers, W. C. Berwick. *Samuel Coleridge-Taylor, Musician. His Life and Letters* (1915).

Simpson, John Hawkins. *Horrors of the Virginia Slave Trade and of Slave-Rearing Plantations. The True Story of Dinah, an Escaped Virginia Slave now in London* (1863).

Smith, Mrs Amanda Berry. *Amanda Smith, An Autobiography* (1894).

Stearns, Charles. *Narrative of Henry Box Brown who escaped from Slavery in a Box* (Boston, 1849).

Stowe, Charles E. *Life of Harriet Beecher Stowe compiled from her Letters and Journals* (1889).

Stowe, Harriet Beecher. *Sunny Memories of Foreign Lands* (1854).

Taine, H. *Notes on England* (1872).

Taylor, Jessie, S. F. C. *A Memory Sketch or Personal Reminiscences of My Husband, Genius and Musician, Samuel Coleridge-Taylor, 1875–1912* (1943).

Trollope, Anthony. *North America*, 2 vols (1862).

Walvin, James. *The Black Presence: A Documentary History of the Negro in England, 1555–1860* (New York, 1972).

Ward, Samuel Ringgold. *An Autobiography of a Fugitive Negro: His Anti-Slavery Labours in the United States, Canada, and England* (1855).

Watson, Henry. *Narrative of Henry Watson, A Fugitive Slave* (3rd edn, Boston, 1850).

Publications of Miscellaneous Societies

The African-Aid Society
The African Times, I–VII (1862–68).

The African Institution. *Ist–15th Report of the Committee of the African Institution,* I–III (1807–21).

Anthropological Society. *Journal of Anthropology,* I (1870–1).

Anthropological Society of London
Memoirs read before the Anthropological Society of London, I–III (1863–9).

The Anthropological Review (includes the *Journal of the Anthropological Society of London and the Popular Magazine of Anthropology*), I–VIII (1863–70).

Baptist Missionary Society
The Annual Report of the Committee of the Baptist Missionary Society, (1857–69).

The Baptist Magazine (includes the *Missionary Herald*), LII–LIX (1860–7).

British and Foreign Aborigines Protection Society
The Colonial Intelligencer; or, Aborigines' Friend, I (1847–8), n.s., II–III (1848–51).

The Aborigines' Friend, and the Colonial Intelligencer, n.s., I (1855–8), and *The Colonial Intelligencer and Aborigines' Friend,* n.s., II (1859–66).

British and Foreign Anti-Slavery Society
Proceedings of the General Anti-Slavery Convention, 1840 (1841).
Proceedings of the General Anti-Slavery Convention, 1843, (1843).
Tracts on Slavery in America: No. 1 – What the South is Fighting For; No. 2 – The Crisis in the United States; No. 3 – British Aid to the Confederates, (1862–3).
Special Report of the Anti-Slavery Conference, Paris, Aug. 26–27, 1867 (1869).
The Anti-Slavery Reporter, n.s., V–VII (1850–2); 3rd ser. I–XIV (1853–66).

British Association for the Advancement of Science, *Report of the British Association for the Advancement of Science* (1831–71).

Church Missionary Society
Memorial of the Committee of the CMS to the Archbishop of Canterbury, (1833).
Conference on Missions held in 1860 at Liverpool (1860).
The Slave Trade of East Africa: Is It to Continue or be Suppressed? (1868).
The Centenary Volume of the Church Missionary Society for Africa and the East, 1799–1899 (1902).
Talks on Africa (?1906).
A Missionary Alphabet for Children, by Edith M. E. Baring-Gould [n.d.].
The Church Missionary Intelligencer, X–XIII (1859–62), n.s., I–IV (1865–8).
The Church Missionary Juvenile Instructor, n.s. IX–XIII (1860–4), n.s., I–IV (1865–8).
Church Missionary Record, n.s., V–XIV (1860–8).

Emancipation Society, *Prospectus* (1862).

Ethnological Society of London

Journal of the Ethnological Society of London, I (1848), II (1850), III (1854), IV (1856); n.s., I–II (1868–70).

Transactions of the Ethnological Society of London, I–VII (1861–9).

Evangelical Alliance

Evangelical Christendom, n.s., I–VIII (1860–7).

Monthly Intelligencer, no. 1–13 (1860–1), continued as *Evangelical Alliance Intelligencer*, no. 15–43 (1861–68).

Freedman's Aid Society. *Prospectus* (1863).

Glasgow Emancipation Society. *Report of Speeches and Reception of American Delegates* (1840).

Glasgow Female Anti-Slavery Society. *Second and Fifth Annual Report* (1843, 1846).

The Ladies' Society for Promoting Education in the West Indies. *The 50th (52nd, 53rd, 56th, 58th) Annual Report* (1877–85).

London Anthropological Society. *Anthropologia*, I (1873–5).

London Missionary Society

Fruits of Toil in the London Missionary Society (1869).

Historical Summary showing the Origin, Growth, and Present Position of the London Missionary Society (1894).

Juvenile Missionary Magazine, XVI–XXIII (1859–66).

The Missionary Magazine and Chronicle, XXIII–XX (1859–66).

National Association for the Promotion of Social Science. *Transactions* (1856–68).

National Committee of the British Freed-Men's Aid Societies. *Speech of His Grace the Duke of Argyll* (1865).

National Freedman's Aid Union of Great Britain and Ireland. *The Freedman's-Aid Reporter*, I (1866–7).

Royal Anthropological Institute. *The Journal of the Anthropological Institute of Great Britain and Ireland*, I–III (1871–3).

Society for the Propagation of the Gospel at Home and Abroad

Work in the Colonies. Some Account of the Missionary Operations of the Church of England in connection with the SPG (1865).

The Mission Field, A Monthly Record of the SPG, V–XIII (1860–8).

Society of Friends. *Negro and Aborigines Fund of the Society of Friends Report* (1850).

United Brethren of Moravians. *Missionary Reporter*, I–V (1861–5).

Victoria Institute. *Journal of the Transactions of the Victoria Institute*, I (1866–7).

Wesleyan Methodist Missionary Society

The Wesleyan Juvenile Offering: A Miscellany of Missionary Information for Young Persons, XVII–XXIII (1860–6).

The Wesleyan–Methodist Magazine, 5th ser., LXXX–XCII (1857–69).

Wesleyan Missionary Notices, 3rd ser., IV–XV (1857–68).

Newspapers

Aris's Birmingham Gazette
The Beehive
Birmingham Daily Post
Bristol Examiner
Bristol Mercury
Bristol Mirror
British Banner
Christian Times
Daily News
The Daily Telegraph
The Economist
Empire
The Examiner
Friend
John Bull and Britannia
The Index
Illustrated London News
Leader
Liverpool Mercury
Lloyd's Weekly Newspaper
Manchester Examiner and Times
Methodist Recorder

Morning Advertiser
Morning Chronicle
Morning Herald
Morning Post
Morning Star
Nonconformist
Northern Ensign
Observer
Pall Mall Gazette
Patriot
The Record
Reynolds's Newspaper
Saturday Review
The Spectator
Star of Freedom
Statesman
The Standard
Sunday Times
The Times
Weekly Dispatch
Wesleyan Times

Periodicals

All the Year Round
The Anti-Slavery Advocate
The Anti-Slavery Watchman
The Athenaeum
Blackwood's Edinburgh Magazine
British Mothers' Magazine
Chamber's Journal
Christian Observer
Cobbett's Annual Register
Eclectic Review
Edinburgh Review
Englishman's Magazine
English Review
The Ethnological Journal
Fortnightly Review

Fraser's Magazine
The Freed-Man
Gentleman's Magazine
The Lancet
Leisure Hour
London Chronicle
London City Mission Magazine
Macmillan's Magazine
Meliora
The Musical Times
Punch
The Quarterly Journal of Science
Quarterly Review
The Reader
Westminster Review

Contemporary Books and Pamphlets

Adams, F. C. *Manuel Periera, or the Sovereign Rule of South Carolina* (1853).

—*Uncle Tom at Home, A Review of the Reviewers and Repudiations of Uncle Tom's Cabin* (1853).

Aiken, George L. *Uncle Tom's Cabin; or, Life among the Lowly, a Domestic Drama in Six Acts, as Performed at the Principal English and American Theatres* (New York, [?1868]).

The American Question. A Lecture delivered in Answer to the Speeches delivered by the Hon. and Rev. B. Noel, Dr Massey, and Others (1863).

American White Man (by D. G. Croly, C. Wakeman, and E. C. Howell). *Miscegenation: the Theory of the Blending of the Races, applied to the American White Man and the Negro* (1864).

Ariel (B. H. Payne). *The Negro: What is his Ethnological Status?* (Cincinnati, 1867).

Armistead, Wilson. *Five Hundred Thousand Strokes for Freedom* (1853).

Arnold, Thomas. *An Inaugural Lecture on the Study of Modern History* (1841).

Arthur, Rev. William. *The American Question. English Opinion on the American Rebellion* (1861).

Asham, Warren. *The Mud Cabin; or, the Character and Tendency of British Institutions* (New York, 1853).

Bakewell, Mrs J. *Friendly Hints to Female Servants* (1841).

Behn, Mrs Aphra. *Oroonoko: or, the Royal Slave. A True History* (1688).

Bendyshe, Thomas, ed. *The Anthropological Treatises of Johann Friedrich Blumenbach, and The Inaugural Dissertation of John Hunter, M.D., on the Varieties of Man* (1865).

Blyden, Edward Wilmot. *Africa and Africans* (1903).

A Brief Reply to an Important Question; Being a letter to Professor Goldwin Smith from an Implicit Believer in Holy Scripture (1863).

Brimblecomb, Nicholas [pseudonym]. *Uncle Tom's Cabin in Ruins! Triumphant Defence of Slavery!* (Boston, 1853).

Broca, Paul. *On the Phenomena of Hybridity in the Genus Homo*, ed. C. Carter Blake (1864).

Brown, William Wells. *The Black Man: His Antecedents, His Genius, and His Achievements* (Boston, 1863).

—*Clotel; or the President's Daughter; a Tale of the Southern States* (1853).

—*The Negro in the American Rebellion. His Heroism and his Fidelity* (Boston, 1867).

Buxton, Charles. *Slavery and Freedom in the British West Indies* (1860).

Cairnes, John Elliott. *The Revolution in America* (1863).

—*The Slave Power: its Character, Career and Probable Designs* (New York, 1862).

Campbell, J. *Negro-mania. . .Examination of the falsely assumed Equality of the various Races of men* (Philadelphia, 1851).

Campbell, G. D. [Duke of Argyll]. *Primeval Man, An Examination of some Recent Speculations* (1869).

Caulfield, Col. J. E. *One Hundred Years' History of the 2nd Battalion West India Regiment, 1795–1898* (1899).

Chesson, Frederick William. *Proceedings of the Public Breakfast held in Honour of William Lloyd Garrison* (1868).

Christy Minstrels. *The Christy Minstrels Second Pocket Songster* (1880).

—*Complete Repetoire of Songs* [?1870–1].

—*Full Report on the Trial for Libel, Matthews Brothers versus Moore, Crocker, and Burgess* (1869).

Civis Anglicus. *A Voice from the Motherland, Answering Mrs. H. Beecher Stowe's Appeal* (1863).

Church of England. Convocation of Canterbury. *Church Work Amongst Sailors in 64 Home Ports* (1878).

Cockburn, Sir Alexander. *Charge of Lord Chief Justice of England to the Grand Jury at the Central Criminal Court, in the Case of the Queen against Nelson and Brand* (1867).

Colenso, John William, Bishop of Natal. *Foreign Missions, and Mosaic Traditions* (1865).

—*On Missions to the Zulus in Natal and Zululand* (1865).

Criswell, Robert. *'Uncle Tom's Cabin' contrasted with Buckingham Hall, the Planter's Home* (New York, 1852).

Crow, Jim. *Humorous Adventures of Jim Crow* [?1840].

—*Jim Crow's Vagaries* [?1840].

—*Mr and Mrs Jim Crow's Collection of Songs* [1836].

Crummell, Rev. Alexander. *The Future of Africa* (New York, 1862).

—*Hope for Africa. A Sermon on behalf of the Ladies' Negro Education Society* (1853).

Cumming, Rev. John. *God in History* (1849).

Dally, E. 'Écologe de James Hunt', *Mémoires de la Société d'Anthropologie de Paris*, 2nd ser., 1 (1873), xxvi–xxxvi.

Darwin, Charles. *The Descent of Man, and Selection in Relation to Sex*, 2 vols (1871).

Davy, John. *The West Indians before and since Slave Emancipation* (1854).

Day, Thomas. *The Dying Negro* (1773).

Denman, Thomas. *Uncle Tom's Cabin, Bleak House, Slavery and the Slave Trade* (1853).

Dilke, Charles. *Greater Britain* (1868).

Disraeli, Benjamin. *Lord George Bentinck: A Political Biography* (1852).

Douglass, Frederick. *The Nature, Character and History of the Anti-Slavery Movement* (1855).

—*Report of Proceedings at the Soirée given to Frederick Douglass* (1847.)

Edgeworth, Maria. *Belinda* (2nd edn, 1802, 3 vols, and 3rd edn, 1811, 3 vols).

Ellis, Col. A. B. *The History of the First West India Regiment* (1855).

Engels, Frederick. *The Condition of the Working Class in England* (Leipzig, 1845; London, 1892; Panther edn, 1969).

Eyre, Edward John. *Addresses to His Excellency Edward John Eyre* (1866).

Fawcett, Henry. *The Economic Position of the British Labourer* (1865).

Finlason, W. F. *Commentaries upon Martial Law* (1867).

—*The History of the Jamaica Case* (1869).

—*Justice to a Colonial Governor; or, Some Considerations on the Case of Mr Eyre* (1869).

—*Report of the Case of the Queen v. Edward John Eyre, on his Prosecution in the Court of Queen's Bench* (1868).

Flower, W. H. 'The comparative anatomy of man', *Nature* (July 1879, May 1880).

Fox, William. *A Brief History of the Wesleyan Missions on the Western Coast of Africa* (1851).

[Free Labour Registration Society]. *Jamaica: its State and Prospects:*

with an exposure of the proceedings of the Freed-Man's Aid Society and the Baptist Missionary Society (1867).

Friswell, J. H. *The Gentle Life. Essays in Aid of the Formation of Character* (1865).

Froude, James Anthony. *The English and the West Indies* (1888).

—*Oceana, or England and her Colonies* (1886).

Garrison, F. J. and W. P. *William Lloyd Garrison, 1805–1869*, 4 vols (New York, 1889).

Gibbon, Edward. *The History of the Decline and Fall of the Roman Empire*, ed. J. B. Bury, 7 vols (1909–14).

Grant, Sir J. P. *Jamaica and Its Governor during the last Six Years* (1871).

Hall, Rev. C. Newman. *The American War. Lecture in London* (New York, 1862).

Harrison, Frederic. *Martial Law, Six Letters to 'The Daily News'* (1867).

Harvey, Thomas. *Jamaica in 1866* (1867).

Hildreth, Richard. *The White Slave. Another Picture of Slave Life in America* (1852).

Home, Henry, Lord Kames. *Sketches on the History of Man*, 2 vols (1774).

Horton, James Africanus B. *Letters on the Political Condition of the Gold Coast* (1870).

—*West African Countries and Peoples* (1868).

Hughes, Lt. Col. R. M. *The Laws relating to Lascars and Asiatic Seamen employed in the British Merchants' Service, or Brought to the United Kingdom in Foreign Vessels* (1855).

Hughes, Thomas. *The Cause of Freedom: Which is to Champion in America, the North or the South?* (1863).

Hume, David. *Essays Moral, Political, and Literary* (1963).

Hume, Hamilton. *The Life of Edward John Eyre, late Governor of Jamaica* (1867).

Hunt, James. *Anniversary Address delivered before the Anthropological Society of London, Jan. 5, 1864* (1864).

—*Anniversary Address delivered before the Anthropological Society of London, Jan. 3, 1865* (1865).

—*Anniversary Address delivered before the Anthropological Society of London, Jan. 3, 1866* (1866).

—*Farewell Address delivered at the Fourth Anniversary of the Anthropological Society of London, Jan. 1, 1867* (1867).

—*Introductory Address on the Study of Anthropology* (1863).

—*On the Negro's Place in Nature* (1863).

Huxley, Thomas Henry. *Critique and Addresses* (1873).

—*Evidence as to Man's Place in Nature* (1863).

—*Lay Sermons, Addresses and Review* (1870).

—*The Scientific Memoirs of Thomas Henry Huxley*, ed. M. Foster and E. R. Lankester, 5 vols (1898–1903).

'Intelligent Negroes', *Chambers's Miscellany of Useful and Entertaining Tracts* (1844–7), VII, No. 63.

Jamaica Committee. *Jamaica Papers, No. 1. Facts and Documents relating to the Alleged Rebellion in Jamaica and the Measure of Repression, including Notes of the Trial of Mr. Gordon* (1866).

Jamaica. *Observations on the Royal Commission and the Disturbances in Jamaica* (1866).

James, Rev. William. *Memoir of John Bishop Estlin* (1855).

Kingsley, Charles. *Alton Locke* (Everyman edn, 1970).

—*Historical Essays and Lectures* (1880).

Kinnaird, Thomas M. *Fugitive Slaves in Canada* (1861).

Knox, Robert. *The Races of Man; a Philosophical Enquiry into the Influence of Race over the Destinies of Nations* (2nd edn with supp. chs., 1862).

Labor, A. B. C. Merriman. *Britons through Negro Spectacles* [1909].

Lamb, Charles. *Essays of Elia* (Everyman edn, 1954).

Langford, J. A. *A Century of Birmingham Life*, 2 vols (1868).

Latimer, John. *The Annals of Bristol in the Eighteenth Century* (1893).

Lawrence, Sir William. *Lectures on Physiology, Zoology, and the Natural History of Man* (1819).

Lewis, George Cornewall. *A Treatise on the Methods of Observation and Reasoning in Politics*, 2 vols (1852).

Lindo, Abraham. *Dr. Underhill's Testimony on the Wrongs of the Negro in Jamaica* (1866).

Long, Edward. *The History of Jamaica*, 3 vols (1774).

Lonsdale, Henry. *Sketch of the Life and Writings of Robert Knox* (1870).

Low, Sampson. *The Charities of London in 1861* (1862).

Lubbock, Sir John. *Modern Savages* (1874).

—*The Origin of Civilization and the Primitive Condition of Man* (1870).

—*Pre-Historic Times* (1865).

Lytton, E. Bulwer. *Speeches of Edward Lord Lytton*, 2 vols (1874).

Mackney, E. M. *Mackney's Songs of Negro Life, as sung by him at St. James's Hall* [1860].

Marsh, J. B. T. *The Story of the Jubilee Singers with their Songs* (1876).

Maxwell, Joseph Renner. *The Negro Question or Hints for the Physical Improvement of the Negro Race* (1892).

Mayhew, Henry. *London Labour and London Poor*, 4 vols (1861–2).

McCarthy, Justin. *A History of Our Own Times*, 4 vols (1880).

Merivale, Herman. *Colonization and Colonies* (1861).

Mill, John Stuart. *Principles of Political Economy*, 2 vols (1848).

—*The Subjection of Women* (1869).

Moffat, Robert. *Mr Moffat and the Bechuanas* [1842].

Moore, Crocker and Ritter. *Complete Repertoire of the Songs, Ballads, and Plantation Melodies, sung by the Christy Minstrels* (1870).

Moore, George. *The First Man and his Place in Creation, considered on the Principles of Science and Common Sense, from a Christian Point of View; with an Appendix on the Negro* (1866).

Moore, George Washington. *Bones: His Anecdotes and Goaks* [1870].

Morton, Samuel George. *Brief Remarks on the Diversities of the Human Species* (Philadelphia, 1842).

The Negro Boy (Religious Tract Society [?1830]).

Negro Comicalities. Laugh and Grow Fat! Nigger Stump Speeches (1884).

The Negro's Friend; or, the Sheffield Anti-Slavery Album (1826).

'Negro Minstrelsy', *Chambers's Encyclopaedia* (1864), VI.

'Negroes', *Chambers's Encyclopaedia* (1864), VI.

A. Neutral. *Uncle John's Cabin (next door to Uncle Tom's Cabin)* (1865).

Nott, J. C. and Gliddon, G. R. *Indigenous Races of the Earth* (1857).
—*Types of Mankind* (1854).

Oastler, Richard. *Slavery in Yorkshire. Monstrous Barbarity!!!* [1835].
—*Yorkshire Slavery. The 'Devil-to Do' Amongst the Dissenters in Huddersfield. A Letter to Edward Baines, M.P.* (1835).

Picton, Sir James. *Memorials of Liverpool* (1873).

Pim, Bedford. *The Negro and Jamaica* (1866).

Pouchet, Georges. *The Plurality of the Human Race*, trans. and ed. Hugh J. C. Bevan (1864).

The Prayer of the Little Negro (1842).

Price, George. *Jamaica and the Colonial Office: Who caused the Crisis?* (1866).

Prichard, James Cowles. *The Natural History of Man*, 2 vols (1st edn, 1843; 2nd edn, 1845; 3rd edn, 1848, 4th edn, 1855).
—*Researches into the Physical History of Man*, 2 vols (1st edn, 1813; 2nd edn, 1826).

Randolph, J. Thornton. *The Cabin and the Parlour; or, Slaves and Masters* [1853].

Reade, William Winwood. *Savage Africa* (1863).

[Reddie, James]. *Scienta Scientiarium. Being an Account of the Origins, and Objects of the Victoria Institute* (1866).

Rejoinder to Mrs. Stowe's Reply to the Address of the Women of England (1863).

Report of the Lords Committee of the Privy Council...concerning the present State of Trade to Africa, and particularly the Trade in Slaves (1789), Part I.

[Richmond, Legh]. *The Negro Servant; an Authentic Narrative of a Young Negro* [1804].

Roundell, Charles Saville. *England and Her Subject Races with Special Reference to Jamaica* (1866).

S. M. *The Adamic Race* (1868).

The Sailor's Home. *40th–51st Reports of the Sailors' Home* (1875–86).

Salter, Joseph. *The Asiatic in England; Sketches of Sixteen Years' Work among Orientals* (1873).

Seeley, Sir John Robert. *The expansion of England* (1883).

Senior, Nassau W. *American Slavery* [1862].

Shirreff, Emily. *The Chivalry of the Old South* (1864).

Smeathman, Henry. *Plan of a Settlement to be made near Sierra Leone* (1786).

Smith, Goldwin. *The Civil War in America* (1866).
—*Does the Bible Sanction American Slavery?* (1863).

Smith, W. L. G. *Uncle Tom's Cabin as It is; or, Life at the South* [1852].

Spence, James. *The American Union,* (1861).

Stephen, Sir George. *Anti-Slavery Recollections* (1854).
—*The Niger Trade* (1849).

Stephen, Leslie. *The 'Times' on the American Civil War: A Historical Study* (1865).

Stowe, Harriet Beecher. *Autographs for Freedom* (1853).

—*The Key to Uncle Tom's Cabin; presenting the Original Facts and Documents upon which the Story is Founded* (1853).

—*Men of Our Times* (Hartford, Conn., 1868).

—*A Reply to 'The Affectionate and Christian Address of many Thousands of Women of Great Britain and Ireland, to their Sisters, the Women of the United States of America'* (1863).

—*Uncle Tom's Cabin, or Life Among the Lowly* (author's edn, 1852).

—*Uncle Tom's Cabin; or Life Among the Lowly*, ed. John A Woods (1965).

A Thirty Years' Resident [Edwin Paxton Hood]. *Jamaica Who is to Blame?* (1866).

Thompson, George. *American Slavery* (1853).

Tylor, Edward Burnet, *Anthropology* (1881).

—*Primitive Culture*, 2 vols (1871).

—*Researches into the Early History of Mankind and the Development of Civilization* (1865).

Uncle Tom in England; or, a Proof that Black's White (1852).

The Uncle Tom's Cabin Almanack, or Abolitionist Memento for 1853 (1852).

Underhill, Edward Bean. *Dr. Underhill's Letter. A Letter addressed to the Right Honourable E. Cardwell* (1865).

—*The West Indies: Their Social and Religious Condition* (1862).

Vogt, Carl. *Lectures on Man, his Place in Creation and in the History of the Earth*, trans. James Hunt (1864).

Waddy, A. *The Life of the Rev. Samuel Waddy, D.D.* (1878).

Wadstrom, C. B. *An Essay on Colonization* (1794–5), 2 parts.

Waitz, Theodor. *Introduction to Anthropology*, ed. J. Frederick Collingwood (1863).

Wake, C. Staniland. *Chapters on Man* (1868).

Watts, John. *The Facts of the Cotton Famine* (1866; facsimile reprint, 1968).

Wellington and Uncle Tom: or the Hero of this World contrasted with the Hero in Jesus Christ (1853).

Weylland, John Mathias. *These Fifty Years, Being the Jubilee Volume of the London City Mission* (1884).

Whately, Richard. 'On the origin of civilization', in *Lectures delivered before the Young Men's Christian Association* (1855).

White, Charles. *An Account of the Regular Gradations in Man, and in different Animals and Vegetables* (1799).

Wilkins, Mrs William Noy. *The Slave Son* (1854).

Williams, Peter. *A Discourse delivered on the Death of Captain Paul Cuffee* (1818).

II. SECONDARY SOURCES

A. BOOKS

Abel, A. H. and Klingberg, F. J. *A Side-Light on Anglo-American Relations* (1927).

Adams, Ephraim Douglass. *Great Britain and the American Civil War*, 2 vols (1925).

Addison, W. Innes. *The Matriculation Album of the University of Glasgow, from 1728 to 1858* (1913).

Ajayi, J. F. Ade. *Christian Missions in Nigeria: The Making of a New Elite, 1841–91* (1965).

Altick, Richard D. *The English Common Reader, A Social History of the Mass Reading Public, 1800–1900* (Chicago, 1957).

Annan, N. G. 'The intellectual aristocracy', in *Studies in Social History*, ed. J. H. Plumb (1955).

Anstey, Roger. *The Atlantic Slave Trade and British Abolition, 1760–1810* (1975).

Arendt, Hannah. *The Origins of Totalitarianism* (2nd enlarged edn, 1958).

Banks, J. A. *Prosperity and Parenthood: a study of family planning among the Victorian middle classes* (1954).

Banton, Michael. *The Coloured Quarter. Negro Immigrants in an English City*, (1955).

—*Race Relations* (1967).

—, ed. *Darwinism and the Study of Society* (1961).

Barzun, Jacques. *Race: A Study in Superstition* (New York, 1965).

Bearce, George C. *British Attitudes towards India, 1784–1858* (1961).

Beattie, Jessie L. *Black Moses, The Real Uncle Tom* (Toronto, 1957).

Benedict, Ruth. *Race: Science and Politics* (New York, 1940).

Best, Geoffrey. *Mid-Victorian Britain, 1851–75* (1971).

Bettleheim, Bruno and Janowitz, Morris. *Social Change and Prejudice, including the Dynamics of Prejudice* (Glencoe, Ill., 1964).

Biddiss, Michael. *Father of Racist Ideology: The Social and Political Thought of Count Gobineau* (1970).

Birdoff, Harry. *The World's Greatest Hit – Uncle Tom's Cabin* (New York, 1947).

Boase, F. *Modern English Biography*, 6 vols (1892–1921).

Bolt, Christine. *The Anti-Slavery Movement and Reconstruction: A Study in Anglo-American Co-operation, 1833–1877* (*Institute of Race Relations*, Oxford, 1969).

—*Victorian Attitudes to Race* (1971).

Briggs, Asa. 'The language of "class" in early nineteenth-century England', *Essays in Labour History*, ed. A. Briggs and J. Saville (1967).

—*Victorian Cities* (Penguin edn, 1968).

Brown, Ford K. *Fathers of the Victorian* (1961).

Burn, William Laurence. *The Age of Equipoise* (1968).

Burrow, J. W. *Evolution and Society. A Study in Victorian Social Theory* (1966).

Cairns, H. Alan C. *Prelude to Imperialism. British Reactions to Central African Society, 1840–1890* (1965).

Carr-Saunders, A. M. and Wilson, A. *The Professionals* (1933).

Cecil, Lady Gwendolen. *Life of Lord Salisbury*, 4 vols (1921).

Chadwick, Owen. *The Victorian Church. Part I* (1966).

Checkland, Sydney G. *The Rise of Industrial England, 1815–1885* (1964).

Chitty, Susan. *The Beast and the Monk: a life of Charles Kingsley* (New York, 1975).

Christie, Richard and Jahoda, Marie, eds. *Studies in the Scope and Method of 'The Authoritarian Personality'* (Glencoe, Ill., 1954).

Cole, D. G. H. *Studies in Class Structure* (1955).

Coupland, Reginald. *The British Anti-Slavery Movement* (1933).

—*The Exploitation of East Africa, 1856–1890. The Slave Trade and the Scramble* (1939).

Cox, Oliver Cromwell. *Caste, Class and Race. A Study in Social Dynamics* (New York, 1959).

Cruse, Amy A. *The Victorians and their Reading* (Boston, Mass., 1935).

Curtin, Philip D., ed. *Africa Remembered, Narratives by West Africans from the Era of the Slave Trade* (Madison, Wis., 1967).

—*The Image of Africa, British Ideas and Action, 1780–1850* (1965).

—*Two Jamaicas. The Role of Ideas in a Tropical Colony, 1830–1865* (Cambridge, Mass., 1955).

Curtis, L. P. jr. *Anglo-Saxons and Celts: A Study of Anti-Irish Prejudice in Victorian England* (Bridgeport, Conn., 1968).

Dalziel, Margaret. *Popular Fiction 100 Years Ago* (1957).

Davis, David B. *The Problem of Slavery in the Age of Revolution, 1770–1823* (Ithaca, N.Y., 1975).

—*The Problem of Slavery in Western Culture* (Ithaca, N.Y., 1966).

De Giustino, David. *Conquest of Mind: Phrenology and Victorian Social Thought* (1975).

Driver, Cecil. *Tory Radical. The Life of Richard Oastler* (New York, 1946).

Duberman, Martin, ed. *The Anti-Slavery Vanguard. New Essays on the Abolitionists* (Princeton, N.J., 1965).

Dutton, Geoffrey. *The Hero as Murderer. The Life of Edward John Eyre* (1967).

Dykes, Eva Beatrice. *The Negro in English Romantic Thought, or A Study of Sympathy for the Oppressed* (Washington, D.C., 1942).

Eaton, Anne. 'Widening horizons, 1840–1890: 10. Magazines for children in the 19th century', in *A Critical History of Children's Literature*, ed. Cornelia Meigs *et al.* (New York, 1953).

Eldridge, C. C. *England's Mission: The Imperial Idea in the Age of Gladstone and Disraeli, 1868–1880* (1973).

Elkins, Stanley M. *Slavery: A Problem in American Institutional and Intellectual Life* (Chicago, 1959).

Ellegard, A. *The Readership of the Periodical Press in Mid-Victorian Britain* (Gotenborg, 1957).

Ellison, Mary. *Support for Secession: Lancashire and the American Civil War* (Chicago, 1972).

Ensor, R. C. K. *England, 1870–1914* (1936).

Fairchild, Hoxie Neale. *The Noble Savage. A Study in Romantic Naturalism* (New York, 1928).

Findlay, G. and Holdsworth, W. W. *A History of the Wesleyan Methodist Missionary Society*, 5 vols (1921–4).

Fogel, R. W. and Engerman, S. L. *Time on the Cross: The Economics of American Negro Slavery* (Boston, 1974).

Foner, Philip S. *Frederick Douglass, a Biography* (New York, 1964).

Foster, Charles H. *The Rungless Ladder. Harriet Beecher Stowe and New England Puritanism* (Durham, N.C., 1954).

284

Foster, Joseph, ed. *Alumni Oxonienses, 1715–1886* (1888).
Foster, Thomas Henry. *America's Most Famous Book* (privately printed, 1947).
Frederickson, George M. *The Black Image in the White Mind: The Debate on Afro-American Character and Destiny, 1817–1914* (New York, 1972).
Fyfe, Christopher. *Africanus Horton, 1835–1883: West African Scientist and Patriot* (New York, 1972).
—*A History of Sierra Leone* (1962).
—*Sierra Leone Inheritance* (1964).
Gainer, B. *The Alien Invasion: The Origins of the Aliens Act of 1905* (1972).
Garrard, John. *The English and Immigration, 1880–1910* (1971).
Gartner, Lloyd P. *The Jewish Immigrant in England, 1870–1914* (1960).
Genovese, Eugene. *Roll, Jordan, Roll: The World the Slaves Made* (New York, 1974).
—*The World the Slaveholders Made* (New York, 1971).
George, M. Dorothy. *London Life in the XVIIIth Century* (1925).
Gillespie, F. E. *Labour and Politics in Victorian England 1850–1867* (Durham, N.C., 1927).
Gohdes, Clarence. *American Literature in Nineteenth-Century England* (New York, 1944).
Gossett, Thomas F. *Race. The History of an Idea in America* (Dallas, 1963).
Griggs, Earl Leslie. *Thomas Clarkson, the Friend of the Slaves* (1936).
Haddon, A. C. and Quiggin, A. H. *History of Anthropology* (1910).
Hall, Douglas. *Free Jamaica, 1838–1865. An Economic History* (New Haven, 1959).
Hankins, Frank H. *The Racial Basis of Civilization* (New York, 1926).
Hargreaves, John D. *A Life of Sir Samuel Lewis* (1958).
Harrison, Royden. *Before the Socialists: Studies in Labour and Politics, 1861–1881* (1965).
Heasman, Kathleen. *Evangelists in Action* (1962).
Hertz, Friedrich. *Nationality in History and Politics. A Psychology and Sociology of National Sentiment and Nationalism* (1944).
Hobsbawm, E. J. *The Age of Capital* (1975).
—*The Age of Revolution, 1789–1848* (1962).
Hobsbawm, E. J. and Rudé G. *Captain Swing* (Penguin edn, 1973).
Hodgen, M. T. *Early Anthropology in the 16th and 17th Centuries* (Philadelphia, 1964).
Hoetink, H. *Slavery and Race Relations in the Americas: Comparative Notes on their Nature and Nexus* (New York, 1973).
Hofstadter, Richard. *Social Darwinism in American Thought* (New York, rev. edn, 1959).
Horn, Pamela. *The Rise and Fall of the Victorian Servant* (Dublin, 1975).
Huttenbach, R. A. *Racism and Empire: White Settlers and Colored Immigrants in the British Self-Governing Colonies, 1830–1910* (1976).
Inglis, K. S. *Churches and the Working Classes in Victorian England* (1963).

Irvine, William. *Apes, Angels and Victorians* (New York, 1955).

Jackson, John Archer. *The Irish in Britain* (1963).

Jahoda, Marie and Warren, Neil, eds. *Attitudes* (Penguin edn, 1966).

James, Louis, *Fiction for the Working Man, 1830–1850* (Penguin edn, 1974).

Jenkins, William Sumner. *Pro-Slavery Thought in the Old South* (Gloucester, Mass., 1960; reprint of University of North Carolina Press, 1935).

Jones, Eldred. *Othello's Countrymen. The African in English Renaissance Drama* (1965).

Jones, Gareth Stedman. *Outcast London: A Study of the Relationship between Classes in Victorian Society* (1971).

Jordan, Donaldson and Pratt, Edwin J. *Europe and the American Civil War* (Boston and New York, 1931).

Jordan, Winthrop D. *White over Black. American Attitudes towards the Negro, 1550–1812* (Chapel Hill, N.C., 1968).

Kenealy, Maurice Edward. *The Tichborne Tragedy* (1913).

Kimble, David. *The Political History of Ghana. The Rise of Gold Coast Nationalism, 1850–1928* (1963).

Kitson Clark, G. *An Expanding Society. Britain, 1830–1900* (1967).

—*The Making of Victorian England* (1965).

Klingberg, F. J. *The Anti-Slavery Movement in England* (New Haven, 1926).

Lascelles, E. C. P. *Granville Sharp and the Freedom of Slaves in England* (1928).

Lillibridge, G. D. *Beacon of Freedom. The Impact of American Democracy upon Great Britain, 1830–1870* (Philadelphia 1954).

Little, K. L. *Negroes in Britain* (1948).

Lockwood, David. *The Blackcoated Worker. A Study of Class Consciousness* (1958).

Lorimer, D. A. 'Bibles, banjoes and bones: images of the Negro in the popular culture of Victorian England', in *In Search of the Visible Past*, ed. B. M. Gough (Waterloo, Ont., 1975).

Lovejoy, A. O. *The Great Chain of Being: A Study of the History of an Idea* (Cambridge, Mass., 1936).

Lovett, Richard. *The History of the London Missionary Society, 1795–1895*, 2 vols (1899).

Lowie, R. H. *The History of Ethnological Theory* (1937).

Lynch, Hollis R. *Edward Wilmot Blyden, Pan-Negro Patriot, 1832–1912* (1967).

McKay, J. *The Life of Bishop Crowther, the first African Bishop of the Niger* (1932).

Magnus, Phillip. *Gladstone, A Biography* (1954).

Mahoney, Thomas H. D. *Edmund Burke and Ireland* (Cambridge, Mass., 1960).

Mannoni, O. *Prospero and Caliban, the Psychology of Colonization*, trans. Pamela Powesland (1956).

Marcus, Steven. *The Other Victorians. A Study of Sexuality and Pornography in Mid-Nineteenth-Century England* (1966).

Marrus, M. R. *The Politics of Assimilation: A Study of the French Jewish Community at the Time of the Dreyfus Affair* (1971).

Marshall, Dorothy. *The English Domestic Servant in History* (Historical Association, 1948).

Marshall, Herbert P. J. and Stock, Mildred. *Ira Aldridge, the Negro Tragedian* (1958).

Martin, James. *The Tolerant Personality* (Detroit, 1964).

Martin, Robert Bernard. *The Dust of Conflict: A Life of Charles Kingsley* (1956).

Mason, Philip. *Prospero's Magic. Some Thoughts on Class and Race* (1962).

Mathieson, William Law. *Great Britain and the Slave Trade, 1839–1865* (1929).

—*The Sugar Colonies and Governor Eyre, 1849–1866* (1936).

Mellor, George R. *British Imperial Trusteeship, 1783–1850* (1951).

Metcalf, Thomas R. *The Aftermath of Revolt in India, 1857–1870* (Princeton, 1964).

Morely, John. *Burke* (1888).

Morrell, W. P. *British Colonial Policy in the Mid-Victorian Age* (1969).

Mowat, Charles Loch. *The Charity Organization Society, 1869–1913. Its Ideas and Works* (1961).

Nathan, Hans. *Dan Emmett and the Rise of Early Negro Minstrelsy* (Norman, Okla., 1962).

Newsome, David. *Godliness and Good Learning. Four Studies on a Victorian Ideal* (1961).

Nichols, Charles H. *Many Thousand Gone: The Ex-Slaves' Account of Their Bondage and Freedom* (Leyden, 1963).

Olivier, Sidney. *The Myth of Governor Eyre* (1935).

Orr, J. Edwin. *The Second Evangelical Awakening* (1949).

Owen, David. *English Philanthropy, 1660–1960* (Cambridge, Mass., 1965).

Packe, Michael St John. *The Life of John Stuart Mill* (1954).

Page, Jesse. *Samuel Crowther, the Slave Boy of the Niger* (1932).

Partridge, Eric. *A Dictionary of Slang and Unconventional English* (5th edn, 1961).

Patterson, Orlando. *The Sociology of Slavery, An analysis of the Origins, Development and Structure of Negro Slave Society in Jamaica* (1967).

Patterson, Sheila. *Dark Strangers* (Bloomington, Ind., 1964).

Penniman, T. K. *A Hundred Years of Anthropology* (1952; 3rd rev. edn, 1965).

Perkin, Harold. *The Origins of Modern English Society, 1780–1880* (1969.)

Poliakov, Leon. *The Aryan Myth: a History of Racist and Nationalist Ideas in Europe* (1974).

Pritchard, F. C. *Methodist Secondary Education* (1949).

Rae, Isobel. *Knox, the Anatomist* (1964).

Pulzer, P. G. *The Rise of Political Anti-semitism in Germany and Austria* (New York, 1964).

Reade, Aleyn Lyell. *Johnsonian Gleanings* (Privately printed, 1909–52), pt II.

Reader, W. J. *Professional Men. The Rise of the Professional Classes in Nineteenth-Century England* (1966).

Reid, T. Wemyss. *Life of Right Honourable William Edward Forster* (1888).

Robinson, R. and J. Gallagher. 'The partition of Africa', in *New Cambridge Modern History* XI (1962).

Robinson, Ronald. 'Non-European Foundations of European Imperialism: a sketch of a Theory of Collaboration', *Imperialism: the Robinson and Gallagher Controversy*, ed. W. R. Louis, New York, 1976).

Roeach, Milton. 'Attitude', in *International Encyclopaedia of Social Science* (New York, 1968).

Sackville West, V. *Knole and the Sackvilles* (1922).

Semmel, Bernard. *The Governor Eyre Controversy* (1962).

Shepperson, George. 'Introduction', in J. A. B. Horton, *West African Countries and Peoples* (1969).

Shibutani, Tamotsu and Kwan, Kian M. *Ethnic Stratification, A Comparative Approach* (New York, 1965).

Shyllon, F. O. *Black Slaves in Britain* (1974).

Simpson, George E. and Singer, J. Milton. *Race and Cultural Minorities* (New York, 3rd edn, 1965).

Snyder, Louis L. *Race. A History of Modern Ethnic Theories* (New York, 1939).

Stanton, William. *The Leopard's Spots: Scientific Attitudes towards Race in America, 1815–1859* (Chicago, 1960).

Stock, Eugene. *The History of the Church Missionary Society. Its Environment, Its Men, and Its Work*, 4 vols (1899–1916).

Stocking, George M. jr. *Race, Culture, and Evolution: Essays in the History of Anthropology* (New York, 1968).

Stokes, Eric. *The English Utilitarians and India* (1959).

Sypher, Wylie. *Guinea's Captive Kings: British Anti-Slavery Literature of the XVIIIth Century* (Chapel Hill, N.C., 1942).

Temperley, Howard. *British Antislavery, 1833–1870* (1972).

Thistlewaite, Frank. *The Anglo-American Connection in the Early Nineteenth Century* (Philadelphia, 1959).

Thompson, E. P. *The Making of the English Working Class* (Penguin edn, 1968).

Thompson, F. M. L. *English Landed Society in the Nineteenth Century* (1963).

UNESCO. *Race and Science* (New York, 1961).

van den Berghe, Pierre L. *Race and Racism. A Comparative Perspective* (New York, 1967).

Venn, J. A., compiler. *Alumni Cantabrigienses* (1944).

Vicinus, Martha. *The Industrial Muse: A study of nineteenth-century British working class literature* (New York, 1974).

Villiers, Brougham and Chesson, W. H. *Anglo-American Relations, 1861–1865* (1919).

Vincent, John. *The Formation of the Liberal Party, 1858–1868* (1966).

Vries, Leonard de. *Victorian Advertisements* (Philadelphia and New York, 1968).

Walker, Frank D. *Thomas Birch Freeman, The Son of An African* (1929).

Walvin, James. *Black and White: The Negro and English Society, 1555–1945* (1973).

Webb, Robert Kiefer. *The British Working Class Reader, 1790–1848. Literacy and Social Tension* (1955).

Weinberg, Adelaide. *John Elliot Cairnes and the American Civil War* (1970).

Williams, Eric. *British Historians and the West Indies* (1966).

—*Capitalism and Slavery* (Chapel Hill, N.C., 1944).

Wilson, Edmund. *To the Finland Station* (1960).

Winks, Robin. *The Blacks in Canada: a History* (1971).

Wittke, Carl. *Tambo and Bones. A History of the American Minstrel Stage* (Durham, N.C., 1930).

Work, Monroe N. *A Bibliography of the Negro in Africa and America* (New York, 1928).

B. ARTICLES

Ajayi, J. F. Ade. 'Henry Venn and the policy of development', *J. Historical Soc. of Nigeria*, I (1956–9), 331–42.

—'Nineteenth century origins of Nigerian nationalism', *J. Historical Soc. of Nigeria*, II (1960–3), 196–210.

Altick, Richard D. 'The sociology of authorship: the social origins, education and occupation of 1,100 British authors, 1800–1935', *Bull. of New York Public Library*, LXVI (June 1962), 389–404.

Anstey, Roger. 'Capitalism and slavery: a critique', *Economic History Rev.*, 2nd ser., XXI (1968), 307–20.

—'A reinterpretation of the British slave trade, 1806–1807', *English Historical Rev.*, LXXXVII (1972), 304–32.

Austen, R. A. and Smith, W. D. 'Images of Africa and the British slave trade abolition: the transition to an imperialist ideology, 1787–1807', *African Historical Studies*, II (1969), 69–83.

Ayandele, E. A. 'Background to the "Duel" between Crowther and Goldie on the Lower Niger, 1857–1885', *J. Historical Soc. of Nigeria*, IV (Dec. 1967). 45–63.

—'An assessment of James Johnson and his place in Nigerian history, 1874–1917', *J. Historical Soc. of Nigeria*, pt I, *1874–1890*, II (1960–3), 486–516, and pt II, *1890–1917*, III (1964), 73–101.

Banton, Michael. 'Kingsley's racial philosophy', *Theology*, LXXVIII (1975), 22–30.

—'Race as a social category', *Race*, VIII (1966), 1–16.

Bardolph, Richard. 'Social origins of distinguished Negroes, 1770–1865', *J. Negro History*, XL (July 1955), 211–49.

Barksdale, R. K. 'Thomas Arnold's attitude toward race', *Phylon Q.*, XVIII (1957), 174–80.

Bartels, F. L. 'Philip Quaque, 1741–1816', *Trans. Gold Coast and Togoland Historical Soc.*, I (1952–5), 153–74.

Biddiss, Michael D. 'Gobineau and the origins of European racism', *Race*, VII (Jan. 1966), 255–70.

—'The politics of anatomy: Dr Robert Knox and Victorian racism', *Procs. of the Royal Soc. of Medicine*, LXIX (1976), 245–50.

Brady, E. A. 'A reconsideration of the Lancashire "Cotton Famine"',
    Agricultural History Rev., xxxvii (July 1963), 156–62.
Burrow, J. W. 'Evolution and anthropology in the 1860's: the
    Anthropological Society of London, 1863–1871, *Victorian Studies*,
    vii (1963–4), 137–54.
Count, E. W. 'The evolution of the race idea in modern Western
    culture during the period of the pre-Darwinian nineteenth century',
    Trans. New York Academy of Sciences, 2nd ser., viii (Feb. 1946),
    139–65.
Cundall, Frank. 'Richard Hill', *J. Negro History*, v (1920), 37–44.
Curtin, Philip D. ' "Scientific" racism and the British theory of empire',
    J. Historical Soc. of Nigeria, ii (1960), 40–51.
Davis, David Brion. 'The emergence of Immediatism in British and
    American Anti-Slavery thought', *Mississippi Valley Historical Rev.*,
    xlix (1962), 209–30.
Deighton, H. S. 'History and the study of race relations', *Race*, i
    (1959), 15–25.
Erickson, A. B. 'Empire or anarchy: the Jamaican Rebellion of 1865',
    J. Negro History, xliv (Apr. 1959), 99–122.
Fiddes, Edward. 'Lord Mansfield and the Somerset Case', *Law Q. Rev.*,
    l (Oct. 1934), 499–511.
Fielden, Kenneth. 'Samuel Smiles and self-help', *Victorian Studies*, xii
    (Dec. 1968), 155–76.
Ford, George H. 'The Governor Eyre Case in England', *University of
    Toronto Q.*, xvii (Apr. 1848), 219–33.
Gallagher, J. 'Fowell Buxton and the New Africa policy', *Cambridge
    Historical J.*, xi (1950), 36–58.
George, Katherine. 'The civilized West looks at primitive Africa:
    1400–1800; a study on ethnocentrism', *Isis*, xlix (Mar. 1958),
    62–72.
Graeber, J. 'Examination of theories of race prejudice', *Social Research*,
    xx (Oct. 1953), 267–81.
Harrison, Brian. 'Philanthropy and the Victorian', *Victorian Studies*,
    ix (1966), 353–74.
Harrison, Royden. 'British labour and American slavery', *Science and
    Soc.*, xxv (Dec. 1961). 291–319.
—'British labour and the Confederacy', *International Rev. of Social
    History*, ii (1957), 78–105.
—'The 10th April of Spencer Walpole: the problem of revolution in
    relation to reform', *International Rev. of Social History*, vii (1962),
    351–99.
Hecht, J. Jean. 'Continental and colonial servants in eighteenth century
    England', *Smith College Studies in History*, xl (1954), 1–61.
Hernon, J. M. 'British sympathies in the American Civil War: a
    reconsideration', *J. Southern History*, xxxiii (1967), 356–67.
Horsman, Reginald. 'Origins of racial Anglo-Saxonism in Great Britain
    before 1850', *J. History of Ideas*, xxxvii (1976), 381–410.
James, Louis. 'Tom Brown's imperialist sons', *Victorian Studies*, xvii
    (1973), 89–99.
Jameson, J. F. 'London expenditures of the Confederate Secret Service',
    American Historical Rev., xxxv (July 1930), 811–24.

Jones, W. D. 'British Conservatives and the American Civil War', *American Historical Rev.*, LVIII (Apr. 1953), 527–43.

Keith, Sir Arthur. 'Presidential Address: How can the Institute best serve the needs of anthropology?', *J. Royal Anthropological Institute of Great Britain and Ireland*, XLVII (1917), 12–30.

Klingberg, F. J. 'Harriet Beecher Stowe and social reform in England', *American Historical Rev.*, XLIII (Apr. 1938) 542–52.

Leopold, Joan. 'British applications of the Aryan theory of race to India, 1850–1870', *English Historical Rev.*, LXXXIX (1974), 578–603.

Lorimer, D. A. 'The role of anti-slavery sentiment in English reactions to the American Civil War', *Historical J.*, XIX (1976), 405–20.

Lynch, Hollis R. 'The native pastorate controversy and cultural ethnocentrism in Sierra Leone, 1871–1874', *J. African History*, V (1964), 395–413.

Maurer, Oscar. ' "Punch" on slavery and the Civil War in America, 1841–1865', *Victorian Studies*, I (Sept. 1957), 5–28.

Musgrove, F. 'Middle-class education and employment in the nineteenth century', *Economic History Rev.*, 2nd ser., XII (Aug. 1959), 99–111.

—'Middle class education and employment in the nineteenth century: a rejoinder', *Economic History Rev.*, 2nd ser., XIV (Dec. 1961), 320–9.

Myers, J. L. 'The influence of anthropology on the course of political science', *University of California Publications in History*, IV (1916–17), 1–81.

Nadelhaft, Jerome. 'The Somerset Case and slavery: myth, reality, and repercussions', *J. Negro History*, LI (1966), 193–208.

Nichols, Charles. 'The origin of *Uncle Tom's Cabin*', *Phylon Q.*, XIX (July 1958), 328–34.

Norton, Mary Beth. 'The fate of some black Loyalists of the American Revolution', *J. Negro History*, LVIII (1973), 402–26.

Odom, H. H. 'Generalizations on race in 19th century physical anthropology', *Isis*, LVIII (Spring 1967), 5–18.

Park, Joseph. 'English working men and the American Civil War', *Political Science Q.*, XXXIX (1924), 432–57.

Parker, Dorothy B. 'Sarah Parker Remond, abolitionist and physician', *J. Negro History*, XX (1935), 287–93.

Perkin, H. J. 'Middle class education and employment in the nineteenth century: a critical note', *Economic History Rev.*, 2nd ser., XIV (Aug. 1961), 122–30.

Quarles, Benjamin. 'Ministers without portfolio', *J. Negro History*, XXXIX (1954), 27–42.

Rehin, George H. 'Harlequin Jim Crow: continuity and convergence in Blackface clowning', *J. Popular Culture*, IX (1975/6), 682–701.

Rice, C. Duncan. 'The anti-slavery mission of George Thompson to the United States, 1834–1835', *J. American Studies*, II (Apr. 1968), 13–31.

Roach, John. 'Liberalism and the Victorian intelligentsia', *Cambridge Historical J.*, XIII (1957), 58–81.

Scott, H. S. 'The development of the education of the African in relation to Western contact', *Year Book of Education* (1938), 693–739.

Shepperson, George. 'Frederick Douglass and Scotland', *J. Negro History*, xxxviii (1953), 307–21.

Sherwood, Henry Noble. 'Paul Cuffee', *J. Negro History*', viii (1923), 153–229.

Stocking, George M. 'What's in a name? The origins of the Royal Anthropological Institute (1837–71)', *Man*, n.s. vi (1971), 369–90.

Tholfsen, T. R. 'The intellectual origins of mid-Victorian stability', *Political Science Q.*, lxxxvi (1971), 57–91.

Whitridge, A. 'British Liberals and the American Civil War', *History Today*, xii (Oct. 1962), 688–95.

Workman, Gillian. 'Thomas Carlyle and the Governor Eyre Controversy: an account with some new material', *Victorian Studies*, xviii (1974), 77–102.

Index